MOUNTAIN RESCUE
CHAMONIX · MONT BLANC

Dear Chris,

The inspiration behind the painting
of The Dru in Montroc is from
the devastating story of Elena.
I can't look at The Dru without
thinking of her.
Hope you enjoy this book.
Happy Birthday!

with love

Christie

(April 2008)

Anne Sauvy

MOUNTAIN RESCUE
CHAMONIX · MONT BLANC

Close observation of the world's
busiest mountain rescue service

Translated by
John Wilkinson and Anne Sauvy
assisted by Sue Harper Todd on chapters 1 to 26.
Chapters 27, 28 and 29 translated by Elin Williams.

Bâton Wicks · London

Also by the Author

in English, French and other languages:
FLAMMES DES PIERRE
THE GAME OF MOUNTAIN AND CHANCE
DARKNESS AND THE AZURE

in French only:
NADIR
CHAMONIX D'UN SIÈCLE À L'AUTRE

Copyright by © Editions Arthaud, Paris, 1998
Copyright in English translation by © Anne Sauvy and John Wilkinson

First published in the UK in 2005 by
Bâton Wicks, London

All trade enquiries to:
Cordee, 3a De Montfort Street, Leicester LE1 7HD

British Library Cataloguing in Publication Data:
ISBN 1-898573-52-2 A catalogue record for this book exists at the British Library

Printed and bound in Singapore by the Kyodo Printing Company

CONTENTS

Contents

APPENDICES

ILLUSTRATIONS

Between pages 96 and 97. All pictures by Daniel Duret unless otherwise credited

1-16 Some helicopter crews and rescuers *Anne Sauvy*
17, 18, 19 Scenes at the Les Bois helipad *Anne Sauvy*
20, 21 *Dragon* above the Aiguilles and Dent du Caïman
22, 24 *Bravo Lima* in action on the Tacul and the Grépon
23 Rescued German climbers at the helipad *Anne Sauvy*
25, 26 Stretcher-lowering; avalanche search team in action
27, 28, 29 A rescue team in 1934 *Frank Smythe*; crevasse rescue
30 *Dragon* in action above the Aiguille du Bionnassay North Face
31, 32 Bobi Arsandaux and Raymond Lambert *archive photos*
33, 34 Armand Charlet and Lionel Terray *archive photos*
35, 36 René Desmaison and Gary Hemming *archive photos*

PREFACE

I dip my pen not into an inkwell but into life.
(Blaise Cendrars, *L'Homme Foudroyé*)

This book is born out of admiration.

Not a particularly fashionable sentiment today.

It is the chronicle of the mountain rescue season at Chamonix in the summer of 1997.

At the start the project seemed straightforward. Three years ago, I obtained permission to spend a summer with the PGHM[1] in Haute-Savoie, so as to collect material for a novel which was based on an imaginary day in the life of the mountain rescue.[2] This experience was rich in discoveries, emotions and friendships, and from it quite naturally evolved the idea of describing what a real season of rescue was about. The objective was clear and precise, the outcome less so.

Why this interest in mountaineering? In rescue?

Mountains:... How should we reply to the eternal question 'why do you climb them?' Some get around it with the old adage 'because they are there'; others avoid trying to provide an answer which is beyond them. So what should we say?

Perhaps that mountains are beautiful, that once amongst them you can escape into another world, a world without norms, a glorious world, a world where nature is still wild, a world accessible only through individual effort, self-mastery, opening up of new horizons. Real and specific horizons, certainly – albeit set in the distant haze and shimmer – but also the horizons of harmony, wonder, joy, and inner fulfilment.

Doubtless it has always been so, even though the evidence is limited. Already St. Augustine was noting:

'Men go abroad to admire the mountain peaks.'[3] And eleven centuries later, the naturalist Gesner wrote:

---

[1] Peloton de Gendarmerie de Haute Montagne which is responsible for mountain rescue.
[2] *Nadir*, Glénat, 1995.
[3] Circa 400 AD, *Confessions*, X, 8.

I have resolved for the future, so long as God grants me life, to ascend divers mountains each year… What voluptuous pleasure we find in them! What the delight of a mind rightly touched, to gaze upon the vastness of the hills and, as it were, lift one's head into the bosom of the clouds. The soul is strangely rapt with these astounding heights, and carried away in contemplation…

I declare him nature's enemy who considers not the high mountains to be worthy of long contemplation… On those lofty heights the effect of the mighty sun is not the same, nor that of the air and winds… The snows are eternal… Everything that nature produces with parsimony elsewhere, she provides in abundance and in its entirety in the mountains, displaying all her wealth and jewels for all to see…

The sight of the mountains seizes me beyond all measure…

But the tide carrying men towards the mountains now runs much stronger. Why?

The age, the society we live in, considers itself the height of civilisation, but it is not what it claims to be. Despite the progress of science, sometimes because of it, and despite so many strident proclamations, the 20th century has been – I speak as an historian – the worst in the history of mankind: cruel, bloody, hypocritical, full of deceit, selfishness, ignorance disguised as certainties and errors disguised as ideologies. It suffices to look at the doubts and aimlessness of today's bewildered youth, which one can only contemplate with a sense of unease. It is a failure. Past generations could refer to values which they considered primordial, yet firmly rooted and valid. That is no longer so.

What are the guiding values of our society today? Money. Information. Speed. Comfort. Permissiveness. Materialism. Politics. So many militancies without substance, unrealistic to the point of absurdity. Or the instruments of oblivion which offer varied and impersonal forms of escapism: television, computer games, jet-setting – or sex, sects, violence, drugs, which in the end provides so little satisfaction. What else is there?

Some are not contented by all this. They look elsewhere, search-ing for more meaningful and healthier values. To attain them, they are willing to accept the inverse of those things just mentioned. So, in the mountains we experience deprivation, solitude, a slower pace, suffering – even risk. We live with discomfort, get up in the middle of the night, are cold, hot, breathless, we force and exert ourselves, we fight, first and foremost with ourselves, we share with others unforgettable moments which help to put the other things in context. Mountains provide one of the chances man has to find new perspectives in a confused and warped world, because they provide a dimension which it lacks. In the mountains one can experience a matchless joy. The rewards are greater than the effort invested.

So why, in the light of such potential pleasure and glimpsed beauty raise the subject of accidents? Why not forget about them, consign them to oblivion?

Straight away, it must be stated; it is not with any morbid intention, quite the opposite. It is not accidents which are the issue, but rescue, a subject that brings together two fascinating worlds: that of the mountains, and that where man helps man. Furthermore it must also be stressed that accidents are only a tiny part of what happens in the mountains. Of the thousands of people who every summer day climb, parapent, walk or ramble, only a very small proportion is involved in accidents and the disproportionate media attention they get often contributes to public misconceptions and the development of false clichés. That has to be shown for what it is.

On a fine day in August, it is estimated that there are about 110,000 people in the Chamonix valley, one of the more beautiful and most popular places in the world, only a tenth of whom are permanent residents. If, on such a day, some ten accidents occur, most of them minor, it will be seen why they must be got into perspective. The myths that develop in the media comment on these events, should be balanced by the fact that for every serious incident large numbers complete their activities without any problems and with great enjoyment and satisfaction.

So it is that very small fringe involved in rescues which will be treated here, because when they do happen, it is inspiring to find such unsung devotion, acts of friendship, smiles between strangers, to see a rescue carried out by professionals who are also mountaineers and who conduct their tasks with deep humanity, willingly, and with a real passion for the mountains.

That is the reason for this book.

On July 1, the day I arrived in Chamonix, nothing existed of the story to be followed except a couple of phrases I had scribbled down during the spring: 'The project is the antithesis of what journalists look for – I do not seek drama, deaths, blood; on the contrary, what I want are successful, albeit sometimes difficult rescues, carried out in emergency situations, but with happy endings and radiant faces reflecting the joy of being saved, of being alive.'

Such rescues I saw during the summer of 1994 and I knew their value and nobility.

But I was not even certain of doing the book. It was a blank space which, maybe, the future would fill. In my publishing contract I had asked that there should be no advance. A summer of bad weather, or a lucky summer when nothing much happened, and there would be no book. Furthermore, should it appear, it did not seem right to receive money arising from future accidents before completing the task. That was my approach. The book, I knew, deserved to exist, for the world of rescue is fascinating, yet I also hoped that circumstances would turn out so that it never saw the light of day.

The season started smoothly, with minor rescues, with interesting discussions. From the beginning however, the constraints were infinitely harder than I had foreseen. If I was to be equal to the task, there would be no days off, no rest. I had to put my own life on hold, in order to be in constant touch with another reality, foreign, unpredictable. And it has proved difficult. In the pages which follow, I have let slip glimpses of the burden I assumed, but much less than in the pages of notes I wrote, without respite, throughout that long summer. Here is an example: John Wilkinson, my husband, who was a don at Oxford University, had just retired, leaving his own country to join me in Chamonix, in a house that still resembled a building site. But that, including him, had to take second place. It was the price of doing the job properly.

Moreover, this background situation, hard as it might be, was nothing compared with everything else, for to be confronted daily by the accidents which were to come, without a break, was a harsh, unforgiving ordeal. It is impossible to predict what life will throw up, it is always full of the unexpected. So the real happenings were as in nature, with its chances, its smiles, its upheavals, its tensions, and sometimes its storms.

Whilst I started my work without any preconceived ideas, envisaging that it would suffice to be an outside observer – as in historical research – it quickly became clear that this was impossible. What was happening was not of the past but, quite emphatically, the present, including events, atmosphere, the reactions of others, my own... I could not just be a mirror reflecting. I too was involved. Thus I became part of the well-balanced, sometimes cheerful, life of the helipad, where rescuers came and went with the same outlook on life. I also spent sleepless nights, shaken by an accident, by its consequences. I had doubts, I broke down, picked myself up. The adventure has also been a personal one.

This book I believe to be full of humanity, because I put all my heart into it, just as those with whom I lived each day, put all of themselves into their missions. To these people I am profoundly grateful, notably Captain Jean-Claude Gin, who does not feature much in the story, being more occupied with administration and public relations, but who, during the writing of this book, gave up considerable time in order to find me additional information, to explain problems relating to mountain rescue, to read and reread the many drafts, rough copies and final texts. I would also like to thank Christine de Colombel, who edited this book for Flammarion, who was always there when I needed her. I must also thank John, who bravely endured and supported me in this demanding adventure. And finally the countless others, whose names are noted on page 4 and 354.

Anne Sauvy, Chamonix, 1997.

LIST OF ABBREVIATIONS

ABMG	Association of British Mountain Guides
BMC	British Mountaineering Council
CAF	Club Alpin Français
CMBH	Chamonix Mont-Blanc Hélicoptères
CNISAG	Centre National d'Instruction de Ski et d'Alpinisme de la Gendarmerie
EMHM	École Militaire de Haute Montagne (originally EHM)
ENSA	École Nationale de Ski et d'Alpinisme
FFME	Federation Français de la Montagne et de L'Escalade (orig. FFM)
GA	Gendarme Auxiliaire
GDB	Groupe de Bleau [Fontainebleau]
PGHM	Peloton de Gendarmerie de Haute Montagne
SAMU	Service d'Aide Médicale d'Urgence A fully equipped doctor who can summon an ambulance if necessary.
SCSM	Société Chamoniarde de Secours en Montagne
TMB	Tramway du Mont Blanc
UIAGM	Union Internationale des Associations de Guides de Montagne

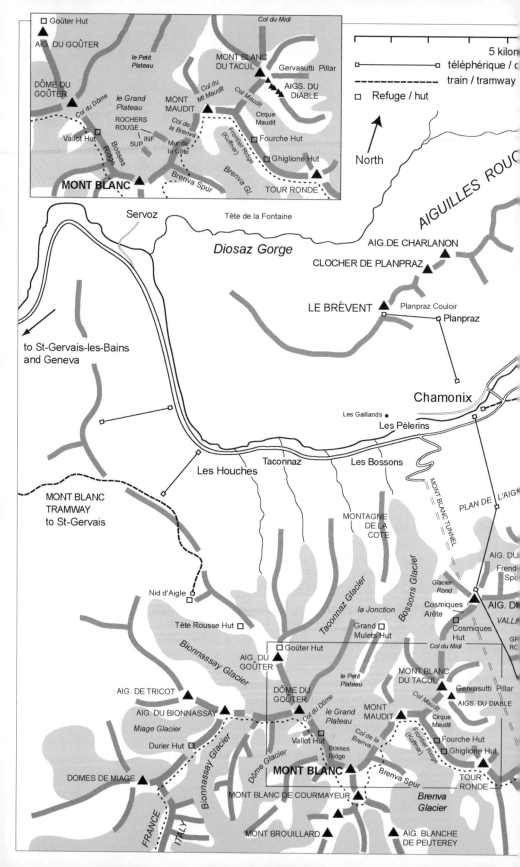

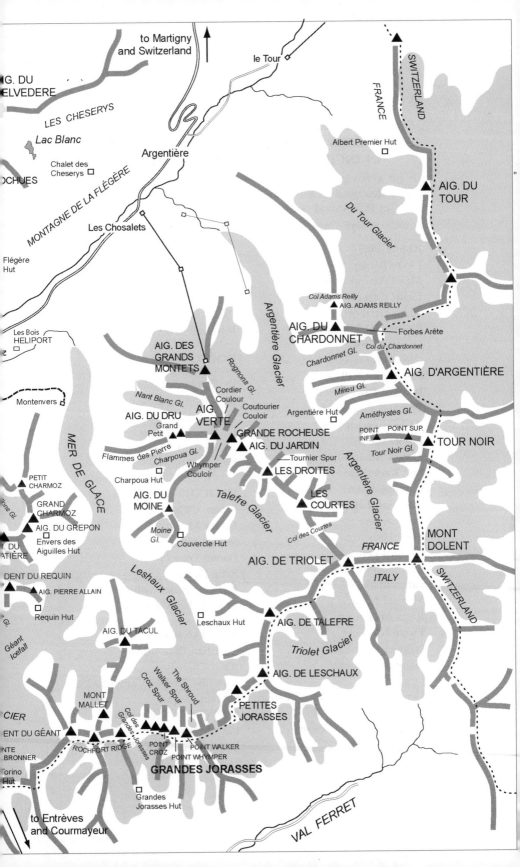

MEMBERS OF THE RESCUE TEAMS INVOLVED
IN INCIDENTS DESCRIBED IN THE BOOK

An aid to navigation through the many names involved in the main
incidents described. It lists only the field activists mentioned – a full list
of PGHM and Sécurité Civile personnel is on page 363

(SC – Sécurité Civile personnel   † – Those who have died in service)

RESCUERS
Pierre Bernier (Bibi)
Max (Maxou) Buttoud
Henri Cazemajor
Alain Darrhort
Philippe Debernardi
Daniel Duret
Olivier Fernandez
Eric (Fufu) Fulbert
Bernard Guérin
Thibaud Ribiollet
Alain (Julio) Iglesis
Lionel Isaia,
Franck Junod
Luc Karleskind†
Philippe Klein
Christian Lafouge
Éric Lazzeri
Marc Ledwidge
Laurent Leteneur
Jean-Jacques Malineau
Gilles Mathé
Michael Medici
Régis Michoux†
Pierre Nicollet†
Jacques Ottonello
Jean-Louis Oustry
Jackie Paillé
Gérard (Gégé) Peyraud-Magnin
Alain Place
Patrick (Hercule) Poirot
Philippe Pouts

Pierre Raveneau
Olivier Renard
Patrice Ribes
Thibaud Riboullet
Pascal Saudemont
Jean-Luc Yvon (dog-handler)

DOCTORS
(often known to the public as 'Dr Cauchy')
Dr Emmanuel (Manu) Cauchy
Dr Benoît Couzineau
Dr Guy Duperrex
Dr François Lecoq
Dr Bernard Marsigny
Dr Loïc Mingant

HELICOPTER PILOTS
Bidon, Gilles (SC)
Didier Méraux
Michel Pierre (SC)
Daniel Poujol†
René Romet
Vincent (Aldo) Saffiotti (SC)
Jean-Michel Vialle (SC)

MECHANICIANS
Christian Bare-Guillet
Alain Charnay
Ivan (the Terrible) Commène (SC)
Sylvain Haquin
Noël (Nono) Rivière (SC)
Pascal Sciberras
Bernard Stoop (SC)

PART ONE

1

ACCIDENT AND RESCUE

The Frontier (or Kuffner) Ridge on Mont Maudit is a wonderfully airy route. There is a lot of space on the right, and even more on the left, and it is not the place to fall.

A couple, Philippe and Marie Claveau, were climbing it on this particular day – August 9, 1994. It was hot and sunny. The föhn was blowing. The mountain was drier than anyone ever recalled seeing it. The two alpinists had climbed the major part of the route and were nearing the Androsace gendarme, moving together, when, probably as a result of a loose block, Philippe slipped and fell over the west side of the ridge, dragging Marie with him. Below them were five hundred metres of void. They started to fall, tumbling. Marie recalled that it was like 'being in a washing machine'.

A fall happens very quickly, and yet you still have time to think, fast.

'This is it,' Philippe told himself.

And Marie: 'The end! For both of us! How am I going to die? If only I could pass out, before I suffer too much. We wanted a child. No, we are not going to die, we must have a child!'

At the beginning of the fall Philippe must have hit a rock which had shattered his knee. Twenty-one open fractures. Marie had her left hand broken, and her arm covered in friction burns. Despite their helmets, they were at once being bashed about prior to what would surely be the fatal blow. Then, suddenly, as though by a miracle, they stopped falling, in the middle of a slope, held by the friction of the rope running through the snow, without even catching on a rock.

They found themselves in two narrow parallel gullies, almost flutings. It was nine o'clock in the morning.

The situation was extremely precarious. Both lying injured, on a steep, dangerous slope, which could avalanche at any moment. Help could only come from elsewhere. Philippe had a VHF[1] radio but the ridge above them blocked any signal. They shouted, but they were far from anyone, in a wild amphitheatre on the Italian, Brenva side of Mont Blanc, and the fierce wind drowned their voices.

Both did their best to secure themselves to the slope of dubious snow and ice.

Philippe could not move, was in considerable pain and losing blood. Marie looked up, towards the ridge, which seemed far away, out of reach in the state she was in. But the only chance of help was from the ridge, where the radio, might well get a signal. The couple had 100 metres of rope. 'Perhaps a hundred metres will be enough', wondered Marie. She had lost her ice axes in the fall, but Philippe still had his, which he managed to pass over to her along with the radio. She set off.

The ascent, actually about 150 metres up steep ice, took her four hours. Shaken, shocked, dragging herself, in pain, Marie was on the point of giving up several times.

'I'll never make it,' she thought. Then: 'If I don't, Philippe will die.'

When she reached the end of the hundred metres of rope and saw how far away the ridge still was, she felt even more uncertain. But, abandoning the largely illusory impression of security, she untied and continued, very alone, step by step and eventually reached the ridge, a bit after one o'clock. In the distance she saw climbers descending Mont Blanc du Tacul, yelled, tried to catch their attention, in vain. It was the radio message, which she then sent and was picked up at Helbronner, that saved them. She heard their reply:

'The person who is asking for help on the Kuffner, I am receiving you, but very badly. Please wait. I'll get up a bit higher'

The joy she felt at hearing this, knowing that all her efforts had been worthwhile, was indescribable.

Although the details were imprecise, once the message had

[1] VHF radios, originally designed for hang-gliders who have no obstructions around them, have variable reception in the mountains whilst the UHF waves bounce between the atmospheric layers.

been relayed, an emergency rescue operation was immediately launched.

On August 9 I was at the helipad, collecting material for *Nadir*.[2] That day had been a fabulous one. The Gendarmerie helicopter, *Bravo Lima*, was on duty, with Daniel Poujol as pilot and Pascal Sciberras as mechanician. Calls were coming in continuously, for serious accidents in various locations with the rescues overlapping, and the helicopter flying from one to another in an attempt to cover them all. Another helicopter had been requested, but the one belonging to the Sécurité Civile, based in Annecy, was not available, nor was any other, and so *Bravo Lima* had somehow to cope with these multiple rescues, whilst not only were the four 'duty rescuers', Éric Lazzeri, Michel Médici, Max Buttoud and Laurent Leteneur, in action, but the first reserves, Gilles Mathé and Bernard Guérin, had also been called out.

A short while before, a dead body had been reported under the North Face of the Dôme du Goûter, but in fact the person had been found to be hovering between life and death, injured, disfigured, hypothermic, shocked, with serious head injuries, but still breathing a little and had been saved.

When the request for help came from the Kuffner, it was given absolute priority over the others and *Bravo Lima* left immediately with Michel Médici and Éric Lazzeri.

Because it was windy, the helicopter had to be lightly laden so as to manoeuvre without too much risk. Despite the calm in the valley, flying conditions at altitude were particularly perilous. It was cold with a terrible wind, causing unpredictable turbulence, squalls and wind shear. With poor flying conditions the risks had to be reduced to a minimum. That meant the helicopter could not carry much fuel, and had frequently to return for refuelling. It also had to make a number of intermediate stops: to drop off a rescuer, pick up another, come back for the first. The whole of the day was played out in such marginal circumstances.

And at the same time as the call from the Kuffner was received, two other requests came in. On the Aiguilles Crochues someone

---

[2] *Nadir*, a novel whose title might well have been *A Day in the Life of the PGHM* has not yet been published in English.

with internal bleeding, near the Col d'Anterne a phlebitis. Three rescues, at widely separated locations, all equally urgent.

Daniel Poujol and Pascal Sciberras left Michel Médici in the Combe Maudite and flew across the ridge to assess the situation and locate the scene of the accident. Those moments, when the helicopter flies towards a casualty and the first eye contact between him and his rescuers in the cockpit is made, with no other communication possible, are often highly charged.

Getting winched down at the beginning of the afternoon onto a steep slope of 50°, whilst being battered by the wind, is distinctly unnerving. That nevertheless was the situation in which Éric Lazzeri found himself, as he was lowered towards Philippe's insecure belay, which he tried to improve before detaching himself from the cable. Stones were falling. The föhn was blowing, the snow in which he was trying to gain a foothold was rotten. Nothing was really holding. He had to clear the unstable snow to a depth of fifty centimetres before he could get any ice screws in. Philippe heard him mutter: 'There we are! Bombproof.'

He felt that his rescuer was as much in need of reassurance as he was himself.

At once, Éric Lazzeri had realized the severity of the injuries and called for the doctor. During his long wait, while Marie was climbing, Philippe had put tourniquets on his thigh, in order to stop the bleeding, loosening them from time to time.

'Don't look,' Éric said to him. And cut his gaiter which, having acted like a pocket was holding half a litre of blood.

'I'll have to cut your trousers.'

'But they're new!'

'Don't worry! My knife's new too!'

A surreal conversation, but it is the act of talking that matters, the human exchange of words, proving that you are stronger than the adverse forces of nature.

While all this was taking place, Daniel Poujol had let Dr Mingant know that he was needed urgently and was coming to collect him from Merlet Park, where he was examining someone feeling ill. He told him that the injured man was bleeding and in a lot of pain and explained the situation in detail. Loïc Mingant had his rescue rucksack and his resuscitation equipment with him. He put on his helmet and his crampons, in readiness to be lowered into the middle of a face in the high mountains.

When they arrived above Éric and Philippe, Daniel Poujol warned Loïc what they were attempting:

'Going to be rough!' he announced.

Pascal Sciberras started winching the doctor down but, just as he was about to touch the snow, the helicopter, at the limits of its power, suddenly shot away from the wall and dropped, nose diving. Gravity had overcome its power to hover. One can imagine what it must be like to be dangling below a helicopter on the end of a cable and just about to get a foothold on a steep, exposed and dangerous slope, to be suddenly yanked off downwards.

'It's not working!' said Daniel. 'We're too heavy. It won't go! We must shed weight.'

They put the resuscitation equipment down in the Combe Maudite, near Médici, flew around a little to burn off ten kilos of fuel and attempted the manoeuvre again. With less ballast on board, this time they succeeded. Once on the slope beside Philippe and Éric, Loïc Mingant made a rapid diagnosis. Philippe had a diagonal wound of about fifteen centimetres. The bone was visible. The kneecap was shattered, as was possibly the base of the femur. The casualty had also lost a great deal of blood. All in a very difficult place to work, attached to a small and somewhat dubious belay, in rotten ice. Speed was the essential. Ideally, in a good position, he would have put the casualty on an intravenous drip. Impossible here. Philippe was in a lot of pain and it was necessary to knock him out to relieve his suffering. Loïc asked Éric to put a tourniquet on his arm, and injected a morphine substitute into the vein. Éric had made the tourniquet so tight that he could not undo it and had to cut it with his Opinel. Loïc then straightened out the leg and the two men put him in the Piguillem[3] stretcher which they held horizontally, so that the helicopter could pick it up.

Hardly had they got the stretcher into position when a snow slide started straight above the belay, hit the doctor in the face and piled up on top of the stretcher and the fractured leg. Philippe, luckily, was out, anaesthetised, and felt nothing. The helicopter, which had gone to refuel, came back. The pilot, the rescuer and the doctor assessed the situation.

'I can only take one at a time!' announced Daniel Poujol.

[3] The Piguillem, known familiarily as a 'Pigui' is a folding stretcher used in mountain rescue.

'Take the casualty, without me' responded Loïc Mingant.

But to get into a hovering position above the belay, Daniel needed more than one try, each time having to shear away suddenly because of the wind. Finally he managed to do so, long enough for Pascal Sciberras to lower the winch cable and the stretcher to be attached. Daniel had to move off rapidly and the Piguillem stretcher bounced and swung about on the end of the wire. Pascal winched it up and pulled it into the machine. They flew straight to the emergency landing pad at the hospital.

Alone and unable to do anything but wait, Éric and Dr Mingant had plenty of time to think about the danger of their situation. While the rescue operation had been taking place the belay had worked loose. Suddenly, to their left, high above them, a huge soft snow avalanche, twenty metres across, broke away and slid down without touching them. If it had started above them, they would have been torn off the belay, as the ice screws were no longer biting. A short while later, another snow slide, just as large, passed them on their right. The wait was long as the helicopter had to go back to the helipad to refuel. But finally it was there and lifted one, then the other, off the belay, each time with a lot of bouncing about, and put them down in Combe Maudite beside Michel Médici.

The latter was then taken up to the ridge, to Marie, whose rescue was more straightforward. She was winched up, followed by Médici.

I saw her arrive at the helipad and noticed her blonde hair. She was taken off to hospital. The rescue finished at 4pm. Two lives which would have been lost had just been saved, first by a small miracle, then by the courage of the casualties, and finally by the PGHM who had carried out an extremely difficult mission.

2

THE RESCUE SETTING

Throughout the long and difficult day of rescues on August 9, 1994, during which I was at the helipad, the suspense had been agonising. Already shaken that morning by the 'dead body' that turned out to be just alive, we expected, at any moment, to hear the worst – in one place or another, or indeed everywhere. Snatches of messages came in, barely audible. The helicopter flew in, landed quickly, refuelled, took off again with another rescuer or a stretcher. You could cut the atmosphere with a knife.

But on this day of many serious rescues there were no deaths. When I left the helipad around 7 pm, the aircrew had not yet had lunch. I was startled to note that Dr Mingant's face, which was a normal suntanned brown in the morning, had, by the evening, taken on a brick red hue as a result of being exposed to the sun and the reflection of the snow. During the day the helicopter winch had been used thirty-two times and the fire service ambulances had been out thirty-five times – to the helipad or other emergencies. And when I left, I didn't suspect that there would be yet one more rescue, which Daniel Poujol told me about the next day, qualifying it as the 'final diapason'.

It involved a young English girl, Katherine Cartwright, the daughter of one of my husband's friends. Open fracture of the leg on the north side of the Aiguille d'Argentière. This rescue pushed the limits. The casualty was lifted off first then, when the helicopter returned to pick up the rescuer, a rogue gust of wind caused the machine to drop suddenly and the cable became caught in huge granite blocks. The helicopter might well have crashed into the slope, but the cable freed itself and the aircraft recovered stability. Then it hovered above Max Buttoud who caught and attached himself to the cable as it was lowered, whereupon it flew straight off at 80kph with him suspended in space twenty-five or thirty metres below the machine. A successful ending. The operation finished at 9.30 pm. It was dark.

That is a day in the life of the rescue service, and an exemplary one! So much at risk, on all sides, climbers, rescuers, aircrew. Not one death but many lives saved, at times almost miraculously. Some friendships formed between casualties and rescuers. Going to visit Katherine Cartwright, in hospital, I recognised Marie Claveau nearby and talked to her. Then I went to see Philippe, who had been operated on the previous day and was on a different floor. I helped them in various ways, such as fetching things from their car. We ended up friends.

August 9, 1994 had been a wonderful and inspirational day of rescue and it was that, I believe, which gave me this idea of writing about a real summer of mountain rescue. So here we are.

But to understand the daily life in such a season, it is best to describe some of the background. The actors will feature bit by bit. I will begin by describing the setting, which is equally as real as the events that will unfold.

The PGHM

First of all, there is the PGHM itself. It is presently sited in the centre of Chamonix, at the bottom of the Mollard Hill, not far from the church of Saint-Michel. Previously it was on the first floor of a building in the Place du Mont-Blanc, at the junction of the road leading to Les Praz. Now it shares an old military building with the CNISAG,[1] of which it occupies the front part.

It is separated from the road by a metal gate, that stands wide open during the day, and a small courtyard with parking for three or four cars. On the front of the building, *Secours en Montagne* is written in large red, white and blue letters, illuminated at night. In the centre is a strong wooden door with triangular windows. It opens onto a foyer, furnished with two low armchairs and decorated with a relief map of the massif, a fine photo of Captain Mollaret, who commanded the unit from 1965 to 1973, and a framed, handwritten quotation from Edward Whymper, which many visitors must have pondered over:

[1] Centre National d'Instruction de Ski et d'Alpinisme de la Gendarmerie (Gendarmerie National Ski and Mountaineering Training Centre).

Climb if you will but remember that courage and strength are nought without prudence, and that a momentary negligence may destroy the happiness of a lifetime. [Curiously left out is the final sentence of Whymper's dictum: 'Do nothing in haste; look well to each step; and from the beginning think what might be the end.']

On the left is a sort of counter with the duty gendarme. Here too is where all telephone calls first arrive. Behind the counter is a small bedroom with a bunk for the man on night duty, a room full of radios and various transmitting devices and a back office, that serves as a command centre for co-ordinating the rescues.

Back in the hall, on the right, are two offices equipped with computers, where formal accident reports are prepared, and also a small foyer for relaxing, drinking cups of coffee, or having private conversations, such as those between a victim's family with the rescuer in charge of that particular operation. From the hall a stair-case also leads up to the first floor with offices for the secretaries, the major,[2] the captain, and a conference room, known as the press room, which in fact has a variety of functions because it is also used for receiving families, or for them to be alone, and various other activities.

And then there is the basement, the equipment stores, of both the PGHM and the SCSM,[3] an armoury, a ski store and finally a room set aside for research, where work is done on the production or improvement of rescue equipment. Finally, right at the very top of the building is an attic where the archives are stored.

At the helipad[4]

So the nerve centre of this organisation is in Chamonix. The rescues, on the other hand, are all carried out from the helipad, which is at Les Bois, a small hamlet not far from Chamonix.

This helipad has quite a story. When helicopters were first used for rescues – with a rather underpowered Alouette II – no one really knew where to park this curious machine, in particular during emergencies. As rescues were then a lot fewer and Chamonix less congested, it used to land, with the help of the Gendarmerie, in the Place du Mont-Blanc. One Friday night it was left there as

---

[2] The highest NCO rank, roughly equivalent to sergeant-major (not a major, officer rank, as in British/US armies).
[3] Société Chamoniarde de Secours en Montagne (see below).
[4] Known as the DZ (=Dropping Zone), something of a misnomer: translated throughout as helipad.

usual, but no one remembered about the Saturday market. Next morning the helicopter was found wedged in between various stalls selling vegetables, fruit, cheeses, sausages and the like. Some stallholders had even tied their lines to the machine, which found itself tied down to the ground like Gulliver among the Lilliputians.

Another solution had to be found. So, for a time, the helicopter was parked on a football pitch, where the ice rink is today. Then it was based for a while at Les Coverays, near Les Mouilles, which caused a general outcry from the local residents. It was moved to Les Pélerins, near the site of the new hospital. Then it was taken as far as Les Houches, more precisely to Taconnaz, in Mr Cachat's sand quarry. It was then brought back to near the Flégère cable-car, before the golf course extended that far. And perhaps other places too.

The town council decided to put an end to these peregrinations by giving it use of the present piece of land, not far from Les Bois. At that time it was simply a clearing amongst tall trees, unfenced, so the helicopter used to land in a hole in the forest. A canvas cover protected it at night. Then, about twenty years ago, a concrete hangar was built to house it, trees cut down, and the curious flocked to look. A wire fence was put up around the site.

Then a modest builder's hut was salvaged and erected on the northwest side of the compound, for the use of the aircrews. A small office was installed in it together with a store and toilets. The rescuers travelled to and from the Place du Mont-Blanc on each occasion. There was no doctor.

Finally, the dog-handlers of the valley decided to have permanent premises there. An opportunity arose. Everyone knows the Piot pharmacy in Chamonix, which is located in a building in the centre of the town. While the building was being restored, the pharmacy moved to a temporary wooden chalet that was erected in the Place de la Poste, and when the pharmacy moved back to its home, the dog-handlers acquired the chalet and rebuilt it at the helipad, a little beyond the hut already *in situ*. The town hall then decided to grant the use of the premises to all rescuers, a decision which seemed to have received a mixed reception from the dog-handlers. Whatever the reasons, the builder's hut is now used as a store for rescue equipment, stretchers, winches, lifting tackle, de-icing equipment, rucksacks ready for avalanche searches, etc., whilst the aircrews, rescuers and doctor are to be found in the Piot pharmacy's old chalet.

'Progress' is now threatening with concrete buildings. The basis has been accepted and it was put out to tender recently. Three plans were submitted. One of them, apparently, would not allow the helicopter to take off. Another, that was reasonably acceptable, exceeded the designated planning area by one metre. It would have been possible to rectify this problem, but as the plan had to be selected in the form presented, the disappointed competitors were sure to take legal action and win. So it was the third plan that was accepted. The finance was finally agreed on October 2, 1997, with a contribution from the EEC.

It is to be made up of three concrete units, constructed in the elegant neo-blockhouse style which has characterised our 20th century, and in which aircrews, rescuers and the doctor would have separate premises. That may seem sensible, but in my opinion is not. I asked if any of the three architects had sought permission to spend a day with those on the ground, in order to understand and study their needs, their wishes. Not one! They had simply worked from the survey maps. Which is how our world runs.[5]

The human aspect is even more important than the architectural aesthetics. People who work together in a difficult, tricky and sometimes dangerous job develop a sense of community, establishing bonds which go over and beyond the simple act of mountain rescue.

'It's going to be like Annecy,' several rescuers told me disappointedly.

I have not been to the Annecy base, but it is easy to grasp that each organisation has its own locale there and few mutual contacts made. Interaction is essential. Not only for the general harmony, the shared jokes, the meals, the coffee taken together and the relaxation that goes with it, but also for the professional side of the relationship. How many times, for example, have I heard a doctor giving explanation and advice to a rescuer? Each person

[5] One notable architectural aberration is that of the French National Library. The whim of a President who claimed to be a bibliophile and the ignorance of an architect would have resulted in the books being visible from the exterior, behind glass panels. It had not occurred to them that light is death to paper and leather bindings. When the specialists eventually made their voices heard, the harm had already been done and it was necessary to greatly reduce the surface area of each floor in order to cover the glass walls with unsightly and costly exotic wood shutters, which are already warping. Did the architect consult the original survey documents? It is doubtful, considering that the first time the waters of the River Seine rose, they flooded the basements, basements that were intended to store books. Now the area is permanently pumped out. The French National Library cost more than a billion euros and its running costs are some 650 million. Compared with these figures, the problems of the helipad at Les Bois are laughable. But isn't public money disposed of more lightly by those who spend it than those from whom it is extracted and who have to earn it?

shares his knowledge with the others. The pilot talks about aerology; the flight mechanicians[6] about winches; the rescuers about the technical issues of belaying and moving in the mountains. Everyone benefits from these exchanges.[7]

Anyway, although it was constructed to house a temporary pharmacy, salvaged by the dog-handlers and finally given over to the rescue service, the present chalet is fine. Let's have a look inside.

It won't take long, as there is only one room. It is a wooden chalet about eight metres wide and ten long, whose walls flare out from the base as was the fashion in the fifties and which has a symmetrical roof made in two sections. The interior is more or less open plan but divided into compartments by joists and bits of partition here and there. Across the room at the back, is a small kitchen. The rest of the space is taken up by three open compartments on the left and three on the right, with, for example, a bunk, a corner for the computers, and desks and workbenches of somewhat ill assorted design.

In the middle compartment on the right, which has a window, is enthroned she who is Queen of the place at times of relaxation: the TV! In July, the Tour de France monopolises and all eyes are on her, although her spectators are often missing, summoned elsewhere by work.

Finding contemplation of the Queen hampered by reflections on the screen, from the glass entrance door, an ingenious handyman solved the problem by suspending a pinkish blanket from the ceiling, between the said door and the Queen, a blanket that, over the years courageously fulfilled its duties. It was not of a wildly decorative elegance and, during the civil war in Yugoslavia, I heard Dr Lecoq lament the 'Sarajevo' effect that this wool rag gave to the place. But, more recently, an even more ingenious handyman has put up an old door that completely protects the Queen from reflections and draughts.

---

[6] Mechanicians do more than mechanics. They accompany the flight, keep a constant eye on the mechanical/aeronautical aspects of the helicopter, and operate the winch at the scene of the incident.

[7] I must point out here that Captain Gin, Commander of the PGHM in 1997, did not share my views. Although he preferred the second plan, he told me that there had been further discussions with regard to the one accepted, between the PGHM, the SCSM and the Sécurité Civile about the interior layout, and it had been modified accordingly. There is to be an 'operations room' where everyone should be able to get together (will they?). He is of the belief that the biggest mountain rescue centre in the world cannot make do with a builder's hut and an aging second-hand chalet. No doubt, but the ideal solution has most certainly not been found. It is perhaps the fault of the law, which does not allow proposers to revise their plans.

What lends charm to a place is not its splendour but its history, the effort put into it by those who have lived there, the life that emanates from it. From this point of view the helipad chalet fears no challenge.

Let's continue the tour! In the centre of the room, lined up or back to back, are three sofas, also salvaged, which have seen better days, and are finishing their time on this earth in fatigued collapse. Never mind! They serve their purpose and are, to use the in term, 'user-friendly'. A bevy of television viewers can be found there on bad weather days. Beside Her Majesty the TV is yet another two-seater couch, for those non-cult followers, who can gaze upon the cult followers, which I have often done.

The floor is covered in lino, second-hand again. The ceiling is wood slats with strip lighting. On the walls, some posters of helicopters and climbing. The south side of the building is mainly glass with a large French window. A big round grey stone acts as a doorstopper.

The place works, in fact, remarkably well. Although everyone is together, it is still possible to find somewhere to converse, talk privately, take a rest, telephone, yet without ever being totally on one's own. At any one time there can be two telephone conversations, the television on, people talking and someone asleep. This is reminiscent of the halls in the great châteaux of the Middle Ages, where everyone lived as a community, but window recesses adorned with stone seats allowed for some privacy. To put it plainly, the place is human.

The day when we get a compartmentalised building, which will, at least partially, shatter the community structure, the helipad will be in danger of losing a good part of its soul.

But that the helipad is essential is patently obvious, and the discussions repeated a thousand times over Chamonix dinner tables attacking it, against McDonald's, etc. seem as shallow as they are unrealistic.[8] Much more important is to form a common front over the real problems in the valley: the survival of the hospital,

---

[8] It would be unthinkable to do away with helicopter rescues and the helipad whose use is solely dependent upon the need for rescue, not on buildings put up for the use of the personnel. The privatisation of the rescue service, on the other hand, might lead to it being used for other purposes. Finally it must be noted that, contrary to what happens in Switzerland, private helicopters are not allowed to land at altitude in France, which limits the number of flights: private helicopters are based in Argentière. The McDonald's project was rejected so the company just bought up an old restaurant in the centre of town instead.

the reduction of traffic in the tunnel, rail-road transport under Mont Blanc.

Today in 2004 the concrete buildings are there. The Gendarmerie group are on their own, separated by two large hangars from the others. Each group has its own room: Sécurité Civile, rescuers, doctors, and press. It would have been impossible to write this book now, running around from one to the other. And several rescuers have told me the whole atmosphere has changed.

Parkinson,[9] amongst many other sensible observations, described a most interesting phenomenon, although the powers that be have ignored his work as being too full of humour and wisdom to be taken seriously. He noted that the most effective organisations live a completely improvised existence:

> The perfection of planning is a symptom of decay. During a period of exciting discovery or progress there is no time to plan the perfect headquarters. The time for that comes later, when all the important work has been done. Perfection, we know, is finality; and finality is death.

The examples Parkinson cited are by no means insignificant: St Peter's at Rome where 'the later Popes lost half their authority while the work was still in progress'; Versailles, which was not finished until the monarchy was in decline; the League of Nations, which was founded in 1920 and whose failure was manifest by 1933, but whose physical embodiment, however, the Palais des Nations was not opened until 1937, by which time 'the League had practically ceased to exist'. Soon the United Nations might well be added to that list, devoid as it is of any real power, but with a huge building in New York, a luxury hotel, countless annexes with an excessive number of staff, while the real problems are left to the care of other organisations like the IMF, ILO, WHO, UNESCO.

It is likely that the present helipad will mark the most solid and interesting period of rescue, the time of a true team at work

Finally, let's not forget that the backdrop to the rescue service is above all the huge and unpredictable mountains which rise high above all human structures, airy ridges, north faces, hostile and frozen walls, glaciers with their streams and moraines, rock rognons, blue-green bergschrunds, gaping crevasses, séracs suspended above unexplored depths, moraines, unstable scree, steep grassy slopes with impenetrable bush, torrents, snow, sky, sun, ice, clouds and wind.

[9] Parkinson, C. Northcote, *Parkinson's Law*, 1958.

3

RESPONSIBILITY IN THE MOUNTAINS

First Views

The helipad opens permanently on July 1 because from this date call-outs are likely to increase. But when the helipad is closed between the winter and summer seasons, rescues obviously still take place when necessary, with the helicopter coming from either Megève, or Annecy. The rescuers themselves remain available in the PGHM building which is only five or six minutes from the helipad at Les Bois, opened up for the duration of the rescue operation.

Thus, from May 31 to June 30, 1997, there were fifty-seven rescues in Haute-Savoie, including the Mont Blanc range. Of these rescues, involving alpinists, skiers, walkers, parapenters, injured workers, there were two cases of exhaustion, thirty-eight injuries (one casualty was found at the bottom of the Whymper Couloir and died the following day), seventeen were ill (heart problems, attacks of cramp, respiratory difficulties, etc. but most commonly altitude sickness), one search for a missing person, the discovery of an ancient body in a ravine and five deaths.

As can be seen, the rescuers may be called out at any time, and not for trivialities. Nor is it the case that deaths only occur in the mountains as the public likes to think. In fact, of the five deaths during this period (not including the body which was discovered or the casualties which later died), none was killed in the high mountains; rather it was two walkers, a hang-glider, a man with a fatal illness who died in his high pasture chalet and a bus driver trying to rescue a child who was rafting.

From this brief introduction it is clear that there is a communication problem. The public often gets the wrong idea about the reasons for accidents and mountain rescue. Journalists as well. The television companies even more so. We will be coming back to this.

July 1

The main summer season has started cold and wet. The snow is down to 2000 metres. The mountains are invisible, lost in grey cloud. Where the pine forests that cling to the slopes are not yet wreathed in mist they are black and wet. The town is dreary. It is only when I arrive at the helipad, under an umbrella, that I am glad not to be elsewhere. The helipad is a place of human warmth, the only warmth to be had in this unsettled weather.

During this first week of July, *Dragon*, the Sécurité Civile helicopter, is on duty. To complete the scene previously painted, it may be added that the Sécurité Civile aircrew wear red overalls, the Gendarmerie helicopter crew khaki, the rescuers blue. It's handy, you know who is who.

The doctors have the privilege of lending a touch of imagination to the proceedings by wearing whatever colour they want: rose, sky blue pink… But this opportunity for originality remains largely theoretical. More often than not they are dressed in red, and the supreme simplification, since Dr Cauchy is the best known of them because he writes for *Vertical*, is that they are all 'Dr Cauchy' 'I was rescued by Dr Cauchy… 'I was admitted to casualty by *Dr Cauchy*', victims have told me, when this was not the case.

In fact, two other hospital doctors, François Lecoq and Guy Duperrex, were working with the rescue service during the summer of 1997, as also on occasion Bernard Marsigny, head of the casualty department, and Benoît Couzineau, army doctor at the EMHM.[1] François Lecoq has adopted a simple approach and when asked his name, replies: 'Me? I'm Dr Cauchy of course!'

Let's take a look at today's actors. Jean-Michel Vialle, known to be an excellent pilot, is dark, with a short beard, very nice. Once he gave me a superb gift for which I remain extremely grateful. Gilles Mathé, one of the two rescuers, has a bright face, fair hair, blue eyes and is very precise. He is a qualified guide and ski instructor. The other, Jean-Luc Yvon is one of the oldest members of the team, and is extremely efficient. He is of average height, with short grey hair and a moustache that curls up at the ends. He is a dog-handler and is always accompanied by Hadja, a six-year-old Alsatian, excellent in avalanche searches, who inspires a

[1] École Militaire de Haute Montagne.

manifest respect in everybody. Yvon is also a parapent expert and is in charge of audio-visual equipment at the PGHM.

So, in this fine company, the conversation turned to the subject of responsibility in the mountains, a serious problem as it concerns accidents, all the more so as it is now tending to lead to legal action.

I brought up the case of Smiler, to see if it was known in France. Smiler is a British mountain guide, who, several years ago, was involved in a sad accident in which his client, a friend, died. The Procureur de la République (public prosecutor) in Bonneville found no case against him. In England, seven years later, a civil action found otherwise. We have not escaped what could become an automatic reflex, like in the United States where the slightest medical error often leads to punitive damages

Now I learned that a French guide, found guilty of various mistakes and negligence in a canyoning accident in which three teenagers died, had recently been given a heavy sentence, including a prison term and a life ban on working as a guide, in a case brought by the parents. He had appealed and was awaiting the outcome.

Canyoning was an issue because the guiding profession is trending towards supplementary activities, starting with skiing, which has now become a compulsory part of the guiding qualification. Here we will concern ourselves simply with climbing.

I also learnt that the accident in the Whymper Couloir, mentioned at the beginning of this chapter, might result in legal proceedings. Here is what I was told.

Three alpinists had set off to climb the Couturier Couloir on the Aiguille Verte. One of them was a good climber, another of average ability, the third, a twenty-year-old, had limited experience. They had not roped up, justifiable when being roped together might put all at risk rather than protecting them, in the event of one falling and pulling the others off. However it is not an advisable technique between partners of different abilities. Each had climbed at his own pace. The weakest either lost or broke a crampon. The others did not wait, another error, but told him they would cut good steps. The best of the three arrived at the summit two hours before the second. Not seeing the third, they decided he must have turned back, so descended via the Whymper Couloir, with the rope that they knew was needed to cross the bergschrund, and made their way to the Couvercle Hut. If at that stage they had notified the PGHM that the third member was not fully accounted for, the outcome might have been very different.

It was not until they reached the valley the following morning, that they alerted the PGHM and requested a search. The missing climber was found, still alive, at the bottom of the Whymper Couloir. So he had continued with the climb, alone, slowly, had probably found some shelter for the night and from the storm, then attempted the descent. He cannot have been far above the bergschrund when he fell, perhaps 200 metres, because his body was hardly marked. He was in a coma, hypothermic at 26°. In Chamonix Hospital, they re-warmed him, but his brain did not respond. He was flown to the neurological department of Geneva Hospital where he was recognised as brain dead, and then on to Lyon, where he was born and where he officially died, when, with all hope lost, the machines which were keeping him artificially alive were turned off.

The conclusions of the public prosecutor, with regard to his death on June 12, were not yet known. He could decide that the two other climbers were responsible and prosecute them for not assisting a person in danger (an offence in France). The family also has thirty years to lodge a formal complaint.[2] We must recognise that attitudes in the climbing world have changed.[3] Far be it from me to say that everything was right in the past, and wrong today. But this development cannot be denied and is perhaps no more than an aspect of a more general trend.

So the law now occupies a place in the mountain arena which it did not have before. Liability can be sought in a criminal as well as a civil court. I know a guide who was offended when the family of his client were asked if they intended lodging a complaint, the client being in no state to decide herself. He was wrong to be shocked. The question is asked routinely, because the law demands it as a logical part of any inquiry involving the actions of a professional. Smiler's case, which we are now going to examine, is one such distressing example of this process.

[2] At the beginning of 1998 the PGHM learned that a complaint had indeed been lodged.
[3] See Chapter 34 where responsibility in the mountains is covered in more detail.

Smiler's Case
Dave Cuthbertson's[4] friends nicknamed him 'Smiler', because of his happy disposition and good nature.

The 1990 accident, and its aftermath, was far from a smiling matter.

Cases such as his, concerning professional liability in the mountains, are likely to become more common as a result of pressure from insurance companies and the financial potential which they present to the injured parties or their families.

Before tackling this subject, I would like to make my personal position clear. I used to climb at a good standard, either with friends, or with guides. I know that no one, even the best, is beyond making a mistake. I have made them myself and seen others do so. At no time would I have lodged a complaint, either against a friend, or against a guide because, knowing the potential dangers inherent in climbing, I took responsibility for the risks, including choice of companions, and was ready to accept the consequences, whatever they may have been. That said, I do not know how I would have reacted if someone close to me, particularly a child, had been involved. As we will see, this event occurred in the summer of 1997.

The problem of responsibility in the mountains is not a new one. We must remember that. Indeed it is almost as old as mountaineering itself.

There are some very well known cases, such as that of Dr Hamel who, in 1820, left to climb Mont Blanc with three friends and twelve guides. Three of the latter died in an avalanche. When the question of responsibility was raised, the finger was pointed at the 'tourists', who had insisted on continuing despite bad conditions. This was the first major tragedy in the history of mountaineering.

The first ascent of the Matterhorn took place on July 14, 1865. Only Edward Whymper, then twenty-five, and two Zermatt guides, the Taugwalders, father and son, came back from the adventure alive. The rope, incredibly thin, had broken. It is on display in the Zermatt museum. The break resulted in the deaths of the four others: Douglas Hadow, Lord Alfred Douglas, the Reverend Charles Hudson and the Argentière guide Michel Croz, although had it not broken it is probable that all would have been torn off the mountain and died. The affair caused a great stir at

---

[4] Not to be confused with the famous Scottish climber of the same name who is nicknamed 'Cubby'.

the time and the question of liability was raised, although in those days there was no question of legal proceedings being brought. But the accident weighed heavily on Whymper all his life, on account of the accusations, justified or not, which it carried with it. There are many such examples to be found throughout the history of mountaineering. But what is new today are the resulting legal proceedings.

Let us go back to Smiler's tragic case, which is liable to be used as a precedent, if not to change legal theory. It will no doubt be one of the first in a long series, in an era when, generally speaking, there is a growing disinclination to accept responsibility.

The accident that involved Smiler Cuthbertson and his client, took place on July 21, 1990, on the North Face of the Tour Ronde. A professional British mountain guide, then aged forty-two, he had been engaged for a week by Gerald Anthony Hedley, who was forty-one. The two men knew each other well and were good friends. They had been climbing together for two years. Having left the Torino Hut at three o'clock in the morning, they crossed the bergschrund at four. Leaving so early, and from a hut, certainly showed that they were cautious, as the North Face of the Tour Ronde is often climbed from the first cable-car. But perhaps they were planning to do several routes from the hut. Whatever their reasons, they started out in good time, as is sensible for an ice route. It should be noted that, despite its being a north face, this route is not excessively difficult. It has an average angle of 52° with a height difference of only 350 metres.

Gerald Hedley was a good ice climber and, after spending the previous week doing training climbs, it had been agreed with his guide that he would lead the climb from the first pitches. Arriving at the narrows in the middle of the face, Smiler Cuthbertson, judging that his client was not moving fast enough and that stone and ice fall, particularly from the parties in front, was increasing, decided to take over the lead.[5] After fifty metres he belayed to an ice screw, brought his client up and, having attached him to the belay with an Italian hitch, continued. As he climbed above the belay, he did not place any intermediate ice screws. Not of itself unusual, since parties often move together on this face unprotected. Naturally it depends on conditions. Smiler's intention was to get rapidly to

[5] At this stage two soloists had overtaken them and there was one team, possibly two, higher on the face.

an area out of the rising sun and falling stones and ice. And there was all the more reason to do so since a party high on the face in front had a short time earlier dropped an ice axe. So their position was not entirely safe and he considered it necessary to move fast.

He was about twenty metres above the belay when he came off. Afterwards, he was unable to explain why. He only remembered having the impression that the ice, which was friable, had given way beneath his crampons. He may have made a cramponing error but he could also have been hit by falling ice. His ice hammer having been knocked out of his grip, he tried to arrest his slide with his ice axe and nearly succeeded, but the axe was wrenched out and he shot off again. By the time the shock came onto the ice screw belay, Smiler had already gone forty metres (twenty above the belay and twenty below) and, even though his fall had been momentarily slowed, the resulting shock tore out the ice screw and his client with it. It was inevitable, considering the force exerted by such a long fall.

The two men were precipitated down the face, cartwheeling, as might be expected. The fall was stopped when the rope caught behind a rock rognon, but Gerald Hedley, who had been catapulted fifty metres further onto rocks, had been killed instantly. Smiler had multiple facial and leg injuries. Another party immediately went to their aid and called for help. Alerted at 8.55 am by the border guards at Pointe Helbronner, the helicopter was there by 9.10 am. The pilot was René Romet, the rescue team members were Jean-Luc Yvon and Luc Karleskind.[6] They could do nothing for Gerald Hedley except confirm he was dead. Smiler was winched off the mountain and taken to Chamonix Hospital. Examining the climbing equipment of the two men, the rescuers noted that it was appropriate and in good condition. Their ice axes and crampons had been sharpened the previous evening. The guide was insured for civil liability through the UIAGM[7] and for professional risk through the BMC.[8] The accident report was sent, as they all are, to the Prefect of the Haute Savoie and to the public prosecutor, who concluded that there was no penal liability.

---

[6] Luc Karleskind was himself to die two years later, almost to the day (July 19, 1992), on the same mountain, the Tour Ronde, as he was carrying out a rescue. Whilst trying to save members of a climbing party who had been caught by an avalanche and swept into the bergschrund on the normal route, he was himself buried by another avalanche.

[7] Union Internationale des Associations de Guides de Montagne.

[8] British Mountaineering Council.

This tragedy turned out to be even more dramatic still. Gerald Hedley was married. His wife, Lynda, had recently discovered she was pregnant and had decided to wait until the end of the holiday to tell her husband, who died without knowing he was to become a father.

In Britain Lynda Hedley lodged a formal complaint and a request for compensation for Daniel, Gerald Hedley's posthumous son.

Judgement was not passed until June 20, 1997. It was severe, concluding that the guide was entirely responsible, that to have used only one ice screw for the belay was professional negligence, and it awarded damages of two hundred thousand pounds to the family of the deceased.

What should be noted in this sad affair, however much sympathy one cannot help but feel for widow and orphan, is that the judgement was made many years later, by a judge who knew nothing about icy north faces. He had recourse to experts but the whole debate turned on the issue of the single ice screw that was used for the belay. Other technical points could have been raised. It is possible, although not certain, that a belay of two ice screws and an intermediate one might have stopped the fall, but it would have meant even more time lost on a climb when speed was becoming imperative.

The main flaw in such a judgement is to rely on rules presented as absolute, in an area as unpredictable and as harsh as the mountain environment. Is it better to climb out of a dangerous area as quickly as possible or to hang around, putting in pieces of protection, at the risk of being hit by falling stones, snow or ice? It is all a matter of judgement. A good professional will make the right decision, taking into account the time, conditions, the physical and technical competence of his clients, without ever eliminating all the risks because the terrain is, by definition, dangerous. To rule, after the event, on the technique that should have been adopted in a situation that is unique and cannot be reconstructed, when the fall of the guide was highly improbable, is a dubious exercise.

During the summer of 1997, we shall see other disturbing cases, even more perplexing than Smiler's.

We will not go into the details of this affair that grabbed the attention of the British press during June 1997. Many other points, in addition to those mentioned, could doubtless be examined and discussed, because it involved a death. With a slight change of events, for such events often hinge on one little thing, the accident would not have happened or have been less serious and no one would have dwelt on that single ice screw belay, a practice which is frequently used.

In conclusion, I record below, with the author's consent, the letter which George Band, President of the British Mountaineering Council, addressed to the press after the judgement which will go down in history as being controversial:

> The judgement in the case ... creates a misleading picture about safety and responsibility in mountaineering ... [it] suggests that placing two ice screw belays and ice screw running belays is a standard safety procedure for climbing routes of the type where the incident occurred and that this procedure is 'universal' and 'elementary' and 'fundamental'. This is not the case.
>
> Depending on the condition, one of a number of procedures may be appropriate. Choosing the best procedure is one of the judgements made during an ascent. The judgement also supposes that if a second screw had been placed then the accident would have been prevented. This is by no means certain; where ice is of poor quality, two screws offer little more protection than one.
>
> It is also stated that 'a fall was foreseeable but the risk of stonefall was remote'.
>
> Falling rocks and ice are a regular and common danger on climbs of this type, and speed is the way in which exposure to this hazard is minimised, whereas a fall is a very unlikely possibility. Ice screw anchors do not offer guaranteed security and any climber who was 'forseeing' the possibility of a fall on such a climb would not consider the route to be justifiable. Because the accident has occurred, it does not mean that any individual is at fault. Risk is inherent in mountaineering and it cannot be eliminated, only reduced.

Smiler Cuthbertson did not appeal against the judgement, although the reasons for it were questionable. In any case he did not have the financial means to do so. The proceedings had been very long. With only modest resources, he had legal aid and the damages were paid by his insurance company.

It should be noted that, on September 28, 1997, the Association of British Mountain Guides, having held their own inquiry, decided that the case did not constitute professional negligence and considered that Cuthbertson's behaviour towards his client was that of a professional and competent mountain guide, every mountaineering decision being taken according to the conditions prevailing in place and time, not a function of the standardised procedure.

This case can be seen as a model, in that it introduces a rigid, legal aspect to an activity where it is impossible to have precise rules and in which each person engages of their own free will. Although a highway code is applicable on a road network created by man, with vehicles he also created, it is not the same in the mountains where climbers are up against a constantly changing, and as yet untamed world. The clash between our civilised world and this other, still more or less natural, is inevitable, but more often than not it translates as a complete lack of understanding.

Finally it should be noted that, at another time and in another place, a tribunal could rule differently. A Californian court, considering the case of an accident following the failure of an abseil anchor, judged that:

> A fall, whether it be due to the casualty slipping, the mistake of a climbing partner, or the failure of the belay system, is an inherent risk in a sport which involves climbing mountains, which cannot be completely eliminated without destroying the sport itself.

But the problem of responsibility in the mountains is a subject that crops up more and more frequently, such as in the disaster at Les Orres in January, 1998.

This tragic accident, well known in France, happened when a school party of snow-shoers was avalanched and eleven killed. The guide alone was held responsible although others were also arraigned. Nowadays, most judges find it easiest to lay the blame on the guide as though he were omnipotent. But people who want to climb and even parents sending children to mountaineering centres have a part in the responsibility should an accident happen. Zero risk does not exist and particularly in mountains.

4

THE START OF THE SEASON

Wednesday, July 2
Although there were no rescues on July 1, there were two this Wednesday: a nineteen-year-old assistant hut warden, who was suffering from measles and airlifted out; then a seventy-year-old female walker with heart trouble was given medical attention and also flown down to the valley.

From this it is clear that a good many mountain rescues are not altitude-related, nor do they concern 'careless young people who go onto glaciers in training shoes, recklessly undertaking climbs which they are not capable of doing, putting the lives of their rescuers at risk, and who deserve to pay for their mistakes, or even not to be rescued at all, etc.', erroneous clichés, which none the less pervade the collective mentality as well as the minds of those who are supposedly responsible for reporting news.

The mountain rescue is frequently called out for 'Mr Average', his family, his children on holiday, his aged parents. Furthermore, a good number of PGHM rescues take place outside the Chamonix valley,[1] often for accidents that are anything but minor. That, too, will also be taken up again.

Thursday, July 3
The weather is ever more gloomy. The forecast says it will be *poor* today, *cloudy* tomorrow and *unsettled* the day after. Nice turns of phrase but the most that can be said of this forecast is that it is a litotes. Covered with fresh snow, iced up and hostile, the Aiguilles are shrouded in a dirty fog. The slopes of dark pines that dominate the valley are hidden in the drizzle most of the time. Lingering banks of mist halfway up look more like monsoon clouds. The wind, for it is windy as well, swirls and blows them around. If it were not for the leaves and the green grass in the valley to remind

---

[1] About a quarter of rescues: accidents at work, walkers falling off footpaths, etc.

us that it is summer, the middle of summer, it would be easy to forget, so icy cold, grey and damp is it. Shivering figures walk around the streets of Chamonix, hunched up under their waterproof jackets.

Impossible to imagine anybody up in the mountains! Impossible? Not enough imagination! Two rescues this morning alone!

The first, a guide's 'exhausted' client on the way to the Col du Géant, which calls for a brief commentary. Ethics dictate that a rescue should not be requested unless absolutely necessary. The exhausted client, who had managed to reach the Requin Hut while a more important rescue was taking place, would in the past have descended to the valley under his own steam after resting for a while. His 'rescue' had principally been so that the others could finish their route.

Returning to the serious accident, it involved a party of Koreans who had decided, come what may, to attempt Mont Blanc and had left yesterday, in rain and snow, for the Goûter Hut. It seems that they had been warned about the bad conditions, but having waited for long, decided to give it a go. They reached the Goûter Hut yesterday. That itself was quite a sporting achievement, but this morning, faced with so much deep snow and bad weather, and doubtless wind too, they decided to turn back. There were eleven of them, split into two groups, one of seven, the other of four. The latter, caught in an avalanche after traversing the Grand Couloir, had fallen two or three hundred metres. Some were buried but the rope had helped the others find them quickly. One was unconscious; he was saved by mouth-to-mouth resuscitation. And the least injured had managed to reach the Tête Rousse Hut to raise the alarm.

In short they had been lucky, as we say of people who might well consider they hadn't been. But their story could have been more tragic albeit commonplace. It was foolish leaving in such weather and conditions; an avalanche, and there could have been four dead. But all finished relatively well as is often the case. The mountains are more forgiving than might be thought.

There are two other rescue operations today, outwith the boundaries of the range but within the remit of the PGHM: the search for a walker lost in the Samoëns area and an investigation of a break-in at a high alpine chalet.

At the helipad the afternoon passes in quiet expectation. It is often like this during bad weather, but a call-out can come at any moment, requiring the helicopter to fly if at all possible, or a team to go out on foot if the helicopter cannot take off.

The helipad has some guests this year whose story can be guessed. A pair of birds, redstarts, who, in the springtime, were looking for somewhere to nest. One of them noticed the eaves of the chalet at the helipad. The marvel of their conversation can be imagined:

'So quiet here!'

'Perfect! Just what we're looking for!'

'And so peaceful!'

'We won't be disturbed here!'

'No people! No dogs! No cats!'

'This place is fantastic!'

'And have you seen that big clearing in front? It looks just made for taking off.'

'To put it bluntly, I've never seen a better place for building a nest!'

The helipad opened the day before yesterday and is still relatively quiet, despite today's occasional interventions. Since it's raining, we're inside with the door closed. From time to time, we see a bird hovering, like a helicopter, in front of the window, before entering its home.

But when the rescue season really gets under way, what will become of the birds?

I start a conversation with Alain Place, a newly arrived rescuer. I ask where he's from, because there's a certain accent in his voice. Got it right! He's from the Eastern Pyrenees, where my family originates. I talk of them and he about his own and his wife, who is from Villemolaque, near Tressères and is writing about the Aspres region.

Someone arrives with a box of small cakes, which we all share. Various conversations ensue, punctuated by bursts of laughter. That's how the helipad is on a rainy day. The afternoon draws to a close. It is almost seven o'clock. The Sécurité Civile put the red helicopter in the hangar and go home. Dr Lecoq and I prepare to do the same. He says to me:

'By the way, this book you are writing, how do you see it turning out?'

'I can't tell yet. It will depend on all of you, on what you tell me, on my reactions to the rescues.'

And I add:

'I'm very much counting on you to convey the human element of it all to me.'

He is astonished, but I didn't say that arbitrarily. François Lecoq is perceptive, sensitive, he registers people's reactions and can put them into words. Of all the doctors, he is the one from whom I expect to learn most. About thirty years old, tall and slim, he has a face which is constantly in movement, laughing, surprised, explanatory, impassioned.

Really just as an aside, I add:

'The Koreans this morning, what was the human element?'

'Ah!' he exclaims. 'Ah yes! There was a human factor to that!'

So the Koreans are back in the hot seat. I don't know what this is about. What could the human factor be? Fear, perhaps, at being involved in an accident far from home, in a foreign country?

No. François Lecoq explains:

'It's terrible with Asians when they can't even speak English. The one I was dealing with couldn't speak French, of course, but no word of English either. Nothing! We could not communicate. It's often the case with Asians, with Japanese, for example. You have to feel your way through. I tell you, it's not proper medicine. Call it what you want – pediatric, intergalactic, veterinary medicine – you cannot communicate! You don't know what's wrong with them, where they hurt, if they hurt, you can't say anything to them, they remain inscrutable, without a word in any language. Italians, on the other hand, oh la la! They spill out everything that's wrong with them and everything that happened. Yak, yak, yak! *Sono disgraziato! E siccura che la gamba e rotta, dottore! E il mia ditta! Guarda! Perde il sangue!* Oh! The Italians! And the French aren't much better! We go and pick them up because they've bust their ankle and they tell you that already they hadn't felt well that morning because they'd drunk hot chocolate. We couldn't give a damn, but they tell you all the same. The Asians, zilch! It's not happenstance, it's cultural.

'The Korean I was looking after this morning, if he'd been French, I'd certainly have given him a jab so he wouldn't suffer in the chopper. But I couldn't just do it blindly. So I stabilised him, rapidly, as I wanted him out of there and in hospital, pronto, because I was *incapable* of finding out what was wrong with him. It's the same with Asians in casualty, they say nothing. They accept waiting on a chair for two hours, not even making a fuss, for it's those who shout the loudest, who complain, those with an obvious problem, that are most likely to be dealt with first. We had a Japanese bloke like that who'd fallen skiing. We were led to understand he'd something wrong with his arm. He had an X-ray, nothing! To have a clear conscience we X-rayed his cervical vertebrae and – Bingo! – it was one of these that was broken! We could well have missed it. So, there's the human element of this morning's Korean accident: no means of communicating. It's like looking after little children, when you don't know if they have stomach ache, headache, or some other ache...'

'Too true!' comments a rescuer. 'One of the Koreans was limping badly when he got out of the helicopter. I tried to find out if he was injured, but he made a sign to show me he was fine. It's like the people from the Eastern Bloc countries, never complain... But the Asians, in addition, smile at you, as though they were joking.'

'Asians,' concludes François Lecoq sententiously, 'are the dread of the rescue doctor!'

Friday, July 4
A cloudy morning, without too much rain, the mountains still lost in cloud and snow. The afternoon and evening a deluge! Yet, despite the weather, there was a rescue in the morning! Someone with altitude sickness at the Aiguille du Goûter, suffering from suspected pulmonary oedema. When I hear this, I can't help exclaiming:

'In weather like this, in such conditions, and that forecast, there are still people other than Koreans who want to climb Mont Blanc?'

God knows I've climbed in bad weather, wrongly no doubt. But when you get a sight, between the drifting swathes of clag, of the present state of the mountains, the huge accumulations of fresh snow, on the faces, the slopes, in the gullies, on the ledges, it seems unimaginable that anybody would attempt Mont Blanc under such conditions.

Well, not only are there people at the Aiguille du Goûter, but there are also others stuck in the Vallot Hut, at nearly 4400 metres. Thanks to the radio beacon that allows those in the hut to communicate with the PGHM and vice versa, that was discovered this morning. Hut is rather a grand word to describe the Vallot. It is really no more than a high altitude shelter, an aluminium cabin which is entered from below. It is always dirty, freezing, damp and pretty foul-smelling.

It's believed those there tonight are Poles. You would certainly have to be Polish to get that far up the mountain in these conditions! The PGHM has barely been able to communicate with them. They just said: *'Frigo... Frigo...'* For them to be cold, it must be cold. What's the temperature in the Vallot? –10°? –15°? The hut only provides protection from the wind. There are blankets but they get wet and freeze.

At the slightest clearing, the helicopter will go for them, but there is no clearing. It's raining harder and harder. It's hoped they will be able to descend to the Goûter Hut, which would seem like the most luxurious of palaces in comparison.

If the Koreans had been killed and then the Poles were found frozen to death in the Vallot when the weather cleared up, there would be an outcry about their foolhardiness, and perhaps with good reason.

But you have to put yourself in their place.

The Koreans: what a voyage to come and climb in the Alps. What sacrifices perhaps, certainly what dreams. Now they find themselves here, in a valley swamped in mist and water, where it has seemingly been raining for three weeks. They are nearing the end of their trip. Are they going to leave just like that? To go home having done nothing other than watch the rain teeming down? Perhaps they'd missed a chance to go up? Had decided not to go on a day when the weather was indifferent? Wanting to wait for the really good weather, which must inevitably come, and climb Mont Blanc in the sunshine and the splendour which they imagined? But the good weather had not arrived. So, they had decided to go, no matter what. They'd somehow managed the climb up to the Aiguille du Goûter, which must have been a pretty taxing expedition, brushing off the fresh snow blowing around in the gusting wind and squalls, flakes sticking to their glasses, ice forming on their eyebrows, on hair unprotected by their anoraks, and fingers numb with cold. They got to the hut, all eleven of them, spent the night there, aware now that the remaining one thousand metres above really was inaccessible.

They decided to retreat and almost succeeded. Descending from the Goûter when it has snowed all night and is continuing to do so, was certainly no pleasure outing. They had done the hardest part, crossed the Grand Couloir without incident. The avalanche that then caught them was pure bad luck.

And the Poles! ... Can one comprehend how much the mountains mean to the Poles? For long, in a country crushed by a dictatorship, which generated nothing but poverty and frustration, the mountains were for some a means of escape from their bleak and meaningless everyday life. It is not their fault if the Marxist economy created an economic disaster. They endured it, they suffered it, they regained their freedom, they can now take advantage of that, they can travel, fulfil long held dreams. Us, we were on the right side of the Iron Curtain...

Now, in a country free but bled dry, the mountains hold the same promises of escape, self-realisation and happiness, and life can be spent preparing for these wonderful moments of fulfilment. Climbers from the Eastern Bloc countries come to Chamonix in coaches in which a place is difficult to come by. Often, they don't have the means to camp. When in the valley, they sleep in or under the coach, or outside. In any case it is no worse on the mountain ... except at the Vallot. They must have spent the year scrimping and saving for this trip, anticipating the forthcoming pleasure. They too, faced with this disastrous weather, set off in it to try and realise their dream, and they certainly achieved something! In this age of soft living, who could cast the first stone? But now – they are stuck in the Vallot and maybe for long...

Saturday, July 5
Rain from morning until night. The mountains completely hidden. Everything drenched, sodden, soaked. No question of the helicopter flying. I haven't even the courage to brave the puddles at the helipad in such a downpour. Anyhow, it would merely have been to watch the Tour de France on the television, which must be harnessing all the energy of the PGHM at the moment. At the Vallot, things can't be getting any more comfortable.

Sunday, July 6
Good weather, well almost. The helicopter was able to go up for the Poles.

Those Poles, someone said to me, informed us that they were there, stuck in the Vallot in the storm, and that they needed to be rescued when it was possible, then during the following forty-eight hours, when it was obvious to them that nothing could be done, they did not contact us again. Others, in the same situation, would be on the radio all the time, reminding us that they were still there, asking us yet again to come, wanting to know when we thought we could. Not the Poles! Once they knew the message was received, they simply trusted us and waited.

It was –10° at the Vallot.

The French sports commentators have recently introduced a fashionable word into their jargon: *le mental* (strength of mind). Let's just say that the Poles have an awful lot.

Another rescue, somewhat curious for the time of year. A Parisien, about thirty years old, had arrived by train last night, hired skis and boots and set off down the Vallée Blanche. In July! He must have thought that with such bad weather, winter had set in again. Nevertheless it's still summer, and he found himself in difficulty at the start of the Géant Icefall, and had become completely stuck when he was spotted from the Requin Hut. Alerted, the PGHM got him out of his labyrinth.

Another rescue, a perennial: a runner in the 'Cross du Mont Blanc' race suffering from hypoglycaemia near La Flégère.

Apart from that, the helipad is relatively calm considering the good weather. The Wimbledon final is on the television. Pete Sampras is beating Cédric Pioline. Amusing, the remarks here on the competitors' girl friends at the decisive moment :

'Bet Sampras's lady is pleased! She can see a convertible coming her way! A dishwasher with twelve different programmes… Oh boy! Is she happy!'

'And look at the other one! Not her! She'll be doing the washing up herself tonight and tomorrow will be signing on the dole. Oh, what a face!'

That's how it is at the helipad. Waiting, relaxing, resting, which can transform itself in a split second into immediate action.

Then we are back to the Tour de France, which doesn't please the Sécurité Civile pilot, Vincent Saffioti, nicknamed Aldo, because he swaggers a bit.

'Huh! The Tour de France, I don't know what you see in it… There are the Fangios and Ferraris who tore their guts out to advance technical progress and then there are the others who still pedal like idiots. Me, what I like are *mechanical* sports.'

But it is an Italian, Cippolini, who wins the stage. And of course Saffioti, who, as his name suggests, is of Italian origin, is delighted. The winner climbs onto the podium. Two pretty blondes stand beside him, kiss him and present him with bouquets.

'Not like us,' remarks Saffioti. 'Every time we come back from a rescue, we imagine that there are going to be two pretty *ragazze*, like those, to congratulate us, give us kisses, present us with flowers. But, no! No one is interested in us!'

Outside, the redstarts continue to feed their brood installed under the roof. Worms in their beak, they perch, to survey the terrain, on the horizontal network of wires and cables, connecting the chalet to the pylon supporting the aerials and the windsock. But often, just as they are about to go into their nest, they are disturbed. By the flight engineer closing the door of the helicopter, or a rescuer coming outside with the binoculars to inspect the mountains, by another who joins him, a visitor arriving. So the bird flies off … and comes back patiently, a little later, finally manages to reach its nest, flies off again.

I can imagine the couple's conversation in the evening.

'I don't understand it. This was a perfectly quiet place when you laid your eggs.'

'Oh yes… Well, I always thought there was something odd about it. I had an intuition…'

'If you had an intuition, you didn't let on… It's not our home any more! Still, what's done is done and the little ones are here. This activity is probably only temporary. These guys and their big machine will soon be off.'

'Think so?'

'Sure! What's to keep them? They don't even sleep here. They'll be going home.'

'I hope so… Because when the little ones start to fly, they'll need peace and quiet.'

'They'll have it! You'll see… That's my intuition!'

What will become of these little birds?

Monday, July 7
Monday is helicopter changeover day. Today *Bravo Lima* is going

to replace *Dragon*. In other words, the Gendarmerie's helicopter, which is blue, will replace that of the Sécurité Civile's, which is red.

During my first days at the helipad in '94, I was curious to know whether the duty helicopter – the blue one – had a name. I was told that it was called *Bravo Lima*. I was blown away. And I thought I had imagination. But never, had I ever been asked to name a helicopter, would I have thought of combining the words *Bravo* and *Lima*... *Bravo*, a word full of enthusiasm, followed by *Lima*, with its faraway exoticism! You had to hand it to them... The Gendarmerie Nationale had a lot more imagination than I.

For some reason the penny didn't drop until my husband reminded me of the aeronautical alphabet where A as *Alpha*, B as *Bravo* etc. As the registration number of the blue helicopter was JBL, it was naturally called *Juliet Bravo Lima*, and by apheresis *Bravo Lima*. Rather disappointing but logical.

As for the Sécurité Civile helicopters, they are all called *Dragon*, each one being distinguished by a number corresponding to the department to which it belongs.

This does not detract from the fact that the phrase '*Bravo Lima* is going to replace *Dragon*' has a wonderful resonance. It carries the suggestion of a coded message that always appeals to me. The impression of a 'great game'. It is full of hints of the mysterious, the esoteric, the wild... Anyway, it is a thousand times better than groups of numbers.

In fact, *Bravo Lima* is being serviced, and it is *Bravo November* that arrives instead. Yet another magnificent name! Apart from that, they look alike, like brothers. All the helicopters, whether *Dragons* or *Alpha Bravo Charlie* etc., are Alouette IIIs.

The pilot is Daniel Poujol whom I'm pleased to see again. He is attached to the Gendarmerie base at Megève. He celebrated his fortieth birthday a year or two ago, at the helipad. He is tall, broad, strong, solidly built and of a well-balanced character. The people who work here must, necessarily, be steady, but he is exceptionally so. I saw him working on that famous day of August 9, 1994 – when the rescues were unremitting, complex, serious, in different locations, a long way from each other, carried out under difficult flying conditions – where he demonstrated mastery and an unshakeable calm. He has regular features, fairly short black hair parted to the side, dark eyes, and a generally cheerful demeanour, but the overall impression he gives is one of strength. When I think that one particular politician, pretty crooked at that, used as his presidential publicity slogan the words 'the quiet force', it makes my blood boil. The quiet force is Daniel Poujol![2]

The weather is good but the mountains are so plastered with snow it looks like winter. So it has been a quiet day.

This morning, two small rescues: a young girl who fell down the stairs at the Albert Premier Hut and someone suffering from altitude sickness at the Goûter Hut.

I am not being uncharitable, but the report of the fall down the stairs delights me. When I was eighteen years old I damaged a shoulder on Mont Blanc and as my mother did not want me to climb, I didn't like to own up to the accident and the resulting treatment. So I composed a veritable masterpiece of a letter, highly credible, in which I described how, on missing a step, I had fallen down the stairs in the student chalet where I was on holiday. This arrant lie was believed… I questioned Dr Cousineau, on duty today, about this stair accident, but it seems that it was a real accident down some real stairs in the hut. Anything is possible!

Benoît Cousineau I am also pleased to see again and to hear that he'll be on the duty roster this summer. He is a military doctor at the EMHM, and served as a doctor with the UN forces in Lebanon, Yugoslavia and Djibouti. A man of some forty years, he has a sensitive and intelligent face, big brown eyes, an expressive mouth and a crew cut, but not too short. He has certainly seen a lot of things during his career. And he has the ability to make himself understood with a simple thoughtful look, a gentle lifting of the eyebrows, the ghost of a smile. He sees deep into people, reactions, situations.

We chat. I explain about the book I am writing, how I see it, and I tell him I'm counting on him too, to convey the 'human element' of rescues. He talks about the altitude sickness case this morning, indicating how difficult it can be to discover the human factor:

'The trouble with altitude sickness cases is one knows nothing about them. They've generally such a screaming headache that they remain silent, and when they do get back down, even if they begin to recover a little, they still feel ill, and hardly talk.'

[2] Daniel Poujol died tragically in January 2004 when his helicopter crashed at the Grands Montets.

Then he tells me about a change which may seem minor but is significant. A change that only recently occurred in the organisation of the rescue service. It is no longer the Chamonix fire brigade who evacuate the casualties or the corpses arriving at the helipad. A decision coming from goodness knows where has decreed that the fire brigade should no longer carry out this service, which they used to do extremely well. Now, either private ambulances or the undertakers have to be called, which is proving much less satisfactory. The casualties sometimes have to lie on a stretcher for half an hour, before being collected.

This state of affairs is aggravated by the fact that the PGHM no longer has the authority themselves to call ambulances, but has to go through the SAMU[3] in Annecy where overworked officials – and what will it be like when we have the thirty-five hour week? – have to deal with all emergency calls in Haute-Savoie. This means that the ambulance for the helipad in Chamonix is summoned when there is time. On average it takes twenty minutes between Chamonix calling Annecy and the return call.

Evidently, there is a problem, which has been partly circumvented in the bad cases, by the doctors deciding more often than before to drop the casualties directly at the hospital helipad.

Finally, I confide in Benoît Cousineau that my real fear in the forthcoming season are the deaths, the idea that there are likely to be deaths and that it would be unrealistic to hope otherwise. I would rather only have to write about successful rescues, in which people are saved, with difficulty but courageously...

It's on death that Benoît Cousineau responds. He knows only too well that the summer will not pass without the usual tragedies.

'Watch,' he says to me. 'When we bring a dead body back, everyone's behaviour changes... It's nobody's fault... We went up there, the guy's dead, we brought him down... But everyone becomes conscious of his own problem of death... Especially here! Then they become different. It's subtle but striking, and it's brought out in the great kindness they show to the victim's relatives.'

Some time has passed. *Dragon*, having left this morning for a week, arrives back at the helipad. It had been called out for a rescue on

---

[3] Emergency medical help service. See page 11.

Les Vuardes, a rock face, above Magland. Henri Cazemajor, who was on duty at Annecy, carried out the operation. He gets out of the helicopter and, coming into the chalet, still somewhat shaken up, exclaims, in his singsong southern accent:

'Bloody hell, what a rescue! Hard! Under an overhang! And the guy's not too good! Twenty metres fall. Lost consciousness and everything ... bleeding from the ear! Bloody hell! Hey, but tell me, who won the last stage?'

'Cippolini.'

'Great!'

The helicopter crews get together. But after renewing acquaintances, Dr Cousineau asks about the casualty, who was taken to Sallanches Hospital. The tone of the conversation becomes serious again.

'He really copped it! Multiple injuries – fractured femur, fractured skull, fractured right hand, one eye closed ...'

The accident had happened on a route called *Henri, tu vas rire*, which has a story of its own. It had first been climbed last spring by members of the Chamonix PGHM: Pascal Saudemont, Philippe Klein and Gilles Mathé. They left for the route in a 4 x 4 and it happens that Henri Cazemajor is responsible for the PGHM's vehicles. Now, to access the routes at Les Vuardes involves going up a rough track to the top of the cliff, and then descending by a gully to the bottom of the climb. But, very unfortunately, the valiant climbers got the vehicle stuck and had to telephone Cazemajor, none too proud of themselves. In order to play down the incident, the one who had made the call had broached the subject by saying:

'Henri, tu vas rire ...' (Henri! You're going to laugh.)

It appears that Henri had not been amused, but the affair had finished OK, thanks to the help of a local farmer and a tractor.

So, when it came to finding a name for the route, it was called *Henri, tu vas rire*.

And now the first rescue to take place on *Henri, tu vas rire* fell to Henri Cazemajor. And most certainly there had been nothing to laugh about this time either.

The climber was an Italian who, together with three companions and an instructor, was doing the route as part of the assessment for his Mountain Guide's qualification. In the lead he had got off route on the sixth pitch, grabbed for a hold that gave way and had fallen about twenty metres. The rescue alert came from Patrick Poirot and Philippe Klein who, climbing on a nearby route, had witnessed the fall.

The accident had happened in an area of overhangs and the PGHM considered reaching him by climbing the route. However the casualty's companions, realising how problematical this would be, had lowered their comrade two pitches down.

On reaching Les Vuardes, the helicopter dropped the doctor and the fireman seconded to the rescue at ground level, then winched Henri down to the casualty now at the second belay of the route, hanging from his harness and drifting in and out of consciousness. Time was of the essence and there was no place for either proper medical care or rescue. The helicopter lowered a Piguillem stretcher, which was held at an angle while the casualty was inserted. Henri Cazemajor prepared him to be winched up horizontally as a vertical position could result in a heart failure. Returning, the helicopter lowered its cable, which the rescuer attached to the stretcher, before cutting with his knife the sling by which the casualty was still attached to the belay, an act that somewhat alarmed his companions.

'The guys were scared!' comments Henri. 'But it was quick and simple.'

Transported under the winch, the casualty was set down near the doctor, who was waiting at the side of the motorway. As soon as he was stabilised and put on a drip, he was taken on the short flight, under medical supervision, to Sallanches Hospital. By the evening, the prognosis was fairly good. The casualty would live and recover.

This technical and difficult operation demonstrates how efficiently a rescue can be carried out, if the alarm is raised quickly – with the use of a helicopter, rescuers trained to cope in all situations, improved winching techniques, and the rapid medical attention given to casualties.

At the helipad, comes another call. Pascal Brun, of CMBH[4] reports that there seems to have been an accident on the Rocher des Mottets, below Montenvers. The helicopter takes off, in an unusual direction, gracefully tilted to its right, towards the Arveyron Gorge.

[4] Chamonix Mont-Blanc Hélicoptères.

Less than ten minutes later, it brings back a little lady, not in her first flush of youth, wearing shorts and large earrings and one arm in an inflatable splint. She had fractured her wrist whilst out walking. The ambulance takes her away.

'The human factor in this particular case,' I suggest to Benoît Cousineau, 'was nothing very special.'

'Nope!' he replies. 'Nothing...'

There are many such accidents and it's out of the question to report them all. They're known as *ramassages* ('pick-ups'). Someone injured or ill, but nothing very serious. They're picked up, treated, brought down; its done with.

No doubt, for the parties concerned, it's the adventure, or misadventure of their holiday and the memory will remain implanted. But it's standard fare for those at the helipad.

5

DR CAUCHY, I PRESUME?

Tuesday, July 8

The rescues begin: two Germans ill at the Goûter Hut, a Frenchman with altitude sickness at the Vallot, an Englishman with a wrenched knee on the Leschaux Glacier, and, as I arrive, a guide, hit on the head by a rock while on his way up the Aiguille du Goûter. He wants to carry on, but needs his wound stitching, and it is simpler to take the doctor up to him than to bring three people down from the Goûter. But that still means two trips, because there are two journalists here filming, and they have to be taken up.

Let's talk a bit about journalists! They come here for a day, rarely longer, hoping to photograph or film something hard-hitting that will supposedly please the public, or at least conform to the rules of the non-political news game: the exceptional. What can possibly be learnt about rescue in such a short time with preconceived ideas? Not a lot! They only see what they have come to see and I don't think they try to understand anything.

It is the motivation of the rescuers, their personalities, and the way the unit lives, that must be appreciated as well as the rescue process itself. The time waiting at the helipad, the sudden rescue alert... And up there similarly, climbers' motivations and their personalities, the expected pleasure of their route unexpectedly cut short by the accident... And what matters in the rescue is the world at altitude that has become foreign and hostile, the fear, suffering, distress, and then emotion as the helicopter approaches. It is the look of wonder and gratitude which is directed towards the cockpit, the human contact established between strangers who are unlikely to see each other again but who share, at times intensely, some moments that might well prove very difficult, for both parties.

Dr Emmanuel Cauchy, known as Manu or 'Dr Vertical' because he writes in the magazine *Vertical*, and also called 'Dr Horizontal' as a joke, in short *the* Dr Cauchy, comes back from the Goûter rescue. It's the first time we've seen each other this summer.

'Ah! At it again?' he asks.

He shows us two extraordinary small pieces of medical equipment that the doctors are using this summer: a blood pressure testing device and a pulse oxymeter for measuring blood oxygen levels as well as heart rate.

Meantime, profiting from the peace and quiet outside, the birds nesting under the chalet's eaves are busy feeding their insatiable chicks. Although now used to our constant human presence, they still disappear whenever someone goes through the door or stops on the doorstep, just below their home.

'It's incredible,' remarks Daniel Poujol, 'how animals can get used to anything! When a chopper flies over a herd of cows, the beasts are terrified, running around, tossing their horns. But near our base, in Megève, there's a farm where the cows no longer even bother to lift their heads when we take off!'

Animals are more sensible than people, who are continually stressed. It makes me think of my grandmother, who lived at Villeneuve-Saint-Georges, beneath the flight path of Orly airport. We simply stopped talking when we could no longer hear each other and if she did comment it was to the effect : 'Well they have to fly somewhere!' She died aged 109, and I doubt she would have lived so long if she had spent her time fretting and protesting, about the noise of planes or anything else.

These small birds intrigue all the helipadians. Theories are put forward about what will happen when the young birds start learning to fly. Someone suggested they would be mutants performing vertical take offs, as a result of observing how one flies when one is a helicopter.

Wednesday, July 9

An incident brings to mind an old book by Saint-Loup, *La Montagne n'a pas voulu*, relating various 'miracles' in mountain accidents, when for example, climbers were left unhurt by a fall, which in all probability should have killed them. This morning, there was a fine example of a lucky escape: an enormous sérac fall to the right of the Grand Capucin. Helicopter and anxious rescuers made a reconnaissance. Two ropes were in the vicinity but the avalanche of ice passed straight between them, missing them completely.

Fortune also smiled on the parapenter whose fall, below the Brévent, was reported by some walkers who had witnessed it. The victim might well be smashed on the rocks. But by the time the helicopter arrived on the scene, unhurt, he had already folded up his 'chute!

The helipad is quiet once more. First one, then two rescuers, followed by the mechanician, start watching the Tour de France. Benoît Cousineau, behind them, is instructing another doctor on the use of some medical equipment, and this is interfering with the sports commentary.

'Benoît,' says Sylvain Haquin, 'how much nicer it would be talking outside... The sun... Nature... The little birds...'

Cousineau gets the message:

'Oh! Your Tour de France! On Monday we got the longest stage ... from half past one until seven o'clock in the evening! Here the TV was on it the whole time. Sure... once the race had finished, the set was at last switched off. But then at half past seven someone suggests watching the day's round-up of the Tour!'

After this diatribe on the feats of the racing velocipedes, he gives up and goes outside to continue his conversation.

'Good!' says Sylvain approvingly. 'Now, the only thing we need to ensure not being disturbed is to disconnect the telephone.'

Fate is on the side of the crew and the rescue team. It is not until the race is finished and the winner rewarded that there is another call-out. A very worried husband reports that he has left his wife, with an injured ankle, below the summit of the Brévent. The helicopter takes off, searches, in vain, calls in for further information, describes what it can see, flies round once again and comes back. Nothing! The casualty has vanished into thin air.

We learn a little later that some English people persuaded her to walk, so she went with them, limping perhaps, but under her own steam.

'There, that would be something to write about' Benoît tells me, 'the story of rescues that never took place!'

In fact there are plenty. The time it had taken for the husband to go for help had allowed the wife to recover sufficiently to carry on, all the more so since time was passing and she preferred to press on before night fell.

Some casualties do this. It is often courageous. But it can also aggravate their condition and make their medical treatment more complicated, and also more costly. It is hard to strike a happy medium.

It is also known, particularly among foreigners, for casualties whose accident is reported by others to hide amongst the rocks, or under bushes if there are any, on seeing the helicopter approaching. It is unfortunate and can have serious consequences. They are afraid of having to pay for a rescue, not knowing that in France, in summer, it is free.

Our conversation turns to the problem of whether or not the rescue service should be free, a subject on which the public always have an opinion without knowing anything about the ins and outs of the question. It would never occur to them to offer an opinion on the chemicals used during an anaesthetic or, even less, on quantum physics theory, although both subjects concern us. They recognise these are matters for experts. But in many other, equally specialised fields, like the economy, everyone prattles on, without knowing anything of the relevant facts, figures, or laws. Sentiment, sometimes generous, even idealistic, with others plainly selfish, takes the place of science. The Social Security, the emergency services and mountain rescue in particular, do not seem to escape this rule.

At the moment, there is an advert on television that seems to amuse everyone. No matter that it is quite wrong and that you immediately forget what product it is promoting. It shows an alpinist hanging from the end of a rope, on an overhanging wall. A Swiss helicopter approaches and the rescuer calls to the casualty, in a suitably Swiss accent, that he cannot rescue him because he has fallen on the French side of the mountain, but if he climbs back up and falls down the Swiss side, they will take care of him and his insurance … or something of that ilk.

Obviously, the unfortunate victim would be rescued wherever he was. Especially on the French side! In any case, rescue has to be paid for in Switzerland and that is hardly a more satisfactory outcome.

One day, skiing above Zermatt, Dr Cousineau saw someone crash fifty metres from the piste, which meant he was off-piste, and the ski patrol were not allowed to rescue him. How we are regulated by inflexible rules! He went down to the casualty but once the rescue had been contacted the victim had first to say how he was going to pay, in cash, by cheque or by credit card, and if this last what was his card number! History does not recount what would have happened had he not had either insurance, or personal funds.

Thursday, July 10
The terrific storms of yesterday evening have given way this morning to relatively sunny weather. So the casualties are mainly walkers or climbers going up to huts, like the person who slipped on a névé at Les Rognes, below the Tête Rousse Hut. Fractured skull, loss of memory, lacerated scalp, bad bruising. Could have been worse… and we suppose all his friends will march into his hospital room saying: 'Hey, you were lucky!'

About four o'clock, the sky clouds over, pitch black in the west. The Brévent turns leaden tinged with shades of iron grey. Around the helipad the branches of the trees toss restlessly from side to side, bend over, spring up, sway and quiver.

The storm had already broken over the Bargy. Some climbers, who had just got down, telephone to report that four others are stuck high up on the cliff. The one who calls adds: 'If the thunderstorm and hail that caught us is anything to go by, they're having a bad time…' Shortly afterwards the alert is confirmed.

'You're going to have a rough ride,' says David – the GA this week.

The down draught caused by the turbine and the rotors makes it even windier. As they take off, the trees bend, toss, crash before returning to the calm that preceded take off.

When the helicopter returns, mission accomplished, with the rescuers and Dr Lecoq, I learn that the four climbers had not been struck by the lightning, as was the fear, but were very shocked, especially a woman amongst them who had been hit once before and was particularly fearful of the storm. They had been removed from their nasty situation and dropped in the valley.

Friday, July 11
Captain Gin and Pierre Raveneau, soon to be promoted major, take their turn on duty. The principle now is that everyone, even if they usually work in the office, should keep in touch with the work on the ground. But there are no rescues.

So much the better!

If there is no book, because the season is too quiet, that means there would hardly have been any accidents and no one would be more delighted than I.

Saturday, July 12

Only five operations today, and not for anyone who could be described as kids.

That is one of the standard fallacies: those rescued are fit, sunburnt young people, who are quite irresponsible, taking wild risks at high altitude and would be better left where they are to teach them a lesson!

So let's look at what happened today.

Take the youngest! A Frenchman, all of 38 years old. A bad case of altitude sickness at the Rochers Rouges, on the traverse of the 'three Monts Blancs.'[1]

Next, in order of age, a Dane, of forty-eight. Same symptoms. But with such severe altitude sickness that he lost consciousness for ten seconds or so. It happened again and he fell in the Goûter Couloir, but not seriously and was uninjured. He was with a guide, who called in on his radio. The sick man was tall, strong and fit-looking, but had never been above 3000 metres before. For him being fit was all that was required. Dr Cousineau explains how people are affected emotionally by the realisation that they cannot, or can no longer, just do anything. Particularly teenagers, who feel they are failures and are despondent, anxious, disappointed.

Then there was a fifty-three-year-old Frenchman, walking up to La Jonction and taken ill with a heart problem at the level of Les Pyramides. His case is the most distressing. Because of previous cardio-vascular problems he had angioplastic surgery, to dilate his arteries. His cardiologist had followed his progress closely and had told him that with gradual retraining he should be able to lead a normal life. A regular in the valley, he got over things, trained progressively and, this morning, decided to attempt the walk up to La Jonction. However, not far from his goal, he felt a familiar cardiac pain. It was a failure. He's going to feel old. Medically, not a major rescue, but one with heavy psychological consequences.

---

[1] There is only one Mont Blanc! However this is the name given to the traverse that leaves from the top of the Aiguille du Midi cable-car, and goes via the shoulders of Mont Blanc du Tacul and Mont Maudit. The whole route is above 4000 metres and is very exacting if one if not fit and acclimatised.

Sixty-two years old. A Scots woman. Overcome by exhaustion at the Tête Rousse Hut and with a painful knee.

Seventy-one years old, the most senior citizen of the day! A rescue, but not too serious, another heart problem, near Lac Blanc. In fact it seems to be more a problem of dehydration and hypoglycaemia. Benoît Cousineau nevertheless had a bit of a fright during this rescue. He took the casualty's blood pressure with his new magic instrument: nothing! No abnormality showing up on the electrocardiogram. Casualty put on a drip. The blood pressure measured 14 with the standard instrument so the new device falls suspect.

Although given by order of age, the list does not correspond with chronological order. Three followed on from each other in the afternoon, indeed overlapped because a cameraman had to be given a lift, which meant extra flights, dropping off the cameraman and a rescuer, flying to another rescue, coming back to collect rescuers… Work at the helipad is often like this: absolutely calm. Then suddenly an explosion of activity.

So, today, there have only been medical cases, no traumatic injuries, although these are still the main cause of rescues. But at this start of July, it must be admitted that it seems to be only elderly walkers calling for help.

I talk to the cameraman. He is young and seems pleasant. I explain the kind of book I want to write: successful rescues, with people saved and satisfied. That, he tells me, is exactly how he sees things too, not looking for sensationalism but the successful rescues. He is working on a television programme about 'holiday guardian angels', lifeguards on beaches, etc. Let's hope that the piece about the mountains will be good. But today's rescues, with an old man or an exhausted old lady, don't exactly fit with the conventional idea. I doubt that rescues will be shown as they are so different from those the media expect.

6

DARK SUNDAY

Sunday, July 13
There are going to be a lot of people in the mountains this weekend. With July 14 falling on a Monday, it's a bank holiday. The weather is good. That's the reality outside, not the forecast, which has changed I don't know how many times for this weekend. In the middle of the week it was going to be very bad. Then they said it would be good. This morning, the prognosis was for storms at midday. Which one to trust?

Three rescues to start the day, one of which is up in the 'serious' mountains: it involves two young people stuck on the Gervasutti Pillar. They had completed the major part of the route, finding snow everywhere. Having overcome the main difficulties, they had an uncomfortable bivouac and, in the morning, the better of the two who was leading the route, was in no state to continue. It's not a matter of foolhardiness in their case. They thought they'd do the route in the day, expecting better conditions. They came out of the adventure alive and unhurt, which is the main thing. Better sometimes a rescue, than obstinacy which ends badly.

Another, rather odd, rescue on the Petite Verte: a prosthetic accident involving a seventy-two year old Savoyard who has continued to climb despite two artificial hips. While refixing a crampon he dislocated one of his hips. One can but admire such a person for his determination to continue climbing, albeit on easy routes.

Then a guide calls in on his radio to report that there is someone ill and alone, shaking and vomiting, on the Bosses Ridge of Mont Blanc. Altitude sickness! The helicopter leaves to look for the casualty and brings back a young man who speaks enough English to allow communication. He has a nice round face, with a small blond beard, a red sunburnt nose and very pale blue eyes which sparkle behind small steel-rimmed glasses with large sun shades.

When the question of sending him to hospital arises, he refuses fiercely. Coming from an Eastern Bloc country, he has neither money, nor insurance. A gendarme reassures him about the rescue he has just been involved in:

'Free! You don't pay!'

He is relieved on this point, but it seems that he has another worry: he has left some equipment, notably a sleeping bag, at the Aiguille du Goûter Hut, which he had intended to collect on the way down. It's explained that he would have to go and collect his belongings, once he had recovered. Yes, but he had hired his boots and that seems to have already heavily dented his budget. So the rescuers tell him that they'll ask the hut warden to get his things ready and next time there's a rescue in the vicinity, they'll collect them. Obviously the helicopter can't be flying just to collect someone's personal belongings. But for people from the East, losing equipment that has cost them dear is nothing short of a catastrophe.

Then come the formalities necessary for the rescue report: details about those brought down. It is an official requirement and is sometimes not very easy. But in the present case, it's very simple. The young man is here, he's feeling better and speaks a little English. His name is Michael Sirotny and he is twenty-five years old. And where is he from?

'Slovak', he says.

And, to help us understand:

'Communist country…'

A rescuer replies reassuringly in English:

'Yes … but no more … finished!'

He smiles.

A gendarme offers to call him a taxi, but he refuses. He has no money. So I say that I'll take him. I often did this sort of thing in 1994. I'll do it again. One can't let this poor lad walk along the road in the hot sun when he has just been ill.

Since the young man does not know where we are going and is only passing through the valley, we have to search everywhere for a campsite whose name and location he can't remember, he only knows that it is on the other side of Chamonix. Back and forth a thousand times trying, as far as Les Bossons, which at least gives us time to chat. He teaches tennis and is travelling with his girlfriend, hitch-hiking, to see the world. They went to Switzerland first, then Chamonix. Tomorrow they plan to go to Italy, on to Croatia, and then home.

He thinks the French are a better lot than the Swiss. With the helicopter coming to pick him up when he was ill and now this lady who is patiently driving him around looking for his campsite, I reflect that he hasn't got too much to complain about.

He also talks about his climb and why he was all alone up there. Perfectly simple for him. In Chamonix there is Mont Blanc. The young man is keen on sport, even though his girl-friend isn't. So, on the way through, he'd do Mont Blanc, while she'd stay in the valley. Nothing very strange about that. But what is surprising is the way he organised his venture. He had very little money. Just hiring boots had been a huge financial outlay. So, no train or cable-car. This courageous young man set off yesterday morning from Chamonix. He first walked to Les Houches. Then he walked up to the Col de Voza. From there, he went up to the Nid d'Aigle, still on foot. That's where others normally start walking. He just went on doing so. He passed the Tête Rousse, climbed the Aiguille du Goûter and there, a little tired, after climbing some 3000 metres, he saw a 'cottage'. He doesn't know the English word for mountain hut, but *cottage* is not the one I would use to describe the Goûter. His experience in the aforementioned cottage had not been happy: one hundred francs for a night on the floor! He had not slept, at two o'clock he'd been woken and had to leave. Some place!

So he left for his Mont Blanc climb. He got to the top in relatively good time: five hours, then started down and he doesn't understand why he was ill! The rest we know.

It was quite a feat for someone with no knowledge of the area, no altitude training, no climbing equipment. Mont Blanc attracts a lot of people like that.[1]

All this time, we are continuing to look for his campsite. Finally, he recognises it! It is at Les Pélerins. He explains to me that they do not have enough money to pay for the campsite and, in any case, they have no tent, so they are sleeping under a tent awning that someone let them use. I wish him a happy holiday. Resource-ful as he is, I think he will have one!

Had I been alone, I think I would have suggested that these nice young people should come and stay until they'd got their equip-ment back. They would have returned home thinking that the

[1] See Chapter 12 *The Case of Mont Blanc.*

French are even more understanding, nice, kind etc. But I'm not sure my initiative would have delighted John.

In fact, even though not accompanied by a tribe of Slovaks, John welcomes me somewhat coolly when I arrive, very late, for lunch.

Daniel Poujol, the pilot, was more of a psychologist than I. When I told him at the start of the week about my new book project, we talked about it for a while and then at one point, he asked:

'And your husband, how does he feel about it?'

The question astonished me.

'Perfectly all right, of course! Well, he's arriving tomorrow, but he'll be fine about it! He knows I write during my holidays. He knows the mountains… It will be like in '94!'

Yes, but then, I wasn't at the helipad all day, every day. And John had someone to climb with.

So his reaction today surprises me. I swallow my lunch, and set off again for the helipad.

During my absence there had been two rescues. One was on the Aiguille Verte for a guide and client who had done the Y Couloir. They were unhurt. They had left the Charpoua Hut at one o'clock in the morning and reached the summit at one in the afternoon, but, after twelve hours on a difficult route, the client was too exhausted to descend the Whymper Couloir.

This type of rescue can be the subject of debate. And sometimes is. If you go for a route you should be able to do it complete, descent included. In this particular case, seeing his client really exhausted, the guide had thought of lowering him down the Whymper, from belay to belay, but it is a dangerous place where no one likes to hang around. If something had happened to the client, people would have said: 'You had a radio. You were well able to see that your client was exhausted. Why didn't you call in good time for the rescue?' Sometimes people are brought down who are uninjured, like those this morning on the Gervasutti Pillar. Sometimes it is justified, sometimes less so. Each case has its own special circumstances.

After this rescue, the helipad is calm again. Daniel Poujol fills in his flight report. Gérard Peyraud-Magnin, known as Gégé, writes

an accident report on a computer. He types with great energy.
'Do you play the piano?' Benoît Cousineau enquires.
'No.'
'You have the potential!'
It's true that Gégé is tapping on the keys *fortissimo*.
But, the job finished, Gégé suggests:
'Let's see what's happening in the Tour!'
'Ah! I knew there was something missing!' remarks Cousineau.
In the end all we see is an interminable car race.

But then comes another call-out. A sprain, somewhere between Les Chéserys and Lac Blanc, pretty trivial if that's all it is. Much less so, is the way the alarm was raised. The lady walker in question had a mobile phone. Finding herself injured, she telephoned Paris and they informed Chamonix. Why make things simple when they can be complicated? It is true that mobiles mean rescue can be called rapidly. But the peaks are now full of people who get out their mobiles and ring round:
'Guess where I am calling from!'
Well, I suppose that's how it is, but to call it *progress* is another matter. The problem with the rescue in question, is that there is no physical description of the casualty or what she's wearing.
'Put in two hundred litres!' said Daniel Poujol to Sylvain Haquin, his mechanician. 'It may take time…'
As sometimes happens during the season, several rescues then start up and overlap. The two on first call in the morning, Michel Médici and Philippe Pouts, came back to the helipad as soon as they knew that their colleagues had left. Then the second reserves were called up.
Someone had fallen on the Taconnaz footpath. Then a climber fell on the slabs above the Arveyron Gorge. A military ambulance arrives at the helipad so that Benoît Cousineau, doctor at the EMHM, can carry out an on the spot consultation… the whole thing becomes very complicated. So as not to get in the way, I stay inside and content myself with watching the comings and goings, the returns of the helicopter for fuel, the various flights with one or another of the six rescuers who have been mobilised. As always, Daniel Poujol copes with these simultaneous operations, putting the right person in the right place, moving the doctor from one location to another etc. Nobody knows exactly what is happening

elsewhere. Only the helicopter crew needs to know everything, as well as Pierre Raveneau, in charge back at the PGHM. There is suddenly an air of that tension which accompanies multiple complicated and serious operations.

The sprain at Les Chéserys turns out to be a fracture of the tibia. I learn that the climber who fell in the Arveyron Gorge was taken directly to the emergency helipad at the hospital. So he must be seriously hurt. I hear the words:

'Multiple bruising… Fracture of the femur… Head injury… Elbow…'

They must be talking about the one they took to the emergency helipad.

Dr Cousineau comes back and announces briefly:

'Yes… One of them was badly hurt!'

'The one who was taken to the hospital?' asks Robert Petit-Prestoud, who often comes to the helipad, as secretary of the SCSM.

'Yes! And there is another one, even more serious…'

I look at him anxiously.

'He is dead,' he tells me.

Information about the surviving casualty reaches me. He is a twenty-year old Englishman. He was climbing on the crag, feeling good, so he didn't clip one or two bolts. But then he fell and now finds himself in accident and emergency. I do not dare think how the mountain rescue would cope if the Chamonix Hospital were closed in favour of the one at Sallanches, which is what is being suggested. The helicopter would have to make longer journeys, leaving other casualties waiting. Some are only just rescued in time as it is.

Fortunately, we have not seen any hint of the forecast storms. They wouldn't have made matters any easier.

I still don't know anything about the person who died, the one who fell near Taconnaz. Other than someone saying to me:

'He's being wrapped up… They're arriving…'

The cameraman was beside himself at the idea of a dead body. The same person who said to me, no later than yesterday, that what interested him, like myself, were the successful rescues, not the bodies. He is overexcited and no one here likes it.

So the helicopter arrives, with the body, which is not in the basket on the outside as is normal.

I ask:

'He wasn't put in the basket?'

Someone says:

'No. Perhaps because he was winched up. Or because of the journalist.'

In fact, the journalist, or rather the cameraman, is outside, his enormous camera on his shoulder, trying to get as close as possible. Robert Petit-Prestoud intervenes and tells him to move away. He goes back as far as the equipment store, but with his big telephoto lens.

Robert mutters:

'They're all the same! When they're here, they want close-ups of the bodies. They have no respect for anything!'

The helicopter does not land in its usual place but touches down gently, near the hangar, with its door turned towards it. The body, which is on a stretcher, inside the aircraft, is immediately transferred into the hangar. Then with a little jump, the helicopter moves back to its normal position. I react in the same way as I did three years ago when a body was brought back. I say a prayer inside me. For some, it may be the only one.

The cameraman is still filming. Someone says bitterly:

'You'll see, that's the picture we'll have on television.'

Poujol comes into the chalet. Pouts and Medici, who collected the remains, also come in, long-faced. Medici is wearing white rubber gloves. He goes past me, giving me a small strained smile. The cameraman hurries after them, with his microphone and his camera. He wants to know everything.

The role I chose is different. He needs live sound and pictures. I slip unobtrusively into the background. I am part of the furniture. What I am interested in are the people, not the tragic facts, although they are part of it all. When I want to ask a question, I watch to see if it is the right moment, and if it isn't, I don't ask it and perhaps never will. Too bad. I'm not doing news reporting; I want to look deeper than the raw facts.

Pouts, free of the film-maker, comes across to me.

'It's starting!' he says sadly.

Yes, it's starting The first death of the season... A woman, I now learn. About fifty-years old. She must have stumbled and fallen off the path.

It's true that, apart from the cameraman, everyone is behaving differently. All are affected. Cousineau went outside to smoke a cigarette in silence. If the rescue service was just about collecting dead bodies, I do not think anyone would stay in the PGHM.

Details emerge bit by bit, when someone has a need to talk, to purge themselves of the memories.

'When I turned her head to see her face,' said Pouts, 'half her scalp came away in my hand… Ah! There was no need to try resuscitation.'

Sylvain Haquin reacts with anger, against the gawkers, already pressing against the fence.

'Let Jimmy loose on them!' he said infuriated, to Gonzalez, the dog-handler from St-Gervais, who, studying the onlookers, replied:

'They're like monkeys in a cage! Except it's us who are on the inside.'

But Sylvain is even more furious with the film-maker who, a moment ago, filmed Gonzalez wiping Cousineau's stained rucksack with a chemical to remove the blood and to disinfect it.

'At least let Jimmy loose on the cameraman!'

The latter is now standing beside the helicopter. The undertaker's car has just arrived to collect the corpse. All this takes place in the hangar and I am not interested in knowing the details. The cameraman films for five long minutes, his camera on his shoulder, feet wide apart, mouth agape.

'It is as pleasant to have you here,' says Sylvain to me, 'as it is insupportable to have him!'

In order to continue filming and perhaps because it is tiring having his camera on his shoulder, the cameraman quickly puts up a tripod. He moves forward. Then, as Sylvain goes outside and advances on him in a way that bodes ill, he moves back to the yellow line.

'For God's sake! You would think we were in the Metro Goldwyn Mayer studios!' growls Robert Petit-Prestoud.

The cameraman shocks everyone.

David, the GA, says he can't take it.

'You have to get used to it,' someone says, 'otherwise you won't sleep tonight.'

'Oh, I'll sleep! But it's not that… It's the lack of respect… He has no respect.'

Helpless, we watch the cameraman who, mobile clamped to his

ear, is phoning excitedly, while pacing round the helipad.

The undertaker's vehicle, sadly impersonal, leaves the hanger and drives off.

Death means failure. Especially here. It is just what they don't want. Of course, dead bodies have to be picked up, but it is to no purpose, only for those still alive. Even when it is to pick up a major injury the rescue has a purpose, for there is still hope.

As yet nothing is known about the dead woman, not even her name. I wonder who she was and whether I will ever know, if she had grandchildren, if there is going to be a devasted husband. This accident illustrates the fine line between life and death. A path, a stumble on a stone, a root, a fall on the wrong side, unable to stop, unstoppable perhaps... Only the journalist will be happy with his day. When I think how yesterday he seemed quite pleasant when talking about his job – but then, of course, nothing much had happened.

After filling in his flight report, the calm Daniel Poujol gives his opinion:

'The journalists that come here are all the same. And that one is as bad as the rest! They are all shits!'

The unexpected harshness of his comment surprised me. It *had* been long hard day.

It's late. I go home. Miserable. A season without deaths, of course, doesn't exist. But it's already July 13, almost a quarter of the way through the summer, with none till now.

7

TEENAGERS

Quite a different story! A cheerful one because it finishes well. Curiously enough, while it was actually happening, I knew nothing about it. But little by little, it took hold. I followed it up, fitting pieces together, faces glimpsed, smiles, and finally I ended up with three well-written essays by the protagonists telling the story of quite an adventure.

Where to start? It all began on the evening of July 13, after I had left the helipad, and had finished before I arrived next day. Finished, settled, affair closed! And when, late the previous evening, John and I had joined the pilots and rescuers, it is likely that, on a day marked by the first death of the season, we talked about things other than rescue and a recce which had taken place as night fell in the lower hills towards the Diosaz Gorge.[1]

Lots of such recces happen during the summer, often fruitless because the lost souls make their own way back or were elsewhere. My notes of July 14 were as follows:

This morning, three youngsters, 14, 15 and 16 years old, who had descended too far towards the Diosaz Gorge were found. On holiday here, one of them, who hadn't gone as far down as the others, realised what was happening, climbed back up and raised the alarm. The helicopter had searched for them yesterday evening, but it was almost dark, and returned without finding them. The youngsters were elated to have been found and brought down. But their parents were far less so.

So that's it! It could have appeared as briefly as that, or not even been mentioned at all, for it is not my intention to establish an exhaustive list of all the rescues that take place this summer! Rather, to try and depict, in their various facets, what seems the most real, the most moving, the most typical too, in a rescue season.

[1] Twelve kilometres west of Chamonix above the main road to Geneva – running down the hillside to the east of Servoz.

All the same, the teenagers' rescue kept running through my mind. I imagined what it must be like to be lost, to say 'Hey! Do you realise what time it is? We're going to catch it!' To watch it get dark, to bivouac without any equipment, then at dawn to hear the helicopter saviour arriving, with the roar of the rotor blades getting nearer and nearer, then to watch it hover, and see someone being lowered on the end of a wire, uncertain of what he's going to say. I know that whoever he was, would have been smiling. Then there are the parents to face. 'Crikey, we're not out of it yet. We're going to get an earful!' Thus, thinking about this rescue, I tried to put myself both in the children's shoes, and those of the parents.

It was Daniel Poujol who had done the evening reconnaissance followed by the morning rescue. But then on the Monday, *Dragon* took over from *Bravo November,* so by the time I arrived, having made a little pilgrimage to the cemetery in Argentière with Captain Gin in the morning, which I will recount later, the crew had been replaced, Daniel Poujol had gone and other rescues or conversations claimed my attention. Nothing or little about the teenagers.

One of my problems is that I can't be present at both the PG and at the helipad, every moment of the day, from dawn until dusk. That was going to be the cameraman's problem next day when he missed the rescue of his life!

The advantage of my position in relation to his is that I can continue to follow events, whereas he cannot film after they are finished. I am less 'up front' than him but, with time, the psychological aspects emerge far more, as do people's impressions, what they saw, observed, thought, all the little details giving colour to a rescue, the touches of humour or distress, the imponderables.

The teenagers' adventure was planted in my head, and evolving. During the week, on seeing one or other of the rescuers again, I asked what they knew about it. Several, in fact, had been involved in the affair: Jacky Paillé, duty orderly, who had taken the emergency call, Pascal Saudemont, who had relieved him in the morning, Philippe Pouts, Jacques Ottonello, Alain Iglesis, who had either been on standby or effected the rescue, and finally those at the PG when the family were reunited.

So, far from forgetting this rescue, it grew on me, the more I found out. I relived the worry of parents who hadn't slept:

'I think,' someone said to me, 'that the next day, their floor must have been worn out with their pacing across it all night.'

I got various impressions picked up from the children:

'Where they were that evening, they could see the July 14 fireworks! That cheered them up. And they saw loads of shooting stars. The girl told me she had never seen so many... They were lucky that the forecast was wrong and it stayed fine! In the morning, they made a fire so we could spot them... Their parents are pretty forceful characters. Mum's a teacher... she wasn't too happy. We did what we could to help the reunion go well, but all the same it was a bit tense.'

The idea of the fire delighted me. These children had certainly kept their heads! What had they read, when they were younger? *Tintin*, Jules Verne, Jack London? I would love to meet them.

Unable to contain myself, on Friday, as I was passing the PG, I asked Jean-Claude Gin if he was allowed to give me the parents' address. After a moment's thought he warned me that the mother had refused the cameraman's request to film the reunion. He didn't know if she would agree to mine, but he realised that I was working differently, had another approach and gave me a telephone number. I called as soon as I got home at midday and was lucky. I learned that the mother and the family were leaving next day!

I rather put my foot in it. Not easy to explain what I wanted in a few sentences:

'These young people,' I say at one point, 'seem to me to have had the presence of mind to light a fire. They were very resourceful!'

'That perhaps is your point of view, but it is not mine!' was the reply. 'We set out certain rules, which they had to abide by if they were to go on this walk, and they broke them... You talk of *teenagers*, you're right, they are teenagers in every sense of the word!'

The tone was by no means one of admiration. The voice at the end of the line most certainly did not share my enthusiasm. But nevertheless, there was some sort of empathy. I had more luck than the cameraman! In spite of their departure tomorrow and luggage to pack, an appointment was set for that evening. I was bursting with gratitude at being received when it would have been so easy to refuse.

So about six in the evening, I left the helipad and drove down to Servoz, asking myself what I was getting into. To arrive just like that at the house of a family I had never met before is rather unusual. I took a copy of *Nadir* to offer as a small token of thanks, and to get the conversation started. The chalet is hidden in the trees. I have some difficulty finding it and am a little late. All right. I ring the bell!

It is the mother who comes to the door. She shows me into the main room where, around a table, five or six young people with shining eyes are busy playing tarot cards. They look at me with a curiosity all too ready to turn cheerful. 'It's the lady who is interested in our blunder!' they say to themselves. And I 'So these are the ones ...' But that is all I'd see of them ...

'Go on, off you go!' they were told. 'Clear the table and go upstairs!'

'Can't they stay ...?'

But no! My feeble protest has no effect. They went upstairs obediently, with much noise and laughter on the stairs.

Only *serious* grown-ups are left: the father, the mother and me! I give them *Nadir* and explain what I am doing this year. The ice is broken. We exchange somewhat derogatory remarks about journalists and praise the rescue service. I'm perfectly at ease with these subjects! Conversation flows naturally.

And then we come to the story itself that the father and mother tell between them, finishing each other's sentences, revealing what it was like, how they felt.

As I am leaving, I see Gaëlle, the 'heroine' of the adventure. She is a pretty teenager, with wild hair twisted into a small chignon and curls round her face. I find her charming. We talk a little. She is two years before her *baccalaureate*, wants to study law and become a magistrate. I am sure she will. She questions me for a moment about the people who left her with such good memories at the start of the week:

'And the nice rescuer who was there in the helicopter? The one with a little black moustache?'

'That must be Sylvain Haquin.'

'Ah ... and the pilot? The big chap who was so kind?'

'Daniel Poujol.'

'Oh! ... and the ones who came down to us.'

The mother, too, is lavish in her praise. There are some people who show no gratitude at all for those who have rescued them. That's not the case here!

In August, I send the family an article which I had promised them: *PGHM*, which *Alpinisme et Randonnée* asked me to write in 1994. I add a few lines saying that if at any time the 'teenagers' felt like sending me their own versions of their adventure, I would be delighted. I do not place much hope in this extra holiday homework, which I tentatively suggest. But in September, I receive the three stories, hot off the press. Which finally allows me to present the true account of what really happened at the beginning. Here it is:

They were four. Pierre-Baptiste, aged 14, and Gaëlle, 15, who are brother and sister. Then there was Samuel, aged 16, who was on holiday in the next door chalet. And there was Guillaume, a local lad.

The holidays were going well. The youngsters form a little gang and decide to go off into the foothills for two days, spending a night in a hut. Their parents do not agree. In any case, relations are not at their best due to an incident involving cigarettes. In short, permission is refused. Two days later, the children submit another proposal: to go off alone for one day. Their objective: to walk to the Villy Hut and to swim in the Diosaz. Conditions are discussed and agreed: departure at 6.30 in the morning and return, at the latest, at 5.30, storms being forecast for the middle of the day. One other instruction: they must not leave the paths.

And so, on Sunday July 13, they rose at six, got quickly ready and joyously departed. The long ascent does not feature in their accounts: except in Gaëlle's as 'pleasant'. At any rate, around eleven the kids are at the Villy Hut, beside the Diosaz. The swim is briefer than anticipated, as the water is glacial. They lunch, share the food around, play tarot cards and decide to start back. Boring to go the same way. Guillaume and Samuel know it by heart. Besides it means climbing back up to 2000 metres in order to descend to 800. There's still lots of time. Why not follow this pretty river Diosaz down to Servoz? They put it to the vote with raised hands. Everyone agrees.

But in that decision lay the big, the huge error. From that moment anything could happen... Because the foothills are a proper wilderness you can't just go anywhere.

The start is not too bad and spirits remain high. Jumping from stone to stone the four accomplices cross the marshy ground happily frequented by frogs. After a while however they hope to come across the path. Ah, here it is! And, after walking a few minutes they spot a bridge and signposts above them. Gaël and Samuel go to look. Helpful! The signposts point to Nice and Amsterdam! The joke doesn't seem very funny. They walk on and realise, after about an hour, that they are not going towards Servoz but towards the Brévent. All the same, they carry on in the hope of coming to a junction. But time's passing. From a bend with a good view, they think they can make out the Tête de la Fontaine Hut. By cutting across the alpages they ought to be able to make it, but time is pressing and it's already half past three... Better to stick with the original plan: to continue to follow the Diosaz and cross by a dam the boys know of. They set off down again, quite pleasant: through trees and bushes, sliding down the grass and finally reach the dam. Only for another setback: still no path.

Gaëlle is tired. She realises, inwardly, that she is a hindrance to the boys. For Guillaume gets across. Samuel and Pierre-Baptiste could probably do it, but not Gaëlle, and of course they stay with her.

'Meet you at Samuel's!' calls Guillaume, who more or less knows how to get to Servoz, once on the other side of the dam. The others decide to go back up, still not on a path. Gaëlle starts to get anxious. She thinks of their parents who must surely be 'worried to death'. And the climb back up, following the track of crushed ferns, goes on for ever.

Down below, the scheduled hour of return has arrived. And no children! Gaëlle and Pierre-Baptiste's parents decided to give them a bit of extra time, before starting to really worry. But at six o'clock, no one... They decide to walk along the path to meet the children. If, by eight o'clock there's no news, they'll alert the rescue. Unhappily, no one on the path. So at eight o'clock, the parents telephone the PGHM. The orderly is Jacky Paillé. An experienced, efficient man. He explains that the best course of action is for the father himself to telephone the huts in the area whose numbers he gives, with a description of the children and what they were wearing. He tries to be reassuring, saying: 'Don't worry, it's under control!' It was also necessary to check with the Guides' office to see if any of the *accompagnateurs* who take walkers in the lower mountains had met them and where... These enquiries all come to nothing. No choice but to send the helicopter out, pretty much at random.

All this time, Gaëlle, Samuel and Pierre-Baptiste have continued to climb up. For four hours and with no path. Gaëlle could go not further either 'physically, morally or mentally'. Without the help of the boys, she would have had to stop. They're all aware of this, particularly Samuel, who wrote: 'We had to constantly keep her spirits up. And during the four-hour climb, I stayed behind her, telling her lies of one sort or another, because I knew spending the night out was becoming inevitable.'

About nine in the evening, having negotiated several tricky sections, the three youngsters found themselves on a sort of ledge. 'A shelf,' said Pierre-Baptiste, 'with a drop on the right, on the left and in front of us and the cliff behind us. I decide to carry on but Gaëlle can't. We are morally and physically exhausted and take the decision to stop there.' Samuel makes a similar remark: 'Gaëlle continually asks me questions, talks of her worries, about those of her parents, imagining that she was going to die here.' And Gaëlle recounts: 'For me, impossible to carry on. I was afraid. I had never been in a situation like that before. I cracked up, I cried.'

But, about nine o'clock, Guillaume has succeeded in reaching the valley, to raise the alarm and explain the situation. The PGHM is immediately alerted. Rapidly, the helicopter, which was about to carry out the reconnaissance, comes and picks him up from the football pitch in Servoz, to show them where to look. But the other three are a long way from the dam. They can't be seen anywhere. But they can see and hear the helicopter. They are dressed in dark colours. 'The young,' the mother said to me, 'dress in black, brown, navy blue... It's the fashion!... Anyhow, who makes fluo clothing these days?' And the gendarmes say the same: 'They were dressed in the same colours as poachers use in order not to be seen!' The three children, on the other hand, had tried to make themselves visible by moving, trying to light a small fire, taking a photo so the flash would go off – which was not seen – all the more so as the mist was rising and they were searching on the opposite slope. Night fell. The helicopter departed.

The three teenagers realise they'll have to stay where they are till morning. Gaëlle was stressed out again. The evening dew falls. Dark. The drop around them. Pierre-Baptiste and Gaëlle are in shorts and cold. The boys make a small fire of dried grass and then attempt to tell jokes and funny stories.

Around eleven o'clock, three firework displays start up in the valley below, and the sight and festive feeling of something familiar helps raise the morale of the little group. For half an hour they light up the night. And then darkness falls again. Pierre-Baptiste thinks about what's going on below and confides to Gaëlle: 'Mum will be off her head with worry!' He also thinks of the meal she would have prepared for them, of the comfort of his bed.

Fortunately, there is no sign of the forecast storms. But they still have to get through the night which, like all nights of unexpected bivouacs, is terribly long. They start counting down the hours. Gaëlle constantly asks Pierre the time, wanting to know how long there is to go… Only four hours… Only three… Shooting stars flash across the sky.

Down in the valley, the situation is no better, worse if anything. At least the children know they're alive and relatively safe. But their parents know nothing, only that the helicopter hadn't located them!

That unending wait, I know only too well. They are hard moments to support for the only reality one continuously comes up against is the abnormal absence, the total uncertainty, the undeniable fact that something has happened, but what? And the imagination runs riot, envisaging all sorts of catastrophes. Nothing can relieve this distress and I am not sure that sharing it helps ease the pain. Going over the same facts, the same suppositions, the same explanations, the same hopes doesn't fill the gaping hole of reality.

But little by little the hours pass. When that dismal moment just before dawn comes, when the darkness becomes grey, cold and hostile without really giving itself up to light, Gaëlle is once again overcome with anxiety: 'They're never going to find us!'

The day breaks, however, very slowly. It needs to get sufficiently light before the search can get underway again. In anticipation of the rescuers' return, the teenagers have prepared another small fire. On hearing the sound of the helicopter, they light it. They see the machine flying around, looking for them. And they are spotted! Through a loud hailer, a voice echoes around them, speaks to them!

'There is a vast sense of relief for us all,' wrote Samuel. Pierre-Baptiste said of this moment: 'I was euphoric.' And Gaëlle: 'The feeling I had at that moment is indescribable, a mixture of sadness and such intense joy that it brings tears to my eyes.'

'The chopper,' writes Pierre-Baptiste, 'asks us to sit down and then hovers above us. Very quickly, a rescuer descends. Samuel and Gaëlle are winched up, and as there is not enough room for all of us in the helicopter, I stay with a rescuer and hear: 'It'll do one flight and then come back.' Whilst waiting, the rescuer made me aware of how irresponsible we had been, but in a very kind way.'

And Gaëlle: 'We were winched into the chopper where the attitude of the PGHM was really nice: a very warm welcome without judgement or reproach, but at the same time making us realise the risks we had run.'

'Immediately,' says Samuel, 'the rescuers smiled at us and comforted us. When we landed, after a few formalities, they gave us coffee. Then we talked about it together, calmly. Not once did they blame us.'

For the parents, down in the valley, the end of the night had been equally stressful. At six o'clock, they rang the PGHM, wanting to come to the helipad. 'No,' Jacky Paillé said to them. 'They might not land there.' In actual fact, it could be at the hospital. The outcome of the adventure was still very uncertain.

'Stay at home,' he added. 'Near the telephone. We will let you know as soon as we have found them!'

And later, he rang them: 'They are safe and sound!'

When I myself asked the mother how the reunion had gone, she said to me: 'Ah, the reunion! The journalist wanted to film it but I wouldn't let him. However, in truth, our reunion was when we had the telephone call telling us: They are safe and sound!'

So the parents got in their car and drove to the PGHM. Jacky Paillé spent some time talking to them, to help things go smoothly: 'Come on! They've learnt their lesson! There's no point in yelling at them! Don't tell me you didn't do stupid things yourselves when you were their age?'

Their mother told me of these moments: 'We so appreciated everyone's kindness! And even before, when we had been waiting with them, they knew how to use a touch of humour to try and put us at ease. They were perfect!'

The conclusion? Each of the teenagers gave one, in their accounts.

Here is Gaëlle's: 'I think I have benefited from this experience. It has strengthened the bond between my brother and myself, and above all has made me realise what a great boy Samuel is. I have tried to tell this story exactly as it was and to portray my feelings to the best of my ability.'

Pierre-Baptiste: 'Several months after the event, I don't regret having had this experience, even though there were bad moments for everyone. I had considered the mountain gendarmes as no different from the others, repressive and doing dirty work. After the rescue, I discovered they were cool and men of great kindness. In short, they are men who have all my admiration.'

And Samuel: 'Once back home, I thought a lot about the rescuers and how to thank them for what they had done. In the end I gave them some chocolates and champagne. Pretty commonplace, wasn't it? But I left with the conviction that they have the finest job in the world.'

8

FOURTEENTH OF JULY

Monday, July 14
When I spoke to Commander Fanet, in Paris, about my plan to write about a season of rescue, he remarked at one point:

'And your imagination will do the rest...'

I replied that my imagination would be turned to low and would not intervene. But, in one sense, he was right, because when confronted with reality my imagination runs riot. This woman who died yesterday while out walking haunted me all night. Particularly those she'd left behind. A husband? Children? Grandchildren perhaps? A tragedy can be so sudden! This particular one being all the more unexpected since walking in the lower mountains is not considered a dangerous activity. Wrongly?

Imagination can go off at a tangent when trying to build up a picture – and the truth, which I learnt today, is infinitely sadder than my night-time chimeras.

This woman, a Swiss, was with a group who went walking every Sunday, competent and well equipped. They had left early to get here and reach La Jonction via the Montagne de la Côte. It is a beautiful walk that I have done often and sometimes alone. There is nothing dangerous about it, in principle. For a change, the walkers decided to return on the Taconnaz side. At about four in the afternoon, while walking down, the unfortunate woman put a foot on some rhododendrons at the edge of the path, which probably seemed firmly rooted, but in fact overhung the hillside. They gave way, she fell and she disappeared from her companions' view. They called her, in vain. Having a radio or a mobile phone they were able to call the PGHM.

No reason yet to suppose she was dead. At this time there were three simultaneous rescue call-outs: the sprain at Les Chéserys, the badly injured Englishman on the Arveyron cliffs, this woman's fall. These three had to be run together and prioritised. As often happens.

When the helicopter spotted the group of walkers, they indicated by gestures the place of the fall. It was her rucksack which was located first, fifty metres down. Then her body, one hundred metres lower still, in a precipitous gully of dank slabs. The rescuers were winched down on this steep, tricky ground and belayed themselves as best they could to some bushes. The victim was clearly dead and at least it had been quick. Her spinal cord was ruptured in several places. I will pass over other details. Rescuers prepared the body for placing it in a Piguillem stretcher. It is not they who certify death, however obvious. They declare a 'state of apparent death'. It is the doctors at the hospital who make the official certification.

This poor woman was fifty-eight years old. Knowing her date of birth, I indulged myself in an experiment that I wanted to do regarding the stupidity of horoscopes. It doesn't make sense that the human race can be divided into twelve categories, each having the same character and the same daily fate, depending on one's date of birth. Absurd! Character, like physical appearance, comes from heredity – and to some extent, education. As for destiny, it is what one makes of it, with a bit of luck thrown in. I checked the horoscope for the day of this first death of the season. It said: 'Just a little tiredness, nothing serious.'[1]

As for the husband who I feared was part of the same group, he did not exist: this woman was divorced. She had two adult sons, more on their father's side, and who had the body repatriated without bothering to come themselves. This affected me all the more because in my circle there is a similar case of two adult daughters who won't go to their mother's funeral, but certainly to the solicitor. And I felt more sadness for this woman now than I had the previous night.

Hardly any rescues this afternoon spent at the helipad. Often one learns a lot during these moments of respite, if one takes the trouble. Just by chatting with people.

I had a long conversation with Dr Cousineau, mainly about the nasty feeling caused by the cameraman yesterday. Benoît gave me his opinion:

[1] The experiment was confirmed by other predictions relating to some of those that died: 'You are on form,' 'Look after your liver,' 'Don't go wild over sweet things,' 'Don't get sunburnt,' 'Have a more balanced diet,' 'Take better care of what you are eating,' 'You are in dazzling form,' 'You will eventually lose those kilos,' etc – a tissue of pathetic absurdities.

'He understood nothing. He didn't understand that the game is played by certain rules. Because here, everyone is affected. Accidents in the mountains could happen to any of us because we all climb: the rescuers, of course, climb to keep fit, and because they want to; as do the pilots and flight crew. They can be involved in an accident during a rescue, while training, when they are out climbing for themselves. Same thing in the lower hills. They have probably taken, or may take, their family up the footpath to La Jonction, where that accident happened yesterday. No one here wants to joke about someone else's death. In medicine today, the oncologist treats his patients unemotionally, as though it could never happen to him. It's the same with the emergency services, when a thirty-five-year-old doctor treats someone with a coronary, he stands back from it and is not affected. In such teams, there is often black humour to lighten the atmosphere. Not here, where there's respect for a death which could be their own ... or of someone close. Here, we all have friends who have been killed in the mountains and there is never a disrespectful or uncalled for word about the dead. Watch, and you will see, when someone dies, a sort of ballet takes place, everyone being affected, does whatever has to be done, yet somehow differently. Isolating themselves if possible by a few feet.'

I was struck by his use of the word 'ballet'. The communal and open space of the helipad, allows each and everyone to move as they wish... Benoît Cousineau returns to the subject of the journalist.

'He broke the rules of the game and then didn't understand why everyone was suddenly unpleasant to him. There is nothing of interest in filming a stretcher with a dead body on it! Including skiing in the winter, we have about fifty deaths here every year. It's not exactly a scoop when one happens! But he seemed to think it was a scoop. The more we tried to get him to move away, the more important he thought it was. But what was really interesting yesterday, was everyone's reactions, the way they behaved, the respect they showed. And their irritation towards the one who wasn't playing the game.'

That was what I felt too. But I also thought that the cameraman was a focus for the ill-humour, the sorrow brought about by this death, even though it was the death of a stranger. They could not rebel against death itself, nor against the rhododendron bushes, or the steep gullies, but they could take it out on the person who was violating death by trying to film it as though it was a curiosity. The word 'violation' which I have just written, I realise, was used several times by Benoît Cousineau when he was speaking to me just now. Because that is what it is. The body of a human being merits the respect that is due to all men, and that includes their remains. To behave badly in front of a body, even when there is no life left in it, is violation.

It is good to know that at least the rules of the game are respected here.

9

A PAST ACCIDENT:
BOBI ARSANDAUX

This is a good time to talk about an accident from the past, lest it be forgotten. It is about the death of Octave Arsandaux, known as Bobi, on the Aiguille Verte, long ago. There are a number of reasons why he should be remembered: his personality, the tragic circumstances of his accident, the immense loyalty shown by his friends. Which is why I mentioned earlier, the pilgrimage Captain Gin and I had made to the cemetery in Argentière on July 14. It was to take the place of his friends, now so old, that they were unable to make the journey this year.

But, in order to introduce Bobi Arsandaux, first of all you have to know about the GDB. The GDB or Groupe de Bleau, was formed in the 1920s by a band of enthusiastic young climbers. Every Saturday, they left for Bleau (Fontainebleau), slept out in caves or under boulders and climbed on the Sunday, training and having fun. The twenty or so members also met during the week. And naturally, in the summer, they climbed in the mountains, where some made a reputation: Marcel Ichac, Pierre Allain and Raymond Leininger to name but a few. There was also Robert Moch, known as 'the Moloch', Madeleine Anizan, nicknamed 'the Marquise', Pierre Chevalier, André Tournon, Henri Brénot, Guy Labour, whom I will talk about in another chapter and, of course, Bobi Arsandaux, the founder, driving force and president of the GDB.[1]

The group had rules. Fierce ones! To become a member you had to be more than nineteen, had to have bivouacked at least ten times, either at Bleau or in the mountains, each of which had to have been in the company of at least five members of the GDB, you had to have done the big Dame-Jeanne abseil, without a safety rope, in the presence of GDB members, you had to have done at

[1] Cf. Sylvain Jouty, *Bleau*, p.122; *Alpinisme et Randonnée*, no.152, March 1992, Ghyslaine Beaux, 'La Belle époque des Bleausards'.

least four mountain routes of more than one thousand metres, and you had to have bought drinks at Bleau, one evening after ten o'clock. In return for which the way was open to join one of the happiest bunches of people you could find in the inter-war years. And watch out! If you quit bachelor life to marry someone outside the group, you were automatically relegated to the sad position of honorary member.

Of the thousands of stories, jokes and adventures of the GDB – some of which were lived in the moment and then forgotten, as life continues – there are others that have survived in the memory of those involved. Whether it was crossing the Boulevard Saint-Michel in Paris with rope, rucksack, climbing boots and a small candle lantern, sounding the ground with ice axes for possible crevasse... Or André Tournon playing at ghosts in the forest, dressed in his white sleeping bag and swinging from the top of an old oak tree while lit up from below by his friends and making groaning noises... It was he too, disguised as a knight with helmet, armour and lance, who stopped the cars on the Route Nationale 6 at the Épine crossroads, offering them the cup of friendship, until three o'clock in the morning, by which time the gendarmes at Chailly-en-Bière, who were no doubt unamused at the joke, were alerted and came to put a stop to these bacchanalian goings-on.

The GDB were also known for having a sort of ritual dance which was called by the fine name of *La Gadouillette,* doubtless imported by Bobi Arsandaux from the Beaux-Arts School. The words had a metaphysical message, which even today, we cannot fail to appreciate:

I'm going to dance la gadouillette
I'm going to dance la gadouillette
Tra la la la la la la, la gadouillette!
Tra la la la la la la, la gadouilla!

Have I managed to put across the sort of joyous youthfulness which characterised the GDB?

The tragedy of 1931 all the more deeply affected them. Bobi Arsandaux had become an excellent alpinist. He had done routes such as the traverse of the Meije, the Mer de Glace Face of the Grépon (the first non-guided French climber to do the Knubel Crack), but above all he was remarkable on ice, taking part in the first serious attempt at the North Face of the Triolet, putting up with Robert Gréloz the direct route on the North Face of the Aiguille d'Argentière and most notably the first ascent of the Lagarde Couloir on Les Droites[1]: all of which classed him as one of the great hopes of French climbing. Unfortunately, his parents refused to provide him with the wherewithal to buy equipment, not through lack of means, since his father ran the French equivalent of *Hansard*,[2] but because they disapproved of their son's love for the mountains and hoped to put a stop to the disproportionate part it played in his life. So in the mountains, Bobi Arsandaux was dressed in rags and his climbing gear was not much better.

In 1931, aged twenty-four and having just finished his architectural studies, he was doing his military service and managed to get leave for the July 14 public holiday. On the 13th he left with two friends, Eddy Stofer and Jacques Jonquière, to do the Grands Montets Ridge on the Aiguille Verte, a committing climb that had only been done twice before. At eleven o'clock, realising they were too slow, they decided to content themselves with the summit of the Tour Carrée, before turning back. Bobi Arsandaux was the last one down, and whilst out of view of his companions, they felt the rope tighten and then go slack, the two strands snapped clean through. It was his rope. 'A rope,' Guy Labour wrote to me, 'whose hemp had become a dirty grey, and which all his friends vehemently refused to use. It only needed once, for a friend not in the know, to accept it…' The long fall, of 800 metres, to the Argentière Glacier could only have one end.

On seeing his friends, Bobi Arsandaux's parents no doubt better understood their son's passion. They had him buried in the cemetery at Argentière, near the Aiguille Verte, where later they joined him.

I have before me his obituary written by Jacques Boell. Some of his words seem premonitory:

> Bobi, dear great friend with your dreaming eyes, sleep in peace amongst the mountains; your memory will stay alive… Our friendship was one that transcends the grave… The small cemetery in Argentière will be much visited, and numerous will be Bobi's friends, I don't doubt, who will come to search, amongst the flowers on the grave, for a scent of the memories of yesteryear.

[1] Arsandaux partnered Jacques Lagarde on this climb, one of the major ice climbs of its day.
[2] The day-by-day Parliamentary record in the U.K.

It's true. Even in these last few years, two of his friends, Guy Labour and 'the Marquise', now ninety years old, still came to Argentière, one from the Drôme, the other from Paris. In January 1997 I asked Captain Gin, who knew nothing of this, to send them a greetings card from the PGHM to show that today's climbing world could reach across the years to them. I think they were deeply touched. Which is why, on the morning of July 14, we went, he and I, to Bobi Arsandaux's grave and we sent a card to each of his two old friends. And so the torch is passed on and perhaps this book will lead the occasional reader towards the grave of a young alpinist they never knew.

Never knew, but worth remembering. Bobi Arsandaux was without doubt an exceptional person. An artist as gifted as Samivel, who was of the same generation. But above all, a striking personality. I go back to what Jacques Boell wrote of him: 'Sometimes a dreamer and idealist, sometimes an urchin and wildly cheerful, sometimes sad and withdrawn, but always an artist and even a mystic...' And this passage from the letter Guy Labour sent Captain Gin on August 25, 1997:

> This boy left us with unforgettable memories. He wasn't a spirit of purity, far from it, a Beaux-Arts student, cheerful, a joker, full of fun and life! But he was pure of spirit, in the sense that he was perfectly honest, upright, of scrupulous judgement, never spiteful, someone in whom you could have total confidence and who had an absolute sense of what was right – and of beauty too ... Sometimes in the mountains, he'd stop and say: 'How beautiful!' and we would carry on happily, in complete harmony.

Don't let's forget Bobi Arsandaux... Nor his friends.

10

TWO DISSIMILAR DAYS

Tuesday, July 15
The weather forecast for July 15 was bad. In fact, it is a lovely day. But as we are always influenced by oracles, we can't help believing the forecast. So no one dared go into the mountains, plans were put back until the next day – and now we have hot sunshine.

Inside the chalet at the helipad, Pouts is typing an accident report, Poirot is reading a Gendarmerie liaison bulletin and Dr Cauchy is writing out a programme on the Sécurité Civile's computer. The pilot comes in.

'Is it normal for smoke to come from your computer?' asks Manu Cauchy equably.

Startled, the pilot approaches only to see, that no, their computer is not smoking.

Pouts has to type the report about the accident to the Swiss lady. One can follow his progress from his asides. Philippe Pouts is from the Midi, often the live-wire of the PGHM, and sometimes perhaps, because he is so lively, talkative, impulsive occasionally to the point of unpredictability, he is the despair of his superiors. But this outward appearance, I know, hides a reliable and sensitive character. This is often the case with people from southern France. I saw he was tense and miserable when he came back from the accident to the Swiss lady the day before yesterday. But he needs to talk and, while typing the accident report, he cannot prevent himself from muttering under his breath.

'Mule track... mule track... but there are no mules any more ... OK! Mule track anyway... Early... Is it an adverb or adjective? Weekend...' He turns to us. 'Do you think that is in the French dictionary? Weekend?'

Poirot and I assure him that it must be (unfortunately!).

'What a stupid word to write, rhododendron! It's nothing but d's! And she worked for a watch-maker ... Poor woman! Her time was up!'

Alain Iglesis, known as Julio, comes by. Alain Iglesis is an amazing person. His list of climbs would fill a book. He is also from the deep south and, furthermore, is from the Eastern Pyrenees. When, a few months ago, I went to Villeneuve-de-la-Raho, where my father was born, I was surprised to find his brother working in the town hall. Alain Iglesis is dark, quite small, with big dark green eyes fringed with long eyelashes, and his eyes have a peculiarity which I don't think I have ever seen in anyone except him. Quite often people who come back down after doing a big route have a special look, a light about them. Their eyes seem to be a living reflection of another world. Alain Iglesis's are like this permanently. No doubt as a result of seeing so many mountain vistas, so much snow, so much sky. But he is not a dreamer. He is reserved but extremely efficient. He is second to none, when he is on duty at the helipad, with the sweeping, washing, cleaning, tidying. In the mountains on arriving at a small grotty refuge everything has to be tidied up. In half an hour, all will be put to rights, the snow thrown outside, the hut scrubbed down, the blankets put out to air in the sun, the stove lit, food prepared ...

Iglesis was involved in the teenagers' rescue yesterday morning, and gives me some details. Where they got into difficulties, was below a mountain called La Coquille. The grassy terrace where they bivouacked was the size of two sofas (the sofa being one of the great reference points of the helipad). It was then that I began to take a real interest in the teenagers.

After Iglesis departs, one of the Sécurité Civile mechanicians tells me how he began climbing and what it means to him:

'It makes you look at things differently. From the chopper, everything seems tiny. But when you are actually there, it's not like that at all! Take the Cosmiques Arête. I have carried out several rescues there and I wondered how the guys could have problems on a route like that. But when on the spot it's quite a different matter! And then the people you meet up there enjoy physical effort ... Yep, it's that! Up there, it's hardship and friendship. Ah! It's very different from meeting up in the valley for a pastis!'

A rescue follows, simple. A fall on the Nantillons Glacier. The casualty is a young girl, an outstanding member, we learn later, of the Swiss rock-climbing team. But rock-climbing is not mountaineering. She and some friends had camped at the Plan de l'Aiguille, intending to do some glacier training. They had helmets, but not on their heads, in their rucksacks. Consequently, when the young girl fell, as a result of not taking the terrain seriously, she banged her head. The helicopter brings her down, in a Piguillem stretcher. She is just a kid and very upset. She wants to get out of the stretcher she's strapped to. It seems that they had a lot of trouble getting her into it. She speaks neither French nor English. She is sulky and unpleasant. Not at all happy to be there. Rebellious, like a teenager towards the adults, strangers, who are around her. The GA this week, Xavier Sonnensheim, who is Alsacien, spoke to her in German, but she refused to listen and reply. They bring down one of her friends who understands French and is cooperative.

'She is fourteen years old?', asks Dr Cauchy, going on how she looks.

'No, seventeen.'

'He must go with her,' says Cauchy. 'Otherwise she will panic. I would like her in hospital as quickly as possible.'

She is already in the ambulance, her small face white and stubborn. Her friend joins her and they drive off.

I ask Manu Cauchy if he had given her a shot.

'No,' he told me. 'We don't if they have head injuries, unless they're likely to be too dangerous in the chopper. Her, we could cope with.'

The impression she leaves with me is unpleasant. What a nasty-tempered girl, after all everyone was doing for her!

'It is often like that with head injuries,' Cauchy explains to me. 'They're restless, agitated, they reject. You saw... she might normally be good natured, but sometimes the parts of the brain associated with aggressiveness are affected.'

In the evening we learnt that she had a badly fractured skull and been transferred to the neurological unit at the hospital in Geneva.

Wednesday, July 16
Today, the weather really is good, as both the forecast and the sky are in agreement. The concord of these two elements means that there is a mass of people in the mountains.

By the time I arrive, two rescues are in action. Cazemajor and Renard are operating on the Envers du Plan Glacier for a sprained knee. But it's nearby on the Aiguille Pierre Allain, near the Requin Hut, where the other is happening, difficult, I'm told, technical, tricky, touch-and-go, urgent. As so often, the helicopter has to go from one to the other, dropping off rescuers or the doctor, returning for fuel, collecting equipment, bringing back a casualty, taking off again. Today will see, in fact, eleven rescues in the range and three others elsewhere in the department.

At the helipad, we wait, only having for the moment occasional bits of news.

Someone from a television channel arrives.

'Is Cauchy here?'

'No. He's out on a rescue,' replies the GA.

'What's the rescue?'

'Two guys are stuck on a route.'

'On a what?'

'On a route.'

'Oh! Well we haven't got time to wait. Tell him everything went well. We're off now.'

And they left, without a by your leave.

Enter Pepito, a council worker. He is more civil, but goes straight to the point and calls cheerfully:

'Hi! How's it going? Slogging away? They're still falling off?'

His dress is markedly less elegant than that of the gendarmes. Pepito wears light grey tracksuit trousers, Adidas, and a long fluorescent waistcoat, decorated with white stripes, out of which protrude his bare arms, reddened with sunburn. He sits down for three seconds, to get a small dose of television, then leaves, saying that he must bring new rubbish bags.

The Envers du Plan team are back. The injured man is a black soldier from Guadeloupe. He is not too badly hurt and, supported by a rescuer, is able to hop to the outside bench where his details for the accident report are recorded. An ambulance takes him away. As for the rescue on the Aiguille Pierre Allain, the helicopter is going straight to the emergency helipad at the hospital. So it must be serious! We learn a little later that it is a broken pelvis, as well as other injuries.

The helicopter evacuates the rescuers from the Envers, then

Pilots and Mechanicians: Daniel Poujol, Michel Pierre (SC), Philippe Buffenoir, Alain Charnay

Olivier Fernandez   Patrick Poirot   Olivier Renard   Alain Iglesis

1-16 SOME OF THE HELICOPTER CREWS AND RESCUERS

Jackie Paillé   Henri Cazemajor   Daniel Duret   Pierre Bernier

Christian Lafouge   Gilles Mathé   Thibaud Riboullet   Lionel Isaia

17-21   PGHM rescuers Franck Junod and Jacques Ottonello (above left) wait at the Les Bois helipad chalet with others on their shift – Alain Charnay, Patrick Poirot, Dr Benoît Cousineau and Daniel Poujol. When an alarm is raised, the helicopter (here *Dragon*) is usually airborne within minutes and (in this example) soon speeding above the Aiguilles (below) to rescue a climber injured on the Aiguille du Grèpon (right).

22 *Bravo Lima* takes off from Mont Blanc du Tacul (4187m) heading towards the Aiguille du Midi. Flying logistics above 4000 metres require adroit juggling of passengers, fuel and equipment.
23 (below) The German party that fell 150m on Mont Maudit (pp 329-330) arrive at the helipad.

24 (above) *Bravo Lima* in action during a rescue on the Dent du Caïman (3554m) – the lower altitude here facilitates more complex manoeuvres. 25-26 (below) A stretcher rescue using a portable winch, and a search dog and rescuer in action amidst avalanche debris where speed is crucial to avoid loss of life.

27 (left) This 1934 fatal accident recovery is a reminder of the slow, cumbersome rescues of the past.

28-29 Crevasse incidents are frequent and potentially lethal if the victim remains jammed in the ice for any period of time. The PGHM has perfected its winch techniques and other skills to speed recovery times.

30 The big mountain accident on the steep face remains the most difficult and hazardous of the PGHM's tasks – the Dru, the Tacul and the Jorasses being regular black spots. This photo shows a rescue on the North Face of the Aiguille de Bionnassay, close under the summit, where loose rock and inadequate belays added to the difficulties.

31 (left) Bobi Arsandaux, the driving force of the Group de Bleau, who died in an abseil accident on the Grands Montets Arête in 1931.   32 Raymond Lambert (seen at the Leschaux Hut with Loulou Boulaz in 1935) the guide who was involved in the 1938 Diables epic (see Appendix IV).

FIGURES FROM RESCUES AND ACCIDENTS OF YESTERYEAR

33-34 Armand Charlet, revered local guide of the 20s-50s and Lionel Terray who briefly quit the Guides Company in protest over the Vincendon/Henry tragedy.

35-36 1966 Dru rescuers René Desmaison and Gary Hemming who used the hard Hemming/Robbins direct route to reach the stricken climbers.

those from the Requin, accompanied by a woman of about forty, in climbing tights, rock boots and harness. It is the wife of the injured man. The necessary information is taken from her. She is grappling with the problem of a key: was their car key still at the Requin Hut? Or was it hanging from a lace around her husband's neck, in which case could she retrieve it from the hospital? Such down-to-earth questions almost always crop up at the time of accidents and generally relate to keys. The couple had rented an apartment in Vallorcine and a car would be necessary for the journeys to and from hospital. Phone calls…

While all this is going on, a guide radios in to say he has a client with a frozen eye on the summit of Mont Blanc.

'A frozen eye!' exclaims Robert Petit-Prestoud, who has just arrived.

'I can only take one for Mont Blanc,' announces Ivan.

'I'm the lightest,' says Saudemont.

But there is now a report that a rope has fallen while descending the Tour Ronde. So the helicopter also takes Malineau, who will be dropped off at the Tour Ronde on the way, while Saudemont will be taken to Mont Blanc.

A taxi has been called to take the wife of the man injured on the Requin to the hospital, but it has not arrived. I can imagine her impatience, despite her apparent calm. She has not had any news of her husband since he was winched off the wall. So, relinquishing the prospect of finding out what a frozen eye looks like, I offer the services of my car and set off with her and the two rucksacks.

On the way, I explain why I am at the helipad with the gendarmes. She asks my name and, by chance, she knows it, but she had preferred not to read *Nadir*, as she did not want to know about accidents. And now she has just lived through one, which is rather worse. She is upset, nice, a bit tense, grateful. She blames herself for having left the belay without hearing her husband, who was leading, telling her to climb. They were out of sight of each other and the noise of a torrent prevented them from communicating. The rescuers tell me later that she had no reason at all to feel guilty, as the rope was tight between them. But there is always a tendency to blame oneself when one has had an emotional shock. She explains that they were climbing a route called *Congo-Star*. They were experienced climbers and had already done many routes on the Envers. She cannot praise the rescuers enough:

'They are amazing! They do everything just at the right moment, without wasting time, calmly… and so nice! They say exactly the right things, the things you need to hear just when you need them. They are extraordinary!'

I drop her off and wish her luck, promising myself to ask for news of her husband in due course, then return to the helipad.

The frozen eye had been taken directly to hospital. Apparently both the cornea and the liquid which keeps it moist, can freeze if it is very cold and the glasses don't keep the wind out. The eye normally recovers in twenty-four hours, but people to whom it happens are usually very anxious, particularly as it can cause temporary blindness.

Pascal Saudemont has joined Malineau for the Tour Ronde rescue. Two people, it seems, with multiple injuries. So it is serious: involving Spaniards. The third team, the reserves, Pouts and Iglesis, arrive to allow Cazemajor and Renard to go for lunch. And the helicopter comes back, with Dr Cauchy and a female casualty from the Tour Ronde. There is now more information about the accident. A Spaniard was soloing, above a rope of three, which included the girl. He fell and pulled them off. He suffered only minor injuries, but hers are more serious. The other two are uninjured. Iglesis, who speaks fluent Spanish, asks the young girl for more information while waiting for the ambulance. She has neck, head and arm injuries. She speaks tonelessly. Manu Cauchy puts her on a drip. The ambulance arrives and takes her away.

The helicopter returns, yet again. The scorching rays of the sun beat down on the helipad. Apparently it is also very hot up in the mountains.

'And there are people everywhere! Now it's really started!' announces Cauchy.

Philippe Pouts resumes his interrupted lunch: a piece of bread and cheese that were heating up nicely on a plastic chair outside. Meaning Pouts and himself, Iglesis says to Saudemont, who has just returned with the other casualty:

'Now everything will be fine! The shock team has arrived!'

'Excuse me!' Pouts corrects him, 'I am the chic team and you are the shock team!'

We laugh. We need to laugh to break the tension. Malineau is still haunted by the Requin rescue, which has affected all those involved in it:

'What a rescue, this morning, right on the face! A great rescue! Don't often get anything like that.'

'You should have cut the rope,' jokes Iglesis, 'It would have saved time!'

'Now the season has really begun!' everyone remarks one after the other, like a leitmotiv.

The helicopter takes off again, towards Argentière this time, with Cauchy and Iglesis.

'The pilot, if you ask me,' says Robert Petit-Prestoud, 'won't be getting any lunch today ...'

Although the ambulance carrying the Spanish girl had only left a moment ago, there are now two others parked in the helipad.

'It's like the taxi rank at Montparnasse station here,' says Pouts, 'ambulances lining up one behind the other.'

Everyone laughs, again.

The Argentière rescue, we learn, is for yet another Spaniard, who was hit by stone-fall and has a smashed hand.

Saudemont in his turn repeats:

'This time, it's really started! And it is by no means finished! There are people all over the mountains today. Everywhere, everywhere, everywhere, everywhere. On all the routes!'

After having dropped the Argentière casualty, the helicopter leaves again for the Albert Premier Hut. The Spaniard, who has arrived amongst us, can walk but his left hand is enormous, very swollen.

'We must take off your watch!' says Saudemont.

His watch is cutting into his wrist, around the swollen skin. The casualty refuses, vehemently. Reactions of accident victims are often strange, particularly when it comes to personal belongings and equipment. As though, injured in themselves, they need strenuously to hang on to their belongings, to that which is 'normal', to that which is unharmed.

Malineau does not argue with him and takes his statement.

The feeling prevailing at the helipad is that of the big rescue days. Lots of people, all the time. A superheated atmosphere. People talk louder, faster. It is difficult to describe. It is not feverishness: that, I've never seen here. But it's born of the intensive action. Of men who have just been in action and who, they know, will be back in it. Whose senses are keyed-up for this action.

Yet four more rescues. At the Albert Premier, a sprained knee, an injury from the previous day which had not improved overnight. At the Nid d'Aigle, a diabetic lady walker has had a hypoglycaemic attack. Then, near Planpraz, a woman in her thirties with a heart problem, but it turns out instead to be an attack of cramp. This is followed by someone with a sprain at Les Chéserys, yet another one!

By quarter to three, neither Dr Cauchy, Michel Pierre, the pilot, nor the mechanician Ivan Commène, known as Ivan the Terrible, have yet had lunch, because they have not stopped for a moment since the first rescue this morning. The young cameraman has arrived and does some filming. Absent this morning, with some snowboarders, he had missed the big rescue on the Requin. Hardly had Manu Cauchy arrived back, than he rushes over to question him.

'I have not yet had lunch! If you don't mind,' he replies. 'I'll lunch first!' Then, softening a little: 'But you can join us.'

And a little later, the cameraman comes to speak to me about the lady who died on Sunday:

'Did I really upset everyone?'

'Yes.'

'But not Poujol, surely! He took me out on a rescue straight away.'

'What do you expect? He's a soldier. He has orders regarding you. He was carrying them out. It doesn't stop him from thinking, from feeling.'

My questioner is stunned. He had had no idea. It had never occurred to him that once having obtained permission to be here, he would only be accepted as a result of having that permission, but not necessarily liked.

'But you, did I offend you?'

'Yes.'

'Even you?'

'But yes! I am close to those who go into the mountains, like them. We are part of the same world. The people who work here are deeply affected by death, have a great respect for it.'

'But I respect it too.'

'No! You were filming everything you could. It grated.'

He doesn't seem able to understand. But I'm glad that at least he asked the question. He is young. If he carries on with this job however, he'll become blasé.

Olivier Renard, newly arrived in the Chamonix PG, and very friendly, marvels at how quiet it now is. Still in his big mountain boots, salopettes and harness full of karabiners, he undoes the top of his salopettes, takes off his tee-shirt and goes out into the sunshine saying in a satisfied voice: 'Ah! Now for some sunbathing!'

It's not likely to be for long. But it's true all is peaceful again. From the small kitchen-diner come sounds of dishes, cutlery and occasional laughter. Even the television is switched off.

'Well!' says Ivan the Terrible, who comes in and sees me writing, 'I'm going to do some writing too.'

'Have you had time to note down some of the rescues?'

'No way! The only breather I had, was a Coke at the Requin. And even then I had to gulp it down.'

Henri Cazemajor, crazy about the Tour de France, has switched the television back on.

But about four o'clock another call-out: a fractured leg, 150 metres below the Goûter Hut.

'A fracture! So I'll have to go!' says Cauchy.

'But stay as you are!' Michel Pierre recommends.

Manu Cauchy is wearing nothing but a pair of shorts and a cap. But in less than a minute he is completely wrapped up in his climbing suit, with boots and medical bag.

And off for the tenth rescue of the day.

Almost immediately there is a request for a reconnaissance flight between the Col du Midi and the summit of Mont Blanc. Later, the circumstances of this diplomatic comedy will come to light.

But a third request for a heart attack at the Bérard waterfall, near Vallorcine, intervenes. These calls grouping together must correspond to some rule of probability.

When the helicopter returns from the Goûter, it does not even turn off its engine before it's off for the heart attack victim. It's in the wind of the rotor blades that the broken leg of the Goûter is taken out. The cameraman is down on all fours filming the face of the casualty being disembarked. He really has not understood anything and will never be liked here. The GA from Strasbourg mutters:

'That one's a real swine!'

The helicopter takes off with Cauchy and Cazemajor. The cameraman rushes over to take more film of the stretcher. He appears nice but he really is incorrigible! I watch him, from inside the chalet, embarrassed for the casualty. Only when he has finished do I go outside. The person in the stretcher is a young Englishman. Only his face is visible. He is unstrapped. His right leg, broken, is in a brace, but his left is also hurting. While awaiting the ambulance I go over to talk to him. I tell him that it won't be very long, that my husband is English, that we are here on holiday, that I'll find out if he needs anything later… He is eighteen. The doctor had given him a shot because he was in so much pain. 'They could not even get his crampons off.' Now, suffering less, he has a smile on his face. He had done Mont Blanc this morning and it was while descending by the Goûter that he'd fallen. I remark that it was better than falling on the way up: at least he has made the summit! He agrees and smiles.

'And he was lucky!' Renard says to me. 'He went about ten metres and stopped. Below there was a twenty-metre rock step.'

The ambulance finally arrives. To transport him, it was decided that a brace should be put on the left leg, as this might also be broken. The ambulance man gets out a transparent plastic brace which is slid under the leg. It has to be inflated with a small pipe and this task fell to the GA who blows hard.

'Hey,' remarks Olivier Renard. 'It's gone green inside! What have you been drinking?'

The pleasant English boy is put on board. The story of these cases frequently come together in bits over the days, so I will jump forward at this point. Next day, armed with an English thriller, I present myself at the hospital where they have never heard of the casualty from the Goûter. Surprised, I went to enquire in Accident and Emergency where they told me that the boy had nothing wrong with him and after all the X-rays, had gone home the same evening! Astonishing! I talked to the doctors who confirmed, once again, because it is not the first time, that reaction to pain varies considerably from one person to another. He was only suffering from heavy bruising. But he had been shocked by his ten-metre fall and really was in pain.

Let's get back to the helipad. While the Bérard rescue is taking place, enter a lady, tall, attractive, of middling age. Fair, quite short hair brushed back over the nape of her neck. Trousers and climbing boots. She asks if there are any rescues on at the moment and if there are going to be any reconnaissances. I explain what is happening. I tell myself that she is perhaps a mother, the one who requested the reconnaissance on Mont Blanc, and who has come here, anxious.

She sits down beside me and explains:

'I was wondering if I could take advantage of a reconnaissance flight to get up to the Envers.'

These words prepare me for anything. There are some crazy eccentrics who land up here. But the rest of the conversation explains things:

'I'm the warden of the Envers Hut. My mother died yesterday. At Sallanches. For ten days I have been down there every day and gone back up in the evening. Today, it was the paperwork. I don't usually ask for help… But if they did have a recce and could drop me off… I don't feel up to going on foot.'

I say to her emotionally:

'You're Babeth! I'm Anne Sauvy…'

We shake hands and remain hands clasped for a long while.

Babeth is the best known hut warden in the range. John holds her in great reverence. And furthermore she is one of my fans! I have written dedications for her in books that have been passed to me but we had never met.

'*Nadir,*' she says to me… I've got two copies up there. Everyone reads them. One of them has got pages missing[1] and whoever reads it rushes to get the other one. Occasionally, at ten o'clock in the evening, someone will refuse to go to bed because he is in the middle of reading *Nadir* and wants to know what happens next! And what strikes me most is that every reader is affected in a different way by one or other of the cases. It's the accidents to the youngsters that get me. But for the young girl who is with me at the hut at the moment it is the case of the Czech. She was distraught about the Czech. The other day, when someone brought us two rucksacks, I saw she was on the point of crying. When I asked her why, she replied: 'It reminds me of the Czech's rucksack in *Nadir…*'

Most authors like to hear that they are appreciated, however I

---

[1] Gummed spine [perfect bound], one of the disasters of modern publishing.

talk to Babeth about her mother. She was only seventy-seven years old, a relatively young age to die these days. But she had not been well for two years now and so it may be felt that her death was something of a release. However, it is still a big shock when it actually happens, said Babeth. I know, I tell her. The funeral is to be in Servoz on Saturday. Babeth wants to say a few words, as the priest has only recently arrived there and had not had time to get to know her mother. She asks my advice on what to say. Should she use the second or the third person singular? We consider this together and discuss what is appropriate. Here at the helipad, everything happens...

The helicopter has arrived back, the heart problem casualty having been taken directly to hospital. The Mont Blanc reconnaissance remains to be done. It concerns climbers who were camping at the Col du Midi, intending to do the traverse of Mont Blanc over the Tacul, and nothing has been heard from them. The mission consists of seeing if their tent is really no longer at the Col, where their friends have been searching for them in vain, then to have a look along the route to see if there has been an accident. Going up to the Col du Midi by the Mer de Glace, the chopper will be able to drop Babeth off on the way.

International excitement
As I left, the helicopter was describing an arc against the slopes below Montenvers as it came in to land after completing the Mont Blanc reconnaissance, the ins and outs of which were not yet known. The niceties of this search were related to me the following day. It was not the run of the mill missing person case.

A group of Japanese visiting Chamonix – they come in droves – had taken the train to Montenvers and the Mer de Glace. One of their number, a lady of venerable age, seventy-eight, had got lost and didn't even have her return ticket. She wasn't exactly in best shape to face the problems that would confront her, given she was hampered by a triple handicap: her age, her nationality – like most Japanese, she could not speak a word of either French or English – and her disability. This third handicap, I have described incorrectly: in today's world, using 'politically correct' terminology, I should have said that she was a 'person in a state of reduced personal mobility'. Awful, but it sounds more impressive and, wrongly, thought to be kinder.

Be that as it may, this old Japanese lady was lost and couldn't be found anywhere. Panic amongst her compatriots. The PGHM alerted, informed the helicopter returning from Mont Blanc which proceeded to look in the gullies where it was thought she might have fallen.

All ended well however, the old lady having reached the valley, either by hobbling down the thousand metre descent, or managing to persuade the counter clerk at Montenvers to calculate the price of a ticket in yen. Opinions rest divided as to these two hypotheses, one of which must be correct. But at any rate, the old lady was by no means out of the woods once she had reached Chamonix, where she felt more lost in the urban jungle than she seemed to have been in the natural one. She had absolutely no idea where her hotel was, nor its exotic name. Some tourists, thinking it strange to see this tired looking old Asian lady wandering around at a loss, realised that she had problems and managed to reunite her with her compatriots.

So when you see the helicopter, it is not always out for brainless foolhardy youngsters… No, it could just as well be for an infirm, almost eighty-year-old Japanese lady.

A serious diplomatic incident averted
The Mont Blanc reconnaissance had revealed even more curious events, which almost caused a diplomatic incident. Here is what happened.

Finnish television had decided to send an exploratory mission to the savages, or the like, to film a major adventure documentary. The Nicolas Hulot-type achieving the exploit of the century. The exploit of the century was the ascent of Mont Blanc by the Tacul normal route. A heroic Finnish climbing team were to throw themselves into the assault of the highest mountain in Europe, with its eternal snows, its glaciers, its sheer slopes, its vertiginous ridges, its yawning crevasses and dangers of all kinds. A fine subject.

The courageous expedition planned high camps, as is appropriate, before the great final assault. No point in telling the Finnish television viewers that the climb can be done in a day from the first cable-car. Advanced base was therefore installed at the Col du Midi, which they probably reached by cable-car, like everyone else. Two brave climbers had pitched their tent there, in order to acclimatise at altitude before the 'Assault'. But without letting anyone know, they had let two days of wonderful weather go by because they did not judge it yet opportune to start their attack. Concern amongst the rest of the team awaiting at base camp in the valley as the two conquerors failed to return. Consequently, two scouts were delegated to see what was happening at the Col du Midi, and then, panic! The brave explorers' tent was no longer in the canvas village! So they had obviously undertaken the perilous ascent and had disappeared, like Mallory and Irvine on Everest, in the most agonising of mysteries.

The Finnish team immediately alerted the PGHM who planned a reconnaissance once the mass of call-outs that day gave them time. A logical priority is accorded to accidents known to be genuine, before searches based on imprecise information that often take up a lot of time. The helicopter, it will be recalled, had already had to deal with a fracture, a coronary and a serious sprain this afternoon. And with the amount of people on Mont Blanc today, any accident would probably soon be known.

In the meantime, the Finn in charge of the operation was going beserk. These French were doing nothing! He could see his heroes dead or dying in the savage mountains and no one was lifting a finger to save them. Deciding that the natives were not acting in a way commensurate with the scale of the drama, he telephoned his embassy. The same panic immediately took hold there. Imagine, if you will, Nicolas Hulot[2] disappearing in some remote part of the Andes and the country having the honour of hosting his exploit doing nothing to find him! The embassy resolved to raise the tragedy which was unfolding in Chamonix at the very highest levels. Panic spread in Paris! Matignon (the Prime Minister's office) called the PGHM who replied that the matter was in hand and presented no problem for the time being and that a reconnaissance was intended as soon as possible.

So, the other emergencies completed, *Dragon* left with two rescuers. After dropping Babeth off, it flew via the Géant icefall and arrived in sight of the vast campsite at the Col du Midi, where the banning of camping is more honoured in the breach than the observance. And there, they noticed one tent pitched apart from the others. Perhaps the Finnish scouts did not go that far? Better check it out! The helicopter landed right beside the tent. But no

[2] French TV personality who takes part in a range of sports (with help, of course, but not too obviously).

one appeared. It must be empty, abandoned... Olivier Renard was left there, charged with seeing if there were any clues inside. The helicopter immediately took off again to search along the Mont Blanc traverse for any climbers in difficulty who had gone unnoticed, or perhaps to find two inanimate bodies at the foot of a slope... But hardly had it reached Mont Maudit than it received a call from Renard.

The latter had opened the tent to find the two missing men, tranquilly lying there, not having thought to show themselves, or even to look outside to see what was happening when the helicopter landed beside them

'Not possible to have been any closer!' Michel Pierre recounted.

'And you know the noise the chopper makes and the snow storm the rotor blades whip up...'

And so, unbeknownst, on July 16, 1997, a serious diplomatic incident was avoided.

11

THE GUIVERECS' ACCIDENT

Throughout this summer of 1997, there were days of intense work, full of emotion, drama and tension, but Wednesday, July 16 was one of the fullest days in this respect, and the Guiverecs' rescue, one that left a lasting mark on the season.

When, one by one there returned to the helipad chalet the pilot, who was Michel Pierre, the mechanician, Ivan Commène, the doctor, Manu Cauchy and the two rescuers, Pascal Saudemont and Jean-Jacques Malineau, each had felt the need to express his feelings and the difficulties they had coped with:

'Great rescue!'

'Hell of a rescue! We don't do ones like that very often!'

'Technical, that rescue was! Real technical!'

'Hey! That was pretty satisfactory!'

'Fantastic rescue!'

The rescue team had been alerted from the Requin Hut after cries were heard from *Congo-Star* [a modern rock climb, 300m/TDsup] on the Aiguille Pierre Allain. The helicopter left immediately. There was no information about the reason for the shouts or the nature of any possible injuries. From the Requin, they could only see a pair of climbers who seemed to be in difficulty and someone hanging from the end of a rope. The Aiguille Pierre Allain is where the statue of Christ the Saviour in the Mountains was placed a few years ago.

The two concerned were Francis and Nadine Guiverec, both experienced alpinists, but it sometimes only needs one little thing to tip the balance. They were on the lower third of the route, on the big smooth slabs but at the time of the accident, separated by a bulge, and could neither see nor hear each other because of the noise of a torrent. Francis, who was leading, had a momentary hesitation over the route-finding, and found himself in a difficult position off-route. With the rope almost fully run out and no longer moving, Nadine thought that she had not heard her husband calling her to climb and so left the belay and started up the pitch.

It was then that he fell. A flake behind which he had found an *in situ* nut, which he had managed to grab, came out. His fall was finally held by a nut that he had placed himself some ten metres below, resulting in a twenty-metre fall. Having bounced several times, he had an open fracture of the pelvis and was losing blood both internally and externally. The flesh of his hip had also been punctured by his climbing gear (a Friend) and a muscle severed. And he also had a fracture and dislocation of the shoulder.

When the helicopter arrived the casualties were spotted almost straight away but it was so difficult to reach them that the helicopter had to hover for more than a minute, while the rescuers took stock of the situation, reviewing the possible belay points on the compact and overhanging slabs. They finally found an answer to the complex problem which needed an urgent solution. There was a lot of blood on the rock below the man, but he was still conscious because he signalled to them with his uninjured arm.

'It took us a few moments to figure out how we were going to play it!' commented Michel Pierre.

The situation was as follows: a steep, smooth wall of about 60°, made up of slabs, overhangs and vertical sections. The casualty was hanging from the rope, held by a nut the stability of which was uncertain, so that the rescuers could not rely on it for their own security. The woman, four metres above the belay, was hanging on by her hands under an overhang, with one leg jammed behind a flake. They are linked by twenty-five metres of rope passing through two bolts about six metres apart.

As they could not run the risk of descending directly towards the injured man or to belay on his nut, the best solution was for them to be winched down to the stance that he had been trying to reach when he got off route, even though it was well to one side of him. As soon as that was decided, Pascal Saudemont and Jean-Jacques Malineau were lowered to the stance, not very roomy but safe with two bolts. Having tied on they got the rope out of the sack.

Only half an hour had passed from the time of the accident to the winching of the rescuers onto the wall, despite the fact that first of all Nadine Guiverec's cries had to be heard from the Requin Hut about 500 metres away, the climbers visually located, the alarm raised, and the accident reported to the PGHM. The rescuers then had to board the helicopter, fly up to the scene, work out what to do and then be winched down to the stance.

While Pascal Saudemont lowered Jean-Jacques Malineau down to the casualty, the helicopter went straight off to collect the doctor with his emergency kit because on the wall they could not manage his sack and a Piguillem stretcher. In the meantime, Malineau had reached the casualty. There was an overhang immediately below him, but not far away a small ledge, only about ten centimetres wide, where the main parts of the operation could be carried out. Drawing level with Francis Guiverec, and holding onto the rock to stop himself penduluming, Jean-Jacques Malineau managed to catch the injured man's rope and pull himself across. Straight away, a relationship of cooperation, almost friendly, was established between them, essential in this kind of tricky rescue.

'Don't worry! We'll look after you now!'

'I've been climbing twenty-two years without an accident and now I'm messing you around...'

'No, you're not. It's our job. There are people who call for rescue for a lot less! We're there to help you.'

'I think I've broken my pelvis...'

'We'll work it out! What's your name?'

'Francis.'

'OK, Francis, stop worrying! You're going to be OK now.'

This sort of conversation is important, indeed a factor for success. It is necessary to establish contact, to talk and get the other to talk, to reassure. The psychological aspect of a rescue goes hand in hand with the technical and medical sides of it.

Francis Guiverec was pale, bleeding profusely and his pulse could be barely detected. The situation was urgent and there was no question of looking for a better belay. But the injured man astonished the rescuers with his calm and sangfroid. He was certainly in pain but did not complain, remained conscious and brave throughout, playing his part in the manoeuvres on the wall.

Pascal Saudemont abseiled down to the upper bolt which he backed up with a Friend.[1] Jean-Jacques Malineau himself was attached to the lower bolt and the nut[2] that had held Francis Guiverec. Once the latter had been securely belayed the two rescuers dealt with Mme Guiverec who was unhurt, but had to be removed from her uncomfortable position. Moreover, she was

[1] A camming device that can be inserted into a crack and will hold solid when weight is applied thereby proving a secure anchorage. Friends come in all sizes, the larger ones being fist-sized and it was probably one of these that punctured Francis's leg.

[2] Metal wedges or hexagons, threaded with wire or rope, that can be secured in cracks. A karabiner then links the nut to the climbing rope to provide intermediate protection during a lead or a secure anchorage at a belay ledge.

inwardly impatient to know what had happened. The noise of the torrent had prevented her from being informed, and the rescuers could only communicate with each other via the radios in their helmets. But she was worried, she had seen the blood on the rock, called to find out what was happening but got no reply, all the more so as the urgency only allowed dealing with the essential.

When it was her turn to move, she surprised the rescuers by the speed she climbed an overhang of V+ or VIa, 'ran up it,' said one, 'flew up it,' said the other. She was then able to belay at the stance of another route, on a good ledge.

The helicopter came back with Dr Cauchy who was winched directly down to the casualty, but because there was little room, the stretcher was set down a bit higher up so as not to knock the victim.

'The winching was done with surgical precision that day!' Ivan Commène recounted. 'The ring of the winch had to land exactly at the spot where they needed to attach it, in order for everything to happen quickly and smoothly.'

Then the helicopter landed at the Requin from where the crew watched developments through binoculars.

Hanging from his harness, Dr Cauchy made a rapid medical assessment, placed a drip into a vein in very difficult conditions and gave the casualty an injection of Nubain to relieve the pain. It was impossible to do more because of the steepness of the wall and the lack of space. While all this was happening, Pascal Saudemont was preparing the Piguillem stretcher in which Manu Cauchy and Jean-Jacques Malineau installed Francis Guiverec, Malineau having to place it almost over him so as to get him inside and strap him in – a very precarious manoeuvre. Fortunately, the casualty remained calm, which made things easier, he did not complain, or hamper them; on the contrary he apologised for being the cause of so much trouble.

When they were ready, the helicopter came back. The doctor, who always travels with the victim, was winched up first. Then the ring was lowered down and the Piguillem attached. Saudemont then detached it from his end, while Malineau cut the casualty's belay. The stretcher left, swinging free. It was winched up in a horizontal position because of the injured man's serious condition. His fractured pelvis and the amount of blood he had lost meant that there was a risk of heart failure if winched up at an angle.

But transporting the stretcher beneath the chopper has a problem that has not been solved: when it is horizontal, the stretcher revolves. The helicopter was about twenty metres above the stretcher when it was attached, so when it was lifted by the winch, it inevitably began turning. However it had to be left like this, five metres below, so as not to risk hitting the basket, until the helicopter got to the Requin helipad where it was set down. There the guardian and a guide helped unhook it, and the helicopter in turn landed. The stretcher could then be placed horizontally in the cabin and Francis Guiverec, on a drip, was taken rapidly, along with Dr Cauchy, to the emergency helipad at the hospital, where Dr Lecoq was awaiting them.

While the two rescuers were finishing their work, the helicopter went to deal with the much less serious accident that had taken place at about the same time on the Envers du Plan Glacier.

On the Aiguille Pierre Allain meanwhile, Jean-Jacques Malineau had abseiled down to Mme Guiverec and immediately put her at ease:

'We've sorted your husband out! He'll be fine! He should be arriving at the hospital this minute! And now, it's your turn. What's your name?'

'Nadine.'

'OK! Nadine. The helicopter will soon be coming to get you and take you down to the valley.'

This news was an intense relief for Nadine Guiverec. She had supposed, that being uninjured, she would simply be left at the hut to make her own way down on foot, which is not difficult but in her present state of shock she dreaded this solitary descent that would keep her away from her husband for several hours.

With her also, as soon as contact was made so too was a sympathetic relationship. Nadine Guiverec was worrying over her own responsibility in the accident. Would it have happened had she not left the belay? Was it her fault? Jean-Jacques Malineau reassured her: the rope was still tight between them and things would not have been any different whether she had moved or not. The rescuers coiled up their ropes together with the Guiverecs' and collected together all the equipment. Then the helicopter, coming back from the other operation, winched up first Mme Guiverec and Jean-Jacques Malineau, then picked up Pascal Saudemont, who had descended to the foot of the wall to collect the rucksack the climbers had left, and took them to the Requin. It was at this stage that I had seen Mme Guiverec arrive at the helipad and taken her to the hospital.

'We were thrilled!' Michel Pierre told me, concluding his account of the rescue. 'Thrilled because we had done a good rescue and brought back someone alive! Cauchy had said not to hang around because the guy was bleeding to death… And he rigged up the drips and all as though in a medicalised ambulance!'

Manu Cauchy confirmed this later:

'His haemoglobin was at 5.6. He wouldn't have lasted another hour!'

The next day, Pascal Saudemont and Jean-Jacques Malineau went to the hospital for news of the casualty, who was in intensive care. They were warmly welcomed. And after learning that the couple had originally intended to do the Mer de Glace face of the Grépon, but had changed objective because of the weather, they proposed:

'Both of us are guides. If you like, next year we'll take you up the Grépon Mer de Glace face to celebrate your recovery!'

But Francis Guiverec, shaken in morale as well as physically by his accident, thought that he wanted to stop climbing.

Just before they left for the Paris area, Francis and Nadine sent the PGHM a letter that was displayed for the rest of the season. Although the rescuers sometimes encounter ingratitude or indifference, they were touched to know that this rescue had provoked sincere gratitude:

Gentlemen
You rescued me, on July 16, after a fall on the Aiguille Pierre Allain. I would like to thank all the team who helped me and my wife. We will always be profoundly grateful to the men who carried out our rescue with such efficiency, such dedication and much kindness and sensitivity.

When, hanging at the end of my rope, I thanked Jean-Jacques Malineau, he replied: 'It's normal, we are just doing our job.' I can assure you that you have done much more. I only need to bring to mind the unforgettable expressions of Pascal Saudemont, Jean-Jacques Malineau and Emmanuel Cauchy to face up to the small and bigger hurdles in life.

We are leaving Chamonix on the August 6, nursing our injuries but retaining a profound gratitude and warmth for the PGHM.

Francis and Nadine Guiverec

12

THE CASE OF MONT BLANC

hursday, July 17

A day of little activity, even though the morning was fine, but storms were forecast, the prospect of which must have emptied the mountains. Only two rescues in the morning.

The storms arrive, as forecast, towards midday, then subside, then reappear about three o'clock. The sky is an inky black. Torrents of rain begin to fall.

'Well!' I say. 'I don't think you will be doing anything this afternoon.'

'You never know!' replies Michel Pierre, optimistically. 'Someone might drown.'

He is in the middle of reading an article in the local *Dauphiné* which is reporting the previous day's events and which makes him melancholic:

'A rescue by the PGHM, A rescue by the PGHM,' he protests, 'it's always the same! They only mention the PGHM, there's never anything about us, the helicopters! It's not fair. The PG boys must have done all that on foot yesterday. They never mention us.'

The helipad settles down for an afternoon of bad weather. The big news is that the redstarts' brood must have flown the nest. The parents are no longer bringing back food and we can no longer hear the insistent squawking of the ravenous fledglings.

Outside, thousands of little needles of rain bounce relentlessly off the flooded tarmac of the helipad and, on the pine-covered slopes of the hillside above us, we catch glimpses of a foreign landscape as swathes of mist creep behind the crest of the ridges or wrap themselves idly around the branches. I would very much like to leave, but I don't, because my umbrella is in my car, which is parked outside the helipad. Walking a hundred metres in a cloudburst is not very appealing and, even though I may be on the best of terms with the gendarmes, it is not quite to the point of saying: 'Excuse me, young man, would you be so good as to go and fetch my umbrella?' So, like it or not, I stay...

Patrick Poirot, sometimes nicknamed Hercule, and the GA, set about constructing, with the help of two large pieces of block-board acquired for them, a two-metre-wide desk for the computers in the compartment on the right just before the kitchen.

All afternoon, they saw, they drill, they measure, they put nails in, they take nails out, they screw, they unscrew, they remeasure, they redrill, they sandpaper, they move sockets and cables... A veritable hive of industry.

When two people are working, it is essential that some unoccupied people watch. Seated on the sofa opposite them, which is my usual place at the moment, I play the role of passive admirer, often assisted by one or two other team supporters coming to volunteer their opinion as to how the construction is shaping up.

'Are you a DIY woman, Mme Sauvy?' asks Poirot.

'Unfortunately not. And neither is my husband.'

'But how do you manage at home?'

'We ask friends.'

I am reluctant to tell him that I count him amongst my very dear friends... But no need!

'Ask me next time you need something doing. I love doing DIY!'

The television is not switched on today. The current entertain-ment is a thousand times more fascinating than the Tour de France! By the evening, coated with a fake oak brown varnish, the desk has the appearance of a table of the Haute Époque style.

'Now, we have to make everything here,' sighs Michel Pierre. 'Even the furniture!'

'Next week, could you change the wallpaper?' asks Cousineau amiably.

But while the artists at the helipad were busy, some of the others were telling stories and these were about Mont Blanc.

Who does not have his curious experience about Mont Blanc? Mont Blanc is a special case. Its height and its fame almost place it outside the normal sphere of alpinism. People want to have climbed *the* Mont Blanc. Many people train specifically for this goal, trample the summit with their conquerors' feet and never go climbing again, as though the accomplished feat of having gone as high as possible in the Alps reduces other mountains around them to nothing. In summer, on every fine day, two or three hundred people go to the summit. They come from far and wide to pit themselves against it. And then they go away again. Now you have to make advance bookings at the Goûter Hut. And I cannot remember which famous alpinist it was, having climbed many routes but never Mont Blanc, wrote that he was the despair of his *concierge* because she could not have respect for him until he had 'done Mont Blanc'. Mont Blanc is mythical.

Fortunately, it is also a very beautiful mountain. Whether by the normal route, the traverse, or by the more difficult routes on the Italian side, it is a special mountain.

It all started more than 200 years ago, in 1760, when a young man of twenty, called Horace, arrived in the Chamonix valley, fell madly in love with this summit, promised a very large reward for whoever could find a way up to it, and lived henceforth with a love of the mountains. You know the rest. In 1786, Dr Michel-Gabriel Paccard and Jacques Balmat made the first ascent, by the Grands Mulets. At the beginning of July 1787, Jacques Balmat, Jean-Michel Cachat and Alexis Tournier made the second ascent. And Horace, whose full name was Horace-Bénédict de Saussure and who had now aged somewhat, succeeded in climbing the mountain of his dreams on August 3, 1787, accompanied by his man servant and eighteen companions who were now starting to be called 'guides'.

Others also took up the challenge. Mont Blanc was visited by various foreigners: an Englishman, Mark Beaufoy also climbed it in 1787; a woman, Marie Paradis, did so in 1808; an American, W.M. Howard, in 1819 and eventually a Frenchman in the shape of Comte Henri de Tilly, in 1834 (the Chamoniards, don't forget, were Sardinian at the time of the first ascent, and Saussure was Swiss.) It was still to be many decades before people's gaze turned to the other mountains. But the pre-eminence that Mont Blanc achieved still holds good today, as it did then.

On July 13 this summer, we saw the case of the Slovak who, without any previous training at altitude, climbed on foot from the valley the 4000 metres to the summit, in less than twenty-four hours. Cases like this happen many times every year without anyone knowing. If there was a machine that could take us back in time so we could examine all the ascents of Mont Blanc that there have ever been, there would be an unimaginable number of epics, comedies and dramas.

At the helipad, everyone of course knows lots of rescue stories and Michel Pierre tells a good one on the subject of Mont Blanc:

'Some English people who were at the Vallot alerted the PG via the radio link that they were needed because there was a 'weird' guy at the hut. And for the English to find a guy weird means he must have been really weird.'

Everyone – including me, Mrs Wilkinson – agrees and bursts out laughing.

Michel Pierre continues:

'We wondered if we should send out the rescue team for a weird guy... We discussed it... All the same, the English had called us out... Feeling uncertain, we asked the advice of Captain Gin, who exclaimed: 'But the Mont Blanc massif is full of weird people! In fact you could say that that's all there were... If we had to go and rescue everybody, it would be never ending! We are not here to bring down weird people!'

'But a little later, the English at the Vallot called the PGHM again and reported that they were with a 'total weirdo' and that the PG really should go. So finally, we send the chopper up. That day, I was the pilot. I land at the Vallot, and what do the rescuers find? A Czech, in jeans and moccasins, with a satchel slung across his shoulder, in which there were two sailing magazines, a map, a pullover and a bar of chocolate ... The front of his moccasins had split open on the way and his toes were jutting out, they were wet but not yet frozen ... The Czech gets his map out. It was a map of Europe. He shows us the town he comes from, then Mont Blanc. From his home, he had bought a ticket to St-Gervais. And he had walked from St-Gervais to the Vallot. Seeing a house, he decided to sleep there and it is at that point that the English, worried about his lack his equipment, alerted us. The Czech himself was in seventh heaven. He hadn't realised that his feet could freeze, that he could fall off the ridge and kill himself... He resisted a little at first when he realised that we were going to take him down, but in the end he joyously got in the chopper... Oh, what a guy! What a guy! Dressed as he was, with his books, you would have thought that he had just fallen out of an aeroplane!'

Then there is the story of the lad from the Auvergne who also wanted to climb Mont Blanc. Jean-Luc Yvon tells the tale:

'He had organised everything, how much he could spend, how much each thing would cost, everything! He could not afford to buy any equipment, but he made do. He was in training shoes[1] with karrimat wound round to protect them. Under his clothes, he had put newspaper insulation. He had thought long and hard about his expedition and had prepared it well. And whereas no one had alerted us about the Czech until the English encountered 'this weirdo', loads of guides who saw this man from the Auvergne radioed to tell us that he was in danger of having an accident. We went to get him. He refused to be rescued. OK, he wasn't injured. We couldn't force him to come with us and so we let him be… But we continued to get reports about him. Well, he made the summit like that! He got back to the Vallot, by sliding down and only then did he realise that if he continued with what remained on his feet, things would end badly. We went to get him. That was better.'

Yvon also remembered a Breton, who also had no money.

'He had arrived from Brittany on a moped, to climb Mont Blanc! Without a penny! He managed to get put up at the presbytery and then set out for the Plan de l'Aiguille to go to the Grands Mulets – on whose advice we don't know. About sixty years old. Town shoes and worn out suit. On his back, for a rucksack, a plastic bag from Payot-Pertin supermarket attached to his shoulders by string! Someone reported him when he was below the Aiguille du Midi near the bottom of the Frendo. He was already soaking wet, his shoes and everything. We had a hard job convincing him to come back with us, explaining that it was dangerous – that he needed proper climbing equipment and that the best route was by the Goûter, etc. Eventually he listened to what we were saying, we brought him down and then he went home, on his moped…

'But wasn't it him that tried again a year later?'

'That's right! He came back next year, still on his moped. Ended up at the presbytery. I think Abbot Dominique had really had enough of him, especially since the guy didn't smell too good either… But he had listened to us, he went by the Goûter, had all the gear, except snow glasses. And he climbed his Mont Blanc. But he got a serious case of snow blindness. He had sort of hitch-hiked up the hill, catching lifts with guides on their ropes on the way, everyone felt a bit responsible for him, but the time came when we had to bring him down from the Goûter because he was

[1] Here, finally, is the most hackneyed and inaccurate press cliché for real!

completely blind... I still remember the stink! It was enough to make you hold your nose! We had to leave the door of the chopper slightly open during the flight. He smelled... like an alpine ibex. Oh! You could say that when Mont Blanc gets to people, it really gets to them.'

The man who knows Mont Blanc's clientele better than anyone, is Guy Bochatay, the CAF's guardian of the Goûter Hut. Nobody is more predestined for this task than he. His father, Henri Bochatay, had held the same job. Guy was born in the TMB![2] He spent the following summer at the Tête Rousse Hut,[3] which his mother looked after, and then all the rest at the Aiguille, before taking over from his father, in 1985. At the age of thirty-eight, he has never spent a summer down in the plain or even in the Chamonix valley. He has always been up there...

At the Goûter, there are 108 bed spaces that can, at CAF's request, sleep 140 people jammed together. You also have to reserve in advance. Many people do not realise this, especially foreigners, as the information is not disseminated outside France. So many more than that actually arrive. They are taken in. Could you, for example, throw outside some Spaniards, who have come from Madrid specifically to climb Mont Blanc, who did not know that they had to make a reservation and who had made the fairly long climb up to the hut only to be told that really they have no right to be there? So they stay and pay, but sleep on the floor, probably not very happy, like the young Slovak on July 13.[4]

The problem has not been helped by the opening up of the Eastern Bloc countries, as it has increased the number of climbers who are drawn to Mont Blanc by its height and its renown.

The PGHM were recently called in to help with a problem of overcrowding which risked turning into a fight. The tramway

[2] Tramway du Mont Blanc that runs from Le Fayet to Nid d'Aigle
[3] Intermediate hut, between the Nid d'Aigle and Aiguille du Goûter.
[4] People nowadays say that the overcrowding of certain huts is a new phenomenon and lament the 'old days' when the huts were almost empty... Nonsense! I remember the old Goûter Hut where we were packed into the bunks or on the floor lying on our sides, in order to take up less space. During the night, feeling as though I was suffocating, I managed to elbow my way up in order to breathe better. When I came to lie down again, the human mass had closed behind me and I had to make a hole with my shoulder between my two neighbours. There must be a sort of filling up law: if a hut is enlarged, the number of people staying in it increases proportionally. And the only possible way of reducing the numbers of people in the mountains and, consequently, reducing the number of accidents, would be to do away with cable-cars and huts... Guido Magnone wrote an article entitled 'Should the huts be burnt down?' but it seems never to have been published. We haven't quite got to that point...

people had reported that ninety Slovenians had caught the train to the Nid d'Aigle. They were not expected either at the Goûter or at the Tête Rousse, both huts being already fully booked. Although warned, the Slovenians nevertheless carried on. They had no tents. There were so many of them that the hut guardians wanted the PGHM to intervene before they started up, but it was too cloudy for the helicopter to fly. And their arrival in strength at the Aiguille du Goûter Hut, where there were already at least 140 people, met a stormy reception, all the more so since those with reservations did not look on this invasion with favour. In the evening, the sky cleared and Captain Gin went up in the helicopter. In front of the hut, he was taken to one side: 'Throw them out!' Inside, he said it was like being in an 'Indian train carriage', as there were people packed in from floor to ceiling. He negotiated with them, sending some up to the Vallot and managed to calm things.

In fact, now, some alpinists camp up there relieving the pressure on the hut accordingly. Furthermore, many do the three Mont Blancs from the new Cosmiques Hut, or even straight from the first cable-car, and so lessen the crowds on the normal route by the Goûter and the Bosses Ridge.

One of the difficulties with Mont Blanc, nevertheless, lies in the approach to the hut prior to the ascent. The dilemma, which has no immediate prospect of solution, is caused by the number of accidents, often fatal, which happen during the traverse of the couloir on the way up to the Aiguille du Goûter, where there is frequent stonefall. Some think a tunnel should be built underneath it. Others object to this on the grounds that it would make access to the summit even easier for crowds of incompetents, resulting in more accidents higher up. The question remains open. Nothing is easy when it comes to Mont Blanc for, far more than with any other mountain, it is so coveted by those desiring to climb it that they easily stake all to reach its summit, their lives included.

We were saying that Mont Blanc is a very particular case. Mountain rescue must in no way be judged by the wild things that happen up there.

Even so, it must be recognised Mont Blanc is something special. Mont Blanc fascinates, Mont Blanc bewitches and its story is far from over.

13

RAIN AND SUNSHINE

Friday, July 18
Incessant rain. There are no rescues and at the PG and helipad, everyone is busy working on reports or accident statements from the past few days. I do the same, asking Michel Pierre or Pascal Saudemont about the technical side of Francis Guiverec's rescue and also about the teenagers, whose parents I meet in the evening.

Saturday, July 19
It is raining.
Rain, rain, rain.
It is still raining. Permanently, endlessly.
When I arrive at the helipad in the afternoon, I ask Pierre Raveneau and Philippe Pouts, who are on duty:
'Surely there is nothing on today?'
'No. All the better for them!' replies Raveneau cheerfully.
But a little while later, we recall that some Koreans are at this moment on the Walker... On the Walker! With the piles of new snow that have fallen over the last few days!
Michel Pierre improvises analysis of a subject which adds to what I said regarding the Koreans at the Goûter, on July 4, a rather more male version, with more imagery and even bluntly meta-phorical in style:
'You've got to understand these blokes,' he says, 'They have come a long way, they've scrimped, made sacrifices... Perhaps they'll never come back... So, they go for it anyway, give it a try. Imagine if some guys here at home saved for years to be able to go once in their life to Thailand and to have Thai massages from beautiful young girls... OK! They get down there only to be told: "There's a problem! The young girls aren't available any more. There are only old grannies for massages." So what do they do, these guys? Ah well, they've come a long way, they've paid their

money, so for want of anything better they have the old grannies…
For these Koreans, the old grannies are the bad weather. And so
they decide they're going to try their planned routes, in spite of
the snow or whatever.'

Everyone present followed the development of this argument
with interest and there is a general sympathy for these Koreans
who have chosen to try the North Face of the Grandes Jorasses
with the old grannies, or rather the adverse elements, while they
were so much hoping for good weather![1]

Sunday, July 20

It is fine! And what fills the holidaymakers with joy instead fills
me with unease. We are always delighted to see the sun shining
over the mountains but what is today going to bring? This is the
agonising question I now ask myself this year on each brilliant
morning.

As the rescues today were not particularly interesting nor
seemingly packed with deep human interest, a brief résumé will
suffice. There were eight call-outs, none of which really fitted the
normal sort of drama conveyed by the media.

The first rescue was for an employee in the Cosmiques Hut,
who was two months pregnant and feeling unwell. She was
quickly taken to hospital.

Other operations were for minor injuries or problems: someone
with snow blindness at the Argentière Hut; a slipped disc on the
descent from Mont Blanc; a twisted ankle on the Améthystes
Glacier; an Italian who broke his ankle descending the Tour Ronde;
a twenty-year-old Englishman who broke his leg on the West Face
of the Blaitière; a twelve-year-old Belgian kid taken ill at the Albert
Premier Hut, probably with hypoglycaemia, and who was brought
down with his father. 'You've never seen the mountains like that!'
the rescuers tell him, as he got out of the helicopter. He grins,
pretty happy.

At lunchtime, there is a strange rescue on the right bank of the
Bossons Glacier. A couple in their forties were having a picnic near
the Cerro Chalet, almost opposite Les Pyramides, and thought they
were in a safe place because there were slabs above them. But

---

[1] Bravely, these Koreans descended alone and unharmed, the next day, without calling out
the rescue.

stones can fall anywhere. And a stone hit the man on the head. He lost consciousness, but when the rescuers reached him, he was conscious again, albeit febrile. His wife and daughter, seriously shocked, were trying to find someone to blame. For them, someone must have knocked the stone down.

I don't know if the helicopter had issued calls when flying in the area, but three hours later, a boy and two young girls appeared at the helipad on motorbikes. Pascal Saudemont wanted to take the young man to the glacier so he could show him where he had been in relation to the place of the accident. There could be a complaint lodged against him. But for the time being the helicopter is occupied elsewhere.

The young people wait outside, then, as it is chilly, ask if they can come into the chalet. All of a sudden, I see my familiar helipad through their eyes. The three rescuers present, all kitted up, dripping with slings, loops of rope, clinking karabiners, jumars, ice screws, a knife, sometimes with a radio slung across their chest, looking very 'professional', almost like extra-terrestrial robots… It reminds me of a little American boy who, seeing my husband climbing on a big boulder at the Dame Jeanne in Fontainebleau, asked his father: 'Is he human?'

To these young people, who can be described as walkers at the very most, such paraphernalia must seem outlandish. They are sitting, huddled together on a sofa, in front of the television which is showing an American film. Médici is writing on a computer. There are brief exchanges of technical words, interspersed with long silences, and even the 'gendarme' side of things shows through: 'Have you managed to get his identity?' Snippets of messages come through on the radio, prefaced by high-pitched musical squeaks: 'Cordial calling Couvercle…' To me, who knows this place and those who work here, their characters, their tastes, often their families, this is a profoundly human environment. When you suddenly turn up here, from another environment, it must seem quite otherwise. I sense that these young people are nervous and I am obviously not the only one because someone tries to relax them by talking about their motorbikes.

Thus the beginning of some sort of contact is established and humanises things.

When the helicopter comes back, it takes Pascal Saudemont and the young man to the spot above where the accident took place.

On the screen, a small American movie star coughs miserably in front of the silent girls. On the helicopter's return, the situation seems to be cleared up. Michel Pierre says to the boy:

'OK, *a priori*, it wasn't you who kicked the stone down! Considering where it was!'

The youngsters leave, relieved.

It's strange that people want at all costs to find someone responsible. Perhaps even compensation. They live in a virtual world, not the real world, where stones can fall of their own accord.

In the evening, we tease the rescuers Médici and Renard who spent the day doing rescues from huts while the other team had more serious and committing rescues, on slabs. Olivier Renard complains:

'I can't believe it! We went to the Cosmiques, the Argentière, the Goûter, the Albert Premier...'

'Hang on a minute! There's still the Couvercle, the Requin, the Charpoua. You might still have some work to do tonight!'

And Michel Pierre, going over all the rescues of the week, enumerated those Renard had done which did not involve huts. 'No! You had a sprain at Les Chéserys... A great rescue!'

Monday, July 21

Fine weather. *Bravo Lima* has replaced *Dragon* and the pilot this week is Didier Méraux, from the base at Megève. He is affable, precise and all smiles.

This morning, he arrived with the essay of a ten-year-old schoolboy and pinned it up on a wall, to the delight of all those at the helipad. This is what it said:

I want to be a pilot.

I will be a pilot when I grow up because it is an enjoyable and easy job. Which is why there are a lot of pilots today.

Pilots don't have to go to school for very long, they just have to learn to read figures so that they can read the instruments. I think they also have to be able to read a road map so they don't get lost.

Pilots have to be brave so they don't get frightened if it is foggy and they can't see anything, or if a wing or the engine fails, they must stay calm in order to know what to do.

Pilots have to have good eyesight for seeing through clouds and must not be afraid of thunder and lightning because they are nearer to it than we are.

I also like pilots' salaries. They have more money than they can spend. Which is why people think that flying is dangerous, except the pilots who know that it is easy.

There is not much that I don't like about it, except that the girls and all the air hostesses want to marry them and they have to chase them away because they get fed up with them.

I hope I don't get air sick, because I get car sick, and if I am ill in a plane, I can't be a pilot and then I will have to go out to work.

The Sécurité Civile have also left a souvenir behind them: someone, and we suspect Noël Rivière, has decorated the pylon outside which supports the windsock and the aerials, with unexpected attributes. All sorts of things are suspended from it, like washing hung out to dry: a bra, brightly coloured panties... Flashy decorations. Which will be quickly removed – not the right thing!

But there has to be humour here, where suffering, failure and sometimes tragedy are confronted daily. Otherwise the burden of all this would make the job impossible. The healthy cheerfulness in the intervals between rescues, is a counterbalance to the more sombre humours.

And when there is no time to make this readjustment, you quickly feel the atmosphere grow heavy.

In any case it is going to be a tough day.

At the time I arrive, the Bernier/Junod team are in action. They bring down two alpinists from Mont Blanc dressed for the high mountains: anoraks, hats pulled down over their ears... One knocks off the snow that is still stuck to his vibram soles on the sunny tarmac. They are a Slovakian guide with a Polish client who has damaged his knee. There is no doubt that the shrinking of the earth – due to transport and telecommunications – has Europeanised, and even globalised the PGHM's clientele. I would be interested to know how many different nationalities have been rescued this season. Let alone those which didn't have an accident!

At the helipad, and most certainly at the hospital, there are always language problems. The ones who have just been brought down, for example, only have some scanty words of German. How we lack a common language! Within the European bodies, every text has to be translated eighteen times! Latin is supposed to be archaic but it was the European language for a thousand years, and moreover easy, logical, brief, and neutral, which avoided any idea of a dominant culture. A real language, not an artificial Esperanto. But in today's world it is sufficient to watch people trying to express themselves in an incomprehensible pidgin, to regret the passing of a time when there really was a second language, a universal one, which we are not even starting to replace.

Having said that, and remembering it as a background problem throughout the summer, let's get back to our injured Pole who does not want to stay on the ambulance stretcher. For people from the East, if one has to be lying down, it's serious. Whereas he does not want it to be serious. It was difficult to get him to remain stretched out.

Rescues follow on each other and, by the afternoon, are overlapping, the duty team working at two sites and the helicopter flying from one to the other: the Tête Rousse and the footpath to Les Pyramides.

The emergency helipad is announced for the victim at the Tête Rousse whom Dr Cousineau was attending.

And the other one, the Pyramides casualty, arrives at the helipad with Pierre Bernier. He has an Arab name and lives in Argentière. He is seventeen, and had fallen about thirty metres from the footpath where he was on his own. Nobody had seen what happened, so he got back as best he could to the chalet at Les Pyramides, from where the alarm was given. Meanwhile he had passed out. He has a blow to the head and arrives with his eyes closed and a vacant expression. The ambulance takes him away.

At ten past four, the helicopter comes back with the three other rescuers and Benoît Cousineau who exclaims relieved:

'It's all right! We've brought him back alive!'

He is talking about the Tête Rousse casualty, a thirty-seven-year-old from Venice.

'But, he's really bad!' he continues. 'While ascending from the Tête Rousse to the Goûter, he started up a gully which he repainted in red for 200 metres... He has broken all four limbs. On one side he has a tibia-fibula fracture, on the other a knee at a right angle, a fracture of the left wrist. On his right arm he has a fracture of the head of the humerus and the other wrist, seven or eight centimetre cuts all over his scalp, an exploded eyelid, his temperature was already at 35...'

'Bloody hell!' Michel Gonzalez adds, 'he was split open on all sides!'

'And when we found him he was conscious and sitting on his arse!'

'What else could he sit on?' asks Alain Charnay...

'And his vocal cords must be severed or dislocated, because his voice was very high-pitched and hoarse,' adds Benoît Cousineau.

'With that lot he should thank his stars that his head is still attached to be able to speak...'

'Well, he didn't talk much... Only: "*Molto dolore!... Molto dolore!*"'

'Fortunately, the doctor was there to give him a shot!' remarks one of the rescuers. 'Otherwise, with his foot perpendicular and the knee of his other leg locked behind him, it would have been impossible to put him in the stretcher!'

'He really copped it!' says the mechanician... 'Even from above I could see he had really copped it!'

The helipad is badly affected by this accident. It is fortunate that there was no reporter here today to take close-up shots of the Italian to be shown to the masses this evening at dinnertime.

Some hours later, I hear Michel Gonzalez, who is still thinking about it, sighing:

'I have rarely brought back someone alive who was in such a state...'

It was a dreadful accident, but a life saved. Just! Considering the amount of blood that he was losing, the Italian wouldn't have held on much longer. The helicopter and the immediate medical care showed all their worth here.

Relaxation. Two women with two small children come into the helipad. I don't know who they have come to see but they bring rhubarb and nectarine tarts. I am called into the kitchen. Everyone has a slice. The atmosphere is lighter.

Another call-out, from Le Chapeau, an easy walk on a hillside facing Montenvers. The helicopter flies off and comes back empty. Dr Cousineau and the rescuers have stayed up there. Didier Méraux busies himself with his paperwork and the two mechanicians do some maintenance on the helicopter. They are called on the radio and asked to request an ambulance for the casualty. It must be serious then.

The 'victim', when he is brought down, is without any doubt the doyen of the summer. His date of birth: 1913! Eighty-four years old. Wearing moccasins, he was out walking with friends, when he fell and hurt his wrist. His blood pressure is 17, but everything else is normal. He explains to the doctor that he is treated for high blood pressure and must have forgotten to take his medications the morning:

'Travelling, you see...'

He left in the ambulance.

Benoît Cousineau comments:

'It's always the same! Every time there is a rescue and I try to speak to casualties to see how they react, to see how their brain is functioning, others always want to speak for them! Yet only the casualties can give you proper answers to your questions. But, every time, someone else replies on their behalf, thinking they are helping. This time, there were a group of four friends, and it was just the same! A conversation with the others!... "How old are you?" "He is eighty-four!" etc. It was the same with the Italian earlier; there was someone else there who didn't know him who had just appeared beside him... "Where does it hurt?" – "You can see he has a broken leg!" It is always, always, always, the same!'

About twenty to seven, Benoît Cousineau telephones the hospital for news of the Italian. When he has finished speaking, I question him with a lift of my chin and eyes:

'He's on the table.'

Other news comes later:

'He was sedated. At the hospital they had to sedate him again... We'll know more tomorrow... I'm amazed that he didn't have head injuries... But when we were with him he was still conscious.'

At the helipad, I learn everything this way, in bits and pieces. There's no point in wanting more or quicker. Everyone can be affected by a rescue without necessarily wanting to talk about it, without straight away describing it or even giving a brief summary.

Nine o'clock in the evening. The sun has set in a triumph of pink and night is softly drawing in. I see *Bravo Lima* flying past, on its way westwards. So the rescues are continuing. I shake myself and return to the helipad.

There were two alerts, at completely opposite ends of the range. At the Tré-la-Tête Hut, a seventeen-year-old girl seems to have acute appendicitis which could develop into peritonitis. On the Argentière Glacier, a young Scotsman has fallen into a crevasse.

The girl is dropped at the hospital, and then taken by ambulance to Sallanches. But it is more likely to be a very bad case of tetanitis.

It was high time to intervene at the Argentière. The Scotsman had been on his way to the hut, with some friends, following the track, wearing only shorts and T-shirt, but with a harness on. To get there more quickly, they took a short cut and left the track. He fell twenty to twenty-five metres into a crevasse. He was unhurt but quickly became cold. By the time his friends had raised the alarm, the rescuers had arrived, set up a winch and sent one of them down to him, his body temperature, when they got him out, was already down to 32°. He was put in a thermal bag.

This piece of equipment is worth talking about. Even in hospital, the temperature of someone who is hypothermic can continue to fall. Dr Foray had the idea of developing a piece of equipment that would allow the casualty to start breathing warm air as soon as possible. The pulmonary surface being large, this gradually rewarms the whole body. The first machine needed a generator, which made it very cumbersome to use. The British developed a lighter model for sailors who had fallen overboard. There was an exchange of information between the different specialisations involved in rescue. The French company, which acquired the distribution license, got in touch with the mountain rescue service. The new machine is light, weighing 1.5 kilos, and consists of a cylindrical box containing quick lime: when carbon dioxide is passed through it, the chemical reaction produces heat and humidity.

So the young Scotsman could spend forty-five minutes breathing under the thermal bag, while the helicopter went off to the other end of the range to pick up the girl. Instead of falling further, his temperature went up to 35°. It was dusk by the time the rescue finished. He was taken to the emergency helipad at the hospital. It is ten o'clock in the evening by the time the helicopter returns. Night has fallen. We all leave, except for the mechanicians who will stay until quarter past eleven to finish servicing the helicopter.

Three lives have been saved today – most likely the girl this evening, the Italian at the Goûter and the Scotsman on the Argentière Glacier, for sure.

14

A PAST ACCIDENT:
CHRISTIAN VAN CAUWENBERGHE

Anniversary of an accident which has remained famous. Mountain rescue has changed so much in fifty years that we should remember what it was like not so very long ago. In 1954, the year in question, things had hardly changed from the time of Whymper in the nineteenth century, or even Saussure in the eighteenth. Everything was done on foot, and the techniques were basic. Rescues involved large numbers and could take a long time, despite the efforts and commitment of those involved.

In this respect Christian Van Cauwenberghe's accident and his subsequent rescue is one of the most interesting past incidents in view of the location in which events took place: the Nant Blanc Face of the Aiguille Verte. It has been possible to reconstruct the story thanks to the account of the injured man, of Philippe Dreux, who was with him, and the guide Gilbert Chappaz, one of the principal rescuers.

The valley at that time was not as we know it today. It was still very rural, despite the big hotels built around 1900. Still many farms, fields and meadows, with cows and very few cars... a relaxed sort of place. This was the world described by Frison-Roche in *Premier de Cordée* because the war had stopped all development between the 1930s and 1950. Many of the guides depended upon agriculture and animal farming outside the season. There were fewer alpinists than today, but their presence mattered and did not go unnoticed.

As for rescue, this was provided, alternately, by the three competent bodies in the valley: the Compagnie des Guides de Chamonix, the military École de Haute Montagne (today's EMHM) and the École Nationale d'Alpinisme (then called the École des Praz because it was in the village of that name, now ENSA). All was on foot, up and down, casualties being carried on stretchers or on someone's back, because the helicopter had not yet proved its worth, nor even been tested in the high mountains. Those involved often included amateur alpinists, usually the casualty's friends. These volunteers were welcome additions to what were long and arduous expeditions. The writer Étienne Bruhl even used this subject for the start of his novel *Accident à la Meije*:

> The rescue caravan is the *bête noire* of alpinists. An ascent is difficult enough as it is when done for one's own pleasure. But to scour the mountain out of a sense of duty, in the search for accident victims, is absolutely hateful.
> Not that any mountaineer has ever hesitated to go to the aid of a friend in distress. The loyalty of alpinists to each other is, on the contrary, one of the most pure and touching demonstrations of real human solidarity. For them it is a sacred duty.
> Sacred duty! Yes no doubt... But also: one hell of a duty!

At this time, the Brévent cable-car, that of Les Houches and the Montenvers train, which still ran by steam, were the only means of mechanical uplift in the valley. There was nothing at the Aiguille du Midi, nor at the Grands Montets, nor was there a chair-lift to the Col du Balme, let alone a tunnel under Mont Blanc.

Equipment was in keeping with the times. Ice axes with straight picks and wooden shafts, which sometimes broke. Ten-point crampons, none with front points, because Armand Charlet, who was chief instructor at the École des Praz, and whose word was God, taught cramponning with your ankle bent so that all points bit into the slope. Nylon ropes had recently been introduced from Britain, but no doubt some still used hemp. Karabiners were heavy, except the first 'Pierre Allains', which were looked on as revolutionary. There were various types of pitons that once hammered in were hard to remove, and if extracted were often too distorted to use again. Breeches were the norm, often worn with Jacquard woollen socks, in the style of Rébuffat. Bad weather clothing included duvets, simple anoraks and also parkas – American surplus jackets left over from the war.

With this sort of equipment, the big routes really were big routes. And so when they decided to attempt the ninth ascent of the Nant Blanc Face of the Aiguille Verte, Philippe Dreux, the instigator of the project, Philippe Laffon, known as Pipo, who was finishing his military service, Christian Van Cauwenberghe and Jacques Soubis were embarking on a major undertaking.

First climbed in August 1935 by Armand Charlet and Dimitri Platonov, the direct route had not been repeated until June 1945 (Jean-Paul Charlet and Gaston Rébuffat) and then again 1947 (Louis Lachenal and Lionel Terray). Which shows what a fearsome reputation it still had, seven years after the third ascent.

The team left Chamonix on Saturday, July 24, 1954 and from Montenvers went up the Dru Rognon. The weather was uncertain, which increased their anxiety. But at a time when all the snow routes were in good condition the quartet had reason to hope that the Nant Blanc, which rarely is, would also be in good nick. As it turned out, since it faces north-west, by late July there was little snow left on the face and the lower part was bare ice.

So it was not exactly with great enthusiasm that they started the climb on the Sunday morning. Indeed Jacques Soubis pulled out as he didn't think the conditions were right, leaving the others to make a rope of three instead of the more flexible two ropes of two. After Philippe Dreux led across the bergschrund and up the first pitch, the twenty-three-year-old Christian Van Cauwenberghe, feeling that his morale needed a boost, asked to take over. In any case they had basically agreed he should lead the ice, Philippe the unconsolidated snow and Pipo the rock. There then followed a steep cone of ice, leading to a narrow gully which, according to Christian was 'hideous, spooky, lethal and overhanging. Revolting... the last place to go!' It quickly became obvious that with the technical limitations of the time, including a single ice axe, he would have to cut steps.

Christian's ice axe, a Simond Aigle, with scarcely any teeth, and Charlet ten-point crampons – were barely suitable for such exploits. So, right from the start, they had to use the traditional step-cutting, pitching it with U-shaped ice pitons for protection. Progress was inevitably slow and Christian had to hack out precarious stances, with the ice piton hammered in at the back.

Having avoided the S-shaped gully with its steep central section, he was tempted to move towards smooth rocks, difficult but hopefully with better protection. They soon found themselves on mixed ground, teetering up grade V rock, in crampons, moving from rock slab to ice, from ice to rock. Pipo, a merry and fanciful lad in charge of removing the pegs, scattered them singly or in clusters. His friends would hear a loud 'Oh, Shit!' followed by the cheerful tinkling of the piton down the slope.

All their efforts were focused on getting above the height of the gully. Christian passed the lead to Pipo for the rock. They continued to progress, slowly, on fairly difficult mixed ground, but always having to cut steps whenever they met ice.

'You couldn't exactly say,' remembers Christian, 'that we flew up the slope on our ten-points, as Armand Charlet would have liked …'

Sometimes they came up against rock steps where they had to resort to étriers. All this took time … and the pessimist in the party began to talk about a bivouac.

They did so near the middle of the face. Christian, wedged in a crack, sitting down, protected, and tired out by the work of step-cutting which he had been doing all day, fell asleep slumped in a heap and had his ten hours. Philippe and Pipo settled down diagonally below him in a spot which was safe but uncomfortable. Did they eat? Surely not much. It is not even sure that the stove had not gone back down in Soubis's rucksack. A lot of provisions did, in any case.

At first light of Monday, July 14 energetic tugs of the rope woke Christian. Philippe Dreux who for the second time had to pass the night besides Pipo, known for terribly grinding his teeth when deeply asleep [bruxism], had not had such a good night. Once ready, the rope climbed three or four steep pitches, through overhangs which led to a funnel running in the direction of the *calotte* of the Verte on the side of which an easy snow ridge allowed them to move together. But then the slope steepened again and Christian took the lead in ice and hard snow. Trending diagonally leftwards and following a line of small protruding rocks, the climbers began to think they might quickly and easily join the Grands Montets Arête. The route seemed in the bag – a successful ninth ascent at hand.

Well rested after his long night, Christian felt as though he had wings and decided to start using Armand Charlet's technique: not to cut steps any more but to bend his ankles and crampons on all ten points. Reaching a steep and exposed spot, he knocked in a U-shaped ice piton for protection and went up, on all ten points and using his ice axe *en piolet ancre* (ice axe pick at arm's length held 'anchored' into the snow/ice with one hand and the other gripping the shaft). It was then that he made the move that was to be fatal: there was a small crack in a sérac, into which he thrust his axe so hard that when he pulled it out, the jerk made him slip.

At the point where he came off he was only ten metres or so from good snow, where the difficulties could be considered as over. It was about 9am. He fell. The piton withstood the shock. Having pendulumed, he found himself hanging below it and noticed that his right foot was perpendicular to his leg, but pointing outwards. 'I've broken my leg,' he informed Philippe in almost a matter-of-fact way.

'You can't have! It's not possible! You're mistaken!'

'I'm not. I've broken my leg...'

Christian then had the presence of mind to immediately try to reduce the fracture, realising that it had to be done on-the-spot because later it would be impossible. He was a black belt at judo, of a positive and calm disposition. Still hanging from the end of the rope, he pulled his foot back down, and turned it into its normal position in relation to the leg. Once the tension was released, his foot went back itself to where it should be.

When he arrived at hospital two days later, the surgeon said to him:

'But someone has reduced the fracture!'

'Yes, I did,' he replied.

And he had done a good job.

Philippe Dreux had climbed up to him and was wondering if the best thing would be to leave Pipo to keep the casualty company and for him to finish the route alone, descend the Whymper Couloir and get down to the Couvercle Hut. But he was hesitating, as he did not know the Aiguille Verte, what problems he might come across. Like Pipo, he was devastated by their friend's misfortune, when success was in sight. In reality, there was only one conceivable solution: the two able-bodied members of the team should finish the route, descend the Whymper Couloir, and go for help.

But first, Christian had to be installed in a better position on this steep slope. Some way below, three rocks protruding from the ice were turned into a sort of seat. They had two ropes, having expected to be four, and one was used to belay Christian solidly with pitons driven into the cracks of the rock. But the operation proved long and complicated, notably the pendulum manoeuvres needed to get him down to the chosen spot.

The weather then turned seriously bad, but the casualty was

warmly dressed: a shirt, a thick sweater, a duvet, an American war surplus khaki-coloured parka and a waterproof balaclava, which came from one of the two Parisian shops specialising in climbing material : Pierre Allain or Leininger's. This clothing, though heavy, was effective and probably provided more efficient protection than the lighter materials used today. The padded duvet's downy bulk retained the heat much better than 'fleece fur', while the parka kept out the wind. In addition, Philippe put him in his own short duvet sleeping bag, a famous Pierre Allain creation. Christian was never cold, despite the severe decline in the weather.

So complex had been all the manoeuvring of ropes and the changing round of equipment in their rucksacks that, by mistake, the other two took with them the little that remained of their provisions. Christian only had a few dates.

The day seemed infinitely long for him. He was not in much pain but his ideas were black. 'Well,' he said to himself. 'There won't be any rescue in this weather ... I've gambled and I've lost.'

His thoughts rarely wandered to the outside world, to his family, but focused on his present situation. He ran through the moves he had made, blaming himself for his technical error and the stupidity of such a fault and, forced to accept the reality, upbraided himself: 'How could I have been so idiotic as to make a *piolet-ancre* in a crack? What exactly happened? What's to be done now?'

The weather was no comfort. It had deteriorated from poor to a full-blown storm. The wind strengthened and then came the squalls, the small hard hail and the snow.

Meanwhile, Philippe Dreux and Pipo Laffon had reached the summit of the Verte, followed the South Ridge, brilliantly descended the Whymper Couloir in one hour, which the bad weather had stopped becoming soft and dangerous, and reached the Couvercle Hut. Very modern for the time, it was equipped with a radio-telephone which allowed them to contact the valley. The EHM was on rescue duty, under command of Major de Thiersant. By the time news of the accident reached him, he had already, based on the likelihood, set in motion an astute and efficient organisation for a reconnaissance expedition on foot.

What had actually happened was that Jacques Soubis, down in Chamonix, was surprised not to see his friends coming back when planned. He thought conditions were not as good as they had judged at the start, he had seen the weather deteriorate and advised the EHM about the situation. Then came the call from the Couvercle, confirming the accident and giving details and, most importantly, the location.

By now it was quite late. It took time to organise the equipment needed for a party of about eight which, because of the location, required the best mountaineers available. Amongst them were the guides Gilbert Chappaz, Maurice Poncet, J.-M. Novel, instructors at the EHM, and Charles Bozon, the famous skier, who was doing his military service there. The caravan left Chamonix at eight o'clock in the evening, with a perfectly formulated plan.

The Montenvers train had already stopped running for the day. A special train was requisitioned. The rescuers, heavily laden, then immediately set off for the Couvercle where they arrived in the middle of the night. They only had an hour or two's rest before leaving again.

Pipo Laffon offered to go with them. His aid was invaluable as the area from the exit of the Nant Blanc over to the Grands Montets Arête is vast, and would take a long time to search in the bad weather and whiteout. The team got up very early to climb the Whymper Couloir and, from the summit of the Verte, descend towards the casualty.

As for Christian, he had watched the coming of twilight in increasingly bad weather. No triumphant sunset, bearer of hope. All was grey and black, icy cold, funereal. It was his third bivouac on the mountain: one on the Dru Rognon, one on the face and now this one, injured. He managed to doze now and again and, several times, vaguely woke up, still partly asleep, partly delirious, thinking: 'Well! I've had enough! I'm leaving! I have to get down!' He tried to get up and found he was stuck, chained, which caused him great frustration. Then, little by little, he realised where he was: 'I'm injured… In the mountains… Alone! Could any rescue come?' Confronted with this situation and at the mercy of nature, he felt helpless. The night was exceedingly grim and unpleasant. If he had not been aware of his broken leg and if he had not been tethered to the slope, he would have done everything to free himself and go down – and would obviously have fallen.

The day slowly dawned on the snow-covered slope. The weather was cloudy, grey and cold. Christian's hood, which he had tightened one side of with his teeth during the night, to protect his face, was covered in a crust of ice. It was the morning of the July 27, three days since he had left Chamonix. The fourth was just starting.

When he vaguely heard murmering and echoes in the mist, and what sounded like voices mingled with the wind, he thought he was becoming delirious again. But they were definitely voices, they were suddenly magnified and he saw a climber coming towards him about ten metres away, who turned out to be Gilbert Chappaz, an army guide whom he knew. Christian asked him:

'What are you doing here?'

The remark was not exactly appropriate as the Nant Blanc is never crowded, even less so in descent, particularly in bad weather... Gilbert Chappaz retorted quick as a flash:

'And you?' Then at once explained: 'I've come to find you!'

The rescue team assembled on the slope. Novel, who was in fine form, suggested:

'We'll take him down the Nant Blanc!'

Christian was vehemently opposed to this:

'Then you'll have to go without me... It is not even to be considered... I'll wait until others come!'

They gave him some tea, put his leg in a wire splint, then, having detached him from his belay, they tried to pull him on the end of the rope, up onto the snow. But on a 45° slope this proved unfeasible. The only possible solution was, helped and supported, for him to climb or crawl himself, on his good leg and the knee of the other. So he progressed like this to the top of the slope, following a trail of steps that had been kicked for him and helped by fixed ropes. His determined approach greatly impressed the rescuers: he behaved courageously, never complaining, although he must have been suffering. Conditions were far from ideal. The weather had become glacial.

From the summit of the Verte, they were faced with a different problem. The snow ridge leading to the top of the Whymper was steeply banked. Something had to be devised in what were almost 'warlike circumstances'. The rescue sledge of the time, the 'Pourchier sledge', was mounted on skis and of no use. They had to improvise as best they could. Fortunately they had brought with them a piece of carpet that they had found at the hut. Christian was attached to it and, the carpet itself attached to the ropes with karabiners and with some pulling and others braking, they hauled him to the Col de la Rocheuse. Lots of ropes were cut into pieces that day, for use as belays and in the different technical manoeuvres.

The descent of the Whymper Couloir presented another set of problems. The route does not always follow the main slope as there are subsidiary couloirs and rock outcrops and the line, sometimes as steep as 55°, has to be picked out. So Christian was left on the carpet, which in the circumstances proved itself to be a relatively manageable sledge. Christian held himself in balance, more or less seated with his leg out in front of him, and was lowered by teams spread out in a star shape and belaying each other. The central belay was always fully fixed, the running belays with ropes and ice axes. Rémi de Vivie, a friend of Christian's who had volunteered for the rescue, remembers the remarkable organisation of it all.

Gilbert Chappaz, went down beneath the carpet-sledge which was held from above by eight pairs fanned out across the slope. At his signal, one team would descend to join the casualty and belay themselves beside him. Then a second and so on. It was snowing. At twenty metres, it was hard to make out the other rescuers who merged into the mist. But the orders came distinctly. When all the teams were back beside the improvised sledge, they loosened their ropes, and the casualty was lowered another rope-length as best they could, and the manoeuvre started all over again.

Armand Charlet, who was at the Couvercle with a climbing course, had offered his help and, knowing the Verte as he did, thought that the plan would work. However, in the Whymper, from the moment they started up it at two o'clock in the morning, the snow had proved soft and unstable and at no point seemed secure. But for such a rescue it was probably preferable to ice. The overcast and snowy weather prevented it from softening further. It held. There were no avalanches or stonefall and the rescue team finally crossed the bergschrund, which fortunately was not too wide, at 4.30 in the afternoon.

Various other volunteers, including a further group of soldiers from the EHM, guides, amateur climbers as well, had offered their help and served as reinforcements, particularly for the easy, but long part of the operation down to the Couvercle Hut and then to Montenvers. Transported on a porter's seat or on the carpet on the snow slopes, Christian arrived at the Couvercle on the evening of the July 27.

There was no question of him being taken down to the valley

the same evening. He was made comfortable in the hut, fed and told to rest. He has good memories of it. But, in his relief, when he declared: 'Well, next year, I'm going to do the Col d'Anterne on the back of a mule, and that's all!', he was sharply told off by Armand Charlet who did not like weaklings.

Next day he was brought down to Montenvers, on a porter's seat, by relays. His parents, extremely worried, were waiting for him. When Christian criticised Philippe Gaussot, a well-known journalist on the *Dauphiné Libéré* at that time, for having caused them great fear as a result of his articles, the latter invoked the 'duty to inform' doctrine, which shows that the problem of the media is not new.

Pipo Laffon had problems since he had left the EHM without permission. Worse! That weekend he should have been on mountain-rescue duty… And although he strenuously pointed out to his superiors that he had been the first on the scene at the accident, this argument had little success and he was confined to barracks for a month, which he did not mind too much since he got on well with the cooks.

As for Christian, he had escaped from a potentially lethal trap, lucky that poor weather had not become a real storm, in which case nobody would have been able to get to him. The newspapers were full of it at the time. One of them, *L'Équipe*, a sports newspaper, even referred to him as the 'Hermit of the Verte', and for some time, his friends gave him the nickname 'Bobet du Nant Blanc' (Louison Bobet being at that time a well known professional cyclist).

The whole operation, including the descent back to Montenvers, had involved thirty or forty men. From the time of the accident to the return to the valley, forty-eight hours had elapsed. Today, an accident like that on the Nant Blanc, assuming of course that flying conditions were suitable, would only take about thirty minutes from the time of the alert being given to the arrival of the casualty at the helipad.

15

FORTY CLIMBERS LOST
ON MONT BLANC

Personal difficulties. They have to be talked about because the experience is taking its toll. The flight crews work in shifts, the rescuers work in shifts, the doctors work in shifts... But for me, it is as though I were 'on duty' every day and it is hard. Much more than I thought, even though I knew it would be a trial. But not like this.

After three weeks, and in spite of several days of bad weather, I am suffering greatly from the constraints that this book involves. I have no time for anything, to the point where for the first time in my life I have written overdrawn cheques, because I had not verified my accounts. Three weeks, and it is already weighing very heavily.

Heavily not just for the time, but above all because it needs great strength to be so close to this daily absolute, the reality of the rescues, to get up every morning in worrying uncertainty about what is to come. Strong, I am still... but last night I could not sleep. I was thinking of the nightmare the Italian rescued yesterday must be suffering. All night I could imagine him screaming 'Molto dolore!' It cut me to the core. Of course, he would have been under sedation, but I also know how much one can suffer when others think you are out for the count – thereby setting their own minds at rest.

Three stressful weeks.

Tuesday, July 22
First rescue, serious, on the Tour Ronde. Snatches of radio messages mention 'a serious traumatism of the spine'. Dr Cauchy is taken with the casualty to the emergency helipad at the hospital. I feel so short of sleep that I wonder if I, too, am not going to doze off on the sofa as I have seen so many rescuers do, for a few moments of recuperation.

The helicopter comes back at half past eleven. Enter Didier Méraux and Régis Michoux. The latter explains:

'One of them has a big hole at the back of his skull. When there are stones falling, you have to do this' – he hunches his head between his shoulders – 'not that' – he bends his head forward. 'He was wearing a helmet, but the stone hit him in the nape of the neck, from behind.'

'French?'

'Swedish.'

'Was he conscious?'

'He didn't even know his name... In fact, he had no idea if he was at the seaside or in the mountains...'

Manu Cauchy comes back and comments in his turn:

'A hole... A huge hole.'

Régis Michoux tells me that the accident happened on the North Face, where three rocks had fallen and one of them hit the belayer who had bent his head, exposing his neck.

The main fear would be that the stone had damaged the vertebrae but the casualty was not paralysed.

'Was the stone still embedded?' I asked.

'No!' said Manu. 'The stone set off again without further ado!'

'That is a flight offence!' exclaims Saudemont. 'Régis! We have to go and look for a stone which has committed a flight offence.'

'And perhaps if we find it,' remarks Régis hopefully, 'there might be the finger prints of the one who dropped it.'

Another call-out, for Les Crochues in the Aiguilles Rouge.

The casualty is a young Belgian girl who was doing an alpine mountaineering course for beginners. It was the second day. Yesterday, it was introduction to rock-climbing. Today – the introduction to moving on snow and arresting a fall. She certainly had been introduced to the falling bit... forty metres, unroped, without helmet, without crampons, just an ice axe. They were going to rope up a couple of metres further on, but she fell before...

'Beginners,' remarks Régis, 'need to be roped if there is the slightest possibility of falling. Still, she was lucky! Only a few cuts on her arm and she lost her glasses which we didn't find...'

Another moment of calm. Television. Storms forecast for tomorrow. A voice comes over the radio, curt, deadened. Manu immediately turns the TV down:

'When the message is in that tone of voice, it's an accident.'

Correct. There is someone with two broken ankles on the Éperon Bayer below the Grands Montets. It is half past twelve. Ottonello and Ribiollet arrive to replace Michoux and Saudemont: it's they and Cauchy who go for the rescue.

On their return, the latter is escorting a man with two bandaged ankles but who is walking unaided, limping badly. It's only cuts and bruises.

In the afternoon the terrain is invaded by a television crew. At this time of year, journalists hope for something big. But in this current period of activity, the afternoon, as it happens, goes by with nothing, except the lamest rescue of the season, which we see on screen a little later.

It is an 'ankle' on the Mer de Glace. A walker in his forties, not even an alpinist. Under-equipped, certainly, but only slightly injured. The whole team went, with Manu, to make it look serious. The TV people want it to appear as much of an 'accident' as possible. Difficult! Manu does his best and asks the 'casualty', who is sitting on a rock surrounded by tourists:

'Does it hurt there? And there?'

Nothing much else he could ask. Then they interview Ottonello. What could he say about so tame an affair? He comments that it is a 'classic' rescue and, since they ask him about the victim's equipment he responds neatly: 'It was the lower limit of the minimum!' This incisive reply is the best moment of the sequence. For our benefit, on his return, he was even more imaginative: 'Any less equipment and he would have been in socks!'

Much later, another rescue does happen. But it is hardly more hair-raising than the first: a broken leg, well and good, but on the footpath to Montenvers? However, the winch has to be used, because of the trees.

It is certainly not amusing, but the casualty is not accommodating either. She bawls out Ribiollet, the rescuer, she bawls out the doctor, she screams when she realises she is going to be winched ('Couldn't they have carried me down on foot? I thought I was going to die!'), and once in the helicopter, she says to Thibaud Ribiollet, 'Would you put your hand up to shield the sun? It's in my eyes!' and adds, suddenly clear-headed: 'I'm a pain in the arse, huh?'

At seven o'clock, Régis Michoux and Pascal Saudemont come to relieve Ottonello and Ribiollet.

'Now the *real* rescuers are here, things are going to look up!' announces Saudemont gloriously.

But the movie-makers have had enough. They have shot enough film for a programme and do not want to waste more time waiting for the possibility of a superb, polytraumatised casualty, struck by lightning and frostbitten. They go.

Pepito and his wife arrive with their little Jonathan. So there are quite a number of us to watch the news on Channel 3: the subject: altitude, the Aiguille du Midi, etc. Then, suddenly, there is Manu Cauchy, in red in front of the red helicopter![1] Laughter in the audience, cheering and much noise.

The current events leave us in peace for a moment. Then Manu takes another call and announces:

'We're going high, boys!'

'Where?'

'The Gaillands!'

Laughter. Nobody can believe that the helicopter is needed for a rescue on a local crag. But yes.

'It's a guy who's had a fall and is stuck on the face.'

The operation is long. Time passes. The helicopter comes back, without the casualty. Dr Cauchy arrives.

'Well?' I ask

'A broken leg, a broken arm, a spine injury,' he replies.

We assume he is joking but it was only the spinal injury that he had made up. The accident was quite serious and could have been avoided. The casualty had a good number of quickdraws on his harness but, obviously feeling good, had not bothered with protection. When he fell, he was seven or eight metres above the belay and so went twice that length before being held. He was not wearing a helmet. It could have been a lot more serious.

July 23

For a long time now, the weather forecast has said that the weather will take a turn for the worse this Wednesday afternoon. Yesterday's evening bulletin had become somewhat vague: alternating sunshine and storms. At five o'clock I get up and go outside. There are a few clouds but the day breaks over mountains free from cloud. And by nine o'clock it is really bucketing down!

[1] This week, it is the blue one...

Three rescues, nevertheless, during the morning. An Italian, a Neapolitan, without helmet, was hit on the head by a block of ice on the Milieu Glacier on the Aiguille d'Argentière. Skull damage. He bravely managed to get back to the hut under his own steam. Two Greeks, off route on the South Ridge of the Moine, on the Charpoua side, had bivouacked, soaked through of course, but more to the point, stuck. Finally, a Belgian climber jumping a crevasse on the Envers du Plan Glacier has twisted his knee.

It rains so much in the afternoon, that I award myself some time off. I am wrong and what happens next proves it. There is no time off in the rescue service.

Passing through Chamonix, I nevertheless go into the PG where I am met with a sad surprise. I have just arrived when Captain Gin comes in. He catches sight of me and says:

'Anne! Perhaps you could help us. Two boys have been reported missing and one of them is English. We have no clues. Perhaps you might know something?'

'To be married to an Englishman does not mean that I know all the English...'

However I am in the back office and there, suddenly, I see on the table a yellow file with a name written on it: Dominic Green. Memories come flooding back.

'But! You have rescued him before! In 1994... on a day when I was at the helipad. He had been struck by lightning on the Petits Charmoz. Iglesis and Ribes did the rescue. Then I went to visit him in hospital, until he went home. We wrote to each other at Christmas ... After that, I lost touch with him. What's happened?'

'He's been missing since July 10, with a Dutch friend.'

'Then they're dead!'

'It's not our job to give up hope... otherwise we wouldn't be doing rescues. Have you any idea what routes he wanted to do?'

'No, I'm afraid I can't help – I didn't even know he was in the valley.'

I learn a few more details. In fact, in the secretary's office, they had already found his name among the rescues in 1994. It was their families who sounded the alarm. Dominic Green and his friend, a Dutchman who was living in England, were due to return there on the 21st, two days ago. The parents had managed to contact one of their friends and he had informed the PGHM. Their tent was found at Les Chavants and was searched for clues. They had left both their passports, which are here. And in their tent were also numerous postcards of the Aiguille Verte. Might that be their objective? Everything points to the fact that they set off for their route on July 10.

Jean-Claude Gin sees I am distressed.

'And that's not all! There are forty people lost on Mont Blanc!'

'What?'

Yes, there are forty people busy wandering around somewhere on the slopes of Mont Blanc. I was so wrapped up in the disappearance of Dominic Green, that I had not paid any attention to the activity, you could almost say turmoil, which reigns in the office.

Disregarding the forecast, forty people left the Goûter Hut this morning, for the summit of Mont Blanc. Among them was a German guide, an Austrian guide, a guide from the Val d'Aosta and a mixture of English, Belgian, Italian, Spanish and French climbers. The Chamonix guides, knowing the hazards in bad weather of the so-called 'simple, normal route', did not want to leave. But every decision is difficult to make. It is such a mixture of balancing the risks, with the psychological side of things. I imagine that there were many unhappy clients, who had climbed all the way up there, paid out money, only to find themselves stuck in the hut while others left. Ill-humour… And perhaps those who decided to go would also be worried, seeing that others had decided that to leave would be dangerous. Yes, every decision is difficult to make where the mountains are concerned.

The alarm was sounded in the afternoon. 'They were saved thanks to a mobile phone,' the television channel TF1 had apparently stated in the evening. In reality, mobile or not, radio or not, if the weather is bad, one should realise that if in trouble you may well not be rescued. Modern technology, in the form of telephones and radios, and the existence of the helicopter tend to make people take things less seriously when they set out into the mountains. One of them had a GPS, which tells your position, and is especially useful at sea, but he did not know how to use it. In any case, the GPS is not really reliable in the mountains because the satellites which relay the signal do not take into account the slope. Furthermore, it only gives a position to within a hundred metres, because of restrictions imposed by the American military, and it still has to find four satellites just to do this.[2]

Whereas, in the mountains, you often need an exact location, and such a rough approximation is not good enough. On the other hand, as the PGHM later reported, many in the group (which included some of the non-local guides) did not have a compass, map or altimeter, and those that did have them did not know how to use them or were already too lost to do so.

The forty had left in dribs and drabs. Nearly all reached the Vallot Hut, with others strung out between the Col du Dôme and the hut. One rope managed to get as high as the Bosses Ridge. Others were forced to retrace their steps. Visibility was bad. There was a strong westerly wind and the wind on Mont Blanc is terrible. You are bent double, hunched over your ice axe; you fight, but the wind is all powerful. It cannot have been much fun on Mont Blanc that morning.

Bit by bit several parties found themselves collecting in the area of the Vallot Hut. Their ascent tracks were no longer visible. All had been walking for a long time, probably in circles, in the white-out, the wind, the storm and the cold. In the course of the morning fifteen or so had congregated between the Dôme du Goûter and the Grand Plateau, about 200 metres below the Dôme, directly in line with the Pitschner Arête on the Grands Mulets side of the Dôme, but did not have the slightest idea of their location. They were tired and demoralised. The guides had made tentative forays in the direction of Taconnaz but with no success. It was at that point that they sent out a call to report they were lost, and to ask if someone could give them a direction. But how do you give people a direction when they do not know where they are?

So they decided to stay put, to hang on in the hope of rescue, digging snowholes to give some shelter from the wind, unroping and sitting on their ropes and rucksacks.

Guy Bochatay, the warden of the Goûter Hut, knew about their call. Realising that a helicopter could not fly in such conditions, he decided, together with one of his employees, Vincent Frossard, to go up to the Vallot himself. He had a bundle of wands which he used to mark their route so they themselves would not get lost, knocking them in every fifty metres or so. Every twenty or thirty metres would have been better, but they did not have enough.

[2] This is no longer the case.

Meanwhile, those who were lost higher up stumbled across the tracks of the others and gradually joined them. They sent out several new calls during the afternoon, the final message stating that there were forty of them.

Down in the valley, they were watching for the slightest clear interval. Sending a foot caravan from the Nid d'Aigle was not the solution, as they were hoping that in the course of time the helicopter would be able to fly the rescuers up more rapidly, which is in fact what happened. The four on duty, Jean-Jacques Malineau, Michel Médici, Régis Michoux and Olivier Renard were at the helipad, ready to leave.

At six o'clock, the cloud lifted slightly at the Tête Rousse. Malineau and Médici were dropped there. If conditions did not improve, they could quickly ascend to the Goûter Hut and continue on from there. Should they locate the group, with the help of Guy Bochatay and his assistant, the four would help the most able ones down and, if necessary, bivouac with the others and look after them. Thick cloud was still obscuring the alternative escape route down to the Grands Mulets.

The helicopter made a second flight to take Renard and Michoux to the same spot. But as they were approaching the Tête Rousse there was a slight clearing towards the Aiguille du Goûter. This allowed Didier Méraux, assisted by the mechanician Christian Bare-Guillet, to make a reconnaissance flight to 4000 metres, but they were unable to spot the lost climbers. The main problem was to locate them so that a foot caravan would at least know in which area to search.

From the Tête Rousse, Régis Michoux, Olivier Renard, Jean-Jacques Malineau and Michel Médici began their ascent to the Goûter Hut, while in the valley, PG members, who were watching with binoculars, spotted the marooned group below the Dôme through a break in the clouds. The helicopter therefore went back to pick up Renard and Michoux, to try and drop them near to the lost party at the first opportunity. It in turn spotted the group but, since the weight was too great to go up to 4000 metres with both rescuers on board, they took Olivier Renard, who had altimeter, map and compass in his rucksack, leaving Régis Michoux at the Grands Mulets. Didier Méraux managed to half-land (balancing one ski track on the slope), a hundred metres from the group. Olivier Renard jumped out of the machine which left quickly to avoid being shut in by the clouds, and went down to the Grands Mulets to pick up Régis in the hope of taking him up as well.

Seeing the helicopter arrive, the group thought that not only were they saved but as good as down in the valley. None of them had really any idea how lucky they were that there had been a momentary interval in the visibility to allow just this one foray. It was quite normal: the helicopter arrives and would now take them away. Climbers know nothing about the constraints on flying techniques. Not one doubted for an instant that the helicopter would make twenty flights to collect them all.

The guide from the Val d'Aosta, Patrick Raspo, had gone to meet Olivier Renard. Together, they joined the group and told the other guides to get everyone organised, roped up and ready to move. That announcement caused great despondency. There was a noise of protest. The morale of the group, which had risen hugely on seeing the helicopter arrive, completely collapsed. In the meantime, Didier Méraux, who was in radio contact with Olivier Renard, told him that if he managed to bring Régis Michoux up as well, he would try to take down the two most tired people. Actually there were three: an Englishman, a French woman, and an Austrian woman. The man said he would stay and let the two women go. They were on the edge of exhaustion and even needed help to walk the hundred metres to the place where the helicopter would land. It had to make two or three attempts before it finally made it. Leaving Régis Michoux, it took the two women on board and flew off, having completed some very tricky flying manoeuvres that effectively ensured the safety of the lost party, which was now under control.

Fortunately, everyone was well equipped, but they were far from happy about having to walk again, especially as they had to start by going back up over the Dôme, a climb of about 200 metres. They also had to hurry because the cloud was coming in again in force. They soon encountered Guy Bochatay and Vincent Frossard coming down from the summit of the Dôme and the four rescuers shared the job out between them: Bochatay and Frossard went first, followed by the most able of the survivors. Renard and Michoux stayed at the back and looked after the weakest, amongst whom were five English climbers struggling with exhaustion.

On his way down, Bochatay had made a direct descent, but

now, in ascent, he had to take a less tiring zig-zag course. In the dense whiteout he put in more wands that had been brought up on the helicopter. The leaders were sinking in to their calves in the deep exhausting snow, but it was easier for those following. It took an hour and a half to climb back up the Dôme. The stragglers were instructed to adopt a Himalayan rhythm: walk twenty steps, rest. Of course, everyone had been fortified beforehand with thermos flasks of hot tea which had been brought up for them.

When they arrived at the top of the Dôme, Bochatay started quickly down the other side, following his uphill track. Some managed to keep up. Despite his detailed knowledge of the area, he still had to use his map, compass and altimeter to find the way at one point where some of the wands had been torn out by the wind and the steps obliterated.

Régis Michoux and Olivier Renard were still the back markers and were principally occupied with looking after the five weary English climbers who were toiling and stumbling. Hardly speaking, they would do ten metres and then stop, sometimes falling. They had to be helped up and encouraged. The rescuers had taken the rucksacks of the two weakest ones. It had been dark for a long time and the batteries of the survivors' head-torches were dead. In the group at the back, Régis Michoux, calm as always, walked in front with a large torch. Where the wands were missing, they could still follow Bochatay's new track. Olivier Renard came last with a headtorch which lit the way for the group. The English, exhausted, lay down on the ground and would willingly have stayed there. They had to be helped to their feet and persuaded to continue. It was midnight when this last group arrived at the hut, about one hour behind the others. When they realised they were finally out of danger, the five English climbers, who had not even had the strength to speak whilst they were walking, gratefully shook the hands of their rescuers.

'Boy, were they relieved!' Olivier Renard said to me. 'And so were we!'

The cook had prepared a big pot of soup. Having already taken off their harnesses and jackets, the other survivors were sitting at the table in the dining room of the hut, eating. The rescuers quickly checked them over: nobody had frostbite, or altitude sickness, everyone was fine, although there was a general air of exhaustion over proceedings. Régis Michoux and Olivier Renard went to eat in the kitchen with the guardian. The room was strangely decorated with dozens of gloves hung up to dry. Two of the survivors, Italians, came to thank them and offer a bottle of wine.

Thus ended a rescue which caused quite a stir. It would certainly have caused even more had conditions not improved sufficiently to allow rescuers to find the group. Forty dead on Mont Blanc! What a headline that would have been.

July 24 – 26

During these three days the weather was mediocre to say the least. On Thursday there was hardly anything other than a reconnaissance flight for a guide who should have passed the Charpoua Hut on his way down from a route, but had not done so nor let them know. So worries unfounded. Everything was fine.

On Friday, at our house, there is a scene that sheds light on the many aspects that exist with young English climbers, however dirty they may appear. Some Oxford students landed up at our chalet at lunchtime, as if by chance. I had not known them before. One of them was particularly striking. Dressed – as only English climbers can be – as a sort of blond Rasta with coloured beads and dreadlocks, which had not known the sweetness of a good shampoo for a long time. In the Underground, one would have hesitated to give him a coin, considering him rather too alarming. Yet, after lunch, it was he who sat down at the piano and played us a Beethoven sonata. And, amongst the routes he climbed that summer was the Central Pillar of Frêney.

On Saturday, it absolutely poured down but when, to set my mind at rest, I went to the helipad and said that I was checking 'that they were not doing anything', they all laughed, because effectively 'they were not doing anything' and there was nothing they could do. But, in the evening, the weather lifted and I started worrying about what could happen at the end of this month, should the weather become really good again, as everything seemed to indicate, including the official forecast.

After twenty-six days

On July 26, it was thus twenty-six days since I started following the mountain rescue service.

Even though there was often grief mixed in with these daily events, even though the daily contact with accidents had been even more dreadful to live with than I had thought, even though my lack of freedom weighed heavily on me, even though the constraints this book imposed were onerous, sometimes intolerable, even though I felt very alone in my task, my assessment of this month was positive. My own difficulties were only personal and therefore, however real they may be to me, were of no account. On the other hand, in spite of the unavoidable suffering of those injured, the rescue service has certainly shown how effective it was.

So many lives saved! And at times it was close: Francis Guiverec on the Aiguille Pierre Allain, the Italian on Les Vuardes, the Italian at the Goûter, the Scotsman in the crevasse on the Argentière Glacier, those on Mont Blanc, others still…

Despite everything, I went to the helipad with pleasure, knowing that I would find different but familiar and friendly faces every day. I felt at home there, I liked the atmosphere, and even though I disliked being stuck down below in the valley, the rescuers, the doctors and the flight crews have given me another form of contact with the mountains. I knew the conditions, the frequentation, the state of the snow. And sometimes even the snow itself appeared on the soles of boots or crampons, when the helicopter returned. The two worlds had been very close.

As I said, many lives saved, and there was only one death, on a footpath. And that in nearly four weeks!

But it must be emphasised that not all the Mont Blanc range is controlled by Chamonix. On the Italian side, the rescues are done by Courmayeur and in the west side of the range by the St-Gervais PGHM. I knew that there had been at least three other deaths over there.

One of them, indeed, was almost within my ambit as it involved some friends who might easily have had the same accident. On July 16, a close friend of John's, Keith Cartwright, a Professor of Medicine, and his son Julian, were at the Ghiglione Hut to do the Cretier Route on Mont Maudit.[3] Leaving a little later than intended, they saw as soon as they went outside, that a French pair, a young man and woman, had been caught in an avalanche below the hut. With the help of two other Englishmen, they dug out the young

[3] Julian Cartwight (an aspirant guide) with his client Julie Colverd died in 2004 in a fall on Piz Badile in the Bregaglia.

woman but had not managed to revive the boy, despite considerable efforts at giving him artificial respiration.

The other fatal accident was on July 22, on the ridge of the Aiguille de Bionnassay. This time it was an English rope. A group had stopped to take photos and had put down their rucksacks. Normally you anchor a rucksack by passing an ice axe through a strap and driving it into the snow. They had not done so and a clumsy movement caused one of the sacks to slide. A young girl nearby tried to grab it but in doing so unbalanced her partner who fell down the slope, dragging her with him.

So a certain atmosphere of drama was not absent in this period, but it seemed to me as though things could just carry along in this fashion, without any major catastrophes, as we were already approaching the end of July.

I did not want to know that the statistics are nearly always the same. I was hoping at any rate, that this year, they might be reversed and that it would be mostly casualties recorded, with few deaths.

Besides, I had not yet taken on board that, although I thought I had spent the summer of 1994 at the helipad, I had not been there every day and that made a great difference. In fact I had deliberately kept away for two days, when there had been an accident on Mont Blanc in which nine people died, thinking the invasion of journalists was bad enough and I would appear intrusive. True, but I did not realise that my behaviour had shielded me from seeing the worst.

These issues are not irrelevant. I had planned to write an eyewitness account, to produce a document. As seen from the outside – impartially – without involving myself.

But it is impossible to be insensitive to events which you are in, daily and unremittingly, like those I intended reporting. The experience I was living also turned out to be personal, human and in a sense new, because the journalists and cameramen only passed through fleetingly. After twenty-six days, I could no longer see the book as the chronicle I had thought of writing four weeks earlier. Increasingly I came to understand that I could not just be the eye of a camera, an impersonal echo of a sound, the mirror of events that lay outside me. I felt totally human, amongst humans. A part of it. Involved in it.

That situation, the continuation of the season was cruelly to bring home to me.

PART TWO

16

A TIME OF TRAGEDY

Sunday, July 27
I must now embark on an account which I fear having to record. I would rather tell readers – who have already seen, from the first twenty-six days of July, what mountain rescue is about and how it is done – that it is not essential to read what follows and they can skip ten days and take up the story further on. What is to come is hard, what is to come is often terrible, distressing and repellent. Having lived through it, I can only approach this account with dread and distaste, for, on July 27, everything plunged into horror.

My chronicle will be done. It will be complete. It is for the reader to decide how far to follow it.

July 27, wonderful weather. A striking contrast to yesterday when, at the same time, it was gloomy and wet, with mist, cloud and drizzle. And there were no dramas. Today, the sun is bright, the air clear and limpid, the sky porcelain blue, the breeze light and nature looking radiant, but right from the start this enchantment is charged with menace.

'Anne, the helicopter is flying,' John said when I got up.

Unfortunately, yes, it was flying.

The better the weather, the more likelihood of crowds of people in the mountains and that some out of this huge number of climbers might have problems.

The first incident I learn of today is awful. A twenty-four-year-old Frenchman fell on the Tacul. From high up, and at speed, he shot over a sérac several metres high. He was thought to have been climbing alone because he had no rope. The truth, which we discover later, is worse still.[1] Several guides told me that they had never seen the snow like it was that day on Mont Blanc du Tacul:

---

[1] See Chapter 34, 'Responsibility in the Mountains', where some contentious cases are discussed.

as hard and frozen as a mirror. Incredibly slippery. If you stayed on the track, you were relatively safe. Out of it, you were not. And it was crowded.

The young man who fell was difficult to find because he was buried in the snow with only his feet sticking out. When extricated he was hypothermic, with blood in his head and his lungs. At eleven o'clock we hear from the hospital that he is not doing well. As he warmed up, he started bleeding badly. To keep the body in a hypothermic state would prevent bleeding, blocked by vaso-constriction, but this risks heart failure. So rewarming has to take place.

Just after midday, Sylvain Haquin comes over to me and says, sadly:

'They don't think he'll get through the day.'

But a little later, we hear that he is slightly better. So he is sent to Sallanches for a scan. Subsequently he was transferred to Grenoble, but unfortunately died a week later, despite all efforts to save him.

The second accident involves two other young people who were climbing the North-East Face of Les Courtes and fell when near the top. The snow had softened. A big slide carried them down the full length of the face – more than 600 metres – to the avalanche cone. Both of them were immediately flown to the emergency helipad at the hospital. They had fractures of the skull and other bones, but will survive. As on the Tacul, the rescuers were Patrick Poirot and Jacques Ottonello with the doctor, Emmanuel Cauchy. Before the second casualty was winched up, there was almost another accident: Manu Cauchy was busy getting him ready for being transported, when the rescuer who had stayed with him saw that another snow slide was coming down the face above them. They managed to get out of its path with the stretcher but their rucksacks were swept away.

At the same time, an accident happened on the Milieu Glacier, on the Aiguille d'Argentière, while descending. Two Frenchmen again as on Les Courtes. Whilst protecting his partner, one slipped. The other had fractured ankles, one of which was an open fracture. The second duty team, Max Buttoud and Christian Lafouge, have to deal with this. Exceptionally, a second doctor, Guy Duperrex, is needed urgently and is transported to the scene of this new accident. The one with the worse injuries is flown to the hospital's

helipad. The other is brought here, on a Piguillem stretcher. His coccyx is hurting and he has a wound on his forehead. Up there he had lost consciousness. Robert Petit-Prestoud and I are alone at the helipad, as everyone is busy elsewhere. The casualty asks:
'Where am I?'
Robert Petit-Prestoud replies gently:
'At the helipad.'
He asks for news of his friend. We explain that he is already in hospital.

As the sun is shining on his face, I shade his eyes, to make him more comfortable. Robert removes his gloves. He is shivering, despite his fleece jacket and the sunshine. It is the fire brigade who take him away without changing stretchers, so as not to touch his back. The ambulances must be snowed under with work today and not only by the mountains.

We'll learn in the evening that his friend has been transferred to Geneva, because he had vascular problems: one of his feet was not responding as two of the arteries in his ankle had been severed. It was saved, I was told later.

At the helipad, we hardly see the rescuers: there are so many accidents that the helicopter flies directly from one location to another.

New call-out for the Tacul. Patrick Poirot and Jacques Ottonello go. We get a semi-coded message saying there is no need for a doctor. Easy, to interpret: they are dead. First of the day because it is hoped that the one who fell earlier will live. Robert goes to the equipment store and comes back with two large beige plastic sacks.

The helicopter lands, bringing back Lafouge and Buttoud.
'A lot happening, today,' Buttoud curtly remarks.
The helipad is full of the tension which reigns on days when accidents pile up.

Lafouge and Buttoud leave for a quick lunch, while Jackie Paillé and Jean-Jacques Malineau, second reserves, replace them. The afternoon looks like being heavy as well.

Rescue at the Vallot for a man with altitude sickness. The helicopter goes off again, with Jackie Paillé, to collect him. When he is brought down, shaken, he goes to sit down on a bank and agrees to go to hospital, because he has a pain in the stomach, but the ambulance is a long time coming. Jackie Paillé questions him about his route: the traverse of Mont Blanc, after a night at the Cosmiques. His group left at two o'clock, 'like everyone else', he tells us. He feels a certain need to talk, to apologise for having been ill. He says he was going so well that he arrived at the summit before the others and waited a long time for them.

'Coming down,' he explained, 'I still felt fine. I went to the toilet. But at the Vallot, I did not feel at all well.'

Very much a teacher, Jackie Paillé tries to educate him:

'You were a long time over 4000 metres and you did not eat enough... Sometimes it is better just to eat bread. Sugar makes acid, while bread puts volume in your stomach, which is better... And if you feel that happening another time, where no one can go to get you, you should take two aspirin, wait until they have some effect and then make yourself go down. At the height of the Grands Mulets, your headache would have gone away. But now, what do you say to a small coffee?'

'Thank you, no.'

'Who were you with?'

'The CAF[2] from Chambéry.'

I make a gesture of surprise... I must explain that after the publication of *Nadir*, I was told that someone from CAF complained that I had not talked about CAF! What? Telling the story of an imaginary day with the rescue service, am I going to put a CAF team in a crevasse? That would not have been very kind!

And this year, when I am doing this for real, here we have CAF involved. True; it is only for an altitude sickness. But I do not know that it was a great deal more tragic than that.

When Manu Cauchy returns, he goes to see the young man.

'A real case of altitude sickness,' Jacky Paillé explains to him, 'Even here he was still throwing up.'

But the helicopter immediately flies off once more to the Tacul and reports to Cordial.[3]

'You can call the undertakers now.'

The arrangements for bringing down the bodies are made briefly:

'Take a rescuer and a stretcher. Same for the second trip.'

Cordial asks:

[2] Club Alpin Français.
[3] Code name for the command cell.

'Aren't you bringing down Manu first who is still at the Col du Midi?'

Manu himself intervenes:

'No! Rescues first! Where they are is spooky...'

This year, when the helicopter brings back bodies, it lands facing the opposite direction to normal: its door towards the hangar, so the transfer between the machine and the hangar is done as discreetly as possible. The gawkers, who hang about the wire fencing, can hardly see anything. Nor can the journalists, photographers and cameramen either, if they are here. Then, with a quick manoeuvre, it lands back in its normal position, with the cockpit facing the chalet.

The funeral car has already arrived. Jackie Paillé goes to help Patrick Poirot get the stretcher which they take into the hangar. The helicopter immediately leaves to collect Jacques Ottonello and the other stretcher. A second funeral car arrives. They both have a sadness and anonymity that frightens me: they are like little vans without windows, one a yellowish colour, the other greyish. Nothing, absolutely nothing to remind us living beings that we are mortal, that death exists, that it is part of life. No! In our society, you have to conceal it, to erase it, leave it to those whom it concerns directly, and for the others, deny it as much as possible. It's worse.

It is nearly one o'clock in the afternoon. The helicopter has been flying since seven this morning without a break, except for technical stops.

Somebody mentions how crowded the mountains are:

'There were eighty people on the summit of Mont Blanc at the same time. A hundred on the Tacul. At quarter past eight, the Mont Blanc ridge looked like a zip fastener!'

We are beginning to find out who the dead on the Tacul were.

'A man. A woman. Young. But what a state they were in... Nothing on them. Nothing in their rucksacks. We don't know who they were...'

Patrick Poirot comes past and says gravely:

'A sad day, Madame Sauvy. A sad day!'

'Were they on the normal route on the Tacul?'

'Yes. Same fall as this morning. Just slightly further on, about fifty metres. But the one this morning was lucky to stop after the first sérac barrier. And these carried on. To another sérac...'

Gradually, further bits of information filter through. The victims were younger than at first thought. The girl was seventeen. The boy sixteen. We learn their names. And that they were with a guide, but climbing independently. And the guide was not near them at the time. One of them lost balance and pulled the other off. At that age, do they know how to belay? Would they know how to hold a fall?

I imagine the pain, the horror for the parents. I think of the parents and it profoundly upsets me… They must have taken a guide, or at least put their children on a climbing course so as to be sure.

Everyone here is affected. No one says much, but the atmosphere is harsh, electric…

Jean-Jacques Malineau comes to say hello.

'Are you OK, Madame Sauvy?'

I pull a wry face.

'Not really… With all this…'

'It's bad today, yes!'

Jackie Paillé in his turn asks:

'What are you going to say in your book, about all this?'

'I don't know if I'll say anything. When there are rescues, well that's fine… But accidents like those today, no! I don't want to describe a day like this!'

'You should also think about all those for whom everything has gone well,' he says to me. 'Today, there were thousands out there, up high and lower down too. Not even affected by the accidents, because rescues are often out of view and so they don't know what has happened. Many were happy with their day… The vast, vast majority!'

Next comes a sprained knee at the Albert Premier and a fractured ankle on the path to the Mottets cabin.

'How do they manage to break themselves like that? I sometimes ask myself.' Manu Cauchy muttered. 'They slip and break up!'

New rescue, on the karst of the Désert de Platé, near Flaine, where a ten-year-old girl has fallen six or seven metres into a crevice, after crossing a snow bridge. She could have gone in deeper but is just cold and a bit shaken. She is safe but would not have survived another hour. Her family and the many others there were powerless to help The arrival of the helicopter and Lafouge and Buttoud's efficient and rapid intervention were met with enthusiasm and the rescuers showered with thanks. In this environment, quite different from the high mountains, the actors involved in this happy outcome appeared like benefactors fallen from heaven.

Yet another sprain, on the névé near the Albert Premier. Yet another sprain, on a footpath in the Anterne area.

Then Sylvain Haquin, who is not flying this week, services the winch. But at ten to five comes another call-out: North Face of the Grandes Jorasses. That is all we know. Then it becomes clearer: two climbers are stuck on the Croz Spur. And another rescue looms – a broken ankle on the descent from the Aiguille du Moine.

But the winch is not ready. It is another quarter of an hour before the helicopter can leave. And we shall see a few days later, in Switzerland, how important it is to have a reliable winch.

Whilst waiting, Manu gets ready. Didier Méraux does some paperwork. Alain Charnay and Christian Lafouge watch the finish of the Tour de France, which is taking place down the Champs-Élysées in Paris, in the sunshine. It is hot here, as well. For entertainment value, the riders make a seemingly endless loop up and down the Champs-Élysées.

The two mechanicians are busy with the winch. It is ten past five. They test it.

I imagine that, sometimes, people waiting to be rescued must get impatient. People who can't imagine that others might be in the same predicament as themselves. 'What the hell are they doing?' Without thinking that they might be busy with another rescue, or doing an essential service on the helicopter. One cannot imagine the huge amount of unseen work which has to be done on the machine when on the ground. It is cleaned, greased, the winch cable changed, and numerous controls and checks made.

At quarter past five, everything is fine, the service is finished.

'So! Is it done?' asks Lafouge, who tears himself away from the Tour, goes outside and picks up his rucksack.

'Didier! Lets go!' says Christian Bare-Guillet, the mechanician. 'Just give me a moment to wash my hands and change!'

'OK,' replies Didier Méraux.

Two rescuers, Gonzalez and Isaia, arrived a moment ago to take over from those who are about to leave, although they are not officially on duty, but everyone is fully occupied. In less than a minute Bare-Guillet is ready and goes off to the chopper that the team have just climbed into. He goes through the check procedure and the helicopter takes off with its usual brief resonant roar.

On the screen, the yellow jerseyed winner, a German, self-importantly receives the final bouquet.

'Shit, that's Europe!' sighs Alain... 'It's the Tour de France and it's won by a German! On the Champs-Élysées! Go on! Show us your bouquet with Crédit Lyonnais on it!... It's us who pay!... Look... There... Tapie is out of prison, but we are still paying...'

Alain generally uses a language that is not really one of refinement. His vocabulary incorporates the thirty common words which refer to parts of the human anatomy and combines them with a sometimes astonishing creativity, which I will not be presenting in these pages.

Six o'clock. The helicopter returns from the Albert Premier. A woman limping, supported by Manu. It is another sprained ankle, not a fracture.

The helicopter has already left for the Jorasses.

At twenty-five to seven, it comes back with two young people. Aiming to get on the aspirant guide course, they were doing the Croz as training, and were not far from the top when they suddenly found themselves blocked as there was too much snow.

'It can't be in condition?' I ask Christian Lafouge.

'No! All snowed up, and bloody cold!'

Another telephone call. Max Buttoud answers:

'Oh... Oh... Are you winding me up... With clients?... And they haven't come back?... We'll do a recce!... Couloir Chevalier ... OK got it!'

It's on the Petite Verte. Surprisingly late for a Chamonix guide. I happen to meet him later and he recalled this adventure with a humility and frankness which I greatly appreciated.

The recce does not take place immediately because this time the rotor attachment needs greasing and cleaning. Fortunately, the anxiety was unfounded. The recce is done as soon as possible but the people they were searching for continued under their own steam.

When I leave the helipad the day is not yet finished. Patrick Poirot and Jacques Ottonello will have to deal with an accident at a bike trial, outside the valley, where someone has been injured. I see the helicopter coming back at ten o'clock, in the dark, unaware, and wanting to stay that way at least temporarily, of what else had happened.

What a terrible day. The morning anyway. That night, sleep will not come. I cannot get out of my mind the two young people who died on the Tacul. I think of their family. In spite of myself, ideas run away with me. What if their parents had given them this climb as a reward for passing an exam? And if they were staying with their grandparents while here on holiday? Their despair, and that of the parents when they arrive... I have risked having very serious accidents several times in the mountains. That's my affair, but I am aware that I cannot bear accidents to others. Whether it affects friends or, like today, strangers and their close relatives.

I can nevertheless, thank God, close this sad day of July 27, with the story of a small miracle. The accident, which did not happen! On the Tacul, again, at the same place as the others. And as the Chamoniard world is a small one, I was put in touch with Marie, who survived this adventure.

So, on Sunday, July 27, Marie climbed Mont Blanc du Tacul with two friends with the idea of skiing down. It had snowed hard in the mountains over the previous days and they had considered other possibilities, but Marie, an excellent skier, thought the Tacul would be in condition for that one day and decided to seize the opportunity. As we have already seen, the Tacul was packed.

They didn't see the first accident, the one to the solo climber, but when about a quarter of an hour from the shoulder, saw the second. The long upward procession stopped, paralysed. Marie thought there would be a wave of panic but considered it better to continue. But since there was a huge queue for the summit and the aim was to ski down, they decided to finish at the shoulder.

They had certainly been surprised to find the snow so hard on the way up, but thought the sun would thaw it, and so waited awhile, having a a bite to eat and drink. Being the best skier, Marie went first, but quickly realised the surface was still hard and icy, offering no purchase at all. She shouted to the others to descend in crampons. But, it was already difficult for her to get back up to them and, being used to skiing steep slopes in winter, she thought she would be able to cope and continued, slide-slipping. And then she said to herself: 'Come on! Get a grip! Do a turn!' The first one was fine. She started a second and lost it. Her friends, busy putting on their crampons, did not see her fall and she did not shout.

The spot where she lost control was only slightly higher than the place of the other two accidents. But, not being roped, she avoided cartwheeling. If a climber falls, he may well be held by his partner, but if the latter is yanked off, the rope is nothing but a handicap. When one manages to brake, or even stop, the other shoots past and pulls him off again. In such a case the rope is worse than useless, except in the rare case where it snags on a rock and stops them.

Marie had two other pieces of luck. She had tightened her bindings fully to make sure she would not lose her skis, and by chance had not done up the waist belt of her rucksack. Shooting over a bergschrund, it had come off, taking with it a glove and her ski sticks, so with her skis and hands she tried to arrest herself and almost did so: 'I've done it', she said to herself and relaxed. But then she started accelerating again and now thought, 'Oh no! I am going to be like the others! I don't want to suffer!' And let herself go. To her surprise she eventually came to a stop.

'How long had it lasted?' I asked. 'An eternity!' she replied spontaneously, then tried to put it into real time. 'One minute? Surely not two...'

She was now in the middle of the icy slope, just above the lower bergschrund, the one which the others had shot. It was about two in the afternoon. Getting to her feet, she traversed over to the track where the crowds were descending, although some were still going up. They looked at her, dumbfounded. She yelled to them:

'I'm fine! I'm fine!'

All she had was some blood on her right thumb, which was split open to the tendon. At the hospital, they would find that one of her legs was very badly bruised but she had not felt it and had been lucky not to hit her head since she was not wearing a helmet. Back on the track she sat down. A Swiss climber gave her something to eat and drink and stayed with her until her friends joined them. It was a long wait. Marie felt 'very, very calm', she told me. 'But even so I didn't feel very clear headed. My mind was blocking it all out, I was like a zombie, I just did things instinctively.'

All this time, her friends, cramponing down the track, were thinking what a great descent she must have had. And then they saw her, sitting on the slope, her face drawn. Although happy to be alive, savouring it even, she was clearly still very shaken. She explained what had happened and they had to accept the improbable: that just after shouting to them to put their crampons on, she had fallen, all the way to here! Looking up, the slope seemed highly impressive, with big bergschrunds. According to Marie, she cleared them easily, because she was going so fast.

The woman friend was a doctor who had worked with emergencies. She examined the injured thumb and put the glove back on. Marie felt shooting pains and started to get tense again, but calmed down with a couple of pills. To such an extent that even though she now had no sack, ice axe, or ski sticks and her crampons had gone with the sack, she felt capable of carrying on. They roped her up, took her skis and lent her an axe. Doing what she was told, she managed to descend the track, hunched over and ill at ease.

Physically, she felt all in but insisted on making the climb back to the Aiguille du Midi, refusing to call the helicopter. 'They had quite enough to do that day,' she commented. After being so close to having an accident in which she might well have lost her life, her thoughts were for the less fortunate: 'There is nothing I can do for the others, but by my asking for nothing, at least the rescuers will have more time to help them.'

So, gradually, stopping from time to time to eat and drink, the little group made its way back up to the Aiguille du Midi, arriving about six o'clock. There was no place on the cable-car until half past seven, so her doctor friend accompanied her to the sickbay. It was only at that juncture, on returning to civilisation, when it really came home to her what had happened, what she had got away with, that she gave way a bit. Tears rose to her eyes at the joy of being alive. She and her friend were quickly put on a cable-car. Someone in the queue who knew her called out a banal:

'Are you OK, Marie?'

'No! I fell... But yes! I'm fine! I'm alive!'

Back in the valley, she was immediately taken to hospital, where she thought she had seen *the* Dr Cauchy, but it must have been Dr Duperrex as Cauchy was at the helipad that day. She was examined and X-rayed. Although hurting pretty much everywhere, all she had was some bruising to her leg. Nothing broken, not even her thumb. She went home the same evening.

I was interested to know her subsequent reactions. She does not remember anything about that evening, which she spent alone, but her family were not far away and she quickly went off to sleep. However, she woke up with a start several times during the night, and that continued on the following nights, suddenly waking up, in a sweat, although she managed to drop off again. Subsequently, her reactions changed. She had trouble getting to sleep, thought fearfully about dying, realising that one day her own body would be cold.[4]

During the time which followed, she felt in the real world but as though floating above what was going on around, the day-to-day conversations, and heard herself speaking with a rasp, in a strange voice. She only really felt comfortable with the two friends who had been with her, as if only they could understand what she'd been through. Others meeting her tended to say:

'What's happened? What's the matter?'

And quickly she would answer with banal words. Or someone would ask :

'So? Are you going to stop climbing?'

No question of that. Why give up what she loves?

Physically, there is nothing to show, but there may be repercussions which will show up later in life, she thinks.

One lesson she draws from her accident:

'When you go into the mountains, you have to realise that death is not an impossibility. You tend to forget that! When skiing, falling is generally a part of the learning curve, a mistake is rarely serious. In the mountains however, anything can be fatal. You need to weigh the possible consequences of every decision.'

It's a lesson in wisdom, which experience teaches but which youth often ignores. Mountaineering is not an ordinary sort of sport. It is not an activity to be trivialised. By choosing to climb, you have access to a wonderful world but it must be done with eyes wide open.

---

[4] This reaction surprised me because I have never experienced it, but rather thoughts in the vein of: what will remain of my memories, my thoughts, my love for those dear to me? Or again: John would be all alone in the world. Marie's remark made me realise that I consider my body not only as a docile, functional, agreeable, private object, but also one that is destined sooner or later to return to dust. Everyone has very personal thoughts on these subjects which it is not customary to broach, and which it is almost taboo to talk about.

17

BLACK MONDAY

Morning
Of course the tele is there. Two deaths yesterday, many accidents and here they are, like piranhas rushing to the smell of blood. They have invaded the helipad.

The two deaths of yesterday haunted me all night. The victims … Their families… Poor kids!

And this book… Can I do it? Can one write about such grief? Not like the media do, but with a real understanding?

It is all too much for me. I'm alone. I imagined that I would have some help, I don't know how… I now see that having written *Nadir* is not an advantage but a handicap. The PG thinks: 'She is able to cope'… But no!

I never stop running around. To copy the list of those on duty for the week, for example. Or to get the weather forecast! To get an updated weather forecast two or three times a day so as to get some idea of what climbers will be doing, I waste so much time going to and fro between the chalet, the helipad and Chamonix, parking the car and all that. I feel totally exhausted.

The weather forecast, what a problem! Other inexact sciences surely make as many mistakes, but we don't know about them whereas the weather is there for all to see. The fault lies not in the fact that the forecasters are fallible, but that they do not recognise it. They assert as truths what are in fact probabilities and when the opposite happens, never explain why. Everyone would like, that until their art is perfected, they behave with the appropriate humility, saying… 'It is likely that…' or: 'we expect that…' But no! The affirmative is the only form used, apparently according to orders from Paris.

So, to try to put a stop to all this running around, I spent this morning at the Meteo office explaining what I am trying to do and ask if they would very kindly fax me a forecast every day. I know it's possible. I know they charge for it and it's not cheap. But I naively imagined that, since the Meteo is a public service, funded through money I pay in taxes, centrally or locally, that perhaps in turn, just for a month, they would help a little... Silly of me! I am told there'll be no help because there's no 'exchange'. What sort of exchange do they want? For me to say that the forecast is correct when it is wrong? Should I perhaps tell these experts, propped up in front of their computer screen, what the weather is outside, which sometimes they seem unaware of. Or what? I cut short the discussion saying, fine! I have never had much good to say about the Meteo and it will go on being like that. Infuriated, I arrive at the helipad to find the television there...

Jean-Jacques Malineau and Olivier Fernandez are on duty. Both young, about thirty or a bit less. Jean-Jacques Malineau is tall, quite dark-haired but his large build makes one forget his youth which is immediately apparent again the moment he smiles. He is an aspirant guide. Olivier Fernandez, has recently arrived from the Grenoble PG and we have got to know each other this summer with what I hope is a mutual liking. He is from the Pyrenees and has the fine accent of the area. He also is tall and slim with wide shoulders. He has brown hair cut short and eyes which sparkle with spirit behind his light framed glasses. He always seems ready to laugh. I find out later that he is a guide.

There have been two rescues already this morning. The first wasn't serious. Three boys and three girls had done the Cosmiques Arête and bivouacked at the grade IV rock step, exhausted and not able to get out by themselves... A classic rescue which other events put in the shade.

But we know more about the two teenagers who died yesterday. They were on a course organised by the EDF (Electricité de France). The training was supposed to have been under guides. Perhaps not enough of them in order to reduce the cost of the course? The parents would not have been worried. Then, out of the blue, this terrible news...

And that's not all. Already three bodies have been picked up. Italians apparently, at the foot of the Frendo Spur.

At some point, Olivier Fernandez comes over to me.

'Would you like to know what I did this morning?'

I know he had gone to collect the three bodies. And, no! I do not want to know. Absolutely not. Especially that!

But suddenly it occurs to me that even though I don't want to listen, perhaps he himself needs to talk about it. He is young. He is supposed to be strong. He probably can't go to a fellow gendarme and say: 'Would you like to know what I did this morning?' No! It is not like that between men. So it is for him, really not for me that I reply:

'What did you do?'

What he tells me is horrifying, and real, and powerful, upsetting, unforgettable. The two of us are cut off from the surrounding world. I take in everything he has to say, torn between distress, horror and immense respect. For him, and for those like him, I will perhaps go on with this book. It is for this I have embarked on it. To tell others that those who rescue are fine people. To tell what they really do, not like in a novel where matters can be arranged. Nor in the manner of the journalists.

Here is what he told me:

'Not a very nice time this morning, you know… I was lowered down on my own, because it was a very exposed position. It wasn't worth risking two people… It was not beautiful, yet at the same time, as I was being winched down over the bodies there was a certain beauty… They had fallen yesterday. But we only found out this morning. So, they were frozen seemingly poised as if dancing… It was extraordinary… But they had fallen seven hundred metres you know… They were smashed up… Their heads had exploded and emptied, no brains left… There was one with an ice axe right through his head, do you understand? He had the ice axe in his head, going in one side and coming out the other!'

As though to refuse the truth, I say:

'Surely they must have lost their gear in the fall?'

'Yes. But it was all attached to them, with lanyards… Bones were sticking out everywhere, one of them had no face left… And the shit, the guts… To describe in what kind of state they were. I took hold of a crampon and the foot came away in my hand… Everything smashed… It really does something to you to see that… During the day you don't think too much about it… But in the evening, at night, it goes round and round in your head…'

'Were you able to put them in body bags?'

'Oh! Not there! It was impossible!… There was a huge sérac above me, you see? I was working under a sérac… I had to be quick… It could fall at any time… And if it had fallen, that would have been my fate. That's it! It would have been my fate... It didn't fall... I attached them at best to the winch cable and they were moved like that... Of course, you couldn't put them in the chopper... They were put down further away, somewhere less spooky... and there they were put in body bags.'

I imagine the scene and say, stupidly:

'And the foot? What did you do with it?'

He laughed mirthlessly.

'The foot? I tied it on with a sling...'

We are silent for a moment, sharing this sad secret.

'Well' he says... 'It had to be done... We had to go and get them... At least, that lot weren't suffering any longer... When they are still alive, suffering and screaming, inevitably you suffer with them.'

All this time, the television people are busy outside. They have got Captain Gin and are filming him in front of the Sécurité Civile helicopter, which arrived this morning. The cameramen film him, in turn, while he is being interviewed. Olivier Fernandez says to me:

'The tele, you know, is false. All they're interested in is carcasses. Oh yeah! They would have loved the carcasses I saw this morning, But what is humane, no. Sensitive, no. What I felt? Not in the slightest. To them, we are just machines. The Captain has to trot out the bland nonsense they expect, always the same, about being careful and all that. But does that give anyone an idea of what being careful means? People watch while sitting down to dinner, chewing their steak and that's it. A book like you intend, those who'll read it, will be those wanting to read it...'

He speaks again:

'A friend of mine was killed on a rescue, three years ago...'

'Not here then?'

'No, in the Grenoble PG, but it was a boy who had done six years in Chamonix, Pierre Nicollet.'

'I remember. Many rescuers went to the funeral. I know that Iglesis was very shaken.'

'Inevitably, Julio and him had done a lot of climbing together... In Chamonix, Pierrot had done the best routes in the area... He was a great mountaineer and a great rescuer... And such personality!... Always in a good mood... Always taking joy in life... Childish eyes, always happy... A passion for the mountains

... Such experience, such calmness... You wouldn't have thought that anything could happen to him... And then...'

'How did the accident happen?'

'It was on the Barre des Écrins... Sheer bad luck... The helicopter had already taken off a young girl with a fracture and it came back to collect one of the others, who Nicollet attached to the winch, with his sack hung below him as usual... The helicopter was slightly off to the side from the winching point and, when it rose, the ice axe attached to the rucksack caught Nicollet under his arm and lifted him up... The ice axe strap on the sack broke, Nicollet fell twenty metres, bounced off a ledge and fell another hundred... He was not in a too bad state, but he was killed instantly... They gave him medals, like for a hero, but after a year, who thinks about him any more?... I looked after his widow, it wasn't easy for her, you know... But that's how it is... I suppose it's better they gave him medals... The guides' medal that's worthwhile, but for rescue work, you know it doesn't mean much...'

At that moment, he is called, because the television crews want to film a rescuer. He goes off saying:

'And you see, I am summoned and I obey.'

When he comes back, he announces:

'There! I'm on TV...'

And he adds with bitter irony:

'I am a hero!'

Other rescues took place, this morning. Before our conversation? After? I don't know any more.

A case of altitude sickness case at the Goûter, seemingly trivial. The circumstances, however, are less so. I perhaps have a tendency, having seen it too often, to be suspicious of publicity seeking, using the latest fashion, currently 'humanitarian work'... Because I know people who do a lot of good work, with children in particular, and who don't shout about it. Who have no need for media coverage. Who make no money from it, nor expect any reward. Who should we believe? I no longer know. Don't certain alpinists do the same sort of thing? I am suspicious until I have proof to the contrary. Was it really necessary to transport whole classes to the mountains on other continents, accompanied by numerous guides, teachers, friends – as they did not long ago?

The school children no doubt enjoyed it, but was it not just a promotional farce?

I recall having seen, a few years ago, a film, which I didn't like, at the Autrans Festival. It was about young delinquents who had been taken out of prison to go on a climbing course with the aim of making an ascent of Mont Blanc. Of course – Mont Blanc! You might suppose that at least they would be pleased to be out of jail, being looked after, by guides etc. Not at all! When being filmed, they said:

'Up yours!'

'They're making us shit our guts out!'

'What a load of crap!'

None seemed to be enjoying it... But was the exercise for their benefit? Or for those who had organised it?

I was much happier to hear, by chance, that Patrick Gabarrou had taken a small group of orphans up the Bishorn, free of charge, with no media attention at all. The Bishorn! Although it's a 4000er, it's not so serious an undertaking so nobody was likely to hear about it. And they didn't, either. Thank God!

Well, this morning, it was an operation of the same sort. Children from an inner city area. On Mont Blanc. Led by an independent guide, who has never been averse to the limelight. Does it have to be Mont Blanc? Wouldn't the children be satisfied with some other mountain? They come from a deprived background... Is Mont Blanc the right thing for them, rather than an ordinary holiday – hill-walking or playing games? Or perhaps the whole thing is organised for the benefit of those in charge? It is not for me to judge. But anyway, one of them, just thirteen years old, had altitude sickness this morning... It will certainly not leave him with happy memories...

Apart from this, it's the daily routine: a sprain at the Envers, a fractured arm on a footpath.

I spend the whole morning at the helipad, my thoughts totally monopolised by the conversation that I had with Olivier Fernandez, his account, his feelings. After he had been in front of the cameras, we didn't continue our conversation. What more was there to say?

Today, at the helipad, Olivier Fernandez talks and talks and talks. I wonder if Malineau and Dr Marsigny, who are on duty today, find him a bit unsettled, a bit 'southern'. Or whether they understand perfectly well why. In any case, I know why he needs to talk. About his home area in Tresbes, near Carcassonne, about the wind that blows there, about his father who is a wine producer, about the Occitan and Catalan languages…

The telephone rings. It's the PG enquiring whether the identities of bodies recovered this morning are known. Fernandez, as it happens, replies:

'No!' he says… 'No, I don't know his name. He had his ice axe where his memory should have been. And although we put the thumb screws on the ice axe, it wouldn't talk either. So that's it!'

He hangs up, and carries on joking superficially. I remember what Benoît Cousineau said to me: 'Watch their reactions, when someone is killed.' This remark is certainly being borne out now. Counselling is available for the families of air crash victims, etc., etc. But who bothers about those who pick up the bits? And who is bothered about a young gendarme who this morning had to pick up three mutiliated bodies whilst under a sérac, in the mountains that he loves? Most probably no one… And anyway, it's better like that. Everyone comes to terms with it in his own way.

Olivier talks. Someone else would close in on himself. And me, as usual, I need to write.

Will the same thing happen to this book as happened to the article I wanted to do, last year, about the Chamonix Hospital? I took its possible closure so much to heart, in the light of what I know about mountain rescue, that I went to great lengths and managed to get agreement to an article on the second page of a major newspaper. A lot of work for a huge nothing. The differences of opinions where I expected a common front for a single objective, left me disillusioned. I sent a text that was too long, that I wasn't happy with anyway… So I dropped it.

This year, I am even more involved in the realities of our society. I wanted the hard facts and I have discovered them but they may not be acceptable. Perhaps not even to the Gendarmerie. It is sometimes said that the PGHM is one of its showcases and that is certainly true, at least as far as its public image is concerned. But the 'real truth' has nothing to do with 'the public'. The truth is with those at the sharp end. It is Fernandez this morning, standing alone under a sérac, holding a foot in his hand. The truth, is the infinitely complex dance which is performed in the mind, an almost imperceptible dance…

That has no import for the media. It feeds the millions of insatiable television gawkers with half truths, without bringing anything solid, true, pure. It reacts only to certain stimuli… Unthinkable for it to turn up because there has been a successful rescue!

People talk about the cost per hour of the helicopter. Rightly so because it is not cheap. But the publicly financed helicopters can fly for the media, whatever the cost and perhaps they are funded because some politician happens to be watching the television at the moment of these pictures being shown, however ridiculous and 'wide of the mark'. It's not sane.

The helicopter has just taken off. For a rescue? Not at all! With two journalists. And to show them what? To show them where the two kids fell yesterday on the Tacul and where the three Italians fell who were picked up this morning.

I don't say this out of pique, because the written word is being supplanted by floods of television pictures and money. Three years ago, I had permission to fly. It was suggested that I ask to do so again this year and I refused. Though the mountains are very beautiful when seen from above. But what interests me is not seeing a casualty being packed into a stretcher. Far from it it! I am concerned with what is going on in his head or in that of the rescuers, like Fernandez this morning, and not the superficial triviality. A curious fact: three years ago, when the PGHM requested permission for me, it was saying 'the writer and journalist Anne Sauvy to fly', the term 'journalist' being the magic word justifying the authorisation!

No! I do not like what the world has become. Inhuman. We are pinned into a corner. We are hamstrung by 'political correctness'. I want to think for myself and I want to say what I think.

It is not death in the mountains that I am concerned with. The mountains are, also, a means of escaping from the world, from this warped society. Up there, everything assumes its rightful place, its true value. For that, the risk is justifiable. But we don't have to impose it on kids, on leukaemia sufferers, those with cancer, delinquents, or heart transplant patients who are taken where? To Mont Blanc, of course! Not for their benefit but for the publicity or for money in the bank… No! Risk is acceptable when you are fully aware of what you are doing and when you are doing it for love of the mountains.

'Risk' – bunjy jumping, scaring yourself silly, skiing, snow-boarding, surfing, riding a motorbike, sailing, paragliding, climbing – no one looked for it in the old days… Life just went along it its natural rhythm. Now if we seek it out directly or by proxy (television) it is because that equilibrium has been destroyed. So we compensate for it. It is absurd. In council housing blocks – often despised but which have central heating, washing machines and sometimes dishwashers and freezers – inhabitants as elsewhere, are exposed to a diet of shooting, crime, petty thieving and thrill-seeking – before being pushed into action and violence.

I don't wish to draw my water from a well or to see icicles draped over my window panes in winter any more than the next person. But I would still prefer it to living in this dismembered and crudely savage world.

Afternoon

I've just had a long conversation with Dr Marsigny. Head of accident and emergency, he sometimes takes a turn on duty here.

The initial impression I had on first meeting him was one of aloofness. I now think this is a façade. I have learnt to appreciate him, to like him and to respect him. More and more. He knows the game. He is someone in direct touch with things. The kind of person I like. One of those men who know their job, hands on people. The meteorologists this morning were not like that, hence their arrogance. They were in an office, not out in the rain, whether forecasted or not.

The thing about Marsigny, is that he knows the cost of getting someone back alive. He tells me about a Canadian rescuer, from Banff, who is in Chamonix at the moment. It seems that in Canada, they either bring back dead bodies or minor casualties, because the terrain is so vast that those who are badly injured die before rescue can arrive.[1] What is wonderful here is that many people are saved who would otherwise have died. It is why I love the work done at the PG, at the helipad and at the hospital.

We also talked, in general terms, of the problem of removing organs for transplant. Anyhow, they can't do it here. Families, which under the shock of a brutal death, have the courage to save someone else, unknown.

[1] The growth of mobile phones will have changed this by now.

And then we talked about death which our age tries to dissimulate. I told him about the feeling of distaste I had yesterday, when I saw the plain funeral cars of the undertakers. I recounted how, when I first came to Chamonix, as a child, there was a great, black, horse-drawn hearse, with black plumes on the four corners of the canopy, which I had found very beautiful. As it passed by, people would stop, cross themselves, the men lifted their hats, their berets... That was respect for death. Now, we do not wish to acknowledge that it exists, we shut it away, people die alone, older no doubt, but full of tubes and alone, desperately alone. My father and mother died in hospital, both in the morning, alone, without me.

I am interested to see that a doctor like Marsigny agrees. That it isn't right. That it's a sham. We do not want to admit the existence of death, but at the same time it is being thrown at us in every television programme made out to be something as unreal as the cathodic dots on the screen.

A quarter to five. The helicopter takes off again for an accident in the Whymper Couloir.

Evening
Obviously I recalled that Cauchy had told me yesterday he was going to the Verte today to do the Grands Montets Ridge with Iglesis, Poirot and Michoux. A thought which I immediately suppressed, as if just thinking about it was a risk in itself. Surely there would be people all over the mountains today?

As always when there is an accident, the preparatory activity is hurried but calm. The helicopter had taken off. I spoke to no one except briefly to Berlioz the GA on duty this week, who is from Servoz, and who wants to join the Gendarmerie. The two rescuers had left very quickly, together with Dr Marsigny who was carrying a bottle of oxygen. The rescuers were, I think, Jean-Luc Yvon and Olivier Renard. Did they know and what did they know? I am used to seeing everyone rush to the helicopter, but this time there seemed to be an extra urgency about it. I thought about this again later.

I was outside the chalet at the helipad, sitting at the wooden table close to where I had been speaking to Marsigny. I was alone, putting down on paper everything which had been going round in my head today.

What happened next was like a Hitchcock film, when the

drama unfolds gradually and theatrically, where things are hinted at but not revealed, thus creating, more meaningfully than any hard hitting platitudes ever could, the reality of a nightmare.

The red helicopter came back from the Mer de Glace and flew the wide arc which brings it back to its tarmac pad. One always watches the helicopter, however accustomed one is to it. The noise swells to a crescendo. Everyone claps his hands over his ears. The thrashing rotor penetrates everything. I watched, like everyone, pinning down my flapping papers with an elbow, and straight away began to understand. Because it didn't land facing us, in its usual position, but, still turning, it landed with its open door facing the hangar.

So it was bringing back a body. A body that was not in the external basket but inside. Fernandez and Malineau ran towards the hangar carrying a stretcher. I didn't try to see properly because I didn't want to. My God! Enough deaths since yesterday… The helicopter lifted and settled back in its normal position. It was Dr Cauchy who descended. So familiar was it to see Manu Cauchy getting off this machine, with his red suit and his rucksack, that it took me a fraction of a second to understand the horror. I don't think it was really a full second, but that flash before the truth hits you. I stood up and heard myself saying in a hushed voice: 'No!… No!… No!… No!… No!… No!… No!' as if denying it could change things. And suddenly this brought to mind the same 'No!' I had hissed in another occasion one night a long time ago, against reality, when the radio had said: 'A man who spent his life guiding others…' and I had realised that Lionel Terray, who they had been searching for, was dead.

Who had died today, I didn't know, Iglesis, Michoux or Poirot. All three perhaps. But in any case I knew that one of them was dead, that I had a real affection for all three of them and that it was unbearable.

Those immediate moments – the helicopter returning and what followed, are fixed in my mind – but curiously I have forgotten the rest. The helicopter must have flown off again. I really can't remember. I suddenly felt like a foreigner. And so fragile. No question of my approaching the equipment store, where Cauchy had gone to sit, not far from Hadja tied up there. It was men's business, for them alone.

At one point Jean-Claude Gin passed nearby. Going or coming

from telephoning in the chalet. My voice seemed strangely rough, as I asked him:

'Who's dead?'

'Régis Michoux' he replied.

I said:

'Oh no!'

Then:

'Anyway! I shall *not* do this book!'

He looked at me. He said:

'On the contrary, you must. That is the mountains. We know. and you know, that they are harsh. Life and death. That's it!'

I told myself he was doing his job as captain. He went back to the others. I was through with this book. Only now could I cry, going off alone behind the chalet where no one ever went. Out of respect, I didn't want to leave before they had taken the body away.

Death in the mountains hits all the harder because it extinguishes those that are truly alive.

For the old, white-skinned, gaunt, the emaciated sick, the ghosts one glimpses on passing in hospital corridors, those slowing approaching death, it is just as cruel that they have to die and, for those who love them, it is just as terrible. But in the mountains, unless there is the long drawn out death of a Vincendon, or a Kohlman, there comes a shift from the most vibrant life to an absolute death and it can't be grasped. One has the impression that it is possible to go back to yesterday, to this morning, to a triumphant life.

Yes, Michoux's death was a nightmare from which one would like to wake and yet had to understand one would not wake. That it was true. That it was final.

Memory is astonishing. How everything turned to despair, from the moment the helicopter first returned. How I cannot place anything that happened afterwards. At no time did I go near the group of gendarmes, who had loosely gathered beside the equipment store. Not that I didn't want to know what had happened. On the contrary I had a terrible need to know. But I had a greater need still, not to do anything which might appear indiscreet. I did not want to surprise a tear, a sorrow.

All the same I learned – but when… from whom… how – that Michoux had been caught in a snow slide in the Whymper Couloir, the top of which was in condition but lower down was slushy. That on the route, Michoux had climbed with Poirot. That they had all descended unroped so as not to increase the risk. That Poirot had been carried away as well but had been fortunate enough to stop himself. I learnt that they were concerned when they could not see him. This all comes to me in flashbacks. Perhaps I had it from Jean-Claude to whom I hardly seem to have talked. I learned that Michoux was married, that he had two teenage sons, a wife, who Jean-Claude Gin described to me as 'quite remarkable'. But you never know how people are going to react.

'Watch the ballet', Cousineau had told me gloomily, at the start of the season.

There was something of the ballet, in these extreme circumstances that affected everybody. The helicopter came back with Iglesis and Poirot. I saw them join the others. I saw brotherly arms around shoulders. Michel Pierre had come. Captain Joubert had come, I was in the chalet at that time and he had comforted me with a kindly 'Bonjour Anne!' Captain Hurtault had come. Some had also left. Jean-Claude Gin early on. He had to tell Madame Michoux before any rumour reached her. One moment, I was sitting on a grassy hummock, at the foot of a tree. At another, I was gathering up my notes. These are flashes, impressions, images. Everything is muddled. What struck me very clearly, at one particular moment, was the division between the reds and blues, grief stricken though they all were, but separately. The blues were outside, having lost their comrade. The reds were in the helipad chalet. Perhaps, like me, they were leaving the others to themselves.

It was a military ambulance that came to collect the body. I was on my feet. I watched it leave. And then I left the helipad.

18

DOUBTS

I have left the helipad. Definitely.
It's difficult. It will be difficult to break off this book, these friendships, but I cannot do otherwise and am astonished that Jean-Claude Gin did not see that immediately.

Before leaving, I tried to telephone John, to see if he was there, because I did not want to go back and be alone. But the telephone was not working properly, I could not get through and I went home, there was nothing else I could do.

John was outside, in the garden. As I was walking up I made the sort of horizontal signs, with my head and my hands, that you make from a distance to indicate that something is wrong. And then I told him about the accident. I told him there would be no book and that I felt delivered from the misfortunes of yesterday and this morning. Régis Michoux, that was much more. It was the loss of a friend. Write a book about all that: no, never!

John did not understand either: 'You have chosen to write about a season of mountain rescue. And that is what this is, a season of mountain rescue...'

'No! It's not at all what I wanted to write about. You can't imagine that I am going to relate all that and the death of Régis Michoux!'

'Yes... On the contrary it is all the more reason to do this book. To help people understand. To pay tribute... In memory.'

He talked like Jean-Claude! What was the matter with them all? I needed to be understood.

So, a little later, I rang Marie Claveau. Marie is pure and upright. She lives closely with life and death. And I think that she is the one who will understand.

Marie Claveau is nearer to it because three years ago she and her husband Philippe survived, thanks to a mountain's miracle and the PGHM.

Marie is close to life because she is soon going to give

birth, after two unsuccessful pregnancies, and that too, is death…
But Marie has been resting for months in the hope that the baby
she is now expecting will live. Calling her, I am sure to find her
in. I tell her what is weighing on my heart and that I am stopping
work on the book. Instead of giving me her approval, she tells me
she wants to speak to Philippe about it.

In the evening, she calls and says:

'Anne, Philippe and I had a long talk and we think you should
go on.'

I would like someone to support me when I say that I am giving
up, because I don't want and I can't write this book. And if I
write that about it, it is because I need to write, not for this book.
Writing, it is my way of thinking.

July 29

So I am stopping this book. It is too much. It is not what I wanted.

I hoped to show what a successful rescue is. I hoped to talk
about the people who were brought down alive, like the Claveaus
and the Guiverecs. The survivors. Perhaps a few deaths are
inevitable. Spanish, or Japanese for example, strangers. Not this
deluge of corpses. Not Dominic Green. And especially not Régis
Michoux.

Sometimes when I was thinking about doing this book, in Paris,
during the last months, there were moments, mostly at night, when
anguish took over. What if a helicopter crashes? Or if a rescuer
dies? Or if they bring John down to me? These were the three
worries that always invaded me. But haven't I been constantly
fighting an over-active imagination all my life? I switched off. I
knew what I wanted to write about: beautiful rescues.

And now reality has merged with these morbid fears. To do
this book has not to be a catalogue of those dramas that the
television companies and magazines adore. So, better to stop.

I telephoned Christine de Colombel, the person in charge at
Flammarion, got her answer phone, left a message to let her know.

There will be no more of this hard daily constraint. I shall see
friends, outside the valley if possible. I shall read. I shall write
short stories. I shall ignore the current events. I shall escape.

It is a relief, but not as much of one as it could be, because I
can find nobody who approves. No one who tells me:

'You are absolutely right! Stop!'

It was this approval that I was seeking, not the contradiction of Gin, John and Marie Claveau. Why don't they understand?

During the morning, a lady from the Maison de la Montagne rang me. About my troubles with the Meteo, now no longer relevant. She was very kind and friendly. I thanked her and told her that, in any case, it was no more important, that I had wanted to write a book about mountain rescue, but a rescuer had been killed, and I was stopping the book. At this the Meteo lady responded:

'Oh, no. Do it for him… do it for them!'

It was a cry from the heart, coming from an unknown woman, and those words, they shook me. As I was saying goodbye, I asked her name. It was Madame Faussurier, wife of Pierre Faussurier of the PGHM.

The roar of the helicopter was incessant.

'They're flying, you know, Anne!' John told to me.

'I shall not go. No more concerned,' I replied.

I could imagine the crowd of journalists and cameramen down there. What a windfall this end of July! Six deaths in two days, including a rescuer! That's news!

Nothing in the world would make me go and join the pack. I would probably never go back to the helipad. It will be a complete break. With people I like and consider friends. Not nice. But that's the way it is.

It needed a man to write this book, not someone like me who spends all their time imagining what it is like for the families, parents, grandparents, wives, children, friends. You can say whatever you like about equality of the sexes. Men are tougher. Full stop. I am not. I fall apart. I cry. I know I do, I admit it. So…

It is the opinion of two other women who sway me most. The gentle Marie Claveau, saved from the Kuffner, and who is going to have a baby, and Madame Faussurier who I do not know but who understands about rescue.

Even so I would like to hear: 'Stop!' And: 'It's too dreadful! You can't carry on!' And I cannot find anyone to say it.

John says to me:

'Look at them, they lost a friend yesterday. And what are they doing today? Rescue work! They don't stop, they don't cry. Perhaps they are crying inside, but they are carrying on. They're there right now. And you? You can't take it!'

Walking round the house like a troubled soul, looking for an answer, a way, some approval, I open Pascal's *Pensées*. What would he say in his wisdom? I leaf through the pages and see these lines: 'Death is easier to confront without thinking about it, than the thought of death when not menaced.'

That is true at least. Our interrogations, our questions, give greater anguish than a sudden and violent accident. But I am looking for guidance and I resort, as I sometimes do, to the words of the day's mass. And Saint Paul says: 'On days of hopefulness, take pleasure. On days of hardship, stand firm.'

Even Saint Paul is starting now! Why are they all so relentless? I don't want to stand firm! It's true I am no longer so sure I am right, but I don't want to continue. I will pick up a life which will be calm and quiet.

Nevertheless there is a sense of commitment once one has started something. In the afternoon I decide to get another opinion, an opinion from those on the ground. Not Jean-Claude Gin, as I already have his advice. And his job is partly public relations, me included. But the opinion of those at the base – what would one of the young rescuers think?

Yesterday morning, when he came over to speak to me, I found Olivier Fernandez very sensitive. Though I still do not know him well, I will ask him what *he* thinks. I look his name up in the telephone directory, he is not listed. Fine, OK! I am relieved because I cannot do more.

Relieved? No, not entirely. A little later I look for his name on the Minitel, and find it. I call. There is an answer machine. I don't have the courage to leave a message and hang up, still tormented.

An hour later, I ring again and this time leave a message, which is somewhat hesitant, asking if we can meet.

In the evening, he calls me, and suggests coming over. I explain where we live and defer any decision to his verdict, whatever that may be. I am anxious. I go and wait for him in the garden. John is playing the piano, inside.

When Olivier Fernandez arrives, about half past nine, we stay outside talking, oddly, about music, then we go inside and, all three of us, with John, chat together, about music or other things. But Fernandez is calm and solid. Simply looking at him and I know that I have to go on … that it's done, I shall go on. It pains me and shakes me, but it is obvious. The broken thread is mended.

We don't even get to the subject until midnight. Olivier Fernandez says to me at one point:

'If you don't explain properly what we do, who will? Certainly not the journalists.'

I make up my mind to return to the helipad on Thursday afternoon, Régis Michoux's funeral being in the morning. Maybe then I will be able to carry on. Till then, rest! Recovering and recuperating.

The next morning, at half past eight, the bell rings. It's Fernandez. He comes to say:

'I know that you will go on. So I suggest you get down immediately. There's a lot happening.'

I feel that I am no more at the controls. I go...

19

WEDNESDAY, JULY 30

Three of them. Young but not friendly. One who does the picture, podgy, hair down over his neck, camera on his shoulder. One who does the sound, with a big hairy microphone, playing the cowboy, in checked shirt, unshaven, strutting about. And the 'chick' directing, with a face like a marmoset, her hair in a little bun, a leather bag over her shoulder, swaying her hips, striking poses, smoking, arranging her hair, chewing her pen or holding forth into her mobile. They are there, 'tempted by the smell of blood'. They film everything they shouldn't. That's the only thing they like. Real birds of prey.

It was they who I saw first. Those three and their casualness. So I went to the back, with Michel Pierre, a mechanician and the GA. We made some coffee. And then the helicopter returned. There was a large grey bag in its basket. It was the sixth death of the morning. One may be Dominic Green. And you should see the TV people, lying almost flat under the rotor blades, filming the bag, the bag, the bag. And the sound man too, recording what? The thunder of the rotors? And the cameraman filmed the rescuers taking the bag out of the basket and carrying it into the hangar. Taking refuge in the chalet, a few of us witnessed it, outraged.

These three made me even more angry than the others I had seen up until now. I reflected that basically no one had the right to say what he thought. Neither the gendarmes, nor the Sécurité Civile, because of their respective chain of command. But me? After the helicopter had left to collect the rescuers, I went over to the three and told them what I thought of them and got it off my chest:

'You are revolting! Revolting! You should be ashamed of yourselves! You just like atrocity! It is not that which matters. What you want is the horror.'

'What?... We know our job!'

'No! You're disgusting. That's all. Disgusting!'

Fortunately Julio came over and said:

'It's true! She's right. There are things that should not be filmed! Do you understand? Should not be filmed!'

We leave them outside and go in. I have tears in my eyes but I have to hold them back. If I do this book, or rather, since I am doing it, I am not going to waste time soaking my notes with tears.

Life, suffering, death, are one thing. Those who rescue, who save, who bring back, who show love, are part of it. And me, I believe I am also trying to say things for the best. But I hate those who are voyeuristic, who pour out this sort of horror on to TV to distort the public eye. They are guilty because they shape opinion through voyeurism. Their indifferent eyes. Robotic urban eyes. Without tact, without benevolence, without respect, without love.

What are monsters? Certainly not huge purple beasts with eight arms and green viscous eyes. Better them than these. Inhuman monsters that our media-loving society creates and who, further-more, seem to be proud of what they do.

There... I have had my say, even if it has no effect. The television companies and the sensationalist magazines should not be allowed on to the helipad. Their journalists are all the same. They only want one thing. Superficiality and blood. Why help them?

Now these three wanted to go out and about. 'To get some mountain shots.' In other words, like the other day: film places where people have died. I said to the crew:

'You should take them to the Tournier, where you rescued those safe-and-sound guys this morning!'

And one of them replied:

'In any case, they couldn't give a damn, they haven't a clue and they'll add the same bullshit to whatever view they take.'

They are taken. Where eventually, I don't know. The worst thing is that, while they are flying, there is a call-out that is con-sequently delayed. It takes a good ten minutes for the helicopter to get back... A parapenter has fallen in Combe Lachenal. And an enormous avalanche is reported, in the direction of the Char-poua; no one knows if somebody is underneath.

How often have I seen people saved in the nick of time? If one day, a casualty dies because journalists have to be flown around, what would people say? Nothing at all, it would be covered up! First and foremost by the journalists themselves.

The helicopter finally reappears, lands, disembarks the parasites, embarks Alain Iglesis, Olivier Renard and Dr Lecoq. As it happens the rescue is urgent, for someone who is seriously injured.

Getting out of the chopper, with her acolytes, the chick is unconcerned and comes bouncing in:

'Well? Now what?'

She talks with affectation.

Bernard Stoop, the nice Sécurité Civile mechanician, replies curtly: 'A parapenter has fallen.'

'Will they bring him here?'

'Perhaps not. Maybe to the hospital. It depends...'

When the journalists go outside, everyone is in agreement about them. And as soon as we are alone, the gendarmes and the Sécurité Civile exchange comments:

'They're all the same, but these three are even worse than the others...'

'Huh! Them! That lot really piss me off!'

They say to me:

'No shortage of things to write about today.'

'I think I've only written about the journalists, so far.'

Everyone exclaims:

'Ah... Well... Yes... Yes!'

But when they are here, asking questions, idiotic ones moreover, the gendarmes, pilots and mechanicians are obliged to reply. Politely. Not me! Whatever I have to say about them, I can say. Oh, relief.

Thank God, the Sécurité Civile helicopter is no longer permitted to take them on a rescue. A sound measure! But now the girl is telephoning Paris. She wants the right to film during the rescues and is trying, furiously, to get permission:

'We're not being helped,' she complains.

No more help to film raw flesh.

She simpers and sucks her biro like a little girl. Little girl! You must be joking!

She asks eagerly:

'Are they bringing the parapenter here?'

'No, to the hospital.'

Disappointment. The trio leaves for the hospital. With a bit of luck they will arrive in time to film the casualty's grimace. What an auspicious day!

A little later, I tell myself that this sort of journalist does have a use. Only one. That of behaving hatefully. Of being hateful. So, we hate them. Perhaps it helps. In time of war, there is an enemy to hate who kills your friends. Here, there is no enemy. The mountain is not an enemy. It is a place, an extraordinary place, which we love. Journalists such as these, with their posing, their insolence, their total lack of respect for the dead, we can detest, rightly, because trapped in a vicious circle, they are influencing a country that has become accustomed to be fed with distorted news. I know there are good journalists, but without being vindictive, I hope that one day these particular three will come to appreciate what sadness and death are really about.

Let us get back to realities and more important matters. Yesterday, when I was not here, there were of course some rescues. Two more parapenters. A snake bite. A fall on a footpath. A hiker who had a heart attack. An accident at work. Et cetera.

But as soon as night fell, there were reports of torches signalling from the Tournier Spur on Les Droites. The helicopter was to take off at 5.30 this morning to investigate. But at quarter to four, the rescuers, flight crew and doctor were woken. The guardian at the Argentière Hut had seen the lights of two head torches falling down the Couturier Couloir. Obviously an accident.

It was not known what the flashing lights on the Tournier indicated. Rescuers had not risked making a night flight yesterday, which is always dangerous, although they go out for climbers if it is certain they have fallen and are in urgent need of help.

They took off at half past four this morning. François Lecoq was dropped on the glacier provisionally while the helicopter, with Alain Iglesis and Olivier Renard, searched. Three alpinists had been climbing the Couturier Couloir unroped. The snow had been made hard and icy by frozen rain. Two of them were dead, smashed up, the third, unhurt, was just above the bergschrund. One of those that died must have knocked the other off on his way down.

With a rescue like this, especially when it takes place in the dark and involves foreigners, it is not easy to find out quickly what happened. Olivier Renard stayed with the two who were dead, so as to prepare them for being taken down to the flat of the glacier on the winch. Alain Iglesis, dropped near the uninjured climber, accompanied him in the helicopter to the Argentière Hut. On the way, the survivor said 'My friend...' in English, but he was Austrian, like one of the dead, the other French.

Then in two further flights, the helicopter dropped Renard, Lecoq and the two bodies on the glacier where they could be prepared for transporting to the helipad. 'Prepared' means being put in big plastic sacks, after ascertaining if there is anything to identify them either in their clothing or rucksacks. Thus the bodies arrive at the helipad relatively unobtrusively.

Meanwhile, the helicopter went to the climbers on the Tournier, who were still calling for help. Iglesis was winched down to them. They were a couple of English, stuck but unhurt. One was taken down to the valley in the chopper, which had to go and refuel, while Iglesis stayed with the other. Both were brought down in the next flight, together with the other climber from the Couturier incident.

A final flight picked Renard, Lecoq and the two bodies. At twenty-seven minutes past six in the morning, it was all over. And it was, at last, daylight.

At seven o'clock, there was another call-out, from a guide. While on Mont Blanc du Tacul, at four o'clock, he had seen a light falling through the darkness and thought someone had dropped a torch. Further on, his client having twisted his ankle, they turned back and, while descending, he noticed some scattered ice axes and concluded there must have been a real accident, which he then reported on his radio.

In the event they were two more dead, and to retrieve them had necessitated some difficult manoeuvres. The victims had fallen 300 metres, crashing over two bars of séracs. Below the second, one body hung in a crevasse by the rope, while his companion lay ten metres further on, stuck in the snow, in a zone of crevasses.

At an altitude of some 4000 metres, it was not possible for the helicopter to lift both off together by the rope. Alain Iglesis organised the difficult operation of picking up first one and then the other. It required the help of the three others on duty: Olivier Renard, Jean-Luc Yvon and Daniel Duret.

Iglesis was lowered down to the one lying on the surface, got his sack off his shoulders and cut his end of the rope, which remained there, loose on the ground. Then he attached the body to the helicopter winch which managed to disengage it although it was half frozen in the snow.

Then came the turn of the one in the crevasse. The portable

windlass had been set up, with anti-friction plates. Carried back to the edge of the crevasse where the rope lay, Iglesis attached a reel of cable to its loose end, whereupon the helicopter took him back across to side where the others had set up the portable winch. The cable was attached to the windlass and wound up until the rope itself started coming in, when a loop of it was attached to the helicopter winch. The end around the portable windlass was cut loose and the helicopter free to lift the body by the rope out of the crevasse.

The two dead men were taken to the Col du Midi where they were prepared for transport. One was English, the other American.

I have explained these technical details because it is necessary to point out that a rescue, even one that is only for the recovery of a corpse, can be a complex operation, which demands each time a new initiative, depending on the situation and the problems involved. Rescues don't usually take place in the relatively friendly environment of a well-trodden route. Falls happen anywhere and follow the shortest line, so the injured or dead often end up in dangerous places. The operation carried out this morning on the Tacul was geared for speed so as not to expose the rescuers more than necessary under the séracs.

During the various flights around the Tacul, two more bodies were spotted on the avalanche cone at the bottom of the Glacier Rond below the Aiguille du Midi. This end of July has been terrible. The help brought to the injured seems to have been replaced by nothing but dismal tragedies. A second team of four was called out to go on this new mission. So eleven people – eight rescuers, a doctor, a pilot and mechanician – were all mobilised at the same time. A rare occurrence.

The two dead climbers that had just been found must have been buried in an avalanche, and then covered by the recent snowfalls. Now that the sun has been shining for four days, they have reappeared. Impossible to know what route they fell from. The ice and the sun had blackened and mortified their bodies. They were identified by their equipment. One of them was Dominic Green.

So, when I arrived at the helipad, in the morning, at half past nine, it was the sixth body they were bringing in and which the television team had been filming with such shamelessness that I had been unable to contain myself.

The rescues continued, but fortunately there were no more deaths.

Only just. The parapenter, whose rescue had been delayed by the journalists going for a spin, had multiple injuries. His recovery was made more difficult by the terrain where he landed: a very steep vegetated slope that made the approach and medical care complex and dangerous. Dr Lecoq explained it to me:

'We had to have the stretcher on our knees! One false movement and he would have been off like a snow-board! One of his bones was sticking out... I sedated him and, as a result, we don't know his name...'

Another accident involving a parapenter, who crashed on take off: he had an open fracture of the wrist.

The sérac avalanche near the Charpoua, already mentioned, could have caused a further catastrophe as nearly twenty people were on their way up but had not reached the spot. It was about 200 metres wide and its debris was a maze of ice. At the request of the security committee at the town hall, the PGHM is asked to put up notices advising people not to cross it as a new avalanche could occur at any time.

A woman suffering from altitude sickness had also been brought down from Mont Maudit. Then a telephone call reported that there was an old lady with a walking stick, apparently very tired, sitting on a rock in the Planpraz Couloir. The helicopter, which was already on its way to the parapenter at Plaine-Joux, dropped Jean-Luc Yvon to look for her, as the information had not been very precise. It was not until quite a bit later that we learnt of his adventures.

Each case, really, is a special one, like this further case of a man, born in 1928, who fractured a leg walking on a footpath.

'He's a delightful old boy,' comments François Lecoq on his return.

I go outside to see him. He is on the stretcher, on the ground, with the GA keeping him company. The ambulance takes half an hour to arrive.

'And this morning, it took one hour!' the GA told me.

This new system of ambulances, is not yet up to scratch! The casualties have to wait. The Social Security is paying. A fine mess!

Gilles Bidon, the Sécurité Civile pilot who is flying today, suddenly notices me. True, he has not stopped since this morning.

'You!' he says to me. 'You should watch out. You are so discreet, that one night you'll be locked in the helipad without anyone realising it!'

'That would make a good chapter!' remarks François Lecoq. 'My night at the helipad...'

We laugh. We need to.

In due course, a long time after Jean-Luc was dropped in the couloir on the Brévent, to look for the exhausted old lady, the pair of them are brought back by the helicopter.

He had not had an easy time. To start with he found himself alone, on a walker's footpath, wearing all his high-altitude mountain gear, big boots, climbing suit, harness, karabiners, rucksack, helmet, etc.

'However,' he tells us, 'I took off the ice screw! That really was a bit too much!'

Then, with the speed rescuers are capable of, he rapidly climbed the couloir, looking everywhere for an old lady, without success. At this stage, the radio called that someone was reporting an old lady of a similar description, but in the Charlanon Couloir this time, and it was most certainly the same one. The first report had been wrong. Jean-Luc joined the Gardes footpath, crossed from one couloir to the other, still dressed in his climbing gear and actually found an old lady, quite stout, sitting on a rock and fitting the description. When the helicopter landed them, this lady, a German with an imposing presence, came and sat down, weary but ready to cooperate, on the big stone used as the doorstep to the chalet. Her name? Her age? To simplify matters, she took her passport out of her rucksack: eighty-four years old!

A taxi was called, and when it came to collect her, she slid a one hundred mark note into Dr Lecoq's hand, with the air of a queen thanking a young groom.

It was collectively decided to put the money into the collection box for new equipment.

'Well!' sighs Yvon, 'wait until I tell my wife that I spent all afternoon chasing an eighty-four-year-old grandma!'

20

RÉGIS MICHOUX

Sometimes, when people die, it is hard to recall what they looked like. On the evening of Régis Michoux's accident, I was haunted by his face, especially his eyes, bright and laughing, surrounded by little wrinkles made by this same laughter. His eyes smiled even more than his mouth. He was a man of about forty, very slender, handsome of face and bearing. His regular, honest features were marked with affability. He had fair hair and a recent blonde beard which he had grown at the beginning of the month, when he was on holiday, and which changed the way he looked so much that one day in mid-July, we saw a cyclist arriving at the helipad whom we did not recognise and it was only on seeing his eyes that someone said: 'But it's Michoux!' He laughed at our surprise.

Thinking about him, I think the expression the 'Petit Prince', which other dead climbers have been called, would suit him perfectly. However, this expression the 'Petit Prince' does not mean he had a delicate personality. Michoux had a big personality and an unquestionable authority. He was an astonishing mixture of steadfastness, kindness and cheerfulness. We understood each other well. I could see it in the smile with which he greeted me when I arrived at the helipad. At the time of his death, I was meaning to ask him soon about the epic of the forty who had been stranded on Mont Blanc and I am sure I would have appreciated his comments.

Although originating from the Chablais, he was not immediately drawn to the mountains. Having done his military service in the Gendarmerie, he had decided to make a career out it and, being a brilliant gymnast, was assigned to the gymnastic section of the Republican Guard. When that was disbanded in 1982, he joined a brigade in Haute-Savoie and started climbing. At the age of thirty-two, he became an aspirant guide and a full guide at thirty-four, in 1990. In 1991, because of his many qualifications, he joined the Chamonix PGHM.

He had big routes to his name, like the Swiss route on Les Courtes, the North Face of the Col Armand Charlet, the Shroud on the Grandes Jorasses, and an expedition to Alaska. He knew the Aiguille Verte well and had already climbed the Jardin Arête, the Couturier and Y Couloirs, so the Grands Montets Arête was his fourth route on the mountain.

He was a calm, reflective, sensible and level-headed man, known for never raising his voice, never losing control and keeping his word. Always available for others, he was patient and a good listener, as much for those he rescued as his friends. He was, in short, one of those rare people, who gets on with everyone and that is why his sudden death was felt so harshly.

The day of his accident he was officially training with Patrick Poirot. To carry out rescues anywhere in the mountains, whether being winched onto a difficult face or on foot, it is essential that the team members of the PGHM and doctors are continuously practising in all sorts of terrain and particularly on difficult ground.

The route selected that day had been decided only shortly before. Alain Iglesis – on a rest day, but often willing to use his time off to climb – had planned to do the Grands Montets Arête with an auxiliary gendarme, and when he was no longer available, Alain had asked Patrick Poirot and Régis Michoux. On Sunday, July 27, the latter had to be in the Chablais for a mass on the anniversary of his father's death, a year earlier, a sad coincidence. Everyone was set for doing the route on the Monday, from the first cable-car, perfectly appropriate for these experienced alpinists. Dr Cauchy, who is an aspirant guide, asked if he could join them, which meant two ropes of two – a more flexible arrangement than a rope of three. It was planned that he would go down from the Couvercle the same evening, as he was on duty at the hospital on Tuesday, while the others spent the night there.

So all four of them set off on Monday morning.

After an accident, we always recall the words, the phrases, the last remarks exchanged, the slightest incident. Patrick Poirot remembers that, when driving on the way to the Grands Montets cable-car station, early on the morning of the climb, Régis Michoux had asked him details about the accidents which had happened the previous day, and about the young people killed on Mont Blanc du Tacul. Hearing this, and because he lived permanently in an environment where rescue is a daily occurrence, and tragedies sometimes happen, he confided that he did not want to encourage his sons to be mountaineers. This is a problem for all climbers: the risk accepted for oneself is less acceptable with respect to one's family.

The ascent passed off well, as it does when professionals are involved. The four had climbed unroped as far as the first difficulties. Then Alain Iglesis, who had done the route before, set off in front with Manu Cauchy, followed by the second rope of Régis Michoux and Patrick Poirot. At the foot of the Aiguille Ségogne, because ice was covering the cracked slabs, the group decided to abseil down the Cordier side in order to get to the Col du Nant Blanc and so be sure of reaching the summit. The first pair got there about a quarter of an hour before the second. When Régis Michoux joined Patrick Poirot on the top, he jested, as though he was a young candidate on the Guides' course:

'Well, I can add that route to my list!'

From the top cable-car station to the summit, it had taken them seven hours, although the normal time is eight to twelve.

Already rested, Alain Iglesis and Manu Cauchy got ready to descend. Conditions seemed good and they could stick to their plan. No reason to change it. On the other hand, they did discuss whether or not to remain roped up. As already pointed out: unless it is being used for belaying, or to help a weaker member of the party, the rope can be a handicap. In the present instance, as all the members of the team were extremely competent, they decided not to rope up and to descend quickly, but keeping a certain distance apart.

Setting off down the ridge, Alain Iglesis announced:

'It's fine! No probs for the descent!'

Patrick Poirot and Régis Michoux had a snack and then followed down the ridge and into the Whymper Couloir. Most of the snow from the last fall had already avalanched, and so there was little chance of it happening again. There was an adequate covering at the top of the couloir and they were able to find good purchase. In an hour they would all be off the slope. They had considered the possibility of abseiling, if the descent turned out to be dangerous, but there seemed to be no need.

On the way down, Patrick Poirot got cold hands, as his gloves were wet. Régis got a spare out of his rucksack and both took the opportunity to have a drink, which left them two or three minutes behind the others. They then set off down again. In the lower third of the couloir, the snow was unstable. As they were now approaching the main channel of the couloir, they traversed down and leftwards to avoid it and skirted above a rock outcrop. The line of their route was obvious.

Suddenly there was a snow slide, not very big, but it happened in a bad place and at the wrong time. Patrick Poirot, who had been avalanched twice previously, heard the characteristic noise of the snow falling from above him. He shouted: 'Watch out!' but was the first to be caught. Régis Michoux, slightly to one side of him and three metres below, was also carried off. Pushed towards the edge of the slope, Patrick Poirot thought: 'I have to stop myself!' and with a considerable effort succeeded in turning face to the slope, forced his axes into the snow and managed to arrest himself. But he saw Régis disappearing in the avalanche, toppled over by the snow. Finding himself alone, he assumed that the other two, who were a little further down, might also have been swept away. He continued his descent for several minutes, but there was another small snow slide and he decided to climb up twenty metres to shelter under a rock.

Alain Iglesis and Manu Cauchy were already almost at the bergschrund and the avalanche did not touch them, but they saw it pass, with a body in it. They quickly climbed down to the avalanche run-out below the bergschrund. The radio was in Régis Michoux's rucksack, which was why the PGHM were not alerted immediately but only when they had dug out the body, whose rucksack was sticking out of the snow. Manu Cauchy took the radio and made a brief call, without giving any details, because others could be listening in. So the rescue was called out without knowing exactly whom it was for. The helicopter was on the spot about twenty minutes after the accident had happened, with Jean-Luc Yvon, Olivier Renard and Bernard Marsigny. They had quickly done what they could, but it was too late – he had been killed in the fall.

Every accident poses questions. In the present case, there was no need for any to be asked, as the four climbers were all professionals of the highest calibre. The mountain environment is not neutral. Choices have continually to be made. Inexperienced amateurs may make illogical ones. Experienced mountaineers try to weigh up the precise conditions at the time – but there always remains an element of chance.

Xavier Chappaz, president of the Compagnie des Guides de Chamonix, paid public homage to the dead man, describing him as a fine mountaineer, which is exactly what he was. I was upset to learn subsequently that another guide, who shall remain nameless, made comments in a local paper which brought credit to neither himself or nor his profession, especially since he is known to have called out the rescue service several times when it was not necessary, indeed improperly.

Better to pass quickly over this shameful incident, and remember that accidents, especially snow slides and wind slab avalanches, can happen to anyone, even guides. The sorely missed Marcel Burnet, one of the best Chamonix guides there ever was, and with whom I had the pleasure of doing several climbs, died in an avalanche on the Haute Route. Toni Gobbi, the famous Courmayeur guide, met the same end. Gérard Devouassoux, whose death is still much lamented in Chamonix, was killed in an avalanche on Everest. And I, myself, was buried in an avalanche, with some others, whilst under the care of a guide.

Of course anybody can make mistakes in the mountains, we have seen examples of them, and we will see them again but in this particular case the decisions were jointly taken by experienced and competent mountaineers.

Régis Michoux's funeral took place on the morning of Thursday, July 31.

It was good that, up until then, the body had been kept, not in the morgue, but at the PGHM, in the room on the first floor, which had been turned into a chapel of rest, where his fellows kept watch night and day, as used to happen in the past.

Many people went to meditate in the improvised chapel. I preferred to stay away, fearing that I might be intruding. But, for those two days, I felt that I was very much there for these final respects.

The funeral ceremony took place, then, on the morning of July 31. It was first and foremost a military ceremony, simple and beautiful. In the interior courtyard, there were many people gathered. The head of the National Gendarmerie, who is always a civilian, had come from Paris. So there were many officials, but it was mainly Régis Michoux's family and friends with whom he worked, doctors, gendarmes and helicopter crews.

The formal uniforms, the gestures, the speeches and the bugle calls all conferred great dignity on this tribute. When there was silence, it struck me as being absolute because, strangely, no noise came either from the valley or from the town. There was only the sound of the swallows flying above us in the blue sky, but there was none of the usual hubbub of civilisation, which seemed to have momentarily ceased.

Everyone felt enormous compassion for Régis Michoux's wife and children, Aubin and Jérôme, and for his ill-fated mother who, having lost her husband a year earlier, had now lost her son.

There was then a cortège to the church of Saint-Michel, where the service was to take place and which was full. The most moving moments were the words that were written and read out by his friends, both present and past and by Captain Gin.

I must quote some extracts from them:

Régis,
No one can claim to have heard you speak one word louder than another.
No one can claim to have heard you speak a word out of place.
You were an example of kindness, of modesty.
You were an example of tolerance and humility.
You were an example of efficiency, of calm.
You were an example of generosity, of courage. You were our model.
And we no longer understand, we don't understand at all…
Why?
Why smiles and joy should suddenly become repulsion, sadness and suffering?
If there truly is a God, may he help us, if not to understand, at least to accept, to overcome this pain by telling us that the day when fate struck you down, you were a happy man.
Happy in those mountains that you loved and which wanted to keep you for themselves.

And this one:

To devote one's life to saving others requires self-sacrifice and courage.
You must challenge yourself to do better, and not be content with what has been done – Then you feel that you have served a purpose.
Perhaps we can help to make the world a better place.
Régis was like that, generous, smiling, affable, he knew the meaning of rescue.
To live a passion, to devote yourself to it simply because its necessary, is in a way the meaning of life.

Today, life has a bitter taste but this bitterness has to give way to admiration, to the one who will remain an example to all of us.

You, our friend, partner in our perilous rescue work, in our joy and our fear, we will continue along the path, and try to be worthy of the friendship that bound us.

And finally a third:

Régis Michoux chose to devote his life to saving those of others in an environment that he especially loved: the mountains. In Chamonix since 1991, he quickly established himself as a strong and accepted leader in the mountain rescue team. Régis Michoux was a great professional.

For all those who worked with him, or simply shared the every day life of the PGHM with him, the joys, the sorrows, the good times and the bad times, up there in the mountains, he will remain a model of strength and stability. Particularly on this day when we all know doubt.

At this cruel time when everything else seems so trivial, Régis has left us a part of his strength, some certainties and a tremendous message of hope and faith in life. The forty people who were lost on Mont Blanc, his last rescue, on July 23, will probably never know how lucky they were to follow his footsteps for several hours, up there in the storm, between heaven and earth.

The mountains are a gift for man, a demanding world where you cannot cheat. Régis, through his passion and his dedication, understood that perfectly.

We will keep with us his perpetual smile, his calm and serenity, his unwavering faith and his humility of every moment.

The evening of the funeral, I telephoned Pierre Leroux[1] to thank him for coming to the ceremony.

He said:

'I didn't know him, but I knew he was a good guy... decent guy!'

And he added:

'In the past, when I had just become a guide, with the Compagnie, I had to do rescues... So I understand what those boys there do... Because each time I found it enriching.'

Time went on, life went on, the rescues went on. But one day, on going home, I found this other piece of writing which a rescuer had left for me and I want to quote this one as well:

[1] Distinguished Chamonix guide.

In the twisted sheets, I toss and turn in my head lots of thoughts. Images march past.

It is hard to watch mates cry, those who are always smiling, those who never falter before a task that is sometimes repellent in a difficult job.

We are all lost, trying to find our motivation again.

Curiously, we feel a need to return to the mountains to get our bearings again, to touch once more the rock we dream about so much, to tell ourselves that nothing is more beautiful than this landscape and return tired out to our homes...

For two days we all found ourselves face to face with our demons, our eyes moist, our hands trembling.

We lowered our eyes, head in hands, we doubted.

Doubt, is somewhat the bad side of life, it tries to come to the surface, a wrong which wants us to abandon our path, our convictions, our work.

However, when I saw this girl, come to Régis's burial place in a wheel chair, when I saw her weep, I knew that we have an exceptional life.

This young woman, who he went to rescue, who he had carried in his arms to the stretcher, who he had lifted off on the end of the helicopter cable, this woman was crying for a man she did not know but for whom she has love.

Another woman, who I met at the hospital and who had been saved by Jean-Jacques and Pascal, said on seeing me: 'I can't talk much today, but I thank you from the bottom of my heart, my husband and I will never forget you.'

Our friend is gone for ever, he will never be here again, will never tap us on the shoulder in the morning at breakfast, will never be roped with us again.

But there is a place where he will always find the way and transmit to us his strength and his warmth: our memory...

Tomorrow, we will continue the work, because injured people need us, because we love the mountains so much that we help them to be less cruel to those who venture into them.

I leave my bed, tomorrow I return to work like all my friends, certain to do what I have to, because it is a task which is a real passion, content to continue along a road where friends have fallen, mortally wounded by their love of others.

21

DOMINIC GREEN

When Captain Gin told me they were looking for him but that he had been missing for nearly two weeks, I had been certain that Dominic Green was dead, that he had fallen somewhere in the massif, and that perhaps, as sometimes happens, he would never be found. Memories came rushing back. It had happened three years earlier.

1994: Saturday, July 23
The cloud was clinging to the mountains. The weather looked stormy, as it had every afternoon. The Sécurité Civile helicopter was on standby, and rescuers on duty in the afternoon were two Catalans, Alain Iglesis and Patrice Ribes.

Suddenly there was a call to the helipad, difficult to hear, crackly, but precise: someone had been struck by lightning, was conscious and five metres below the summit of the Petits Charmoz.

As always, there followed a minute of rapid preparation, hurried words. Despite the cloud and the storm, which could start again at any time, the pilot thought he could attempt the flight, but quickly, without the doctor so as to keep the chopper light. Because, unusually, the exact location had been given with such precision, someone jokingly said:

'And remember, if you see someone six metres below the summit, don't pick him up! It won't be him! He's five metres down!'

The rotors were already turning, the men quickly jumped in the machine with their equipment. The helicopter left.

I stayed with the doctor. During the rescue, some news came to us over the radio:

'*Dragon* to Cordial... We've found him. Bringing him down. He's conscious but has lost a boot.'

Bizarre... It is pretty rare to lose a boot in the mountains. Perhaps he had been struck on the foot and it had taken it off? There are times, at the helipad, when anything is possible.

The helicopter came back. The doctor and Iglesis helped the young man, who had a short Christ-like beard, out of the machine. His left leg was bare. They put him on the sofa, hardly a metre from me, for a first medical examination.

He was a foreigner, shocked but nevertheless making an effort to express himself in French, which showed character. The doctor listened to his heart and questioned him, in French and English. The lightning had stripped his leg bare, burning the skin and all the hair, and torn off his boot. Entering by his right shoulder, as he was starting to abseil, it had gone right through his body and come out at his foot which was burned, swollen and very red.

He was twenty-two years old, English and called Dominic Green. His friend, nineteen-year-old Stuart Gould, had been thrown against him by the impact. Both had lost consciousness, but, when they had come round again, Stuart Gould descended and ran to the Plan de l'Aiguille to call for help, quite a feat, considering he must have been in a state of shock.

The ambulance had arrived at the helipad and had taken charge of the casualty, who must have been suffering, as he was complaining a little.

Owing to the weather conditions, the helicopter had been unable to collect Patrice Ribes immediately. So he had spent time up there alone in a very stormy atmosphere. When he was being winched, the static had been such that it had hit and melted his radio microphone. He brought back the English boy's rucksack, in which he had put the missing boot, found close by. He took it out of the rucksack. It looked as though it had exploded! All the eyelets were pulverised and half of the inner boot was missing, burnt. The two navy blue socks, worn inside each other, were in complete tatters.

We were stunned.

'And I know what he smelt,' said Iglesis. 'Hot tar.'

Next day I asked Dr Cauchy for news of the casualty. He didn't know but suggested I went to the hospital to find out.

I learnt that the young man was in intensive care but that I could see him because he was bored. I went, afraid to disturb him if he was in pain. Dominic Green was surrounded by apparatus of all kinds, small screens, tubes, machines, but was very conscious. We chatted. He was glad to be able to speak English, to be distracted, to know that I could lend him some English books and I felt he was grateful for the time I had spent with him. Pain does not prevent boredom, as I know from experience. He was glad, of course, to have been rescued. But also very put out by no longer having a pair of climbing boots. A common reaction, typical even, and of course understandable. To know one is alive, but that the new boots, the pride and joy, that cost two hundred pounds were gone...

After that, I went to see him every day. His climbing partner was camping far from Chamonix and did not have any transport. He came, of course, as and when he could, but for the patient time passed slowly. Once I took him some apricots, another time chocolates and, always books or English magazines, but only to do with climbing. Nothing else interested him. He knew my name, through the English translations of my books. We talked about it all. He was the age our son, who died shortly after birth, would have been. I liked the way he loved the mountains and the way he spoke of them.

The hospital kept a close eye on him and, at the start, did many tests because lightning can cause complications later on, with damage to the heart or kidneys. Dominic had problems and pain with one of his ears, but that, I think, was the only lasting effect of the accident.

On July 26, he left the intensive care unit and was put in a little room of his own. He particularly appreciated the fact that, from his bed, he could see Mont Blanc.

On July 30, I met another young man at the helipad who had been struck by lightning and he told me about the moment of intense light and terrible noise when he was hit.

The PGHM had entrusted me with the burnt boot to return to Dominic. It had been the object of much astonishment. When he saw it, Dominic was amazed he still had a foot... A foot which nevertheless had third degree burns.

He talked about mountains all the time, about the season now lost, because of the accident, and about all the routes he hoped to do next year! He was a student but it was the mountains that seemed to be his immense and overriding passion. This accident did not appear to be the first he had had, as he told me once that his friends thought of him as another Joe Simpson.

I spent some time with him each day, up until 3 August when he was repatriated to England.

He sent me a very nice letter of thanks. He was still in hospital, but hoped to start walking the next day and return home a few days later. His parents also thanked me and sent me a souvenir from their home town. In December, we exchanged Christmas cards. And then our lives went their separate ways ... I had heard nothing more of him until, in 1997, I saw his name written on a file.

1997: Thursday, July 31
The day of Régis Michoux's funeral. I was hardly at the helipad, where in any case there were only minor rescues.

The day before, at Leysin in Switzerland, a helicopter winch cable broke. The casualty and the doctor, who were both attached to it, died in the accident, which shook the rescue world.

At the PGHM I had a long talk with Jackie Paillé. He brought out that the links rescuers sometimes establish with the rescued and which persist is often their greatest reward.

Friday, August 1
Bad weather.

I go to the PGHM for a meeting with Jean-Claude Gin, but he is seeing Nicole Michoux. I stay downstairs, watching, seeing the things that follow on from events at the helipad, things that are yet more difficult. At least at the helipad there is action, often lives are saved. Here, people come to make statements, for example, and there are also bereaved families. Receiving them seems to me the hardest part of the job.

I see a man go past, not very young, white hair and wearing a tie. A father no doubt. He is very dignified but from time to time displays that tensing of the jaw, with the mouth half-open to hold back his emotion. I hear a woman's voice asking about a wedding ring ... No, he was not wearing one. While the rescuer, Iglesis, goes to get something, Jean-Claude Tissot joins the family and speaks to them a little, so they are not left alone. At times like this, it is necessary to make small talk in order to avoid a terrible silence. I get snatches of conversation. There is the matter of a wallet containing papers and a little money. There is the matter of a car found unlocked, with the radio no longer in it, stolen perhaps ... All this seems pathetic, compared to what everyone is thinking about, but it is better to fill the time up with something.

Enter two large bearded men, well into their forties, scruffy, with battered shoes and small rucksacks. I get the impression that they have come to enquire about the belongings of a friend who has died. Fernandez and Malineau speak to them, in English, and everything starts over again. There are still problems with what has or has not been found. There was no money... They forgot to look if there was anything in the side pocket of his trousers... The rucksack was burst open... The rescuers go off to find out about something or other. Left to themselves, the two men stop speaking English and drop into a language I cannot identify. Slowly they pace the entrance hall, back and forth, near the map of the massif. They are huge, looking a bit like over aged hippies, nice. Saudemont comes back to join them and they go outside.

When he returns, I ask him what accident they had come about.

'The ones who disappeared,' he tells me. 'Those we have just found on the Glacier Rond.'

I give a start:

'But I knew one of them! I'd like to tell them how sorry I am. Have they gone?'

'Maybe not.'

We hurry out. They are still there, looking at the memorial to the dead of the PGHM.

I go over to them, upset, wanting to say something that might help. We talk. I explain how I came to know Dominic Green, three years ago, when he had an accident. They are the father and the uncle of his Dutch friend, Arne Vanderzwan, who was twenty-three. We mainly speak in English. How to lessen the pain? With small things, little words, exchanges, to let them feel that there are others, outsiders, who can feel for them. I tell them that I have climbed a lot, that it is such a wonderful thing to do, that we all know it is dangerous, but that it gives such happiness.

They are fine people. They understand. The father understands. Between his abundant beard and his unkempt hair, he has a penetrating look, a sensitive, intelligent and refined face. I ask him if he has any other children. And it is awful. He has five. Or rather he did have five, three sons and two daughters. But the eldest son was killed in a motorcycle accident. And here the second is being brought down from the Glacier Rond. I admire him even more for having accepted his son's love of the mountains.

Arne was coming to the end of his studies in astro-physics at Leeds University. He was to have been awarded his degree on

July 24. It was the fact that he did not come back for the ceremony, which alerted everyone, that something must be wrong. They ask me if I have children. I say, alas, no. They are suffering at having lost them, and myself for not having. Everyone suffers in one way or another.

Then they tell me that yesterday evening they went up to the Plan de l'Aiguille, with some of Arne's friends, and climbed up higher, in the direction of the Glacier Rond, towards the place where the bodies had been found, in a location away from the path but accessible. And there they had erected a cairn, a cross, and left some messages.

I ask them if Dominic's parents are going to come. They reply: 'They are here!'

My heart stops. I must go and see them, say how much I feel for them. I learn they are staying at the Hotel de l'Aiguille du Midi. If I were in their place, in a foreign country, what I would most appreciate, would be someone to show me some affection. But would they? I find the hotel, go inside, ask for them… The father is pointed out sitting near the reception, speaking to the owner. Hardly have I started to say that three years ago, when Dominic was struck by lightning… when he realises who I am. He stands up, shakes my hand and takes me into a lounge where his wife and his two other sons are sitting. I start telling them again that three years ago…

'You are Mrs Wilkinson!' cries the mother.

She hugs me. We kiss. I sit with them. How I admire these people, whom I do not know, but who are so controlled, so digni-fied, in their comportment and what they say.

To discover the family of someone whom I have known and who has died, has happened to me at least twice before, and both times it was deeply moving. What inner strength the Greens have… The parents must be nearly fifty years old; the sons are twenty-three and sixteen. The eldest had come out earlier, when the search for the missing climbers was taking place

We talk. Now the senior, the twenty-three-year-old son, is married and works in computing. While the parents and the youngest son will leave tomorrow, from Geneva, he will stay on to escort the body on Monday, which will leave from Lyon. The formalities are complex. The father is very exact, and goes out from time to time, to sort out new problems, which he does calmly and efficiently, coming back in to explain them. The eldest son is worried about his dress: he has come wearing jeans and casual jacket, and thinks he should be more formally dressed to accompany the body. The father tells him it does not matter, that it will do. We talk about the love of mountains. I tell them that when Dominic was in hospital he only wanted books on mountains to read. That brought a smile to their lips. We talk about Dominic. They tell me that at Leeds University, where he was president of the climbing club, he had studied Russian and Philosophy, but that his main aim was to become a guide, to devote his life to the mountains. They tell me his other passion was music, that sometimes in Chamonix he played the trumpet or the violin in the street, not for money, but for the pleasure of entertaining passers by.

I explain the new book I am writing and say that I shall speak of Dominic. They are pleased and touched. They tell me that Dominic had two notebooks, one listing routes he had done, the other listing routes he had failed on but would try again.

We have to leave each other. Mrs Green tells me that there will be a religious service for Dominic this evening. I ask where. It is to be at the church of Saint-Michel. My evening is full, but I'll attend. Just as we are going our separate ways, while I am standing close to Mrs Green and we are holding each other's hands, I say to her with deep admiration:

'Mrs Green... You are so brave...'

Her mouth trembles a little and she replies:

'No... Really I am not...'

We kiss goodbye tenderly.

I leave, deeply distressed, and go via the hospital to get news of the Guiverecs. They are improving. Francis is in an armchair, with his arm in some large piece of equipment. When I tell them that I am going to carry on with the book, Nadine's face lights up. She says:

'You are doing the right thing.'

Undoubtedly, opinion is unanimous. They are still coming to terms with the decision to give up climbing and everything that it has done to their lives. I learn they do not have children. I suggest they think again about their decision, because there is still pleasure to be had from doing easy things in the mountains. They are probably going back home near Paris at the beginning of next week.

I go to advise John that I am going to the church service. He decides to come with me, to meet the Greens, then return home straight away, as the Cartwrights are coming to dinner.

It is a beautiful mass, taken by four priests. I wondered whether, for the Greens, this was a conventional gesture in the local church, but I see from the start that all four are practising Catholics. They join in the service. But that does not mean faith eases pain. Perhaps the contrary. But it does bring hope. The four Greens and myself take communion, then at the end of the service, in which Dominic's name was specifically mentioned, Father Dominique brings the parents a lighted candle and invites the hundred or so people present to show their sympathy, that they are not alone in their hardship, and the whole Christian community is with them, suffering and praying together. It's beautiful this love shown by so many strangers.

Before leaving the Greens, I have a question for the eldest son. At one point we find ourselves alone. I say to him:

'Do you have children?'

'No.'

'Do have babies, for your parents…'

He replies thoughtfully:

'True… Now I am the eldest son…'

Let us hope that life carries on, that youth will rekindle it, in this suffering family.

22

TWO PILLARS:
THE GERVASUTTI AND THE BONATTI

Saturday, August 2

Again!...

I don't deliberately want to attack the press. But there is a kind of journalist whose job is to report about 'squashed dogs' – they are not usually of the highest calibre. The ones sent here are those reporting on 'squashed climbers'. And they are not the best either, not by a long chalk.

So, here we are again. The present specimen is cocksure. The lines that are starting to show on his face are not kindness lines. He talks familiarly to everyone, calling by their Christian names people he has never seen before and will never see again. He thinks the world revolves around him. He is a photographer who works for a famous magazine. A reporter accompanies him.

A long time ago, I knew a journalist in Chamonix, working for the same magazine, who was all too delighted to report mountain accidents. One day, when some of my friends were caught on the Frêney Pillar in bad weather, I heard him say to the small group that hung around him because he bought the drinks: 'If they are dead, it'll be champagne all round!'

And that's how it still is. It is not of my making, I am simply reporting what I see, what I hear. If it is nasty, too bad – this book is not being written to lie.

As it happens, a pilot, off duty today, recounts what happened before I arrived. As I already said, the Sécurité Civile took the sensible precaution of forbidding journalists to fly during rescues: they complicate matters, add weight and cause delay. And further- more, they regard the dead, the injured, those in distress, with cold, even cynical eyes. A look devoid of love.

But the ones we have here are not used to obstacles being put in their way. They took over the helipad telephone and one made a call, outraged. Called who? Someone high up in the new government. A man reputed to be civilised but who immediately gave in to them: 'Monsieur, you have permission for anything you want!' So the photographer is flying during rescue operations.

I merely pose the question: even though the rescues have been difficult this morning, even though a rescuer died this week, even though a winch cable broke the other day in Switzerland killing two people, even though it is turbulent and flying conditions difficult and at times impossible, even though there are serious casualties and some deaths, they are taking him up. Is it right? Is it proper? Is it in the public interest? Is it what the public want?

Ought I to tell the truth about what I have witnessed? In this country, that claims to be free, how much is censored! Admittedly there is no censorship committee. No need. Self-censure is the most reliable form of censorship. It is an organ, nameless, faceless, formless, all powerful, driven, rightly or wrongly, through fear. That was the only form that existed in the USSR. Silent though it might be, it is more effective than the pleasant little practices of the *Ancien Régime*.[1] Individual liberty is superficial, whereas the press itself is free. The politician who decided to give these journalists permission to fly is hardly going to worry about the votes of a few climbers in danger, but when it comes to the press, that's a different matter. It's a curious sort of world!

Enough talk about journalists. When I arrived this morning I was told that there were probably two people dead, one on the Bonatti Pillar, near the Flammes de Pierre, the other on the Gervasutti Pillar of Mont Blanc du Tacul. Their bodies are still up there.

All rescues are postponed for the time being, because of the conditions. Despite the good forecast, the mountains are shrouded in cloud. And cloud is not the only problem, there are strong winds blowing at altitude.

The first call-out came at half past seven this morning. Two climbers had been caught yesterday by the bad weather on the Gervasutti Pillar. One of them was unable to carry on. His friend managed to get out and go for help. A flight was possible this morning but could not get close enough. A body was spotted hanging on a rope, upside down.

[1] My specialist subject.

Manu Cauchy is the duty doctor today. Seeing him, I got the impression that, during the week following Régis Michoux's death, his hair had greyed. Outwardly, everyone seems to be coping, but it's impossible to know what is really going on inside, one can only speak for oneself.

Manu hoped that the person glimpsed from the helicopter might not be dead, only hypothermic. The gendarmes are less hopeful. The body is near the top of the Pillar. The clouds closed in again before they could see any more. They're waiting for a clearing.

The helicopter then became involved in the other rescue. Red flares had been set off from the Flammes de Pierre, near the Dru. They were fired by Christophe Profit, who was climbing with a client when he realised there had been an accident on the Bonatti Pillar. The helicopter left, with the photographer on board. They saw one man, who was alive, and someone else, lying beside him. The machine climbed higher, with difficulty, making two or three passes along the wall. Michel Pierre, the pilot, was struggling to find enough power to fight against the wind. Then, just as it had on the Tacul, the weather closed in and put an end to the reconnaissance.

Everyone anxiously keeps an eye on the sky. Time is ticking by. At one o'clock the mountains are still shrouded in cloud. The Brévent is hidden in a thick grey mist. Only the Dôme and the Aiguille du Goûter are visible, against a background of blue sky. Everything else is hidden.

I talk to Bernard Stoop, an agreeable person, who is a mechanician with the Sécurité Civile. He asks me about *Nadir* and I tell him how even that had been painful at times to imagine and write, but now this present book... My voice breaks as I tell him about Dominic Green, I can barely finish my sentences when I speak of his family. We hardly mention Régis Michoux, whom he knew well and helped bring down. Bernard simply says: 'The atmosphere inside the aircraft was... I can't tell you... I can't talk about him.' And I don't want to hear either. We all feel as though we have been flayed alive this week. Bernard Stoop tells me how he discovered the mountains and found his calling in rescue. He, too, thinks I should go on with this book, which at times is proving a hard cross to bear.

There are also reports coming in of one, or maybe two bodies, very high, somewhere between Mont Blanc and Mont Blanc de Courmayeur. The Italians are dealing with it, doubtless with the same problems of cloud and wind.

There are times when love of the mountains seems questionable. Yet they have nothing to do with it.

The rescue on the Gervasutti Pillar takes place at midday. Very difficult. The man was dead. He was a Chilean. His companion, a Frenchman, who had left him the day before to go for help, had spent the night out in the snow at 4000 metres. Then, by a stroke of luck, when he was going the wrong way, had stumbled upon a tent on Col Maudit occupied by two Englishmen, with a mobile phone.

Michel Pierre gives details and recounts this morning's reconnaissance.

'The first time we went up, we got within five or ten metres of him. The wind was very strong. There were clouds swirling all around us. The second time, we actually found ourselves in them for four or five seconds. That wasn't much fun. You'd better not mention it… We're not allowed to fly in cloud. But we didn't do it on purpose… Oh why not! Yes, write it down. They have to know what it's really like at times.'

Then he moves on to the actual rescue.

'We took Henri, you know who I mean? The little old man with the walking stick…'

Have I only introduced Henri Cazemajor solely in connection with the route called *Henri, tu vas rire*? Henri Cazemajor is a handsome, athletic young man, with chestnut hair and blue eyes, who, according to the registry office, is fifty years old. However the records must be mistaken, since the person concerned has the appearance of being ten or even fifteen years younger. It is doubtless because they are jealous to think that Henri possesses an elixir for eternal youth that his mates tease him, but he gives as good as he gets.

Hearing himself called a little old man, Henri, who is busy typing up an accident report, indeed retorts with vigour.

'It had cleared up,' continues Michel Pierre, 'except for a lenticular cloud over Mont Blanc.'

'But fortunately there was Henri!' says Henri.

It appears in fact that it *was* fortunate they had Henri with them, because I gather, from a somewhat hesitant and interrupted account of the rescue, that it had been an extremely tricky operation.

Manu had been put down on the Col du Midi, with the Piguillem stretcher. This sort of manoeuvre is common when working at altitude, in order to lighten the aircraft.

'Then I winched Henri,' said the mechanician, 'on to the top of the Pillar, thirty or forty metres from the body. Closer was impossible.'

'Oh boy! Being winched down over the Gervasutti like that,' comments Cazemajor. 'Do that to Nicolas Hulot and he'd die of fright!'

'So Henri got to him by the pillar and prepared for the arrival of the doctor.'

Manu Cauchy was, in turn, lowered onto the pillar. He and Henri announced that they needed a while to get sorted. The helicopter went to collect Marc Ledwidge, the Canadian rescuer, who was to look after the other man. When the latter took off his gloves, those who saw his hands were appalled. They were frozen, cracked, white.

'His hands,' they told me, 'were like something out of a horror movie. They were so swollen that his wedding ring had disappeared into his flesh.'

He and Marc were dropped on the Col du Midi, because the weather was closing in again and Cazemajor and Cauchy wanted to be picked up quickly, before it became impossible.

The rope manoeuvres carried out on the Pillar seemed to have been rather more than tricky. They were described with so many asides that it gave food for thought.

'Ice everywhere! The 8-millimetre ropes were so iced up, they were as thick as my arm...'

The helicopter winched up the body, with the hope that there might still be some life. At the hospital a team was ready and waiting. When a person is hypothermic a defence mechanism within the body allows the surface to cool down, whilst conserving any remaining heat within the body core, to ensure the survival of the vital organs. Cases where the body temperature has fallen as low as 22° have been resuscitated. This one was 2°. No hope.

Then, having taken on more fuel, the helicopter went back up for Henri Cazemajor and Dr Cauchy, who had been left on the Col du Midi while Marc and the frostbite casualty were rapidly taken to the hospital.

Sometime later, Henri Cazemajor gave me some details about this unfortunate pair, telling me that the Chilean who died was well known. He had climbed Everest and was a real expert in the Andes. But he was carrying hardly any bivouac equipment in his rucksack.

'Well, what do you expect?' asked Cazemajor. 'A climber like that would have expected to do the route in a day. If I went climbing with Christophe Profit, I wouldn't go checking what he had in his rucksack!'

He and his friend had left on Thursday. The forecast was good and there was no mention of the bad weather that came in on Friday. When the Meteo gets it wrong, the consequences can be appalling.

Several months later, I met the Frenchman, Xavier, who told me about his partner and about what happened. Twenty-eight years old, Xavier had started climbing young, following in his father's footsteps, and got bitten. He had done many fine routes, mainly in the Mont Blanc area. He had hoped to become a mountain guide. The Gervasutti Pillar was well within his capability.

He had met his friend, Dagoberto Delgado, when he was working in Chile for two years. He was one of the best Chilean climbers. Forty-one years old, which is often an age of peak fitness and endurance, his list of climbs included the Kangshung Face of Everest, the first Chilean ascent of Cerro Torre and numerous big routes in the Andes, many of which were first ascents, comparable to the North Face of the Matterhorn. Passionate about mountains, but modest, he spent his time teaching young people to climb and was as loved as he was respected in his own country. There, his death was announced on the front page of the big daily newspapers, *La Tercera* and *El Mercurio*, whilst a whole inside page was devoted to him. This is how France felt, on the death, for example, of Lionel Terray.

I am saying this, not only to explain that he was perfectly capable of climbing the route, and much harder, but because the press and the media did not bother to investigate and spoke of 'a Chilean' wheeling out the same old clichés about 'reckless climbers'. And imagine the feelings of the young Frenchman who had just lost a greatly respected friend, when he saw from his hospital bed, news reports that talked about two 'foolhardy climbers'... one of whom was a Chilean, who died, whilst the other, a Frenchman was rescued. Well! The term 'foolhardy' is certainly uncalled for. And what pictures did they show? Those of tourists in shorts on the Mer de Glace! What sort of message does this send out and what must the public think? That the alpinists are tourists like these, who chance their luck attempting walls which really only the big stars can climb.

And it's not acceptable. Either one reports correctly, or one does not report. But such blatant misinformation, conveying false ideas, just cannot be tolerated.

'They are either heroes or reckless,' said Xavier Chappaz, president of the Compagnie des Guides de Chamonix: the two categories used by journalists who have no knowledge of the subject and who can't be bothered to try to understand it.

Here is the true story of what happened on that route. Two protagonists, two competent climbers, who weren't on their first route of the season. They knew what they were tackling and had climbed many of similar standard. The weather forecast was good when they left on Wednesday, July 30, simply stating 'conditions will be anticyclonic for the next five days', with, on the Friday 'some passing bands of cloud, which on the whole will not come to much'. No mention of the bad weather that they found themselves caught in. On the Wednesday evening, they talked to the warden of the Cosmiques Hut, who told them that the route had been done recently and that the latest forecast was good. Fit as they were, they expected to climb it in the day, but if it was still a bit snowed up, bivouac near the top and finish next day.

They started very early on the morning of Thursday, July 31, climbing the first pitch by the light of their head-torches. There were no signs heralding bad weather (mare's tails, lenticular clouds, etc.). It had frozen well during the night. On the other hand, they found all sections facing north still plastered, which slowed them down. They swung leads, in other words took it in turns as the lead climber. About seven or eight o'clock in the evening, having done the sixteen difficult pitches, the cloud came in and much to their surprise, it suddenly started to snow.

Certain that the deterioration in the weather could only be temporary, they decided to bivouac where they were, at the brèche, and finish the climb in the morning. It was a long hard night. It snowed continuously in big wet flakes, which got into everything. The storm intensified instead of stopping.

Their equipment? The standard sort of thing. Xavier had fleece trousers and jacket, plastic boots, balaclava, double gloves, over-trousers and a Gore-Tex jacket. Dagoberto had nearly the same, the difference being that his jacket wasn't Gore-Tex, but was fleece with a windproof internal membrane. Too confident in the Meteo's forecast perhaps? He must have got much wetter than his friend during their night's bivouac. They both did what anyone in that situation would do, getting up and moving about now and again, stamping their feet to warm them up, eating bars of chocolate.

The next morning, in the snow that was still falling, they did the ten-metre abseil that leads to the next part of the route. Dagoberto Delgado, tired, asked his friend to lead the rest of the climb. The pitches that followed, usually considered to be easy mixed climbing, had become very tricky because of the snow, and took time.

Xavier wasn't worried: 'We're getting there, we're near the top, I know the descent well,' he thought. The route finishes up a final grade IV arête, the same exit as for the Boccalatte Pillar. And there the two found themselves faced with Patagonia-like conditions. Everything was frozen, a carapace of ice covered the mountain. Xavier battled up this pitch, sometimes having to take off his gloves, but finally managed it, relieved: 'In two hours we're at the Col du Midi!' Even with a tight rope, Dagoberto took an hour and a half to do the pitch and arrived exhausted, his speech slurred, feeling nauseous, dizzy and becoming incoherent. It was then that things took a dramatic turn.

Xavier had a radio and tried to call the rescue but couldn't get a signal. The top was only fifty metres away but Delgado was in no state to continue. Only one solution remained: to secure him and descend rapidly for help.

So he made sure Delgado was well tied on and climbed up to the top, where he found himself in a complete whiteout. To begin with there were some old tracks. Then nothing, zero visibility, a white world. He knew he had to descend to the right and started down, but when visibility is that bad, it is sometimes difficult to know if you're going up or going down. Finding some seemingly fresh tracks, he thought perhaps they were his own. He had an altimeter, but considered it better not to get completely lost and risk falling, so he dug himself a snowhole for the night, having to take his gloves off to do so. He hoped that in the morning he would get down and his friend would be rescued. He dozed off, but waking he saw that the weather was still bad.

He set off again at first light. It was thick mist. He found a track which he followed and stumbled on a tent. He was on Col Maudit. In the tent two English climbers, some thirty years old, who took him in and helped him. They had a mobile telephone and the alarm was given. They put him in both their sleeping bags and made him some tea. Before parting, they swapped names and addresses, verbally, not having anything to write with, but they have slipped from his memory...

That was this sad and painful story.

In front of me a journalist is asking Cauchy to explain what happened.

'His mate,' explains Manu, 'left him at six yesterday evening. He was still all right, although already becoming a bit incoherent. The guy was probably standing up, but when he dropped asleep, fell upside down. He's dead... body temperature 2°! We found him jammed in a crevice, hanging... It was a hellish rescue. In a deep freeze. Rime and ice everywhere.'

'Shit!' says the photographer delicately.

Michel Pierre interrupts:

'You, stop surrounding us with corpses. The reason we are here is to save lives!'

'Contrary to what you hear,' the journalist retorted, 'we don't write about deaths. All that belongs to twenty years ago.'

'Oh, yeah!' retorts Michel Pierre. 'We've just had two TV crews here... They said exactly the same thing, and then they filmed nothing but the bags which we use to bring back bodies in.'

Virtuously hypocritical, the journalist denies it. Outright. Without having been there. He trots out the same patter he no doubt gives everybody:

'Deaths. That's not what interests us. No way! Besides, we were taken to court[2] and the public prosecutor found us guilty because

[2] Twenty years ago?

there is a legal article[3] prohibiting showing pictures of the dead, blood, violence, etc.[4] So you see...'

The other journalist agrees. But would either of them have been here if there had not been twelve bodies brought down between Sunday and Wednesday? Isn't it manna from heaven for them?

I don't think it's the result of public demand. The public can be fashioned and formed. It has in it the seeds of good and the seeds of bad. The bad cannot be denied. There were those who enjoyed the spectacle of capital punishment. There were our women during the Revolution, who settled down the whole day, knitting (*les tricoteuses*), to watch heads being cut off. It was a fringe of society, albeit an inglorious one. Now it is to that fringe that we are sacrificed, the lowest elements. And to satisfy them, claiming that they are 'the public', we are all subjected, first in the 19th century with the written word, now with horrendous pictures. The phenomenon has only got worse, thanks to the advances in technology.

What happens at the helipad is but an upsurge of this depravity. But since it is so, why not proclaim it as such?

The Dru is still in the cloud. The gendarmes are writing accident reports. 'This paperwork is crazy!' remarks Henri Cazemajor. 'It's sometimes more complicated to find their identities than it is to go and look for the guys!'

Although they can see he is busy at the computer, the journalists pester him about the Vuardes rescue. They offer him a coke, address him familiarly although yesterday they didn't know him, and ask stupid questions about what he is writing.

'But didn't he have a rope? *Bolts?*'

'Yes, but he still fell...'

'If that's how it is, better to stay in the bar,' sniggers the specialist of the text.

[3] I searched in vain for the relevant information. No one connected with the Law seems to have heard of it.
[4] When I bought the magazine in question – out of necessity – I opened it to see a wild face filled with fear, covered in blood, the body too. 'So there it is!' I thought. In fact it was the wrong article, but it still showed the blood-covered face of a child and bodies lying around, equally bloody. The article talked about cries of pain, shredded bodies, with limbs torn off etc. This was in Jerusalem. Doesn't the law also cover this type of news? As for the article about the mountains, it only showed the bloody arm of a corpse stuck in a crevasse and the photograph of a casualty and another body taken with a telephoto lens. We will see later why there was not another photo, as extraordinary as funereal. In the text, the Chilean's body was described as the 'prey' as it was attached to the winch, and the rescuers were called the '*guerilleros*' of the squad.

Apart from the two main rescues of the day, there are some minor ones; to which not much attention is paid, so great is the concern about those on the Dru. At one point, there are two casualties waiting and an ambulance arrives. But they are not allowed to be put in the same one... A second has to be called.

Bernier says that these rules drive him crazy! And no wonder the Social Security is in deficit, when things like this happen. Someone suggests:

'We could call a taxi for the other one! It would be cheaper.'

Manu intervenes:

'Yes, but that wouldn't work because it wouldn't be *reimbursed*.'

Has no administration ever thought, whilst working out ever more complicated rules, that perfection is the enemy of what works – simplicity?

Half past six. The Dru begins to clear. The helicopter winch is tested. The one that broke in Leysin weighs heavily on everyone's minds.

The wind blowing at altitude is a fierce north-westerly, its violence indicated by the swirling clouds.

Henri is pessimistic:

'We won't be going tonight. Not with this wind...'

He telephones the PG:

'Yes!... At least try, to keep their spirits up, and show that we haven't forgotten them. If not we'll have to leave it and get prepared to go tomorrow morning, early.'

I think about the man waiting. At the first attempt this morning, they saw him with his partner stretched out. They are in a niche – sheltered from stonefall – a bit to the side of the route.

The winch tests are finished. They are going to have another go. The journalists aren't joining. It's dangerous enough without their added weight which is considerable.

Dragon takes off. In the chalet, there is a picture on the computer screen, annotated by some anonymous artist, showing a climber on what looks like a moraine, with the caption 'Henri Cazemajor: Grandad of the glaciers'. But the helicopter comes back, without having been able to do anything.

I ask Bernier :

'The person you saw this morning, was he definitely alive?'

'Definitely alive?' he replies, doubtfully. 'Difficult to say...' He gestured with his arm... 'If he's already spent one night beside his dead friend... and if he has to spend another...?'

At half past seven, the helicopter has to go out again for a rescue on the Mer de Glace. A forty-year-old gentleman, with a painful back, near the ladders at Montenvers. The pilot calls to Henri:

'This one's yours! We've to go and fetch a forty-year-old grandad!'

In two trips they bring back a group of people, including the grandad, several little ladies and even a real climber, with crampons on his rucksack. He wasn't with the others but had gone to their assistance when he saw them in difficulty, and he'd been brought down with the rest of them. As I am about to go home, I offer him a lift to Chamonix to save him the walk. The grandad and his little ladies will no doubt go in an ambulance and a taxi.

As I walk over to my car with the climber, he says:

'My dream would be to spend a day at the helipad, to watch them working.'

'Well, you'll envy me! I'm spending the summer there!'

'What?'

'I'm writing a book about the rescue season.'

He stops suddenly and asks:

'What's your name?'

'Anne Sauvy.'

'Ah! You are *the* Anne Sauvy!'

He says this as if he was saying: *the* Billy the Kid or *the* Calamity Jane! How flattering…

In the evening, as John and I are eating, the Dru seems to be clearing. I ring to ask. A third attempt is being prepared. I drag John along to the helipad. It is nine o'clock. Bernier puts on a fleece jacket under his rescue suit in case he has to spend the night with the casualty. The light is fading and it is unlikely he could be brought down, even if they reach him. The helicopter takes off. Everyone is tense. Captain Gin and Marc Ledwidge are here as well. The mountain is almost clear but flying conditions are still bad.

The helicopter comes back. They weren't able to do anything.

'Another half hour of daylight and we'd have cracked it!' Bernier tells me.

We are all distressed by what is happening up there. A fourth attempt is planned for six o'clock tomorrow morning. I will be here. This rescue is haunting me.

We all leave the helipad in the dark, in a procession of cars and headlights.

Despite taking a pill, I hardly sleep. Around half past three I see the sky covered with stars. It will be fine for the morning.

Sunday, August 3

At four o'clock, Bernard Stoop, mechanician for this rescue, got up and went to the window. It was still completely dark, but there were stars. Going back to bed, he lay thinking about the unknown person up there, in distress, looking at the same stars, and doubtless the lights of the valley, a world so near and yet so far away.

As for myself, I had hardly slept. All were keyed up for what was to come. I got up at quarter past five to see that the clouds had come back in force. Despair.

About six, I am at the helipad and the rescue is on. The cloud level has dropped, and there is no wind.

I arrive as the helicopter is about to leave. The pilot today is Gilles Bidon, the mechanician is Bernard Stoop, the rescuer Olivier Fernandez.

And the photographer, on board too. He has permission. We're all upset about it, but that's the way it is. Then suddenly, just as they are about to take off, he gets out and the aircraft leaves without him!

I didn't learn what had happened until later. At six o'clock, worried about the photographer's prying eyes, Jean-Claude Gin telephoned headquarters and said:

'Stop the journalist from going.'

'Captain', replied Pierre Faussurier, 'he must already be in the helicopter. Only you can stop him.'

So he called the pilot up on the radio, and said to him:

'The photographer doesn't go, for security reasons.'

It was the right thing, as we would soon appreciate.

Olivier Fernandez alone carries out the rescue operation. He is winched down a few metres from the wall and he sends the casualty off, who is flown to the emergency helipad at the hospital. Then they return for Olivier and the body.

And it turns out to be a girl.

Several days ago, my morale cracked and now, this time, I start to crack physically. I can't cope any more. I just get home in time to be sick and empty myself from all ends, shivering, lie down, ill. Even if I can force my mind to continue with this task I have set myself, my whole body seems to revolt and goes on doing so for days. But I must see it through.

23

ELENA

So it was a girl that they brought down from the Bonatti Pillar. And the man who had waited beside her body, for two nights and one day, was her fiancé.

She was called Elena. He was called Alexei. They were Russian. They were to be married in September.

They had decided to spend the summer in the Alps and do two particular routes: Mont Blanc, for its height and prestige, and the Bonatti Pillar, because of its elegance and history.

They had found Mont Blanc easy, but symbolic. As for the Bonatti, although a much more technical, difficult and committing route, their standard of climbing fully justified tackling it. Alexei had been dreaming of doing the Bonatti for twenty years, since first wanting to become a mountaineer as an adolescent, but at a time when the idea of climbing in the West was unthinkable. Twenty years to imagine this granite shaft, thrusting towards the sky, in a country beyond his reach. In the meantime, he did what was permitted – climbing in the Caucasus in a regime of rigidly imposed rules, check-in and check-out times, with nobody allowed to excel, each climber progressing at the same pace as the other – neither brilliant nor bad. Then, the Wall came down, and he could go to the Dolomites and the Verdon. Finally with Elena to Chamonix, to realise his lifelong dream.

They left for the Dru quite confident, with supplies for five days, which would allow them to wait for good weather if necessary and enjoy the mountains. In fact, after leaving the Charpoua on the first day, they made a route-finding error, and, not being in any hurry, had decided to come back, bivvy on the Flammes de Pierre and set off next morning, getting it right this time. On such things does life hang: the exact hour and place where one is at a given moment in the strange game of destiny.

The second day, they made good progress, got quite high and found, close to the route, a good bivvy located under an overhang and consequently protected from any stonefall coming from above. From this niche Alexei could descend on the rope to a patch of snow and replenish their water supplies. Sheltered, they held all the aces, perched almost in the sky, the valley deep below their feet, dark green, with its noise and its hubbub, its doubts and its constraints, but all that seemed far away. Attached to the side of the Aiguille, safely sheltered, they prepared for a beautiful night out in the mountains. One has to have experienced it to understand how they felt. Imagine being in an eyrie, lofty and remote, with only the basics, where the world is reduced to what it is, tiny, whilst one has for neighbours the essences and the stars. That is what they had. And nothing should have happened to them. Not there.

Nothing except the unforseeable. And the unforseeable was a gigantic rockfall, thirty metres to the side of them. So huge, so immense, that the rocks bounced off the slabs all around them, ricocheted and hit their shelter. The wall behind them was scarred with their impact, the ledge where they were covered with dust. They were hit, it was inevitable. A stone shattered Alexei's left shoulder, another broke his right wrist. Elena seemed to have been spared. She complained only of a blow in the back, but once the rock bombardment was over, she busied herself dressing Alexei's wounds, supporting and bandaging his shoulder. Then suddenly she felt faint, lost consciousness and collapsed, very pale, her big blue eyes wide open, a strange rasping in her throat.

In this further misfortune, Alexei, not knowing what was wrong, tried to help her, but, hindered by his injuries, it took him forty seconds, maybe fifty, to move across to her, lean over, give her artificial respiration, try to save her. For a quarter of an hour, twenty minutes, he tried, but he could feel that, despite all his efforts, Elena's lips were becoming cold, that in his arms she had ceased to live, and he gave up his hopeless battle against death.

He sat beside her, not much better off than she, injured as he was, with no way of alerting the rescue. What must his terrible watch have been? Night, day, night again…

Yet when one speaks to someone of such things, even if he recounts what happened, one cannot push further, to probe into his memories, cries, tears, despair, things that are too secret, the words, perhaps, he addressed to Elena. The joy of the route, the joy of their forthcoming marriage, all suddenly snuffed out. And he was left there, faced with this loss, faced with this frail lifeless body, faced with his shattered love, faced with a future no more, faced with his probable death beside her.

The night passed. In the morning, Alexei saw climbers emerging on the Flammes de Pierre, quite a long way away, but within earshot. He shouted to them.

The person he saw was Christophe Profit, guiding a client. But there was too much wind to hear properly. However, Christophe could hear Alexei's voice, pinpointed his location and was able to make out one phrase that he was shouting in English:

'My friend is dead!'

So he set off red flares as a signal. Then himself went back down because the whole wall seemed dangerous and unstable after the rockfall, and told the PGHM what he knew of the situation.

This was on the morning of Saturday, August 2. And all that day, the helicopter was unable to reach the injured man.

The first flight was at twenty past nine, after the reconnaissance flight to the Gervasutti Pillar. The rescuer, Pierre Bernier, spotted them: 'One man sitting down, who had weakly moved an arm, and a body stretched out at his side.' The magazine photographer who had just obtained permission to fly, using the means which I have already described, was in the aircraft and took a photograph with his telephoto lens: probably a dead body, and an injured man who would perhaps soon be dead himself. The clouds and wind made flying conditions at altitude very difficult. However a little later, and at some risk, it had proved possible to bring down the dead man and the casualty from the Gervasutti Pillar. As for the Dru, there were two other attempts to fly up, but nightfall put an end to any further hope of rescue. Alexei spent his second night at the bivouac. He was no longer feeling well.

So it was on Sunday morning, with a clear sky and a dropping wind that the rescue was carried out. Only three went, lightweight. At the last moment, Jean-Claude Gin had made the inspired decision to forbid the photographer, already in the aircraft, to fly. Gilles Bidon, the pilot, and Bernard Stoop the mechanician had arrived together. Olivier Fernandez was the rescuer.

Bernard Stoop: 'I am very glad to see it's Olivier who will be with us. Because I know that the operation is going to be tricky and technical, and it is important to have someone equal to the task and with whom we have a good rapport. I don't show my feelings, but I am happy.'

Olivier: 'It isn't too windy. The helicopter climbs slowly through the morning mist. I know that behind the clouds the Drus will be in sunshine. I sense it, I hope it's so.

'Wisps of mist slide across the plexiglass of the cockpit, the turbine is humming, the rotor blades cut the sun into thin slices. *Dragon* circles above the Dru Glacier, hugging the contours, in search of rising air to help it climb towards the wall. We don't have much fuel, just 150 litres.

'In the cabin, it's quiet, concentrating. Our eyes are already peering upwards. Each runs through the expected scenario in his mind. We know there's one dead person. That's all.

'The Flammes de Pierre pass beneath the little wheels of the helicopter. The summit of the Dru is well in the sun, in front of us. But a huge cloud hides us from the valley, a natural screen shielding us from prying eyes. The setting is almost intimate.

'In the midst of this great expanse of red granite, we spot the ledge, below the overhang, the injured man moving slightly, the body stretched out beside him. The helicopter turns away for a moment while we talk, working out what we're going to do.'

Bernard: 'I think it was Gilles who saw them first. We climb a little higher. Gilles flies past and judges the power; the conditions are favourable and we are not too heavy. We work back slowly, level with the ledge and clearly see the man who gestures to us. As we approach, the downdraught of the aircraft blows away the anorak of the person lying down, revealing the face of a young woman.

'We make a rapid assessment of the place and situation: it's simple, we have to stick as close as possible to the face, twenty-five to thirty metres above the ledge to be able to winch and, because of the overhang, there promises to be a little exercise in penduluming for Olivier to reach it. Once down, Olivier will despatch us the injured person, who we'll take straight to the hospital, whilst he will prepare the second person.

'Already Gilles is moving a bit away from the wall, climbing. I get ready to winch, automatically reciting my actions, whilst guiding Gilles into position thirty metres above the ledge. Then I attach Olivier.'

Olivier: 'O.K., there they are! I'm about to go down on the cable ...
Get closer, Gilles, start penduluming and if I manage to grab a
bit of their rope I can pull across to them. Is that all right with
you?'

'Fine with me!' replies Bernard

'He settles himself well in his seat, clips on his leash and puts
on his leather gloves.'

'O.K. my end!' Gilles calls.

'Good! Let's go!

'The side door of the helicopter opens. The aircraft starts hovering. The trap door swings down and, with a smile from Bernard,
I let myself be lowered into space, like a diver plunging into the
water, losing all points of direction.

'I swing through the moving air that separates me from the
mountain, towards people I don't know, towards wounded beings,
towards an equation with several unknowns.'

Bernard: 'The tips of the rotor blades are two or three metres from
the rock. Because of the overhang, I can't see the ledge to put
Olivier down, so he signals me when at the right height. I stop
the winch and begin shaking the cable to induce a swinging movement. At this point, Olivier must be about five metres from the
ledge. The pendulum gradually builds up, although the length of
the cable and the wind from the rotors don't help much.'

Olivier: 'The cable starts to swing... When I am almost within
reach of the man, I signal him to throw his rope. He throws it once
and misses... Twice... Three times... Four times... Finally, at the
fifth attempt, I manage to catch hold and haul myself onto the
ledge.

'The look in the man's eyes is chilling, empty, with no hint of
warmth, or hope, or fear. Immense eyes turned to me, to the sky.

'The look of a soul drowned in grief, destroyed by the waiting.
It's two days he's been there. His helmet is askew across his face.
If we hadn't been able to come, he wouldn't have lasted much
longer.

'On the ledge, we are wrapped in silence. I know the person
on my right is dead.

'Dead, because the man, a Russian, tells me in good English
that it was his girlfriend who is lying there, beside us.

'He tells me a little about their climbing plans, their life, their forthcoming marriage. He's shaking, he's suffering, he's cold. His shoulder crushed by rocks, his wrist broken and a fractured skull. But he will survive...

'*Dragon* slides smoothly away to the right, disappearing down towards Chamonix and the helipad to pick up more fuel.'

Bernard: 'In a brief radio call, Olivier informs us all's O.K. A few minutes later, he calls again: he's ready.

'Then everything happens rapidly. Gilles and I are at the 'get set'. I manage to swing the wire in to reach Olivier and a few moments later, the survivor is winched up and hauled aboard. His arm injured, I seat him just on the edge of the trap door without unhooking him. During the winching operation, Olivier took the precaution of tensioning the casualty with a rope, in order to gradually bring him directly below the winch, without swinging. Gilles reports back to base and is already diving towards the valley. The climber utters some words that I do not understand. 'It'll be all right!' I tell him, wanting to reassure him. It's not much, but what else could I say? In fact there's really nothing to say. This guy is at the end of his tether. His dazed face and drawn features reflect the physical and mental suffering he has endured and is still enduring. You could see it in his eyes. *No comment*, as the English say. It's faster descending than climbing and it only takes a few minutes to reach the hospital where an emergency team is already waiting.'

Olivier: 'On the ledge, alone, I gaze at the young woman. Her features are very delicate. Her hands are slender, she's slim, well-dressed, youthful, unmarked by the accident. Her lovely curly fair hair cascades over her shoulders under her helmet. Her splendid blue eyes are wide open, expressive. Delicate, she seems like a ray of beauty amidst all this emptiness.

'I know she's called Elena. I lean over to secure her, to get her ready, before she's lifted off this uncomfortable bed of rock. Her skin, which I brushed while tying the rope, her skin is soft, cold, too cold. To attach her, I support her by each wrist, ankles and neck. So she will be removed gently.

'In order to spend the least time possible on this ledge exposed to stonefall, I am going to leave her on the end of a sixty-metre rope.

'The helicopter returns, having left Alexei at the hospital. Bernard sends down the cable and hauls me into the aircraft. I ask him to be gentle when lifting this young woman whom we are going to take back down to the valley with us.

'The machine climbs, the rope uncoils and tightens. The cabin is hushed. The body leaves the ledge, slides into the air. It glides as though guided by an invisible hand, gently.

'Sixty metres below us, the rope describes an arc. I lean my head through the trap door. The sun is shining. The wind whips our faces. With reddened eyes and racing pulses, Bernard and I watch.

'The sight is dazzling, surreal. A beautiful woman flying and dancing. Our hearts share emotions of pain and tenderness while a ballet unfolds. The body miraculously comes to life, moves, rocked by the currents, majestically, with subtle gestures. And beneath this body as it dances, unrolls fabulous scenery, glaciers, screes, moraines. The light is sublime. A few clouds make this vision yet more noble. The wisps part before her. We gaze with wonder, Bernard and I, witnessing an unreal spectacle.

'For the two or three minutes it takes us to descend, we feel Elena alive, dancing in the air with a dazzling grace. We no longer know where reality begins and ends. These are moments of tenderness.

'Arriving above the Mer de Glace, where we will be able to put the body down, we instruct Gilles, as though it were a living person:

'"Carefully, Gilles! Gently! Come down gently! Be careful with her ..."

'Gilles lifts the nose of the aircraft up, holds it steady, and carefully puts the body down on the smooth, white flawless ice. Then we land beside her.

'"No question of using the basket," says Bernard. "She comes inside!"

'I concur, get out, take Elena round the waist, then lay her down in the cabin on the aluminium floor and gaze at her. I am uncertain, I no longer know if she is really dead or I am dreaming, I don't know if we should have watched the beauty of that descent as presented to us to admire. My thoughts seem to be in a vacuum. I am gripped by coldness. The helicopter takes off and we head towards the helipad. Outside, the sun is shining, bathing us in sunlight.

'I will never forget the expression on her face, her gracefulness, the mysterious dance choreographed by wind and death.

'I can still see in my mind, the sparkling colours of that summer morning, the ethereal scene of effortless grace and beauty which unfolded before us. I remain sure that there was a message to be read, a significant moment when death and its horror became inextricably linked with the majesty of that move through the air, with its purity and elegance.

'I will continue doing this work because it provides moments of such contradiction, moments that make me realise that we will never know all the secrets that life and destiny hold.

'I keep in memory that piercing look in Elena's blue eyes, which seemed to cross the divide between us and thank us for coming for the man she loved and by whose side she had laid down, for ever.

'I keep in memory the image of that body which seemed to live, free from all the oppressive constraints of our world, that body which was simply passing, but which in death, for the space of a moment, wanted to appear in its full beauty, before leaving us for ever.'

Elena...

Those who saw her will never forget the dead girl floating through space, between heaven and earth, her big blue eyes staring into infinity, and who seemed to come back to life through some mysterious grace.

There will have been no material record of this immaterial descent. And it is better so.

We learned later that Elena had died of internal bleeding. We saw photos of her, alive and happy. On the way up to the hut. On a trip with friends, in the Moscow countryside, where she had adorned her hair with a crown of pink thistles and May blossom, which suited the pure beauty of the young fairy she was.

Elena will always live in our memories.

24

DANGER AND DEATH

Why? Why death? And why death in the mountains? That of Régis Michoux, rescuer who had saved so many lives at risk to his own? That of Dominic who wanted to devote his life to the peaks he so loved? That of Elena who came to discover the Alps, just before her marriage? Those of other victims…

It is particularly difficult to evoke death in a period when everything is done to make it a taboo subject, ultimate absurdity since it is the only certain thing that faces every living creature.

No past civilisation, however arrogant, has ever had the insane and sterile audacity to banish the notion of death, or even the final act of respect due to earthly remains. Everywhere, always, death has been the object of customs and rites. But in our present society, it is not even thought of as natural. It is brushed away, which only increases the disarray when it happens.

Since the 18th century, the philosophers, whom we are taught to revere, imposed ideas about progress and happiness. Since progress supposedly leads to happiness, attention has shifted from the essential, the human condition (*la condition humaine*). Technical progress *has* been achieved, but at what price, and has it brought happiness? As for moral progress, it did not follow, quite the opposite. And the minds of men, at a loss and without an answer, do not know what to turn to, or where to find the way. To avoid despair, the easiest course has been to erase death, in every way possible. To deny, to forget, to remove, to wipe out the only certainty each one of us has: that of dying. As if to exorcise it.

Little ritual today. No more black hangings on house doors. The yellowy or grey-coloured funeral cars of the undertakers are funereal in name only.

Often there is no ceremony: bodies are put in the ground or cremated and it's done without ever wearing the apparel of mourning to show grief.

Everything is devised to circumvent this problem of death. Medical progress is constantly referred to, as though preparing our immortality! But much other behaviour appears to have the same aim. Which makes one wonder what underlies the abolition of the death penalty, knowing without admitting it, that in certain cases of second offenders it will end in yet further deaths. Perhaps this suppression has its source in the collective subconscious which is trying to deny that death exists? Isn't forbidding it, as in capital punishment, giving the impression that little by little the phenomenon is being abolished?

The Catholic Church has itself followed the trend, for the appropriate rituals are no longer considered essential, which is staggering. The Extreme Unction that prepared for the last passage has been replaced by a 'sacrament of the sick', soothing, softening, comforting.

Nevertheless in certain hospitals one discovers, as though it were a novelty, 'accompanying the dying' which has always existed and been of good comfort.

Long gone is the time when the epitaph 'I was what you are, you will be what I am' was used as a stark reminder to the living. Gone is the time of the *Artes moriendi* (the art of dying), widely used booklets, whose object was to prepare for death, warning the dying to beware of various temptations, precisely described. No one knows the *Litanies for a Good Death,* a forgotten literary masterpiece that must have greatly consoled many people. A 'good death' was prepared from childhood. Cemeteries were at the heart of towns and villages, not relegated to the sad outskirts. Death was in some measure a part of life.

It is true that today death is better controlled – that people thought about it more in times when infant mortality was greater, when pandemics, like the plague, threatened everyone, when medicine was more or less ineffective. It is still as much there, but it has become the adversary, a matter for the medical field, as though it were a scientific phenomenon that has not yet been mastered. It is kept at bay as much as possible from the living, from children. Life prolonged, hope. Yet we are shown in photos, films, television, everywhere, murders, wars, accidents, as if they were fiction to distract and which certainly only apply to others.

And, when death does happen, we are completely thrown

by the manifestation of its power as though it were something scandalous.

How then speak of death today? Of death in the mountains? It rouses indignation, all the more for appearing avoidable. All that is needed is not to go there! For the layman, it seems crazy to run a risk that is not necessary. And the initiated are no less shaken since death in the mountains is rare and all the many precautions that are taken are precisely to avoid it. The mountains seem more like a place where life triumphs, where one finds strength, fulfilment, effort rewarded, a place of flowering, of youthfulness, of joy, of everything that death is not.

And its penalty is instant. The smoker knows the inherent risks for a future that he chooses to ignore. Death in the mountains hits by its very suddenness. It strikes those who are so alive. Which is why it seems so powerful and terrible. How can so much beauty, so much grandeur suddenly lurch into grief?

But isn't the taste for risk, for life ventured and regained part of the pleasure of climbing in the high mountains? That is sometimes claimed, but it is not basic. What is true nevertheless, is that when in a terrain that involves danger you are at least spared other fears… Who worries about cancer, coronaries, embolisms, car accidents, old age, Alzheimer's, when committed on a route? Then, every moment is lived for itself. Everything takes on its real value away from so many other threats. Which is not irrelevant. You live for the moment, conscious of your fragility and stripped bare of the superfluous.

If you die in the mountains, it is nearly always quick. Anyone who has had a fall stopped knows how fast and quick it is: the attempt to stop oneself, successful or not, living the instant.

Suddenly, the snow collapsed from beneath my feet and my hands. An awful fear, quick as lightning, and instantaneously, an incredible calm; a presence of mind, an astonishing lucidity… I made a desperate effort not to topple over backwards; at the same time, I thrust my hands into fresh snow, and did my best to keep my crampons parallel to the slope. But they skidded on the ice and, first one, then the other, my feet shot off. At that precise moment, I felt the rope bite into my skin. 'Paul has been pulled off with the shock,' I thought, 'it will all happen very quickly now.' Already I had got purchase with my feet again. Stupor. The rope remained tight around my waist… At first astonishment gained the upper hand, then a sort of physical joy, quite outside me, like a ray of sunshine on my skin, then a huge fear. Finally I lift my head. Fallet smiles. Me too. In short, it is not so difficult to die: we had done the hardest part.[1]

Admittedly, if man were immortal but could be killed in the mountains, to approach them would certainly be blameworthy. That is not so. Man is mortal. And this risk is not taken just to 'go up and come down'. It gives the entry into a world which is different from that below, a true world, a simple world, where only basics matter – a mouthful of water, a piece of bread, a halt, a smile. All of which puts everything into its proper perspective and renews the taste for life.

What is this world for which we should give up the magic of the mountains? Adverts, beeps, zips, clips, racists and anti-racists, Serbo-Croatian conflicts, druggies, electronic drills, fundamentalists, terrorists, price of petrol, shopping trolleys, vandals, strikes, mad cows, bar codes, credit cards, pollutants and environmentalists, weed killers, tribal wars, DSS, PAY, SIMS, ID, IDS, AIDS, Footsie One Hundred, Opinion Polls – Isn't this, more or less, what the present-day society has to offer us?

Those who choose effort, cold, burning sunshine, remoteness, bracing air, distant horizons, snow studded with sequins, the sunbeam on a sérac seemingly giving birth to an emerald, the serrated ice, the light and the azure – if they die for their passion, they died not for nothing, however tragic and distressing their death may be. For they are part of those through whom mankind keeps its grandeur.

[1] Robert Tézenas du Montcel *Ce Monde qui n'est pas le nôtre*, Gallimard, 1966.

PART THREE

25

IT GOES ON

Sunday, August 3

Having left the helipad ill in the morning, I went back in the evening to get my computer. On arriving, I saw a poor man, tired and heavily laden, leaving on foot. Robert Petit-Prestoud said he thought was a Pole, who had just been brought down from Mont Blanc. Exhausted myself, I had all the more pity for those in a similar state, and I went to get my car to catch him up, two or three hundred metres further on, bent under his rucksack and give him a lift.

He was in fact a Slovak, a bit surprised to be helped like that, voluntarily, or perhaps a little worried that he would have a bill to settle at the end, but finally so pleased to put his rucksack in the boot and be driven that he did not need persuading. He spoke neither French nor English and we were unable to exchange a single sentence. He showed me where to go with gestures and must have found it strange, this country where, bingo, he is brought down by helicopter, bingo, a little lady acts as chauffeur and saves him a good five kilometre walk along a sun-baked road. Poor chap, he was going almost as far as Les Bossons and would have been shattered ... On arrival, by dint of signs, he gave me to understand he wanted my name and address. It was to send me once back home, a touching letter of thanks which he must have asked someone to translate. His name was Peter Rehak and he lived in Trnava.

On getting back to the helipad, I learnt most of what had happened. He had done Mont Blanc, badly equipped like people from the Eastern Bloc generally are. No point in blaming them for not having our smart climbing suits and our super-boots. He certainly didn't. He had black rubberised boots, like postmen must have worn at the beginning of the century, poor quality trousers, a big sweater, a junk store anorak, a karrimat rolled up on his rucksack and crampons like those of the 1930s, perhaps, with points only a centimetre long and leather straps.

So, he had done Mont Blanc and, whilst traversing towards Mont Maudit, one of his crampons lost a screw and came off. Two good Samaritans took him on their rope, but realised that there was a risk of all becoming goners. The helicopter was called. True, the Slovak had nothing wrong with him. But was it not better to take him off alive than dead a little later? Indeed, it is a good thing that when necessary the rescue can take this preventive sort of action.

At the helipad, the Slovak had refused to let them call a taxi. He had been lucky to find me to give him a lift.

The other rescues of the day were odds and ends, if one may call them that: sprains, sunstroke, altitude sickness, blisters, cramps, fractures; to walkers, climbers, and parapenters, French, Italian and a Chinese. Can't find out about everything.

Monday, August 4
Weather, fine but heavy, less good than forecast. Busy in the morning, and passing by the PGHM about midday, I ask:

'Were they flying this morning?'

'Yes! They were busy!'

'Sprains?'

'Oh! No! A major fall on Mont Maudit with one dead and another with multiple injuries, and three people have disappeared on Les Courtes and can't be found.'

'On which route?'

'The traverse – but there are no signs of a fall anywhere?'

My God. It just goes on and on.

I go home. We have three English students for lunch. Climbers in perfect health! It is comforting to see them! Young, alive, happy. Julian Cartwright, a red-head I don't know and the rasta blond, pretty dirty, pretty astonishing, who had played a Beethoven Sonata the other day.[1] The red head and the rasta have just done the Central Pillar of Frêney. Their faces are gaunt with the effort but their eyes are still full of the sky, still full of a light from another world, eyes which justify everything there is about the mountains.

[1] Jamie Fisher and Simon Milward. Jamie was later to die in tragic circumstances on Les Droites (see Jamie Andrew *Life and Limb*, Portrait 2004). As mentioned elsewhere Julian Cartwright also died in a climbing accident (in 2004).

They left on Wednesday, with a good forecast, bivouacked that evening and started to fight for it on Thursday, getting caught in serious bad weather, not forecast by the Meteo, in the same evening that it overtook Dagoberto Delgado on the Gervasutti Pillar, but also took the lives of a German and four Spaniards, who had been with them in the hut.[2] They bivouacked again for a second night, highly uncomfortable since the rope, tied to pegs above them, channelled the snow pouring down the face right into their duvets. Soaked through, they were caught in Friday's storm at the top of the Chandelle. On Saturday they set off again with difficulty, wet, freezing, but finished their route.

There they are, very much alive, sitting opposite me. The pleasure they are radiating is witness to the fact that real happiness is earned at the price of physical effort, determination, sodden and freezing duvets, and sometimes danger.

In the afternoon at the helipad there is much concern over the climbers missing on Les Courtes. They are assumed to be dead since they were expected back the day before and had not arrived. By dint of patient investigation, information starts coming in. They were seen on the route. A guide found a crampon under the Col des Cristaux, therefore after the traverse. Various reconnaisances brought no further clues. But Alain Iglesis, who is on duty and took part in the searches, with five other rescuers, thinks that they must be in the big crevasse at the bottom of the Col des Cristaux, on the Talèfre side. He describes it to me. It's enormous, the first snow bridge is twenty-five metres down but there is nothing to be seen on it. Impossible to descend into it today with the heat and all the stones and snow slides which might fall. Tomorrow morning, at dawn? If so, they'd have to go through the snow bridge at the only point where there is a hole. But it's not even certain that they will be there.

'And perhaps they will never be found,' he sighs.

Another rescue. On Mont Maudit, at exactly the same spot as this morning.

'It's bizarre,' remarks someone, 'sometimes it's the Tacul, sometimes it's the Maudit.'

Be that as it may, in the morning, it had been serious. A rope

---

[2] Those incidents were dealt with by the Italian rescuers as the climbs were on their side of the range.

had fallen. An Irishman was dead; his French friend was seriously injured, with a fractured skull.

The helicopter leaves with Dr Lecoq. And, phew, comes back with two lads who only have grazes, are fine, can walk, but their faces are a horror, covered in blood. They are Czech. François Lecoq takes them to sit down near the equipment store. There is still a cameraman. I hadn't spotted that one. He films their heads close-up. I'm seething, but I am wrong. François says:

'That one's OK! He only wants successful rescues. He's French but working for Pioneer Productions, an English set-up, who do work for the Discovery Channel, which is American. And he has been asked to do the opposite to the others: to show the use of rescue.'

The three of us chat. I ask François Lecoq if, all the same, this season isn't worse than the others. He thinks not, that each year here there are fifty deaths, sixty at most, of which thirty or forty in summer, and that there will be this year roughly the same number, but that it is concentrated in one week, which is what is shaking us all. He says that in the end, it's a matter of statistics. One death, approximately, for 6000 climbers but it is easier to calculate the figure for skiers, because of ski passes...

As it's a matter of statistics, let's talk statistics. How easy to pick on the deaths in the range! Although they only represent a tiny proportion of the thousands, the hundreds of thousands, of those walking the footpaths, the mountains routes, and the ski runs.

But why is nothing ever said about of the 650 drownings, or the 9000 French road deaths amongst whom are many children.[3] Then there is the 10,000 deaths a year due to infections contracted in hospital, the 12,000 suicides, and the 65,000 smokers' deaths. The latter is talked about a bit. But not a lot! Because tobacco brings the State fifty-four billion francs a year in tax.

Then there is AIDS – not a pleasant way die.[4] But it has been inculcated into the minds of the public, that it is tragic and noble form of death whereas it considered absurd and even criminal to be killed in the mountains. Make sense of that if you can. The world is mad.

---

[3] Since 1997 the number of road deaths in France has considerably decreased.

[4] The figures for this are: 2989 deaths, in France, prior to 1989. For the years 1989-96, a period of eight years: 25,398 deaths, which is an average of 3175 a year (figures from the Institut National d'Etudes Démographiques). Twenty times less than the number of deaths attributed to tobacco. Is that proportion respected? Does the media talk twenty times more about tobacco than AIDS?

I have to go to the hospital, to say goodbye to the Guiverecs. Since I am going there, I ask Alain Iglesis who, a minute ago was holding the passport of one of the two Czechs which needed to be returned, if I couldn't take it. He only has that of the one called Kunicki, the other being Tuma, and he gives me a rucksack lid, which has the passport in it, saying that if I could get their addresses for the accident report, it would save time.

En route for the hospital. Traffic jams. At reception, they have no record of Kunicki or Tuma, and I am sent to emergency. At the reception there a none too pleasant woman tells me that I must wait.

Since waiting is not all I've got to do, I go up to see the Guiverecs. There, I am welcomed with a smile. Madame Guiverec has a lovely smile. I am so happy she did not lose her husband! I am so glad that he is there, on the road to recovery! As on each visit, I give them news of the latest rescues, not brilliant today, the Maudit, the Courtes, the Maudit again, plus an Englishman who has been on the Frendo Spur for three days and there is no news of. Even for an English climber that's a long time.

It matters little what I write on these pages. I know sometimes it's about horrible things. But I write because I need to get it out of my system, like Olivier Fernandez the other day, needed to talk about the ice axe in the head.

Once again, I ask myself: what will I make of this book? How to do it? No easy answer comes.

A long time ago, I read a work by Georges Sonnier who described an accident he had witnessed. It was terrible. What I am writing must sometimes be worse. I am being drawn into talk of death and suffering as they really are, not about those of the drab funeral cars. Our society prefers not to know about the reality. And, when pictures of horror are shown in magazines or on television, one has the impression that they are made to seem as though they were fictional, nothing to do with those comfortably installed in their armchairs, but something that happens to others. They seem ultimately have no other goal than engendering in all of us a false sense of well being and security. But unfortunately, it does concern us all.

What is certain, is that this experience I am living, absolutely every day for more than a month, with never one off to collect myself, to think of other things, has left me staggering.

Such a book, I only carry on with to show the work of the rescuers, the doctors, the crews. But from this hecatomb where I find myself this week, can a book be made? To transcribe it in conventional phrases is in no way suitable. Indeed unacceptable.

One thought at least comforts me, that the countless notes I am taking will not be lost. They will go to the Bibliothèque Nationale (National Library), as I have just learnt this summer that they want my manuscripts and the journal which I have kept since childhood. And all of this, what is real, what is human will remain there as a complete record of the accidents and the mountain rescue in 1997.

With the Guiverecs I talk about their future life, of the mountains. If you ever have really loved the mountains, you keep some ties with them, in some form or other. We take leave of each other. Madame Guiverec kisses me. I realise that I do not even know her first name! Yet she and he, and their problems and their opinions, have mattered much to me through the summer. We exchange addresses.

I go back down to emergency where there is now a more pleasant woman and, furthermore, a nurse, who takes me into the department.

One of the Czechs is being treated in the first room. He really is scraped raw. Frankenstein! I show him the rucksack. He's not interested.

I go to the other room that has been pointed out to me. Second Czech. Second Frankenstein. A nurse is sewing up his arm. His face is still bleeding. When I show him the sack, his face lights up with joy. He obviously feared that he lost that in the fall. He is Kunicki. A pleasure to give him pleasure. Now, I try to find out his address. I write the word in capital letters on a piece of paper, in French and English, even though it is more or less the same. He does not have the least idea what the word 'address' means. He takes the piece of paper, looks at it carefully, gets blood on it, but he still does not understand. Enter a charming nurse, whose face is familiar. She tells me her name and she is Olivia Lasserre. I think it is she who gives me a sheet of paper with a curious address which I proceed to copy down. Enter, in turn, Manu Cauchy who jokes:

'You here!'

Then Bernard Marsigny comes in, who adds:

'We'll have to put her in PG uniform soon!'

I give up trying to get Tuma's address which no one seems to know. I say my thanks and goodbye. I've got blood on my paper, I've got blood on my hand, I've got blood on a compress which some good soul has slipped me to wipe off the blood. But it is not the blood which upsets me nor these weird raw faces. What distresses me is the suffering of those who are in pain and above all it is the love. The wounded love of those, parents, spouses, friends, children, who love those suffering or dead. The love of those who worry about what their suffering might do to those they love. There is only that which is beautiful, or terrible, tenderness and love.

But in truth, after all this, what would I like more than anything? To be fit, to be twenty years old and to go into the mountains!

It's what I miss. I would like to leave the hut at one or two o'clock in the morning, with a sky full of stars, the stones of a moraine scrunching beneath boots, the glow of head-torches lighting up the moving scree slope, then hard snow. Crampons being put on without talking. Then we'd rope up. Continue to walk. The slope would steepen. There would be a bergschrund to cross. Then a couloir. That's what I loved. Comes the moment when the great slope under our crampons is revealed with the first glimmering of dawn, grey at first. And slowly it gets lighter, the mountains emerge all around. Just a few of us, to live this moment of intense joy. For an instant the rising sun would turn the cast of our shadow azure. We would arrive at the summit when all below are still asleep. And we there, with the beauty of the world before us.

If I could, that is what I would do. Tomorrow!

26

AMONGST FRIENDS

Tuesday, August 5
'We're not going to lose this one, at least. It's not her last evening?'

They are talking about me and I am touched at Lucien Berardini's solicitude. This kind of reflection does more good than any amount of polite compliments and, furthermore, makes me laugh. Berardini is having dinner with us, along with Robert Paragot, Captain Gin and Hélène, Captain Joubert and Caroline, Mark Ledwidge, who is the Canadian rescuer, Jean and Lorraine Afanassief and Sylvie and René Brochard who are staying at our house. It's a good thing that Sylvie is here! She has got everything ready like a good fairy. I spent the day in bed, exhausted, still ill. Sylvie has been busy making dinner when I come down, groggy. No need to explain what's wrong, an unremitting month at the helipad and its consuming effect on body and heart.

But one piece of good news: Marie Claveau had a baby yesterday. This little miracle of the mountains and the PGHM is called Samuel and was born three years less five days after his parents' accident.

Lucien Berardini is still his old self, remarkably so. I have never known anyone more natural. He must shock some. Myself, I have always admired him. And continue to do so. He says what he thinks, without inhibitions, outspoken. He is a human phenomenon. He continues to climb, with his stumps of feet and fingers, which were amputated after Aconcagua, when he was how old? Twenty-five? He must be nearly seventy now. He recently did the Nose of El Capitan. He is fantastic.

Obviously, given the gathering scattered around the sitting room as there wasn't enough room at the table, the talk was of mountains and rescue.

I learn that the search is still continuing for the three who disappeared on Les Courtes. Alain Iglesis went down into the crevasse this morning. And found some gear lost in the fall. Not the bodies. Would they ever be found?

On discovering that there is now a *via ferrata* in Chamonix and that the phenomenon is growing,[1] Berardini gives his opinion, without subtleties:

'It will make more dead meat!'

Then the subject of free rescue comes up. For long I shared John's view: a fixed rate, of say one hundred pounds. He maintains in an emergency even the poorest English student or workman could find that, but it would dissuade those who don't really need it. From what I've seen this season, I've changed my mind. The people from the Eastern Bloc are sometimes so poor that, to avoid such a payment, they would go without rescue and perhaps die. And then Robert Paragot, now president of the FFME, comments with his usual good sense:

'Once you stick a finger in, the rest of the body follows!'

It is Marc Ledwidge and Lucien Berardini who come up with a reply that has nothing 'politically correct' about it:

Marc starts:

'The best solution, is to prohibit the poor from climbing! That would sort out all the problems!'

Lucien caps it:

'Forbid fools and the poor in the mountains!'

It is good to escape the censors now and again!

Wednesday, August 6

Yesterday, when I was unable to get up, as well as the Courtes search, ten rescues took place in the range, fractures, sprains, altitude sickness, French, Greek, Belgian, British, Spanish, Japanese, Slovak, Danish, plus a woman walker killed falling from a path at the Tournette. I haven't the time to find out more and get on with today.

This morning, same sort of rescues, altitude sickness, fractures, etc. Outside the range, Philippe Debernardi, from the St-Gervais detachment, rescued a parapenter stuck in the top of a tree.

At the helipad, Dr Marsigny is on medical duty. I like him more and more. Under his dry exterior, each time his human side becomes more apparent to me. He is very strong, as a mountaineer,

---

[1] And what to say about the most beautiful ridge of the Matterhorn, the Zmutt, threatened with being equipped?

in medicine, in everything. He is a tall man, quite thin, embarrassed perhaps in the past by his height which he still tries to hide, like a big teenager, with a stoop. But he can't avoid it, he is tall. He has a striking face, highly intelligent. A mobile mouth. Dishevelled hair. He is not concerned with publicity. He is a fighter – for his casualties, for his threatened hospital, for the rescue service. Today, returning from a difficult medical rescue on the Dent du Géant, he said:

'It is essential to get out on the ground, to understand! I need to do it yet more.'

Shortly after my arrival, two rescues. Because of the clouds, they were difficult, but successful. It's of that kind of rescue alone I'd hoped to speak.

For the Dent du Géant, the call-out was imprecise. Someone had reported comings and goings. That's all. The helicopter leaves, with Alain Darrhort and Michel Gonzalez. *Bravo Lima* is apparently searching, as the clouds permit, in the indicated area without seeing anyone. Finally the group is spotted.

Immediately the doctor is called, and the chopper comes back for him. For us, at the helipad, the ballet of the helicopter's return and quick refuelling unfolds. At the start of the alert it wasn't even known if there was an accident. Now that the resuscitation equipment has been requested we realise that it is very serious.

The casualty is an Italian who fell leading. His protection came out. He fell in total about thirty metres. His partner burned his hands and took the top off one of his fingers trying to hold the rope as it ran out. The casualty has a back injury and probably a fractured skull. The mist hid all that was going on. For mist read: no helicopter. On his return, Bernard Marsigny explained:

'I saw myself spending the night with him. And in another two hours he would have been in a coma ...'

But luckily a clear interval allowed Daniel Poujol to go and take casualty and doctor to hospital. Then, a little later, to collect Alain Darrhort and the other man. He's an Italian, in his forties and rather stout. He is from Aosta but does not speak French. On his return to the helipad, Bernard Marsigny bandages his hands outside, on the wooden table.

When it's fine, casualties are not brought inside. Theoretically, they are immediately evacuated by ambulance. In any case, in summer, it's as hot outside as in, so they are put in the shade of the pine trees, which avoids getting them up the steps and unnecessarily moving them around. Thus they can easily be shifted from one stretcher to another. It also avoids problems of hygiene. For example, on this particular day, I was sitting on one of the sofas in dark green imitation leather, its springs broken like the others, and I was leaning my head against it.

'Is that blood?' asked Alain Charnay at one point. 'Mind where you're putting your head!'

We had a look. There were some brownish stains that could be anything and date from who knows when.

'It must be the Spanish girl who was in here this morning!' said someone. 'Her scalp was bleeding.'

'They shouldn't come in here!' remarked someone else.

Alain Charnay wiped the stains off with a damp cloth and the matter was closed.

So Bernard Marsigny is treating the Italian outside. He does not seem in much pain and is smoking cigarillo after cigarillo, no doubt stressed, thinking about his friend. What goes on in people's heads? Perhaps he doesn't know the other man well and is annoyed not to have done the route? Or is he in despair and doesn't want to show it? So many different feelings, sometimes even conflicting, are able to coexist in the mind.

The other rescue is on the Cosmiques Arête, on the IV pitch, which should be regraded VII, in view of the number of problems it causes: bivouacs, accidents, rescues, by air and on foot. The clouds dictate a party on foot now, with rucksacks, rescue equipment and stretcher. Pierre Bernier and Jacques Ottonello get to the casualty, an American, who has also fallen and has a back injury, but is able to move his legs and has feeling in them, which is a good sign.

For this rescue on the Cosmiques, the solution seemed to be to winch him up the IV step and finish the rest on foot. But once again a break in the weather allowed him to be lifted off. The rescuers made their own way back to the Aiguille du Midi with the rest of the equipment. As it was late in the day, I imagine a special cable-car had to be put on.

During the afternoon I had suggested to Daniel Poujol that he come and eat with us from yesterday's leftovers. He had declined, saying:

'We're just going to have a quick bite at the tennis club, you know, amongst ourselves ...'

Perhaps he said this out of tact but, of course, they may all want to be left alone, quietly. I didn't press him. This summer, I simply comply, listen, keep in the background, try to be ready for anything.

Later, after chatting a bit with Daniel Poujol about the difficult rescue on the Géant, I repeated:

'I know you've reserved at the tennis club ... If you change your mind, the invite is still open and you only have to ring. We were twelve yesterday and I think there was enough for twenty-four! So it would be no trouble ... And you would be very welcome, at whatever time you like, leaving when you like, eating without saying a word if that's what you want!'

He laughed and immediately accepted.

In the evening, I called into the PGHM. It was a fever of activity. The PG was besieged by journalists only interested in deaths.

Fernandez had taken over from the orderly who'd gone for dinner. While I was near the reception desk, speaking to some-one else, what is all too frequent happened. The telephone rang. Fernandez answered and said:

'Chamonix PGHM.'

He listened, then responded ...

'No.'

And then he put the receiver down, raising his eyes, and explained:

'That ... That was a newspaper ... They asked: "Have you had any deaths today?" I said no and they hung up!'

In the evening, Olivier Fernandez comes to our house with the helicopter crew who arrive when it is dark, about ten o'clock, because Daniel Poujol does not shut up the helipad until dusk.

A good evening. To use an old-fashioned word, we're all on the same wavelength. How does one describe a good evening? Good is hardly a story, it is an atmosphere, a mutual trust, affection, cheerfulness, memories shared with others. John goes to the cellar to bring up bottles, better each time. We tell them of Monsieur Père, at Varennes, near Beaune, who used to go out to his pigeonry where he kept his wines, coming back with dusty old bottles, unlabelled and unsealed, saying to John:

'Taste that for me, Monsieur Wilkinson! That's the real thing!'
And we didn't know, not even him, what it was, Pommard, Côtes-de-Nuit, Corton-Charlemagne, but whatever, it was always delicious. When John produces bottles of ever better kind it is a sure sign that the company is going up in his estimation!

So a happy evening, which ended at 12.30. I am left with the striking impression of how lucky I am to know such people, and it was but a chance meeting that put me in their path. Daniel Poujol, in the course of talking, asked me, having lived in so many different circles, the Sorbonne etc., how I saw them. The Sorbonne, some of my old teachers, yes... before May '68, and even then... But I thought of others, no doubt very intelligent, but otherwise? As people? From the Sorbonne and other centres of scholarship I can only think of a few, really worthwhile.

It is true that I have experienced quite a lot of events, often thanks to my father. Replacing him, just before his death, I had to give a speech in the great hall of the United Nations, in New York, in front of forty ambassadors, Perez de Cuellar, the Secretary General and others. Where haven't I been? Fine. So what? It's nothing, nothing at all, what most think of as 'importance'. My small band of friends at Bleau in the old days, my groups of friends from the Premier de Cordée Chalet or at the Biollay Hut, that really was something, that was special... We were people apart, ready even to die for our love of the mountains. The beauty of a tiny hidden hut and a sunset, was worth more to us than all the palaces on earth.

With the people of the PGHM, I have rediscovered something rather like my bands of friends from long ago. They are straightforward, they love the mountains and do not take themselves too seriously, as Fernandez showed in something he said, this evening:

'Those who treat us as heroes simply don't understand. We are ordinary human beings who try to help others. That's all.'

That is the reply I didn't give Daniel Poujol at the time, but is the right answer. That is how I 'see' them.

Thursday, August 7
At the end of the morning I meet Jean-Claude Gin and explain my plan for this book and how it's taking form; chronologically, because time is the basic factor in a season and sequence is affected by what happened previously. I tell him the sort of information

that I will need. About midday we're finished, but just as we stand up to go our ways the conversation starts again, less formally. He teases me about my antipathy towards the media, which I justify, giving him examples and telling him that I am not alone in thinking thus. Sometimes I feel that I serve for all, even as an agent for liaison. Leaving aside the helipad, where some days I seem to be the resident 'Shrink'. More the regiment's canteen woman. The woman who is told many things, which have nothing to do with rescues, and which, obviously, I do not record.

Our meeting has eased certain tensions. The death of Régis Michoux, the concentration of tragic rescues, all in some ten days, the winch breaking in Switzerland, a helicopter crash in the Pyrenees, all have created a general pressure, controlled, of course, but noticeable even at the surface, in the same way as a volcano may look the same from the outside but is full of lava whose molten mass is quivering, seething and boiling.

Today, the weather, pretty stormy, has led to caution. There is hardly anyone in the mountains and, when I leave, hardly any rescues. So I decide to take a big step, although it cost me a lot. Olivier Fernandez has spoken to me about the Russian, Alexei, whose fiancée had died. He had paid him a visit in hospital and said to me:

'Go and see him. He speaks English. His eyes are red with crying, and the tears glint in their corners. It is hard to know what to say, but he is alone and he is unhappy ...'

He's right, I must go, but it made me feel ill, quite literally, and ever more so as the day advanced, so distressed was I about this visit. And I don't know what to say to him either, even less so than Olivier, who had rescued him. And yet what days must he be spending. It's Thursday afternoon. Four days since he was brought down, alone with his dark thoughts.

To break the ice, I decided to take him a rose, to pick the most beautiful in the garden and give it to him. I took a small vase to put it in, which I'll leave there and I chose a white rose, still closed, tinged with pink. This, I tell myself, must be tried – hoping he will think it a nice gesture, but still I wonder how things will turn out. I would so regret the approach if he did not appreciate it. I would not like to make him feel worse still.

At the hospital reception desk I was told:

'Boldyrev! Room 21! Bed by the window!'

I climbed the stairs, with my rose in my hand, feeling silly. There are mirrors everywhere in this hospital, on the right of the staircase, and then opposite me, when I arrive at the top. I did not want to look at myself, I walked up looking at my sandals, a knot in my stomach.

I knocked and entered. In the nearer bed, there was someone who had had a mountain biking accident, English, a climber in fact. But, on a day when the weather was bad, he had hired a bike and taken a fall, fractures etc. Only moderately agreeable since he was watching sport on the television and did not lower the sound.

Alexei was lying in the other bed, near the window. He looked surprised when I went towards him. I began by showing him the pretty rose and busied myself with filling the little vase, and putting it on the table near him. It was a way, I don't know how to put this, of showing him that I came in friendship. I did not want to announce myself as a writer of mountain literature, I did not want him to think I was a journalist greedy to know about others' misfortunes. The rose was also for that. I told myself that having lost his fiancée, he was, apart from Fernandez and Bernard Stoop, all alone in his mourning.

He is a tall dark man, forty years old, but looks young, quite a thin face, black hair, a black moustache and a beard that has covered his chin and cheeks during the eight days since he left for his route. His eyes *are* red-rimmed ... he must weep often.

I sat down beside him, near the window, I smiled at him while wanting to cry, and I began to introduce myself, to talk to him, to tell I had climbed a lot, that his accident had touched everyone, and then that I was at the helipad when they were brought down, he and Elena, and that their accident had terribly distressed me. That was why I had come to see him, that I know Fernandez, his rescuer, who had spoken about him to me. And if I know Fernandez it's because I write about the mountains and that I had found the rescuers were such fine people that this year, I am writing a book about what they do. Conveyed like this, everything is said, it isn't offensive and contact is established.

His neighbour's television is annoying, and having a fracture of the otic bone, Alexei does not hear well out of his left ear and being tired, a little dosed up with painkillers, he speaks low, but in good English. I was shocked, later, to see the magazine which, at the time of the accident I had so disliked, talking disdainfully of 'his get-by English'! I doubt if the journalist's English was any better and I don't know if he had even seen Alexei at the time. Why belittle people like that?

Alexei tells me about the rescue, how it happened, with the technical details as he had seen them. I realise that I was right to come, that he needed to talk and that he needed someone to listen. In fact, that's all I have to do: listen, listen, listen. And then, from the rescue, he came to the climb, the circumstances of the accident, and everything that has been going over and over in his head.

He talks then about his life, in the USSR, about being able to leave freely. I know from experience that the Russians are inexhaustible when it comes to talking about their relationship with the Soviet system and I think it is good that he talks about something other than the accident.

He speaks low, but without interruption. He tells me that his father was a writer acceptable to the regime, that he'd had opportunities in life, access to dachas, to smart hotels for holidays. But he explains how he had discovered, little by little, that the communism which was held up to him as the perfection of the world, was not. He tells me that he thought about it secretly and rejected it but had retained one error: to believe that at least the USSR was still the most beautiful country in the world and was astonished that the free people elsewhere did not rush to go there once they could.

He was born in 1957. At the age of eleven, he was shocked by the repression of the Prague Spring. He talks to me a lot about the Czechs, about the guilt of his country concerning them. He went to Prague, and talks much of it and how sad it was that Europe had been divided in 1945. All this, which might seem irrelevant to mountain rescue, is in fact not. The conversation is interrupted by the passage of nurses, of blood pressure and temperature readings. And the casualty is making a psychological step towards abstracting himself from his tragedy.

He talks continuously, almost soothed. He says if there had been no Stalin, there would have been someone else, as bad. He says that the Soviets killed at least twenty million people, perhaps even double that figure. I know that, but I let him say it because he is happy to express himself. Since the collapse of the Soviet Union, in 1989, he had read two utopian works which he thought exactly applicable to communism: those of Thomas More and George Orwell, both of which enthused him.

Then, briefly, I tell him about my doing the trans-Siberian journey and the incredible adventures I found myself involved in. He understands my allusions and I amuse him. He laughs several times. I wonder if it is the first time he has laughed since his accident. It's good to laugh…

I ask him what he does for a living. He is a computer programmer for a company whose head office is in Switzerland. And that brings him back to communism. He tells me that when you develop a program, you have to think laterally, to see what might arise from each step. And sometimes you realise there is too much data, too many interlinking factors, and you have to nullify the research, because the program is not properly thought out, since it has too many unknowns to be coherent. Communism, in his eyes, was similar, no one had understood it or been able to stop the program. I reply that communism also missed the fact that men have both good and evil in them and had been conceived as though men were only good, and so it could not work.

Our discussion of all this was very much on the same wavelength. Long gone is the moment when I was pacing the corridor with a rose in my hand. We are now acquainted.

Alexei worked for several years in artificial intelligence and puts forwards other comparisons for me. He cannot understand how there were, and still are, communists in Western countries, when they had the facts to see.

After having spent almost two and a half hours with him, during which I think he relaxed, felt less alone, I leave him, promising to return.

27

THE ATTENTIONS OF THE PRESS

Friday, August 8

The helipad is overrun by journalists of all nationalities. They have taken entire possession of the whole chalet. Their equipment too, cases and machines everywhere. The rescuers and doctor are outside because inside there is no more room for anyone else. Even their vans, stuffed with machines full of knobs and keyboards, real travelling television studios, are filling the helipad site. Why aren't they made to leave them outside? A bit of inconvenience might make them rather less high and mighty.

The helicopter, with unshakeable regularity, continues to take off in the middle of all this, comes back to collect equipment and refuel, leaves again, lands with a casualty, flies off once more, and basically does what it has to do. There are in fact several operations: a Greek with snow blindness on Mont Blanc, an Italian, accompanied by a Swiss guide, who has altitude sickness on the summit of the Aiguille Verte, another Greek likewise on Mont Blanc.

On my way here I bought, unwillingly but out of necessity, the magazine of the journalists who so infuriated us last week and which has just come out. It's what might be expected. Photos, which happily do not feature, for reasons explained, the body of Elena gliding under the helicopter which might well have 'made' the cover picture. As for the accompanying text, it is nothing but a jumble of errors. Manu Cauchy, on duty today, Bernard Marsigny and Olivier Fernandez who are passing, and myself study it. At least it has the merit of being almost funny, for it is difficult to accumulate more mistakes, platitudes, and ill-digested information. What careless work, what disregard for others! So many periodicals are satisfied to fill their pages with rubbish. Doubtless care is taken that the photos are perfectly clear. But for the rest, no standards, no style, no accuracy, no nothing. It is illogical. Similarly, on television one can imagine a whole bevy of sound and image technicians, intent on getting perfect quality, but of what … broadcasts that are all too often mediocre. This pre-eminence of technique, of the superficial is doubtless a characteristic of our *fin de siècle* and is nothing to be proud of.

Olivier Fernandez and I have better things to do. One of Alexei's worries, one of his main regrets which in his deep unhappiness most concerned him yesterday, was his camera, in his rucksack, which he believed was still at their bivouac on the Dru, for it contained the film with the last pictures of Elena alive. The previous evening I had telephoned Fernandez and learnt that on his way back from the searches on Les Courtes he had got himself winched down to the spot to recover the sack and it was now at the PGHM. Off duty today he was going to pick it up and we had arranged to meet here. The camera is covered with mud and splashes. We put it to dry in the open air and decide to go in the early afternoon together to see Alexei at the hospital and show it him. In that way he will have two moments of pleasure, the first when he knows the camera has been recovered, then when he gets the photos.

Which is exactly what happened, his face lit up when he saw us coming into his room with the camera.

He is a bit better than on the previous day. Rested, and doubtless in less pain. The nurses have shaved him, which makes him look very different, but his face seemed even more sunken after what he had been through. Olivier takes charge of having the pictures developed. He takes one of Alexei before removing the film. We stay a bit with him.

No major rescue during the afternoon: a Croatian with a broken ankle on the Goûter, a case of acute altitude sickness on Mont Blanc, a Spaniard with a wrenched shoulder, a Dutchman in difficulties on the moraine.

In the evening: Opening ceremony of the mountain book festival at Passy which I attend to see friends. I decided to forego book-signing sessions in the following days in this baking heat.

Saturday, August 9
Very calm, when suddenly there is a call out for snow blindness on Mont Blanc.

Almost comical, for since yesterday Manu Cauchy, duty doctor, has been working here wearing dark glasses. The day before he had done Mont Blanc from the Cosmiques where he forgot his first aid kit and dark glasses... If the medical corps experiences what the sick suffer from that can only make them all the more understanding.

Someone calls out: 'Manu, take your white stick with you!'

'Manu's first rescue yesterday,' someone explains, 'had also been a case of snow blindness.'

And he imitates the doctor casting around trying to find his patient:

'Where are you...? Where are you?'

The helicopter leaves with Jean-Louis Oustry and soon comes back with the 'victim'.

'It's very painful,' Manu informs her, based on his own experience.

Two cameramen have entered behind the young girl and film the whole conversation. In fact she is not suffering but sees everything white, and no longer can tell the difference between various colours. It is more a case of frozen corneas. Manu telephones Dr Blein, the ophthalmologist, who can see her, but straight away, before closing his surgery. Can she get there that quickly? Now the helipad's quasi-official chauffeur, I solve the problem by offering to take her immediately. No point in her hanging around awaiting a VSL (ambulance car). I have certainly played my bit this summer in helping reduce the Social Security deficit.

The young woman is from the Ardèche and very agreeable. On the way she tells me she had never been mountaineering before, but had signed on for a week's course with a woman guide. With Mont Blanc as the climax. Plus a super climax of frozen corneas.

Nevertheless, she had got her Mont Blanc, and once her eyesight has recovered, it will doubtless be a good memory.

How many are there, each summer, who decide to go on this kind of course, without any particular desire, as they might do for sailing, riding, canoing, rafting, caving, pottery making, basket weaving, country dancing? I can't help wondering... At least about those with no burning desire. Tens of thousands probably, who are going into the middle or high mountains. I was reading yesterday, that there are 1,300 officially posted guides in France alone. So now they need to work. Like the property market has to. Like the campsites have to. Like the sports shops have to. And the manufacturers. Etc.

On the other side, there are a large number of people with free time who don't know what to do with it... We are all aware of holiday-makers, students, those taking early retirement or retired young, those in part-time work, who need to so something with their leisure. With enjoyment sometimes. But sometimes also because they don't know really what to do with themselves.

Between these two sides there is naturally a potential market.

There are occasions when I shock people by saying that the greatest ecological disaster of the century in France was the introduction of paid holidays. I do so deliberately to provoke those who try to make politics out of ecology. But there is an element of truth in it. How many places and sites have been destroyed, or irredeemably damaged by buildings, roads, motorways, lay-bys. parking lots, chair lifts and cable-cars, huts even. That's the cost we make nature pay.

And then there is the price humans have to pay. And it is by no means done with. Certainly not in the mountains. You can't launch tens, perhaps even hundreds of thousands of people, particularly into the Alps, with nothing going wrong. That is the reply to give those who start querying the number of mountaineering accidents. It is simply a matter of mathematical probability.

For the mountains are not and cannot be a commonplace. They demand a special motivation. They require being loved, desired. Not to be consumed, like a 'product'.

Certainly, there has to be the opportunity to discover them. But that can happen during a holiday in the valley when one is a child or teenager, as was the case of Jean-Marie Choffat, sent to a Peugeot holiday centre at fourteen, an experience which changed his whole life.[1] Or through a purely personal approach; to take a guide once, and have a go.

Of course one cannot hope to go back to the period of Saussure or Henriette d'Angeville; but the idea of a standardised mountaineering packet brought down to the level of a simple pastime is something shocking.

These general reflections have nothing to do with the particular case which brought them to mind. The young Ardèche lady was nice, and who knows, will perhaps become one of the rare cases who are suddenly bitten by the mountains through going on a course.

A fall on the ordinary route on the Tour Ronde, an easy outing, all the more so as it does not entail spending the night at a hut,

[1] See his *Brodequins du soleil*, Alzieu 1977 – a set of climbing memoirs.

but catching the first cable-car. In any case the accident was of no consequence: a guide who was unhurt and his client who has a simple sprain.

Eight versus seven! That's the score of the number of journalists and those involved with rescue. The journalists have won. They're crawling everywhere, talking at the top of their voices, and, like yesterday, have all their vehicles on the site.

A rescue on the Moine Ridge of the Aiguille Verte, on the way down. Four French, one of whom is ill. The whole lot are brought down. Physically or psychologically unwell? When the first, the ill one, arrived at the chalet it was Jean-Claude Gin, passing by, who took his details, but as he was called away to the telephone, I asked the lad if he wanted something to drink and what was wrong. He shook his head and replied:

'Nothing! I was stupid ...'

He seemed unhappy. I went and got him a glass of water which he gulped down. Then the others arrived. Formerly, it's true, ill or afraid, the whole lot would have had to make the best of things for themselves. On the other hand ...

'We prefer to bring them down when they are in that sort of state,' one of the rescuers said.

And rightly ... Thinking about those four, I imagined a whole range of situations. Perhaps they had fallen out with each other? It's quite common, but it's not the kind of thing we discover down here.

Whilst this was going on, a more serious matter, a thirteen-year-old who went out walking with his family in the low part of the mountains near Bérard. Fell on a scree. Head injury, lost consciousness, semi-coma. Conscious again but agitated. Transported direct to the hospital.

It was a family outing. The boy was racing another on a scree slope.

'There were at least ten of them there, and no one keeping an eye on them,' I was told.

It is not particularly simple to 'keep an eye' on a thirteen-year-old boy, who considers himself independent. The problem lies, once again, in this popularising of the high and mid-height mountains. It is necessary to say it and say it again, because it is the reason for numerous rescues. A path is easy. But the edges can be steep. Scree slopes, by definition, are unstable.

That evening we will learn that the child was taken to Grenoble, to a specialist neuro-surgery service, with a cracked skull.

We continue, amongst ourselves, to complain about the journalists, considering this year there are really too many, swarming like flies. Even Manu, who answers their questions quite willingly, explains that he was being hampered – and each time it is always the same thing – for when he got out of the helicopter and went over to examine the child stretched out and surrounded by his family, there was a cameraman walking behind him filming everything.

In the duty chalet, later, five journalists of whom four speak only English are quizzing Manu. He is looking for the right word from time to time: when necessary I try to help and we joke, in French, to relax things. So, how do you say *une grimpeuse* in English? I invent 'a she-climber' like one talks of 'a she-wolf', for *une louve*.

Always *à propos* these bloody journalists, the overheard remark of a rescuer that day –

'It makes you lose concentration.'

I think it came from the one who was listening to details of a call-out on the telephone: locality, nature of wounds etc. Fifty centimetres from his face two cameramen were filming him. But it was not a film! It was a matter of getting as best as possible, the details of a real accident. But for the producers it was simply cinema. That's the nub of the problem. One cannot mix two quite different professions. God knows, those who are in the rescue business, gendarmes and support services, need to be fully concentrated.

Another rescue, for the female client of a guide. Nothing much. A Spanish woman who had a minor fracture coming down from the Envers Hut. The guide, French, came into the chalet to give the details necessary for the report. Dark haired, perhaps thirty. Thoroughly disagreeable. Peevish, unpleasant, impolite, uptight, hostile. Oh, how I would not want to be the client who, when the draw is made (*tour de rôle*), gets a guide like that. The *tour de rôle*, is something of a lottery. One can get someone quite outstanding. One can get someone like him.

In the meantime, a sprain on the Albert Premier moraine, and another at Les Chéserys. The Chéserys path is a veritable crucible of sprains.

Jean-Louis Oustry comes in laughing and announces:

'I've just dropped a clanger!'

Two ambulances had arrived at the same time and had asked him:

'Where are the wounded?'

'Not yet arrived, I think.'

'Pardon,' said the two sprains who were chatting on the bench outside the store cabin, 'It's us, the wounded.'

About 4.30, there came by a quite young woman, in black tights. She's a guide and was looking for her client, the one with the frozen corneas of that morning, whom they can't find anywhere. She's not at the gîte where she is staying; she had no money. Manu Cauchy explains what happened and that he had sent her to Dr Blein, directly. I state that I must be the last person to have seen her alive, as it was I who dropped her off there. But it is Saturday afternoon and the surgery is closed. The mystery remains unresolved, but must in due course have been explained, as the client came the next day to thank us all, me included. A nice case, with a happy ending. A pleasant victim, all the more so since it is not everyone who takes the trouble to say thank you.

Daniel Poujol enters the helipad chalet, and asks if I would like to meet his wife, who is outside, visiting. Of course! I go out and we sit at the wooden table where the journalists don't come much. Brigitte Poujol is quite delightful. She is slim, beautiful, with a bright look. They form a remarkable couple! And there are their children, Alexandra, 7, who is very motherly towards her brother, Nicolas, 2, incredibly lively. A real little boy, never still... He runs around the place, picking up pebbles, tearing at the grass, falls, gets up, his knee bloodied, without crying and does not do so when Olivier Fernandez delicately cleans the graze, sets off again, running around, picking up more pebbles... We five or six adults are transfixed, hypnotised by this unbelievable need of a child to be active.

Children, thanks be to God, and here come others. A friend of Daniel Poujol arrives with four more, each smaller than the other, to be shown the helicopter.

'The Daltons!' Robin Joubert said the other day, talking of the children at the Rue du Lyret.[2]

---

[2] The notorious band of outlaw brothers, distinguished only by their height, in the *Lucky Luke* comics. Rue du Lyret is where the PGHM is quartered.

Alexandra comes and takes Nicolas in her arms. Six children! Seeing them, a tourist outside tentatively comes in with two more and asks if it is possible for them also to be shown the helicopter. Eight children! Astonished, agog, eager and happy. Suddenly, it occurs to me that it adds to the glory of *Bravo Lima* to give so much pleasure to little children, after so many flights, often for life, sometimes death, nearly always dramatic. At the moment only innocence and happiness reign. The helipad has become a terrestrial paradise! Aside from the journalists, naturally.

And then comes another call-out. No rescue is funny, but this one causes hilarity among the rescuers.

'It's Maxou!'

'What?'

'We're going to rescue Maxou!'

Maxou is Max Buttoud. Today, off duty, he was going to take his wife and a female friend of hers to Mont Blanc. They left by the first Aiguille du Midi cable-car, did the traverse to the summit, and descended via the Grands Mulets. And there on jumping one of the last crevasses Mme Buttoud hurt her leg. Later we discover it was a bad twist and a cracked fibula.

'Go alone,' Bernier and Fernandez, the duty rescuers, tell Manu Cauchy. 'That will make one less in the helicopter and Maxou will be able to help you!'

Manu takes a splint and rucksack, and off goes the helicopter. Wide eyed, little Nicolas watches his father flying away.

Pierre Raveneau is there, always smiling, conciliatory, even with the journalists. Craftily, he says to the others:

'I trust you will fall in as a guard of honour for Maxou when he comes down!'

Then he disappears. His new promotion to Major doubtless prevents him from taking part in this practical joke, and there must be much work waiting for him at the PG. But the idea takes hold and they get organised. The two duty rescuers in uniform, go and get their ice axes. The second mechanician in khaki jumpsuit, finds a yellow axe from somewhere. Alain Charnay, who is also a gendarme, but in shorts as he is serving as secretary, takes a snow shovel. While Robert Petit-Prestoud, who for many years ran the fire service at Chamonix, also finds some sort of implement.

All line up, very correct, but from time to time one or other comes up with a new idea and goes to find an improvement.

Olivier Fernandez gets an old wheeled stretcher, very dusty, from the hangar. Bernier, known as Bibi, calls out:

'If we bring out a sack for corpses, do you think Maxou will be unamused?'

It was considered this might be going a bit far. But all are hugely entertained by the preparations.

It should not be forgotten that the helipad is full of journalists, English, German, French even. Not one moves to film the scene. I am astounded. But don't they understand anything? Do they have no sense of events? Of all events?

I say to various of them:

'But don't you get it? It's that too you should be filming! The human side of the helipad ... Life.'... It's funny. Go on!

I say it in French, I say it in English going from one to the other. They are uninterested. It does not fit into their fixed patterns.

A fat lout, to whom I say it in English because he is working for the Germans, replies in a tight voice that he is French-speaking. In fact, Swiss. I try and get him to understand, him at least. Waste of time. He or someone else responds:

'In any case it wouldn't be shown.'

That's how they are. It is either 'shown' on the sacrosanct screen or it has no chance of appearing and, in that case, nothing else is worth bothering about. They live and only react as a function of 'demand', or what is considered as such, which I am by no means sure is that of the public.

'If they can't sell it, it is of no interest,' Gilles Bidon comments later when I recount the incident.

They are robots!

Up to now there are only two journalists I have found worth-while out of the whole lot. I took their names and can pay them that tribute. They are those working for Pioneer Productions, making a documentary film for British television: Gilles Perret, the producer, and Ben Duncan a redheaded Englishman.

The guard of honour lines up, facing where the door of the helicopter will be. It can now be seen. It approaches, rumbling, roaring, shaking and finally lands in front of us, its blades still turning. There was no call to 'Present arms' because of the noise, but it was all but. Thumbs along the seams of their trousers, ice axes and various tools at the present, the five fallen in to honour the arrival of their comrade.

A comrade who from the helicopter gives them the two fingers but then, seeing the cameramen are filming – because a victim is being brought down, and that enters into their category for recording – immediately stops.

Perhaps, all the same, there will be a photo. Bibi had gone to get the official camera, used for judicial records, and given it to Gilles Perret, for an unique picture, sighing:

'It's processed by the service in Paris. We'll get a bollocking... Never mind!'

Then Mme Buttoud is helped to the ground, a bit shaken by the adventure. She manages a smile, just. She seems very tired.

There, my imagination runs away with me again. I have known too many women whose husbands have pushed them into going into the mountains, forcing them against their will, incapable of realizing that they can't share their passion, or even understand it. For such women, the mountains mean nothing and never, to my knowledge, have such efforts been successful. Perhaps this is another case. Happily, I am wrong, as I learn next day.

In order to put the wheeled stretcher away, Fernandez scoots it along the tarmac, and when it has gathered speed, jumps flat on it, just like a kid.

That's what one finds at the helipad, a balance in life... Men who are capable at any moment of carrying out a rescue on a big wall, highly technical and dramatic, or can meet with the distressed families of the injured, the dead, and treat them with marvellous tact, but who also know how to recharge their batteries, to have fun, in a childlike way.

That evening, on the way back, I visit Alexei, as I do every day now. Olivier Fernandez, who had taken charge of having the photographs developed, told me he would wait for me and that there were two Alexei wanted to give me, one of which was of Elena. In fact, he goes through them all, explains them, comments them, offers me some. I in turn discover the beauty of Elena.

It is half past eight when I leave the hospital. Heavy days...

28

A LONG SUNDAY

August 10.
A very busy day, typical of a sunny Sunday in the first half of August.

Yesterday's weather forecast was – correctly – for good weather with 'blazing sunshine'. As it also predicted a deterioration and storms to follow, many climbers and walkers have decided to take advantage of an opportunity that might not be repeated.

To start with, a case of acute mountain sickness or appendicitis at the Aiguille du Goûter: a fairly young and only moderately pleasant Romanian. He has to be taken to hospital quickly, and I'm glad that Ben Duncan, the Englishman from Pioneer Productions, who is just leaving, decides to give him a lift and spares me the trouble of transporting him myself, something I had been getting ready to do in order to save time.

There's a brief moment of respite at the helipad. François Lecoq tells me that he had a daughter this year, called Marouchka, and that her arrival has changed his attitude to mountaineering – and to calculating and taking risks. There have been so many births since that summer of 1994, when I first got to know them all. François's daughter, Manu's daughter, Daniel Poujol's son, that of the Claveaus, and others too. It's such a breath of fresh air to hear about births! Particularly here.

Then the alarm is raised. Someone has fallen into a crevasse at La Jonction. Filmed up close and recorded, as is becoming the norm here, Daniel Duret tries to concentrate enough to register the information transmitted to him by phone.

Whenever there's an emergency, whenever there's an issue of understanding the frequently imprecise details about the location and circumstances of an accident, this confrontation of manners becomes increasingly shocking. I think about it every day, because it's repeated every day, as if the real is being distorted by the virtual. What is this 'duty to inform'? Does it exist on the same level as the 'duty to rescue'? Does it exist at all?

The differences between those who practise one and those who practise the other are also striking. Now, that would be something interesting to film – the disparity between them! On the one hand the rescue team: tall, slim, bright-eyed, fast-moving, precise and productive. On the other, the journalists and film-makers: slow-moving, generally overweight and expressionless. Perhaps it's not entirely their fault. The news must take them from football stadium to lorry roadblocks, from troubled council estate to helipad. They collect mileage, hotel rooms, restaurant menus. Nowhere do they have the time to understand things fully. So why should we be surprised to see the daily news repeated with such painful similarity?

Pioneer represents an interesting variation on the theme. Rather than too often demanding transport to the rescue scene, the two young men have attached a miniature video camera to one of the helmets of the rescuers, who is certainly a little weighed down by the device, but doesn't have to operate anything: everything he does from being winched down to taking care of the injured is filmed automatically.

Daniel Duret and Marc Ledwidge, together with the crevasse rescue equipment, are already in the helicopter, which is taking off. Dr Lecoq and Malineau are collected a little later. A long and apparently complex rescue operation.

Even before Place and Iglesis arrived to take over from them, a walker came in to report that he'd seen a red parapent falling between Planpraz and Flégère. The sighting is confirmed by a phone call reporting the crash of an orange and yellow parapent. Doubtless the same. There's often a discrepancy between the eyewitness accounts of a single accident. It turns out that the parapent in question was orange and purple. And the accident very serious.

The helicopter has by now picked up the rescue team, who have spotted the injured man on a steep and unstable scree slope scattered with bushes. As soon as they see the condition he's in, they request the doctor. *Bravo Lima* picks up Dr Lecoq from the crevasse, to which a second doctor, Marsigny, is mobilised, as one is needed at each site – a rare, but not unheard of, situation.

In the crevasse, there's a German wearing a T-shirt, stuck between the ice walls and rapidly getting colder. It's taken a considerable amount of work and de-icer to get him out. He's suffering from hypothermia and transported direct to the hospital helipad.

On the scree slope, the parapenter's eye socket has been stoved in by a branch and he's in a coma. The rescue is taking place on a steep slope in the lower hill terrain, on scree where nothing grips and which is riddled with *varosses*, tall, tangled bushes about ten feet high, which have simultaneously saved and injured the victim. Away from the paths at this altitude, the mountainside is often in a state of chaos – in the original sense of the word. It was impossible to winch anyone into these bushes. So the rescuers were lowered to a position higher up the slope, where Iglesis found a large boulder to belay from. Then they had to get at the injured man, who was suspended by his own cords and thus posed a difficult problem: if freed before being secured he would fall down. Instead he had to be reached, attached and put in a harness.

It wasn't a particularly technical rescue, but nonetheless extremely difficult because of the terrain and the state of the casualty. Dr Lecoq requested the resuscitation, oxygen and perfusion (drip) equipment. Then the doctor and the rescuers had to take the injured man lower down the slope, away from the bushes, in order to winch him up. The operation was so difficult that it took two hours in total to rescue him.

'And I thought it only took twenty minutes!' exclaimed François Lecoq when he came back. 'In an operation like that you concentrate so hard that you lose track of time.'

Then he added: 'I thought he'd gone the way of Henri II except that it was a branch instead of a lance.'

'In the eye?'

'No, just above it, but that means it could have reached his brain. He's in a bad way. Very bad.'

Iglesis, who has seen many missions and rarely comments on them, used strong words to sum up the operation: 'We worked like slaves on this rescue! It was a hell of a fight!'

But the calls continued to come in while these two big operations were taking place. There was information from the Conscrits refuge that footprints had been sighted leading up to a crevasse near Les Miages, while someone else had described a 'slip' in the same area. Reports do tend to dovetail because of the number of people who travel with radios or mobiles.

On top of that, there's a sprained ankle near Lac Cornu.

Malineau is dropped there but, as it's nothing serious, he and the casualty have a long wait until the helicopter has time to pick them up. 'Not such a bad thing!' says Fernandez. 'You get to bond with people. You don't often have time for that.'

He's not on the first or even second duty roster, but has been brought in as a back-up, because so many rescuers have already been called out this morning. At one point when the chalet is free of journalists, who have gone outside, he can't stop himself from sighing: 'That lot really give us crap with their fifty deaths a year in the mountains! A hundred and seventy-five people have just been killed in Algeria, kids and all, but it's easier for them to come here to get their blood offering for the masses.'

At that point a report comes in from Vallot that someone is 'in a state of total exhaustion and can't stop falling into torpor'.

As soon as they finished at La Jonction crevasse, Marc Ledwidge and Daniel Duret were sent to Les Conscrits with Pierre Bernier, which means they're on the other side of the massif. There they find a happy ending. A rope had in fact fallen into a crevasse, with no damage, and had just managed to get out under their own steam.

By now, seven rescuers and two doctors have been mobilised at the same time, which is quite a rare occurrence.

The sick man is brought down from the Vallot. He's thirty-three and from Grenoble. He's still a bit groggy when he arrives at the helipad. While they're taking his details, I ask him if he'd like something to drink. Yes please! I bring him a glass of water. He's still thirsty. A second glass and then a third. It's as if this helps people acclimatise to the valley where they've landed so suddenly. When it comes to calling for an ambulance or a taxi, I don't hesitate to offer him a lift, because he seems so tired to me – so obviously tired that I carry his rucksack to the car.

He's a typical Mont Blanc case. Nearly everyone is under the impression that Mont Blanc is easy. Technically that's true. But it's very high. The man from Grenoble has trained on 2,800-metre peaks, but 4,800 metres and 2,800 metres are not at all the same thing. Mont Blanc requires altitude training that very few beginners can do without. What's more, you have to remember the dangerous passage of the Aiguille du Goûter, which has nonetheless been very merciful this year. Not a single death! Mont Blanc is also nearly always cold, windy and dazzlingly bright –

and the combination of these factors can be deadly. Yet it's so good to climb when properly fit!

I drive off with the case of altitude sickness from the Vallot. His friend is still up there, having been accepted by another rope. The main problem is that he doesn't know Chamonix – and not even the name of his campsite. Round we go ... again! We take the route des Pèlerins, but to no avail. Half an hour later, almost back where we started, at the end of a tiny little road he recognises where he is. The invalid has three children, ranging in age from seven years to nine months, and he's camping with them and his charming wife, who is pretty surprised to see him brought back under escort.

Off to the hospital now, to see Alexei. I only mean to drop off an English translation of one of my books, which he's requested, thinking that reading will keep him company, but I end up staying a good hour, as he needs to talk. The more he regains his strength, the more time drags for him. He wants to show me some new photos that someone has had developed for him. Photos of Mont Blanc emerging from the clouds, when their plane was approaching Geneva. Photos of a climbing competition held on boulders below the Gaillands, and which they found amusing, but a bit stupid, given that the real mountains were all around them. Photos of Le Brévent, which they climbed in thick cloud. Photos of their ascent of Mont Blanc. Photos of Elena in the country, crowned with a garland of flowers straight out of the Middle Ages – so graceful an ornament. Gradually getting to know someone after their death, when you know they don't exist any more, causes an extremely painful sense of melancholy.

Alexei asks me questions about the book that I'm to write. I explain all the doubts that I've had – and that I'm still experiencing. He tells me I must go on, but can't find the right word to describe the perseverance that he's advising until he looks in a little English–Russian dictionary and finally points to it: *wisdom*. Another one who wants me to write this book which is so painful. But advice like his is what keeps me going.

Back to the helipad. A rescuer is asleep, sitting at the wooden table outside with his head in his arms. It's Julio and his incredible capacity for recharging his batteries. He can sleep anywhere for just a minute at a time and wake up in a fraction of a second ready for action. It's a real gift from the gods to be able to sleep like that!

In my absence there's been a fractured ankle caused by jumping over a crevasse, near La Jonction. At the moment Marc Ledwidge and Malineau are near the Pointe Percée dealing with a fall off the beaten track: two broken arms, I'm told, plus head injuries with delirium. Dr Lecoq is there too.

Iglesis has woken up and we chat. I really appreciate him. As well as being an excellent mountaineer, he's decisive and wise with good judgement and a passion for his job – but sometimes reveals a wicked sense of humour.

Daniel Poujol was saying to me recently: 'Have you noticed all their differences in personality?' In fact, as time goes by, I'm more and more struck by this. Gone are the days when I used to feel as if I was visiting the Smurfs, with all these gendarmes dressed in blue and all the same. To do this job – as indeed to want to climb – you need personality. There are so many banal, ordinary, colourless people in everyday life. But not here. That's probably why I like it so much.

A new rescue: a parapenter near La Pointe du Tricot. François Lecoq, who was taken straight to the scene from the hospital at Sallanches, where he'd gone with the casualty from the Pointe Percée, returns full of admiration: 'That parapenter, what class! An open fracture of the knee, a broken femur on the other leg, and he was waiting for us – sitting there calm and courteous without a single complaint. A real master! That's how pain is. Different people feel it and react to it in very different ways.'

Another rescue – on the Verte. A man with a hand injury who has been waiting for some time above the bergschrund of the Whymper Couloir. But it doesn't sound serious and other rescues have taken priority. 'They may well end up top-roping him and coming down on their own,' remarks Iglesis.

But they waited, and the rescue took place.

Today, from half past three onwards, Pioneer has chartered the CMBH Lama, piloted by Pascal Brun. The Pioneer journalists finally make me think – and more so with every passing day – that it *is* possible to practise this profession properly. It's true that they try to film the rescues that have a happy ending: rescues in the right sense of the word, those that bring help rather than gruesomeness. What's more they've taken the trouble to hire a private helicopter, rather than trying to get a seat in the rescue helicopter. So, there is a way of doing the job correctly after all.

I find it reassuring to know that. It means that all the distaste and irritation, inspired in me by so many of the journalists and film-makers I've seen at work here, are nothing to do with an unconscious prejudice on my part but are caused by their way of doing things.

And so Pascal Brun takes Gilles Perret and Ben Duncan to the Whymper Couloir. Having consulted Daniel Poujol, he takes off first in order to film the departure of *Bravo Lima*. The sight of this aerial ballet from the helipad is stunning. And apparently the flight that follows is even more so. Captain Gin, who is off duty today, has a place in the Lama and returns full of enthusiasm. The flight of Daniel Poujol followed by Pascal Brun must have been like Paganini with a Stradivarius. And it seems that the arrival of *Bravo Lima* at the Whymper and its flight over the landscape on the way were breathtaking. At last, some TV pictures that will be worth the wait!

The Whymper 'casualty', who is apparently hardly injured at all, arrives in rather a fit state. In the old days, of course, he would have managed to get down himself. When he sees that he's being filmed he makes an almost wild gesture, as if to protect himself. People tend to react to the capture of their likeness on film as they would to a physical attack, especially if they're also in a weak or dependent state.

François Lecoq examines the hand, which isn't badly hurt, it seems. I ask the injured man if he'd like a drink. He refuses. He's not very nice in any case – or having a bad day. He has brown hair, a face that's red with sunburn and very blue eyes, but a way of looking at people that's devoid of all friendliness. And so, as he's waiting for the requested ambulance, no one takes any more notice of him. Sitting on a bench, he leans his head against the wood of the external wall of the equipment shed and sleeps – or sulks.

Every day is rich with new lessons. Everyone is given a good welcome here, even those with only very minor injuries, but they need to show a minimum of co-operation in return. What's the point in unpleasantness? What a difference between this evening's man with minor injuries and this afternoon's seriously wounded parapenter – the one whom François Lecoq described as a 'master'.

That's all for today, in Chamonix at least, as Michel Médici is still to collect the body of a fairly old man, who fell from the Dent d'Oche, and an injured man from somewhere else. A reconnaissance flight is requested too, a little later, but there's no sign of trouble.

It's been a long day, which has given me the opportunity to speak to many of those who work here – like Pascal Brun, who wanted to know how I was going to structure this book, or Marc Ledwidge. And others too. Towards the evening, there's a visit from Max Buttoud, his wife, with one leg in plaster, and his wife's colleague who was with them on Mont Blanc. They bear bottles of champagne and biscuits to celebrate yesterday's rescue. Soon there are fourteen of us, even though the journalists have left. Robert Petit-Prestoud is there, Olivier Fernandez and his wife Christine, a nurse in the casualty department, the rescuers, the mechanicians, Alain Charnay … everyone in fact. We sit down outside around the rustic table, we talk, we laugh. Madame Buttoud tells me that she works in a tax office, which means that they're a couple with nothing to recommend them: a policeman and a tax inspector! She also says that she and her colleague had really wanted to do this ascent of Mont Blanc and that they'd trained seriously for it. She takes the verdict of misadventure well, with humour and pleasantness.

The stars come out one by one. We had moments of fun, under the blue and cloudless sky, with the feeling that all was perfectly at peace in the mountains. This is how things should always be at the helipad, or anywhere else… relaxed, simple, friendly and in a beautiful setting.

29

PECULIAR RESCUES AND THE MADDEST OF THE SUMMER

The previous chapters should give an idea of what a mountain season is really like. Of course, it's certainly not over by August 10, but the rest will have to be presented more briefly, leaving out many of the rescues and only keeping dramatic, novel or significant events – otherwise this will continue to be an enumeration of sprains, fractures and minor altitude sickness, even if each of these is a genuine adventure for the casualty concerned. So the rest will be treated more succinctly.

Monday, August 11
Uncertain forecast. For some time now, big storms have been predicted – to last for a night and a day. Even yesterday, they were announced as 'violent'.

'Come quickly, desired storms!' as Chateaubriand[1] said. Everyone is wishing for them, after so many intense and exhausting days. But morning comes, then evening and the following night, with no sign of a storm. The only outcome is that climbers and walkers having deserted the mountains, the rescue day is peaceful.

Nevertheless, this morning, very early to minimise the dangers, the epilogue of a tragic story is played out. In the crevasse of Les Courtes, where it's presumed that the bodies of three missing climbers from August 4 are to be found, the main snow bridge which is regularly monitored, has collapsed, and a rope sighted yesterday at the bottom. A search has been planned for this morning and, as it's well above freezing point, there have been fears for the safety of the operation. But all went well. Alain Iglesis told me about the expedition, which he took part in. Two of the bodies were successfully retrieved. The third was still under perhaps five metres of snow, but they were able to attach its rope to a large block in the slope above. That way, it won't fall any further, and if there's a thaw, it stands a chance of being found.

---

[1] Vicomte de François René Chateaubriand (1768-1848) – French prose writer.

'It's so much better for the families,' Iglesis said. 'And even for corpses, it's worth making the effort. Otherwise people think, 'they couldn't give a damn.' They have no idea... Anyway, it's all right because we brought two of them back. But yesterday, what a day! And we had to start all over again at six o'clock this morning. Exhausting!' If he, the indefatigable one, says this, it must be.

Elena's body has left the morgue and departs for her homeland, via Geneva, tomorrow. Alexei insisted on seeing her again. He'll be leaving the day after tomorrow or on Thursday, with his brother who's due to arrive.

The hardest thing for him, he explained to me, will be to return to the flat where he lived with Elena, where he'll be surrounded by all her things. He once told me about some geraniums they had planted together on the balcony before leaving. I think about her clothes, her books, her things in the bathroom, her bottles of perfume and goodness knows what else. And to learn to live there without her... For some types of bereavement there is no consolation.

Fortunately, Alexei isn't alone when I arrive, but with another Russian, Igor, who came to visit when he heard about his ordeal. Alexei and Igor speak Russian, Igor and I French, Alexei and I English – a rather complex but friendly conversation.

Igor turns out to be an interesting character. He has an incredibly strong and stocky physique, like a kind of Neanderthal man, with a compact head that nonetheless radiates intelligence through piercing blue eyes. He's a qualified guide and a member of the Groupe de Haute Montagne, so he must be a good climber. At the moment, though, he works in Moscow, organising trips to the Alps. All in all, he's one of the emerging capitalists from the new Russia, the first I've ever met. I don't think he knew Alexei before, but his misfortune has been so great that it's brought distress to all those who have heard about it.

Tuesday, August 12
Nine rescues, including those outside the range, most, and the most serious of them, involving walkers.

A striking case was a sixty-three-year-old Belgian who complained of 'heart problems' at the Col du Brévent, but turned out only to be tired. The symptoms he described weren't even very worrying. He first called at 12.30, but as other rescue operations were underway, he wasn't picked up until one o'clock, which isn't bad for a day like this. He's very displeased not to have been brought down sooner. His reaction is a good illustration of the 'rescue-consumer' – extremely demanding and unaware that there might be other casualties. This is the attitude that would probably develop if people had to pay to be rescued, creating a 'saved-and-insured' clientele.

Another case, that of a brave yet stubborn carpenter who cut his finger seriously while working at the Platé refuge and who insisted on being stitched up on the spot so that he could finish his work. Despite his attempts to influence medical opinion, it was absolutely essential that he receive proper treatment straight away.

The highlight of my day at the helipad was a long conversation with Benoît Cousineau who was just back from his holidays. He had been absent throughout the intensely dramatic period that we had been through here. I tell him about the strange summer that I'd experienced – my doubts and vicarious suffering. He understands and offers an analysis. As a former 'blue helmet' doctor in Lebanon and Yugoslavia, he believes that the rescuers' encounters with death and suffering are equivalent to the psychological traumas of war. But this isn't recognised, and the medical check-ups that they undergo in Chambéry or Annecy are performed by doctors who often have no idea about the mountains. As they're unlikely to be understood, the rescuers don't try and explain. They can't really discuss it with each other either, or burden their families. And so they're on their own to survive the ordeal.

I too have had to survive the summer alone, and I understand what he means. Of course, it wasn't me picking up the dead and the injured, but I involved myself in this process day after day, as far as my strength – which is real but nonetheless fragile – would allow. And I've seen the outcome.

Benoît also tells me that the violent death, encountered in such close proximity here, confronts each with his own death. I've experienced this too and, surprisingly, much more so than in the case of the death that had the most devastating effect on me – that of my father, which was long, cruel, terrible and painful. But then I was also suffering from the end of a great love, while now, as

I watch strangers die, I sometimes feel that it's myself on the edge. You need to have been through it yourself to understand.

This summer I have completed my own crossing of the desert, without thinking about it too much either, due to lack of time, and, most clearly this week, I've taken refuge in spiritual resources, like thirst gives need for a spring. Every ordeal is a crucible and I'm emerging from this one, which was a real trial of fire, with far greater clarity of vision. I felt the same way several years ago after a pulmonary embolism, an unimaginable physical hell of two weeks' extreme suffering. I then saw with a luminous clarity the need for prayer, even though my condition did not allow it.

With almost no personal physical suffering this time, except for a general malaise and an attack of high blood pressure, the compassion that I've been feeling for all the mental and physical suffering of others has given me a great spiritual need that finds solace in church celebrations. This particular evening I go to a service of collective penance taking all my sorrow, helplessness, my fear of not being able to write the book the way it deserves to be. I feel as naked as the day I was born – and as on the day I'll die. Father Dominique directs our thoughts towards our failure to give to others and then, thankfully, I feel I *have* given, given as never before, never so intensely. But how great is human weakness, especially my own. I stay for the mass that follows and receive communion, forgiven. That's how writing about a mountain rescue season leads to a spiritual adventure. I am being carried along by a current and I let myself run with it. In any case, the current is stronger than I am.

Hospital. A visit to Alexei. He's expecting his brother. It's good that he's returning to his family circle. He gives me the photos of Elena with the flowers in her hair. He'll get some more printed in Moscow. I'll keep them with me for the rest of the summer. Perhaps this is the big difference between what I'm trying to be and the journalists I've seen this summer. I'm sure they'd have liked to get hold of these photos. They might even have bought them and sold them on. But Alexei gives them to me in return for the friendship that I've shown him and the tenderness that I feel myself for Elena's memory.

His brother arrives. Very Russian, very warm-hearted, speaking quite good French and understanding English. I want to leave them alone together, but we take some time to exchange addresses. This is probably our final farewell. But Alexei and Elena have entered my life to remain anchored there for ever.

Wednesday, August 13
The weather is quite good. Ten rescues, ranging from the typical to the surprising.

First there's an accident at the Posettes avalanche defences, near Le Tour. Pascal Brun, who is working at the site informs us that the foreman has been hit by a stone on the back of the head and that he's bringing him down. The injured man arrives, but bizarrely it's the front of his T-shirt that's covered in blood.

Manu brings him into the kitchen to dress the wound.

'That's it!' says Rivière. 'Do it on the table where we eat.'

Nothing serious. The casualty leaves holding a dressing over his newly disinfected wound. He'll probably get an X-ray to be sure.

'They ought to wear helmets!' says Pascal Brun to Jean-Louis Oustry. 'You're lucky to spot one helmet on a council construction site. I know it's uncomfortable and hot. But sometimes the accident happens so quickly. OK, I know I work in shorts... It's really difficult to do everything you're supposed to in readiness for all eventualities.'

This observation is true for all environments and especially the mountains. Fortunately, sanctions are rare. But if you really observed all safety measures without exception and in their entirety, in a kind of work-to-rule, the inconvenience and time wasted would be so considerable that accidents would actually be caused. That's why it's sometimes an advantage to move together on a route, without belaying, without wasting time by pitching it. Guides are all too aware of this. The longer you hang around, the greater the risk. But if there's an incident and insurance companies get involved, 'experts' or otherwise, it's always easy to say that no – or insufficient – safety measures were taken, as in the case of Smiler. Only the highly competent are able to decide what to do for the best at a specific moment, circumstances and conditions, but their judgement won't be infallible.

It's 11.20 am. A call on behalf of a 'kid' on the shoulder of the Tacul, in other words at 4,000 metres. He's supposedly ten and a half and the only information given is 'hurry'. Visibility up there is only so-so. There are lingering clouds. And it is necessary that the helicopter will be able to get through and find the spot. It takes off with Manu and Thibaud Ribiollet.

Ribiollet is a newcomer, or almost, young. With light brown hair, a long straight fringe, green eyes and long lashes. You can tell exactly what he looked like as a small boy. He is youthfully slim, but already has broad shoulders which one day will probably give him an impressive stature.

Jean-Louis Oustry explains how the alarm was raised:

'The call came in from a guide, but the guide's surely not with him. A guide would never take out a child of that age! It's insanity to do so! Their heart and lungs are insufficiently developed. My own eldest waited until he was eighteen to do Mont Blanc. The second's the same – he'll do it this summer for the first time at the age of seventeen. Hell, you could hear the kid screaming over the radio. People just don't realise ...'

Gilles Bidon reports that they're coming down to the helipad. But suddenly there's a change of destination towards the hospital. So Manu must have felt there was a deterioration during the flight. But when he arrives, he describes the symptoms to us

'The patient said he wasn't getting enough air to breathe, so he started panicking, and that causes a secretion of hormones leading to vasoconstriction, especially in the lungs ... resulting in even less air getting into them. A vicious circle, you see!' He was describing a 'panic attack' ... an English term also used in France.

In the afternoon, after a few rescue missions of only moderate seriousness, there's cause for concern on the Dru. Shouts have been heard from the North Face. The helicopter has gone out twice, and twice it's failed to get through because of the clouds. The forecast this morning was for 'lots of sunshine with a few clouds' and instead, there are lots of clouds with a little sunshine. Everyone is dreading an incident like that of the Russians.

Time passes. The clouds get thicker and darker. The one in which the Dru is currently swathed is dense, compact and dark as anthracite. There's a storm rumbling: an echo of thunder and large, heavy drops of rain begin to fall. Perhaps lightning is striking the Dru. One's so helpless in the face of the elements. If it starts to clear, which is often the case at the end of the day, the rescue will take place. Otherwise it will be tomorrow at dawn. The storm is dramatic, then suddenly calms and passes.

A new emergency. Unbelievable! This time it's for a six-month-old baby near the Lac Blanc ... at 2400 metres. Manu explains that a child is more vulnerable at six months than it is at two, because all the mother's haemoglobin has been lost. And babies' ears, especially their Eustachian tubes, are tiny and fragile. Now that the storm has passed, the helicopter will be able to fly, taking just one rescuer.

'The only thing to be done,' says Manu, 'is to bring it down – and quickly!'

Later, I heard some of the details about this disgraceful expedition from Lorraine Afanassief, who happened to be at the Lac Blanc that day. The parents were apparently oblivious. During the afternoon, the two men in the group had been seen venturing on to the steep grassy slopes that lead down to a line of rocks. Someone had commented:

'They're going to end up at the helipad!'

Then, when the group began the descent towards La Flégère, Lorraine advised them to give a drink to the children – as there were *two* of them, one aged six months and the other eighteen months!

'Haven't got any dosh,' they replied.

They left, got caught in the storm and came up again – with difficulty. The children were soaked. The baby girl's lips were purple, her face bright red and her hands and feet white. No jumper or anything. Lorraine wanted to undress her to wrap her in dry clothes.

'She'll get all cold, if you take her clothes off!' said the mother.

But Lorraine insisted, trying to dry the child and rub some warmth into her, while the alarm was being raised and the parents objecting: 'It'll cost too much!'

One trip was enough to bring the two young women and children down – all of them soaked through.

As for the kid on the Tacul this morning, the blame lies with the lift system and the access they give. No parents would ever dream of dragging a child of ten up to 4000 metres from the bottom of the valley. And the others wouldn't have taken two babies up to 2400 metres if they'd had to carry them all the way up from the bottom. But if you reach altitude easily, it seems simple to go further. That's the main thing that tourists must be made to understand. Rescue operations like the two today would provide a good lesson, if they were shown on television.

The firemen have arrived even before the helicopter touches down. The six-month-old girl has calmed down, but the older boy is still crying. Someone produces a piece of chocolate from goodness knows where. A fireman blows into a surgical rubber glove to make a toy and ties a knot in the end – it makes a strange fat balloon with tiny fingers. The women in their shorts and cagoules are young, a little bewildered and not particularly concerned about their children. One of them asks:

'Wha'do we owe you?'

'Nothing at all!' replies Duret.

The ambulance leaves with its charges. The matter is closed.

Then the Dru emerges from the clouds. The flight finally takes place. At the beginning we think the climbers are unharmed, but a message from the rescuer mentions a 'victim', who's brought down. This turns out to be a Dutch chap, about whom Peyraud had given an alarming description:

'He's pissing blood all over.'

He must have made that comment after touching the man's harness, as he only has one large flesh wound, in his thigh. He was wearing a helmet, but got caught on a peg or a bolt as he fell, ripping a twenty-centimetre Y shape into his skin.

Manu administers some initial treatment on the bench in front of the equipment shed. He begins by cutting through the man's trousers, then suddenly interrupts his work to enquire politely:

'Is it OK to cut?' Everyone laughs. The trousers are already ruined from the accident anyway. The injured man laughs too, as if to say that his trousers are of negligible importance compared to the rest.

That's true, but it's not everyone's reaction. Occasionally there are complaints about a fleece jacket that's had to be cut. It's a fundamental human reaction, I suppose, even if it's totally out of all proportion. People get attached to their equipment, as if it were a link with ordinary life.

There was one amazing case in Britain which has remained notorious. It's the story of the climber Antony Rawlinson, who later became President of the Alpine Club. He had taken a huge fall while attempting the first ascent of Zero Gully on Ben Nevis. He was picked up, with grave injuries and in a coma. He was still in this state when he arrived at the casualty department. He was wearing a rather splendid cashmere sweater, which he'd just been given for Christmas and liked enormously. 'We'll have to cut through the jumper!' remarked the doctor to the nurse, whereupon the victim suddenly sat bolt upright, cried 'Oh no you don't!', took off his sweater and then fell back again, as unconscious as ever.

It's 7pm. Bernard Stoop is today's back-up mechanician. We talk about Elena and Alexei, about whom I provide the latest news, including the fact that he's leaving tomorrow. The couple and their sad story have had a lasting effect on Bernard. He'd like to see Alexei again, but has some routine maintenance to do on the helicopter, which will take about a quarter of an hour. After that, there's a reconnaissance trip to Les Droites for which he's not needed. So we decide to go and see Alexei together, as soon as Bernard is free.

Surprisingly, Alexei isn't in his room. His new neighbour tells us that he's been allowed out for the evening and is having dinner with his brother in town. We leave him a friendly note but, as we're heading for the car park, we bump into him and are able to say our farewells in person. I find Alexei's warmth very moving. He tell us that, if ever Bernard, Olivier or I go to Moscow, we'll be welcome in his home.

There's something that can't be denied about mountain rescue operations: they're very human interactions. And if people usually lose touch after the event, largely due to the huge number of rescues, sometimes they're the basis of long-lasting friendships, of the kind that a guide can form with his client selected by the luck of the *tour de rôle*.

That night I'm invited to a large dinner party at some friends' house. It's a chance for me to gauge the extent to which public opinion supports the idea of paying for the rescue service – without any understanding of the problem and with no attempt to find out more about it.

This is when you find yourself producing the arguments: 'So, we should leave the bodies of those whose relatives can't afford to bring them down up there, like in the Andes or Himalayas? ... So, even humble holiday-makers who want to go for a walk on the Petit Balcon should be forced to take out insurance? ... So, if a walker sees a parapenter fall, he might be advised not to report it to protect himself from receiving a bill, if the victim isn't insured? … Wouldn't that be a step towards society renouncing all responsibility? What about human solidarity? … It would mean deaths and injuries of those difficult to retrieve – who could so easily have been saved. And the costs of the deaths and injuries will themselves be significant. … What about today, then? The two babies brought down from the Lac Blanc. I saw the mothers. They certainly weren't up to paying for a rescue operation, not even insurance. They would have tried to walk down with their babies frozen and soaked to the skin, regardless of the consequences. Is that the kind of thing you want to see?'

When you give concrete examples, you realise that people are only thinking in abstract clichés, with no idea whatsoever about the realities. And it's the realities that count.

Coffers of public money are disappearing without trace as we speak, and for some reason people alight on the mountain rescue – as insignificant to the total as a grain of sand, and as noble and useful a task as it's possible to imagine.

And just as this dinner and these conversations were taking place, so was the most crazy rescue of the season – not to mention the fact that, on the other side of the valley near Samoëns, Major Darrhort was helping to free twenty-six ramblers, trapped by a rising torrent.

But let's get back to the crazy rescue – which would have been droll if it hadn't been so dangerous.

It took place where else but on the North Face of the Grandes Jorasses.

The helicopter had just been on its reconnaissance mission to Les Droites, where the people who were giving cause for concern were only late, rather than in danger. That was when they picked up a call from the Leschaux Hut, requesting assistance. Two Koreans, who were attempting the Walker Spur had just lost all their equipment and their rope! They were in radio contact with two compatriots at the hut, who had alerted the warden.

The helicopter, piloted by Gilles Bidon, happened to be in the vicinity and descended towards the Jorasses to assess the situation. It wasn't exactly encouraging. The Koreans were separated and clinging to a wall at around 3400 metres. The helicopter immediately went down for refuelling but, on the way back picked up another emergency call, this time from the Charpoua Hut.

The low-fuel warning light came on, indicating that there was only a quarter of an hour's flying time left, but the machine nonetheless stopped off to rescue a trainee guide, who had injured his calf with his own crampon. They picked him up at top speed, as time was running out.

Then, having dropped the casualty at the helipad and refuelled, the helicopter quickly took off again with Noël Rivière as mechanician and Jean-Louis Oustry and Thibaud Ribiollet as rescuers. The latter was left at Leschaux to lighten the load and the machine headed for the Jorasses. The wind had risen and there was a layer of threatening cloud. Ribiollet was charged with monitoring the cloud and report how it was developing.

So how did these Koreans, Kim Song Ho and Roy Ile Hee, end up hanging without a rope on the North Face of the Jorasses, attached to the wall only by the sling through their harness? The answer is both simple and stupid: after failing on the route, or caught in the storm, they'd tried to abseil down … and the rope had slipped from their grasp. Koreans are reputed to be very stoical. But it's interesting to speculate whether exotic curses could be heard echoing around the Walker when the rope slid to the bottom.

Whatever the case, they hadn't moved since they'd been sighted. They were positioned 300 metres above the start and twenty metres to the right of the route, on some smooth, compact slabs with few holds. Steep slabs – not vertical, but very steep indeed. They were three metres apart, one protected by a Friend 4 which was barely holding, the other by a size-three nut that had been put in upside down, which meant he had to pull it upwards to keep it in. Between them – quite a large flake.

That was after the storm. Now night was drawing in. Half of the Walker – The Shroud side – was enveloped in cloud. Noël Rivière had to lower Oustry down from a great height, complete with a large rucksack which would allow him to spend the night with the Koreans if necessary or, even, if he managed to get them winched up by the helicopter, to fend for himself.

'Bugger me! If it wasn't the best rescue of my career!' I heard him tell Iglesis the next day, still overcome with emotion. 'Even Nono was terrified, when he winched me!'

In fact, as it was getting rapidly darker he'd been lowered forty metres directly down to the Koreans. The angle of the wall meant that the helicopter couldn't get any lower. From that moment on, there were four of them experiencing the same intense situation, but from totally different perspectives: Ribiollet, who was monitoring the clouds from the refuge as they drifted to the scene of the rescue, becoming increasingly dense and menacing; Gilles Bidon, the pilot, who realised how close he was to the rock face and that the clouds were forcing him closer with every moment of fading daylight; Noël Rivière, the mechanician, who kept checking the cable on one side and the helicopter on the other, calling out, 'Watch out for the blades!' from time to time; and finally Jean-Louis Oustry, who had not only to invent but also to carry out the moves that would save the Koreans – at top speed. Meanwhile, who knows how intensely these two were experiencing the same situation?

Oustry had been lowered down to the flake that had been spotted between the two men, a short distance above them, and from which he hoped to make a belay. But when he arrived, still hanging from the end of the cable, and grabbed it, it moved, proving unstable. He let go and, as he still had a little slack in the cable, slid further, to the great consternation of the rest of the crew. The two Koreans watched their saviour arrive, but were too terrified to help him. With no ledge in sight, Oustry finally managed to place his foot on the face just above them on some minuscule holds and to establish a belay on a tiny spike and a nut worked into a shallow crack, and with this protection unhooked himself from the cable.

For those in the helicopter, the five minutes or so that he took to make himself safe, must have seemed like an eternity.

Oustry saw what the Koreans were holding on to – and it wasn't much. Via his helmet's integral radio, he requested that the ring at the end of the cable be sent down again and gestured to the Koreans how to attach themselves. To complicate matters further, while this was taking place, his radio earpiece fell out and no further dialogue was possible, as he couldn't hear a word the crew were saying.

'Just a small thing,' he said later. 'Stupid! But what a cock-up.'

He managed to put it back in, held out the ring to the nearest Korean, checked that he was properly attached and took out the Friend to which he was attached.

'That bloke,' Gilles Bidon told me, 'was held a little bit by the Friend, but mainly by the Holy Ghost...'

The Korean was taken off in the helicopter and dropped at the Leschaux Hut.

Meanwhile, Oustry took over his place, which was an improvement on his own. He collected the remaining equipment that was lying around, including some rusty karabiners and pegs that the Koreans must have salvaged from the route. The unstable block was between him and the second Korean. Still using sign language, he once again explained how to attach the winch. *Dragon* returned. Noël Rivière sent down the cable. But the earpiece fell out again, leaving Oustry unable to communicate once more. He put it back in again. Time was passing. The darkness was intensifying.

The ring at the end of the cable reached Oustry and he threw it to the Korean, who caught it very skilfully and hooked himself on. By reaching across, Oustry succeeded in releasing the nut, and it was the second Korean's turn to be hauled up, hanging from the cable. Oustry retrieved his own equipment. The earpiece fell out once more, but by now he was getting used to putting it back in again quickly. But he was so absorbed in doing all this that he didn't see what everyone else was all too aware of.

And this was, according to Gilles Bidon, the fact that: 'The clouds were continuing to envelop the scenario and that night was continuing to fall, leaving the action to unfold between the clouds and the wall, as if at the bottom of a well.' Indeed the clouds were now rolling in from the Col des Hirondelles via The Shroud.

The ring was dropped down to Oustry.

'Nono directed it just right! Not two or three metres away as so often happens when winching. The moment I was attached, they shot off from the wall at sixty or eighty kilometres an hour. Apparently they already had the headlights on, but they only told me afterwards – I didn't even notice at the time. The wall was rapidly disappearing from sight and I was swinging around horribly, but I'm used to it by now! When you're at the end of a cable you just have to put up with it!'

'The clouds posed such a threat, that we didn't dare waste the minute it would have taken to winch you right up.'

'Those bastards really took me for a ride! And when they finally winched me up, it was the first time during the whole operation that I could actually see Nono and the helicopter. Or perhaps I'd seen them out of the corner of my eye, but I hadn't really looked at them. You get so preoccupied with what needs to be done. I've never been in such a tight position to perform a rescue! Places that treacherous are really rare, anyway. And no belay!'

Everyone was reunited at the Leschaux Hut, where they left the Koreans.

'I'm sure they said thank you,' remarked Gilles Bidon, 'but we had no language in common. I think they were a bit oblivious to the danger they'd been in, anyway. Or perhaps they've got a different concept of life from us? It was a bit like the time when we rescued some sheep! They didn't struggle, they just let themselves go. That's what the Koreans were like, but with smiles to split their faces!'

Whatever the case, the next day the two survivors came down to the rescue base. They were delighted to get their sling back, together with the rusty karabiners and pitons. Pierre Bernier, who greeted them, tried to reprimand:

'Next time, it could be the big one!'

'But as they are a race who are fond of fun,' I was told later, 'they just laughed, gave a little bow to say goodbye and left – still laughing.'

The following day, we learned that they'd got hold of another rope, had gone back up to Leschaux and that one of the friends, who spoke a little English, had told the warden that they were leaving for the Walker again.

Did they manage it this time? We never heard any more of them.

30

THE FUTURE RESCUEE

Wednesday, August 14

Ten rescues – eight of them in the Mont Blanc range. A serious accident in the morning on the Dôme de Rochefort. Dr Duperrex, Olivier Fernandez and Gilles Mathé carry out the rescue – of some German climbers led by a German guide. Two of the clients were roped to him and two others formed an independent rope. It's the guide who was injured as they were climbing back down through an area of steep unstable rocky ground. Why did he fall? No one knows. The clients saw him fall past them. The rope caught on a spike and stopped him. So it's pretty lucky really. All three of them could have fallen to the bottom if it hadn't been for the fortuitous spike. Even so, the guide fell thirty metres. He wasn't wearing a helmet.

'With a helmet,' Duperrex told me, 'he'd probably be uninjured.'

In fact, he was seriously hurt. With head and spine injuries, he was losing lots of blood and had stopped breathing. The second rope went down to him and gave him mouth-to-mouth while waiting for the rescue, which is probably what saved him. In the afternoon, he's transferred to the neurology unit in Geneva.

The morning's other accident took place at the Charmoz-Grépon bergschrund. An Italian this time – another head injury, but less serious. This victim was wearing a helmet, in which a rock made a hole 'as big as a tennis ball', but saved him all the same.

I have a slightly tense conversation with a guide who drops in. As I know him, I tell him about what I'm planning to write. He feels that no one should talk about anything to do with mountain accidents. I point out that it is right – given the number of journalists, working for TV or mass-market, sensationalist magazines, who pass through here saying God knows what and with no respect for the truth – to try to show people what really happens, to dispel all the prevalent myths, to talk honestly. I add that the circulation of a book is insignificant, compared to the millions of people who make up the audience of the television and magazines, and finally of the respect with which I intend to write this book. He recognises this, but remains entrenched in the belief that problems should be hushed up. A polite conversation, but with no real communication.

This makes me think of an incident that took place at the helipad the other day, when I had just left, and which I regret not having witnessed. A woman came to complain to the rescuers, claiming that she was going to lose business as there was so much coverage of rescue operations on the television! It hadn't occurred to her to take it up with the media – and how would she have done so anyway? Who can? Not even the guide I've just been talking about. So she took it out instead on those whose mission is to save people. A strange reaction indeed.

Towards the end of the afternoon, there are fears of a major accident on the Dru, below the American Direct. The first on duty this afternoon are Cazemajor and Fulbert. Eric Fulbert is new here – tall, young, dark-haired and pleasant. The helicopter leaves with Cazemajor on board, but it turns out to be almost a false alarm – just a sprained ankle. This makes Fulbert laugh.

'An exposed rescue operation on the Dru, which might as well be a common or garden pick-up at the Planards!'

The injured man is a giant of a Pole, called Matteus Marcinkovski.

'That means Cazemajor in Polish,' explains Fulbert.

They make him write out his name for the statement.

'Do it cle-ar-ly!' says Fulbert, pronouncing every syllable and commenting for our benefit: 'It looks like Arabic, the way he's writing it!'

Pronouncing every syllable is of no help whatsoever to the Pole, who doesn't understand any French. But he gets the picture, smiles and starts again.

'In the right order!' demands Cazemajor of the questions that have to be asked. 'I've been working in that order for twenty-seven years, and I'm not going to change now!'

'It's such a pain to work with grandads!' sighs Fulbert.

The atmosphere is relaxed. The ambulance arrives. The Pole is placed, sitting upright, on a stretcher. But his feet are still sticking over the edge. And when the stretcher is wheeled inside his head brushes against the roof.

'Careful of the head!' shouts Cazemajor. 'We brought him down for an ankle and you nearly took him to hospital with a fractured skull!'

Everyone laughs, except for the Pole, who hasn't understood. If only all rescues could be like this one!

Another call-out, this time to a crevasse on the Argentière Glacier.

Later, a little before eight o'clock, we hear the details: a case of hypothermia, with a broken leg, straight to the hospital helipad. Olivier Fernandez, who arrives for the night shift, tells me: 'You've got to see Fufu, he's soaked through!'

I go outside. Fulbert's certainly soaked. He had to go fifteen metres into the crevasse with water running over him. The rescue was a delicate operation – they were already deep down and the crevasse plunged a further thirty metres or so. The situation was made all the more worrying by a wider gap close to the spot where the victim had stopped. All in all, a long and difficult rescue under running icy water, which had soaked Fulbert's overalls and even the T-shirt underneath. I offer to make him something warm.

'Hey, he's not going to die!' interjects Cazemajor.

Gilles Bidon, the pilot, takes me to one side and dares me to ask Henri Cazemajor a question that will make him react. I rise to the challenge and approach him, but cautiously all the same.

'Monsieur Cazemajor … Monsieur Bidon claims that you won't hit me if I ask you whether the rescue you've just completed is your 2001st or your 2002nd.'

Cazemajor does react:

'OK, so you're starting too! You've got away with it this once, but watch out next time!'

Friday, August 15

Fourteen rescues in total, nine of which take place in the range.

Among them a bad case with multiple injuries on the Brioche: a young soldier of twenty-two adores the mountains but had gone without permission. This is likely to cause him further problems.

But if he loves the mountains so much, doesn't he at least have an excuse? He's certainly paid for it dearly enough with his accident: a fall of thirty metres, facial injuries, loss of consciousness, fractures of the eye socket, jaw, pelvis, spine and lumbar vertebra, at least four broken front teeth and a 'Glasgow' of thirteen. The Glasgow, as I now discover, is the scale for measuring head injuries, which goes up to fifteen. But the injured man had regained consciousness and was making every effort to speak, despite his difficulties. When Dr Cousineau telephones through his report, he finishes with:

'Say "in a satisfactory condition", so that no one panics, especially his family!'

Towards lunchtime, while I was attending pre-lunch drinks during the Guides' Festival, there was a relatively mundane rescue that nearly turned into a crisis. It took place on the steep bit of the Col du Chardonnet – just a broken leg. You learn to put 'crises' into perspective here: a broken leg becomes even for me 'just a broken leg', because it's easily mended!

Yes, but. Before the helicopter arrived, someone had covered the casualty with a survival blanket, one of those thin metallic films which help to conserve body heat. But when the machine arrived the wind created made the blanket blow away and up into the rotors. There was a dreadful noise. The pilot Gilles Bidon thought (in such cases the power of thought is very direct and blunt) 'If it shits things up, we're goners.' He set off back, but because of the strong sunlight couldn't see one of his flight instruments, the temperature gauge. He thought that it could end in disaster if the sheet was stuck in the turbine. When he was finally able to see the temperature, it was normal and he managed to land on the helipad at the Argentière Hut. All that remained of the survival blanket after it had been shredded by the rotors was a piece the size of a page from a book, which was duly removed.

And then they set off again to carry out the rescue. The victim screamed as soon as he was touched. He was suffering greatly and appeared to have a fractured tibia. That evening after the hospital tests, he turned out to have no injuries and no fracture, just bruising. I've been told again (and have had several chances to verify it this summer) that pain levels are completely different from one person to the next and are nonetheless genuine, even if someone else with exactly the same injury feels little.

Now for another rescue out of the ordinary – in Sixt. A fall at the Cirque des Fonds with no further details. This is given priority over another request (rightly, as will soon become clear): a workman with a lumbago attack on one of the ski lifts. Stuck on a pulley, but quite comfortable in this position he can therefore wait.

It is Alain Place and Benoît Cousineau who went to Sixt. A fifty-three-year-old woman rambler wearing good boots and belonging to a group that had been walking along a path in the schist, rather steep, narrow and sloping. One false step. She slipped on the schist dust, fell, slid on her bottom, then rolled fifty metres, before finally tumbling into a ravine – and straight into a torrent. Her friends pulled her from the water, probably taking the right precautions for her neck and spine, yet risky, but no more than to leave her in forty centimetres of freezing water.

The helicopter had to use the winch, as the steep, schistose terrain prevented it from landing. The wind from the rotors threw up stones all over the place. So Noël Rivière lowered down Place then Cousineau, who tried to find a vein to inject the casualty as soon as he reached her. But her veins refused to comply, due to the vasoconstriction caused by the cold and the injuries. There was no pulse to be felt and the victim's temperature was only 33° Celsius. All this took place in water, mud, falling rocks and black dust. Benoît Cousineau put a needle in each arm twice, with no success, before finally finding a small vein in the top of her wrist. The woman was in great pain – everywhere. He administered a Nubain to ease her suffering. Then she was fitted with a surgical collar, followed by a Ked (a slatted corset which immobilises the wearer from the neck to the thigh and fits into the Piguillem). She was winched up and taken to hospital.

The news that evening wasn't great: a fractured spine and probably skull too. At the scene, the injured woman couldn't move her legs and everyone feared the worst, but she'd regained some movement in the hospital. However, she was complaining of tingling, due to a medullary œdema that was building up pressure. She possibly needed an operation on the vertebrae to alleviate the pressure. Anyway, *Bravo Lima* later transported her to an emergency neuro-surgical unit in Grenoble.

During the mission to Sixt, the workman with lumbago on the pulley was freed and the rescue was no longer necessary.

But then a new call comes in from the Nid d'Aigle: a dislocated shoulder.

'Crikey!' laughs Iglesis who went that way yesterday on the way down from his fourth ascent of the Peuterey Intégral: 'I know it well. I'd have left my sack there if I'd known!'

He leaves with Cousineau and they return with the prettiest accident victim of the summer! A dusky and curvacious twenty-two-year-old with long black hair: Miss Helipad of the year with no contest... She needs support and has a bandaged knee. Her shoulder is wedged with clothes and padding. She's in distress and seemingly a lot of pain. In fact, she later turns out to have no real injury. She's French, born in Nantes, but has an exotic name like a princess from the *Arabian Nights*. As he reads her name later, Julio remarks, 'She really was of a certain type, wasn't she?'

Yes, but *what* type? Mediterranean, certainly, Byzantine perhaps? Her mother-in-law, who was on the scene, was apparently very reluctant to let her leave in a helicopter with – horror of horrors – *men*!

The ambulance carries away this extraordinary beauty, leaving us to wax lyrical about her charms.

'You're the one with all the luck!' Place tells Iglesis. 'I got a right dog just now!'

Towards eight o'clock, it looks like the day's over, but I go on. My friends, the Angels, are taking me to the Eden for dinner, affording me the rare privilege of eating with a 'future rescuee'. It's certainly original!

He's a film-maker whom I've met once before at Autrans and who is preparing to do Mont Blanc du Tacul tomorrow. Jean Afanassief – also in the party that evening – is booked up and, as a result, has referred him to the Guides Company, who have found him someone else. But the 'future rescuee' is extremely freaked out by the idea of his route. He's not exactly what you'd call a mountain expert. Afa has lent him some crampons and, when he tried them out on his boots, he put them on upside down... The helipad is a frequent topic of conversation that evening and I'm asked a lot about what happens there, the atmosphere and everything else, including the accidents...

During dinner, our 'future rescuee' is a source of much mirth. Everyone showers him with advice for avoiding the probable accident. Afa explains to him that things can happen very quickly on the Tacul: 'You slip, you fall over a line of séracs – and there you go!' The 'future rescuee' forces a laugh. I take the list of tomorrow's rescuers out of my bag, give him their names and suggest that if he should come across one called Henri Cazemajor, he can strike up a good relationship by asking him if it's his 2003rd rescue...

Then, as the opportunity presents itself, I suggest taking down all his details now: surname, first name, date and place of birth, address and so on. I'm beginning to learn the routine. This will simplify the identification process, which is often painstaking and complex for the gendarmes, especially when the victim is not in a state to talk properly. I might as well take down the name of the guide too, but the 'future rescuee' only knows him as Antoine. At least we have that!

It's a joyous occasion, which Afa enlivens by regularly treating us to a song which he practised that morning in the Guides' choir and which seems to have made an impression on him: '*We are the little goatherds ...*' The 'future rescuee', who is thinking of all the tomorrows when perhaps there'll be no singing, is the only one who doesn't seem thoroughly entertained.

I have an idea to make him relax and suggest that if he's lucky enough *not* to arrive at the helipad by helicopter tomorrow, then all he has to do is turn up towards 7.30 in the evening with two bottles of champagne to celebrate his non-rescue. At which point, he proposes to walk the kilometre that separates us from the helipad right now, to sleep on the doorstep and to tell the first rescuers on duty:

'There, I saved you some time, by coming straight here!'

He's joking but remains worried. Dominique Angel and I have another laugh at the thought that, if he really does have an accident tomorrow, we'll feel extremely guilty for having joked about it all evening but that the 'dinner with the future rescuee' would be a hell of a good story for the book.

By the time we take our leave, the 'future rescuee' has decided to take a sleeping tablet to stop himself thinking about it during the night. I tell him, 'See you tomorrow at the helipad – either way!'

Perhaps that'll make him bring some champagne at least...

Saturday, August 16
Only six rescues. A few moments worth recording.

The first rescue – of two reportedly exhausted climbers – took place on the Gervasutti Pillar. And they sure were exhausted! They'd probably attempted a route a bit out of their league, which they thought they'd polish off in a day, but at 11 pm, towards the top and only fifty metres from the summit, they were forced to bivouac rather uncomfortably on a slender arête thirty metres away from each other. There was a good ledge only twenty metres below them, but they were too tired even to go back down in the dark. The pair of them were lucky that the weather was good.

Towards four in the morning, they let off red flares. Then, when dawn finally broke, they tried to set off again but couldn't take any more. The rescue request was transmitted in an unusual way: a tourist plane saw the flares, alerted Annecy airport, which telephoned the operations centre of Annecy police station, which in turn notified the PGHM.

This rescue was the first of the day, with Cazemajor and Ribiollet. As the helicopter needed to lose weight in order to use the winch at 4,000 metres, Henri Cazemajor was dropped at the Col du Midi while Thibaud Ribiollet left to undertake the first winching operation of his career as a rescuer, although of course he had an apprenticeship behind him.

'It was just like training,' he told me, 'but with the pleasure of really saving someone!'

Once he was lowered near the mountaineers, he anchored himself and gestured to *Dragon* that he'd be a little while. I think he'll always remember the face that greeted him and the grateful, ecstatic look in its eyes. They struck up the usual conversation.

'Good morning! How are you?'

'Thanks! We're OK ... nothing broken. But just can't go on.'

'What's your name?'

'Christophe.'

'OK, Christophe, this is what we're going to do ...'

He retrieved their scattered equipment, put it in their sack, prepared and checked the harnesses, then called *Dragon* back to winch up the lead climber and then himself, before going down to the valley to refuel.

To reach the other climber, the operation had to be repeated. Ribiollet was winched down to him. This second climber was more exhausted than the first. He was protected only by a small Friend and the rope from above, even though there was a good spike of rock not far from him. But in the darkness that prevailed when they decided to stop for the night, he probably didn't see it. He seemed much more frightened by the idea of being winched up by the helicopter than his companion, but was taken up the same way, followed by Ribiollet.

The 'future rescuee' wasn't far from there and must have seen the helicopter. Was he worried? Or had the effort of climbing for real exorcised yesterday's imaginary demons?

There was also a rescue near the Lac Blanc, where a woman had broken her leg. Her foot was twisted through 90°, which meant that she had to be moved as little as possible and the Piguillem had to be placed directly onto the ambulance's stretcher. She didn't cry out at all. Benoît Cousineau nevertheless gave her a shot of Nubain and then politely enquired: 'Can you see pink elephants?'

'No,' she replied, 'but if they walked past, it wouldn't surprise me.'

I love the way that a mountain rescue allows people to escape momentarily from their own drama, holding out the lifeline of a human relationship which diffuses all tension.

Then there's a call from the Pouce. A guide has heard cries for help. Benoît Cousineau comments:

'It could be the rescue of the day or nothing at all!'

Gilles Perret and Ben Duncan are dubious. The white Lama of the CMBH is free, piloted by an Italian. They can hire it and would very much like to, as it's their last day here. But it's a doubtful case and they hesitate – for budgetary reasons. Finally, they make up their minds. *Dragon* takes off with Franck Junod and Gilles Mathé on board, followed by the Lama.

Left alone with Benoît Cousineau, I enquire about the way rescuers react to medical procedures. He tells me that it varies greatly. Some concentrate on the technical side of the operations, leaving the medical aspects to the doctor, while others have a passion for this element of mountain rescue. Régis Michoux was so interested in it that Benoît is of the opinion that he could almost have done the job of the medic – he prepared syringes and assisted perfectly. Those 'beyond the first flush of youth', Yvon, Cazemajor and Paillé, are often more interested than the young ones, for whom it's the thrill of the mountains that reigns supreme.

The helicopters return. The answer is 'nothing!' They've been right around the Pouce and saw numerous ropes, but everyone was fine. A false alert. It happens. The guide meant well. But here's a question for those who think the rescue service shouldn't be free: who would have paid in this case? The guide? But then, no one would dare report an accident!

A little later I notice a group of people outside near the gate, verging on an altercation. I go out, but it's too late! I've missed an interesting scene. They tell me:

'It's a taxpayer who's cross that we've returned without a casualty or a dead body!'

'And boy, did he yell at us! He said that this valley was polluted from below by the lorries in the tunnel and from above by the helicopters and that it was spoiling his holidays.'

'Apparently, he's got a fabulous chalet at Les Praz. He must have been a 747 pilot who's been polluting all his life and now he'd like to ban helicopter rescues!'

'Or a bloke who owned a cement works or a big factory, but now that he's retired has become a champion of the environment, because he feels that nothing should disturb him, even the mountain rescue!'

A moaner, in other words, whom I imagine will be very pleased with himself tonight: 'I told those 'copter pilots what I think!' Yes, but when his wife has a heart attack on the way up to the Petit Balcon or his son hits a rocky patch on his mountain bike or his grandson is stuck in the Vallot with altitude sickness, he'll be the first to complain that 'they' aren't going faster or can't take off in the fog in the middle of the night. There's a total lack of awareness, especially amongst the second-home owners, who are there so often that they could at least make the effort to be better informed.

The relative calm that day makes me think of autumn. No breeze. Stationary clouds hovering over the peaks. The first yellow leaves on the paths. Perhaps the season is already coming to an end, even though the forecast is for good weather during the next days.

Towards 7.30 pm, the 'future rescuee' hasn't yet been rescued. In that case, did my suggestion to come to the helipad anyway to celebrate his non-rescue strike a cord?

Success! Having become a 'non-rescuee', the 'future rescuee' appears with two bottles of champagne and Jean Afanassief. It's the time when the shifts change over. The Sécurité Civile helicopter team has arrived, as well as the four on duty. We are twelve, maybe fifteen … I don't know exactly.

General surprise at the generosity of the 'non-rescuee': 'Well, if they start to bring us champagne, when they *don't* need us …'

'That'll be 5000 a day!' points out Benoît Cousineau.

'We would drink a lot!' concludes Henri Cazemajor jovially.

'Is *that* the grandad?' the 'non-rescuee' asks me. 'But he looks so young!'

'Of course he's young. But that hasn't stopped him missing out on his 2015th rescue today!'

The champagne has come at just the right time for Thibaud Ribiollet, who is celebrating his first rescue winch.

Sunday, August 17
A rescue from a crevasse on the Rognons Glacier under the Aiguille Verte on the Argentière side. A young guide from Chamonix and his client were on the descent. The guide had the rope coiled around his hand. The client fell through a snow bridge and into the crevasse. The guide had the presence of mind to drop the loops of rope and to jump to the other side to act as a counterbalance, but the client was falling too quickly and dragged him down too. They're more shaken than hurt. The client has a sprain and the guide scraped his face. A former member of the PGHM, now an instructor at ENSA, saw them a moment later, as he was passing the crevasse, and raised the alarm. In any case the guide had a radio and, as soon as he had pulled himself together, would have been able to call himself and even get both himself and his client out, but by then they would have been very cold.

The rescue was an unusual one. Gilles Bidon, the pilot, started by dropping Jean-Louis Oustry next to the crevasse, but, as the hole was wide, Oustry decided they could manage without instal-ling the portable winch on the ground. So he was taken back up then winched directly into the hole by the mechanician to a depth of twelve metres or so, where he detached the rope from one of the two victims, hooked him onto the sling, allowing them to be lifted out of the crevasse together. The same manoeuvre was used for the second man.

'That crevasse!' remarks Jean-Louis Oustry on his return. 'As long as the bridge over it remains, even with its hole, others are going to fall in it. It looks so well covered and the bridge is so wide.'

Later there's a request for a recce from the warden of the Couvercle. Two Germans, who left some equipment at the hut, set off yesterday morning for the Whymper Couloir on the Verte and still haven't returned. Perhaps they'll come back after all, other-wise there'll be a reconnaissance mission, which is impossible for the moment because the Cirque de Talèfre is filled with clouds.

Towards 11.15 am when the weather lifts *Dragon* sets off and reports some time afterwards that the two climbers have been spotted at around 3500 metres but that it wasn't possible to get close to them because of the clouds. The radio transmits Gilles Bidon's message:

'It must be those two. They gestured to us that they didn't need help … either that, or one of them had a broken arm!'

The helipad erupts with laughter. One raised arm means: 'We don't need help', while two raised arms are the sign for a rescue request. Obviously, if someone has a broken arm or shoulder, he can't raise both arms. But there's less risk that this signal for help should be confused with all the one-handed waves that people habitually make when they see a helicopter passing.

It seems that there's almost no one in the mountains. The forecast was for fine but cloudy, generally brightening up in the middle of the day, possibly followed by rain, but it's the opposite of what actually happens. At one o'clock in the morning I could see that it was already raining in the valley. In the middle of the day it's raining too and in the evening the sun returns.

This isn't the only ray of sunshine at the helipad that evening. Pouts arrives too – during a day off from his trainee-guide course.

Philippe Pouts is as good as a sunny spell. You never know if he's making things up or telling the truth, but he's such a good laugh!

This time he tells us about the April Fools' Day when he was on office duty during miserable weather and answered the phone saying:

'Hello, this is the presbytery. I'm listening.'

He remarks: 'There was no problem. People just thought they had the wrong number and rang back.'

And he mimics the conversations.

'Forgive me, father. I meant to call the mountain rescue!'

'No harm done, my son.'

And then, one of the callers turns out to be Colonel du Trémollet, who's in charge of the EMHM.

'It's the presbytery here, I'm listening.'

'It's Colonel du Trémollet here, but … but … what have they done on the switchboard? I asked for the PGHM!'

To avoid getting the switchboard staff into trouble, Pouts humbly admits, 'April fool, colonel! This is Gendarme Pouts. Please accept my apologies.'

Is he making up the reply?

'Well then, Gendarme Pouts, eight days CB … April fool!'

Pouts has an amazing talent for telling stories. I get him on the subject of one of his other anecdotes:

'And when you're on phone duty, you always answer, "To whom do I have the honour of speaking?" Why's that?'

'Ah … it's since I called a senior officer a donkey! It wasn't my fault, he was from the Toulouse region and had exactly the same accent as Darrhort. He asked to be put through to the captain. It was Captain Thimothée at that time. I replied:

'Too bad, he's not here.'

'Put me through to Major Mathieu then!'

'No luck again, he's just left.'

'Who *can* you put me through to, then?'

'Hey, stop it, you donkey! Do you think I haven't recognised your voice? Stop arsing around! Didn't you know it was me … Pouts?!'

'What the devil? It's Commander Métairie here, Assistant Commander of the Haute-Savoie region. Put me through to a senior officer at once!'

'And we continued like that. I was still convinced that it was Darrhort, who was having me on. Eventually he hung up. So, I asked one of the blokes who'd been here longer:

'There isn't a Commander Matari or Motori, is there?'

'Oh, Métairie! Yes, he's the Assistant Commander for the region.'

'I start to feel worried. So then, I phone Darrhort. They tell me he is out in the mountains. I ask where. What a disaster! He couldn't possibly have called me from there!'

'And then all hell broke loose. Faussurier first, demanding a written apology. Then when Major Mathieu came back:

'Pouts, get someone to take over your post and come up to my office right away!'

'What had I gone and done! I picked up the phone and asked for Commander Métairie in Annecy. I said, 'It's Gendarme Pouts, Commander. I beg you to accept my apologies. I mistook you for Darrhort from St-Gervais, who has the same accent as you. There are lots of us from the Pyrenees, aren't there? So it's easy to get mixed up.'

'Oh, I swallowed all my pride! Finally, I made my apology in writing and he was nice about it. He put the matter to one side and, as he retired five or six months later, it's still there.' 'It's like the Balladur incident!

'We all know the story, but it's such a splendid one! It took place during my first day at the helipad in 1993 and made a great impression on me. That's one of the things about the helipad – telling and retelling funny stories, strange rescue missions, and keeping yourself sane through humour. As Gilles Bidon said the other day: If we didn't have a good laugh from time to time here, we'd end up killing ourselves! '

Pouts then carried on with the story:

'Can't remember what I'd done to the mechanician that day, who must have been Nono, but he'd said to me, "I'll get you for that!" And then, we got a rescue request from the Montagne de la Côte. It was Balladur's dog, well, not exactly his dog, but his bodyguard. Edouard Balladur, who was Prime Minister at the time, always had to be escorted by a bodyguard. He was also with Jean-Claude Charlet, the President of the Guides, and his dog. The dog got into a scrap with another dog. The bodyguard tried to separate them but he's the one who ended up getting shoved off the path. Crack! His ankle. They call for us without giving details. So we arrive above a clearing in the trees, where we see people waving their arms about. I attach myself to the winch and begin to go down, when suddenly the helicopter shifts four metres right into the middle of the fir trees. The bastards! I get branches stuck in every part of my body (he acts out this bit), then I reach the ground all covered with twigs, needles and resin. I run to the scene of the accident and who do I see? The Prime Minister!

'At your service, Mr Prime Minister!'

'God, I must have looked an idiot with all those branches! The injured bloke had already been prepared for rescue by the guide. I check everything and attach the ring. He's winched straight up and they send the ring back down to me. I hook myself on. They start to bring me up and for a second time the helicopter moves four metres to the side and I find myself fighting with the trees again (he acts it out). I arrive in the helicopter and tell them:

'Don't be such bloody idiots! It's the Prime Minister down there. And the injured bloke is his bodyguard!

'Yeah, yeah,' they answer. 'And we've been asked to tell you that the Pope is waiting to see you at the helipad!'

'So then I tried to get them to believe that Balladur was going to drop by in person to say thank you to the rescue team. Can you imagine! Everything would have to be ship-shape with perfect uniforms... The dog was called Titus – they made a puppet of him for one of those satirical TV shows.'

Then another rescue comes up – a mountain bike accident near La Flégère. It's only an arm, but a full rescue is needed because the casualty's blood pressure is falling rapidly. He's an entertainer in the children's holiday camp of a big nationalised industry. He was partying last night and hardly slept for some reason or another. He woke up in bad shape, took a Lysanxia tablet (which is some kind of tranquilliser), then set off on his mountain bike and ended up in the bushes. Not very glorious! But once again, it brings us back to the recurring theme of the free rescue service. Shouldn't our society, with its famous motto of liberty, equality and fraternity, also take care of people like this, who certainly have neither insurance nor the means to pay to be rescued? Should this poor boy have been left on his own to recover? Perhaps, but given his state of stress, there was risk of a major collapse. He appeared to be very agitated and panicked when he realised he had a wound on his arm, screaming: 'I'm losing blood, bleeding to death!'

They had difficulty calming him down. He wanted them to telephone his parents immediately and when he was told he'd be able to do so himself, he shouted: 'But I've only got one arm!'

'Don't worry, you can use a telephone perfectly well with only one arm – and the other one will soon be better!'

That's also what rescue's about. Taking care of everyone, whether they're pleasant, responsible, sensible, brave, grateful, or irresponsible, cowardly, unpleasant, grumpy, surly, ungrateful. And to do the best possible for all of them.

After that there's a gourmet interlude. A lady has brought in a lemon tart. Everyone gathers round in the kitchen and Pouts reappears:

'There's heaps of room next door and you're all in here where there's none! As always!'

And, as he mixes with lots of Chamoniards on his aspirant guides' course, he tells us a joke that they tell against themselves:

'At last! I'm beginning to get the rudiments of the local patois into my head. Madame Sauvy, do you speak any Chamoniard?'

I purse my lips expectantly.

'For example, do you know the Chamoniard for: "Please, kind sir, I didn't fully catch the meaning your last question. Would you possibly be ever so kind enough to repeat it?" Well, can you translate that into Chamoniard?'

There's a general silence, before Pouts gives the answer:
'Whaaaaaaaa?'

31

A PAST ACCIDENT:
THE SURVIVAL OF GUY LABOUR

Anniversary of a famous rescue – the week-long ordeal of Guy Labour, seventy years ago.

His name has already occurred in connection with the story of Bobi Arsandaux,[1] but he himself was the subject of so extraordinary an adventure that it is appropriate to talk about it in this book and to contrast for a third time an accident of the old days with those of today.

The story in any case has gone down in the annals. It had a place of honour in Saint-Loup's *La Montagne n'a pas voulu*,[2] the climax of that book.

But the two didn't exactly get on together. Their meeting took place at the Argentière Hut. 'He struck me as a bit of a bore,' Guy Labour wrote me. 'He asked for an interview and I couldn't refuse, but I rather played the cold fish. Hence his judgement!'

It is certainly true, Saint-Loup is not exactly enthusiastic:

> Faced with the perspective of doing a route alone, Guy Labour shows no emotion, no fear. He is twenty-seven. He is a cold man, almost icy, despite his youth.

And further on:

> Guy Labour is now nearly forty. He is still cold, exact, as on the day of his fall. What is his memory of his adventure? 'Generally rather unpleasant ... not exactly one that makes one want to talk about it,' he replies with the ghost of a smile. And Mr Labour, who still mountaineers, despite losing eleven joints, gets out his calculator again ...

Guy Labour, cold, icy? A member of the GDB, a man who when over ninety still came to the tomb of his friend, Bobi, at Argentière and who writes such sensitive letters to me and Captain Gin?

---

[1] See chapter 9
[2] *Paris and Grenoble*. Arthaud 1949, pp 167-205.

So, it is to add a little something to Saint-Loup's book that I briefly tell the story of that outstanding case of survival.[3]

It began on a Friday – August 17, 1934 – the day when Guy Labour, who found himself alone at Chamonix after his partners had left, decided to attempt a solo traverse of the Grands Charmoz. It seemed a reasonable objective in a range that he knew well. The season had suffered from bad weather. But now, at last, it was fine and Guy Labour wanted to profit from his last two days of holiday. He told the lady receptionist at the hotel where he was going 'just in case', and left to catch the Montenvers train.

That evening he bivouacked in his sleeping bag, not far from the Nantillons lake, on the moraine. Next morning: 'Left in dark. Solitude and silence. Sunrise. Daylight spreads. Pleasure of being alone.' He started the route proper, had a bit of difficulty at the Burgener Chimney where his sack ripped and he lost some of his food, but was stopped by the gendarme on the ridge, where traditionally the leader stood on the shoulder of the second. He had hoped to climb it free but after several failures had to give up without going to the summit, since the wind prevented lassoing it. On the descent he met some Parisians he knew at the Rognon, among them the famous mountaineer Micheline Morin.

He carried on down with his ice axe under his arm and was approaching the moraine, when suddenly one of his feet went through the old snow piled up by avalanches. He tried to throw himself forward but was unable to do so and, falling into the crevasse felt two violent blows before coming to stop on a layer of snow and ice, eighteen metres down, without knowing what was below, but without doubt more nothing.

It was Saturday, August 18, 3.15 in the afternoon.

The hotel receptionist was unconcerned by the climber's lateness. On Monday the 20th his family, alarmed by not seeing him, rang his office to find he had not appeared there either. He must have been delayed. Next day, Tuesday the 21st, they got seriously worried. The hotel was telephoned. The receptionist remembered that the young man had left on Friday. Where? Climbing… The guides were alerted and prepared the stretcher for bringing back

---

[3] The following information does not derive from Saint-Loup's book, not very accurate and somewhat romanticised, but from the letters I received from Guy Labour and the text of a lecture he gave in 1948 on the subject and which he kindly showed me. This chapter was read and approved by him before his death.

corpses. Four days ... What else could one expect? And where to look for him? It was not the epoch when helicopter recces were made.

The brother of the missing man came straight away. His mother joined him. They were prepared to fight, not lose hope, to do everything to ensure a search took place and continued. The guides did not really believe in it. Certainly they were paid for the days spent, but were of the opinion they were wasting time, time which passed and with it any last chance.

The delay in raising the alert and starting the search, obviously meant that the news did not get out. It was not until Friday, August 24 that the Paris papers reported it, that his disappearance became known, confirmed and made public. Micheline Morin learnt about it at Zermatt where she now was. She sent a telegram to Chamonix to say she had seen Guy Labour on the date concerned at the Rognon Nantillons, on his way down. At least they knew where to start looking. But after all that time ... Despite the pessimism of the guides and their desire to give up, the family insisted they continue. Paul Mugnier and Camille Ravanel set off on Saturday, August 25.

'Hey, a rope in the crevasse,' one said whilst searching around the glacier. 'And a call "Help!" ... It's Labour!'

'Don't be an idiot! ... Labour's been dead for ages!'

But it was him. His eighth day of waiting.

But how had he spent the time?

He had first surveyed the situation.

Where I am, it's some four metres wide. Above? The wall against which I am leaning is perfectly smooth, even overhanging. The other side is not much better ... Yet, rather like a column, a protrusion of ice some five or six metres high sticks out. Above, the wall is less steep, perhaps even a shade under the vertical. And then up high, at fifteen or sixteen metres, four or five 'landings', and some sort of edge.

Higher still, like the dormer by which a tiler gains access to the roof, is the ceiling of a sixth landing as seen from the bottom of a stair-well, with a round hole, my door of entry! A little splinter in that hole, my ice axe which caught on the surface.

So now, how to get out?

The ice protrusion on the wall to my right seems to be the best chance.

But all I have is a large rock piton as a tool and two painful wrists to operate it.

Guy Labour decided to have a try. When he stood up he staggered and realised he had been more shaken by the fall than he had thought. With great difficulty, in a couple of hours' effort, he had cut two or three steps and deemed it better to get organised for a bivouac so as to start again next day, rested.

Not much in his rucksack: a pullover, a waterproof cag, a spare pair of socks, a hundred grams of raisins, eight Novaltine tablets, thirty grams of almond paste, a candle end, two boxes of matches.

He was shivering. He lay down, curled up on his abseil rope, a puttee under his head as isolation from the ice.

Another try the second day. He managed to reach the first buttress, formed by the upper part of the ice column. Then bit by bit, by dint of much effort and time, gained a further fourteen metres and reached what he believed would be an ice ledge, but turned out to be no more than a bit of a bench with a lip. Without ice axe, it was impossible to cut a passage beyond. He stayed there a long time, refusing to acknowledge defeat, heard the sound of distant voices and yelled, without reply.

Leaving the rope hanging on either side of the ice buttress, he decided to climb back down, knowing that rescue could only come from outside, trying to work out when. He began losing feeling in his feet, despite rubbing them.

The second night was very long. And the day that followed also. All the time Guy Labour passed in the crevasse, seemed infinitely long to him. He was continually shivering, yet without really feeling the cold, and reckoned that the body was defending itself by a nervous reaction. From time to time, he called out, almost as a duty, knowing perfectly well that in crevasses sound does not carry upwards, or not far.

Third night. Always shivering but with the absolute determination not to 'be cold' and mulling over the accounts of Alexandra David-Neel he had read, sure that one could fight cold other than by purely physical means.

When he woke the fourth morning he decided to climb back up, to see if from the ledge he had reached there might not be some sort of exit. The steps he had hacked out two days before allowed him to get there fairly quickly. Determined to make it work, whatever the cost, he cut holds for his hands and excavations for his feet; it took him an hour to make a single step, and he would need twenty-five or thirty. Coming back down to the shallow bench with its edge he noticed that at its back was a kind of crack in the ice, some three metres high, with perhaps snow at the top. He started jamming up it, but suddenly slipped and fell over backwards. He found himself hanging by a heel, with the foot trapped in the crack by its crampon, head down, over the wall.

After some unsuccessful attempts to catch hold of the edge of the bench, he realised he had to do something quickly; he was going purple and exhausting himself. Here is his account

> I grab the knee of the leg that was jammed with my hands, and then by my teeth, and so crawl up it to the level of the heel and finally get my hands on to the hold cut on the lip of the ledge; but I am completely doubled over, head against the leg, and I can't budge the foot. I'm choking, my hands are numbing on the ice and I am losing feel, in a moment they will start opening, leave go and it's all over… I make one last desperate effort, yank on my hands and the jammed leg, and violently arch my body over.
>
> The leg frees itself and I am left hanging by my hands. I manage to get my feet back into the holds and onto the ledge, almost unconscious. My hands are by now completely numb and I've lost all feeling. The only thing I am conscious of is the need to get back down, and that urgently.
>
> With my teeth I close my fingers so they can hook on to the holds, and trust they won't open of themselves. Through sheer will-power I descend. I get some help from the rope left hanging either side on the ice column five or six metres from the bottom, collapse over backwards, having probably passed out at the end.

The waiting starts again, now almost semi-comatose. Guy Labour struggled to fight off the torpor. He heard calls, yelled back, but in vain.

At five in the afternoon his ice axe falls beside him from where it had been hanging. Too late. Guy Labour was shaking too much to act and couldn't remain standing. He wrote in his notes: 'Feet freezing more and more… Even so still hope.'

The fourth night was long, broken by bouts of shaking. The slow passage of time became obsessive. On the fifth day, despite his sparing use of food, he had none left. His toes became a black purple, his limbs grew cold. He had a raging thirst, probably fever, was cold to the knees. He tried to lie quite still, apart from the spasms of shaking, curled up in a ball to preserve such body heat as he had.

A fifth night passed thus.

Sixth day, unending:

Nothing ... shouts ... Growing colder. My legs are quite dead. I remain unmoving, eyes closed. This evening, a storm, magnificent, lightning, the thunder roaring, fantastically, outside. Snow and hail fall. I am covered by five or six centimetres during the night, the sixth.

I have hardly the strength to shake it off, and am not much concerned anyhow. To quench thirst I eat hail. It melts in the mouth, much better than snow or ice.

Seventh day:

135 hours. Despite being covered by hail, I am not really cold, even though my feet are frozen and the lower body numb to the thighs. And this continuous shaking ... Is it this idea that remains absolutely primordial: I MUST NOT be cold. And yet, what good is it?

I am certainly in a fever, I am thirsty. On the other hand, I am not hungry, despite eating hardly anything for five days and nothing at all for two. But I imagine nice things; pineapple in syrup; a good underdone leg of lamb etc.

Also a desire for sunny, warm places. Memories of Hossegor, the sun drenched beaches.

From time to time, despite being in a semi-coma, I shout, but I am aware my calls are ever feebler. A clear impression I'm sinking seriously.

Pretty awful night, it is the seventh. Extreme weariness, curious desire to get it over with ... It's been going on too long, lost will.

'Eighth day starting. A partial collapse of the edge of the snow on which I rest, early in the morning.

One leg more or less hangs down. Is there yet more emptiness below me? Eleven o'clock ... One hundred and sixty-four hours I have been here and how much longer will I go on counting the hours.'

Nearby, a voice.

Hey! A rope in the crevasse!'

Immediately, instinctively I yell. I have the time to think 'Quick before they move away.' Then, 'my voice is pretty feeble.'

I hear the same voice: 'Someone's calling ... Help ...!'

And then something deep, deep inside me 'IT'S OK. CONTACT'S BEEN MADE.' It is for a moment a prodigious shock, almost electric, instantaneous, extraordinary. It's a turning upside down, a feeling, at a vast scale (what words to use to explain it?) that the 'story is finished'. And then, as quickly, a total and absolute relaxation of the mind. I know that, 'now it's in the past, memories to be recounted' ... And it is calmly, almost technically, that I say, 'It is Labour!' And the other voice stating 'It is Labour!' And then another voice, further away, replying 'Don't be an idiot! ... Labour's been dead for ages!

The long story of this survival epic finished therefore on Saturday, August 25.

Guy Labour lost eleven joints of his toes. He spent four months in hospital, but a year after his accident, in August 1935, he led a rope up the Grands Charmoz.

The reasons he came out of it so well are various. In the first place, a positive outlook, collected and calm, meant that he was not overtaken by fear, did not imagine the worst. Then, the will to find a solution for himself and, once that failed, the refusal to despair: on the contrary to keep the confidence that help would come from outside eventually. Finally, his physical reactions, coupled to the certainty that, as Alexandra David-Neel had observed in Tibet, one can defend oneself against cold more effectively than is the usual practice; to curl up into a ball, to concentrate the mind. He remembered a solitary bivvy at Bleau, when wet and frozen, without a stove, he had the impression of warming up, rolled in a ball and drying out. He also thought about a bivouac on the Dru where, while the others never stopped fidgeting about, dancing around, singing to keep warm, he 'curled up' motionless, and found himself no more chilled in the morning than they, and a great deal less tired. Learning from these experiences, he drummed into his mind that he 'did not want to be cold'.

'That certainty [he wrote me] was both rational and instinctive, something fixed in me: I had no need to 'know that I must' any more than 'oblige myself' to breathe. This 'not to be cold' was also a part of myself. It was a fight, certainly, but it was 'a part of myself'. All that is terribly difficult to explain. It's the first time I've tried to put it down on paper and write about it.[4]

A final point concerning cold: of all the doctors I've spoken to about it, whether friends, experts, or general practitioners, I have never had a reaction. Always a total silence and a change of subject.[5]

Finally let us mention it is Guy Labour's story that inspired Roger Frison-Roche's famous novel *La Grande Crevasse*.

[4] Letter of December 7, 1992.
[5] Today the phenomena of hypothermia are better known and controlled. In the summer following receipt of that letter, or the one after, I had the pleasure of introducing to each other, Guy Labour and Dr. Foray, then a surgeon at the Chamonix Hospital and particularly interested by the phenomena of hypothermia and frostbite.

32

UNDERESTIMATING THE COSMIQUES

Monday, August 18

Five rescues. Plus a reconnaissance of the crevasse on Les Courtes where a body remains: a new snow slide has made it unlikely that it will be recovered this year, even though the rope that was tied on to the victim is still there.

Serious: the accident of a young woodman electrocuted whilst cutting down a tree under a high tension line. A branch touched it and the current passed through the saw down his arm to his feet. His father who was with him, ran down to give the alert at Saint-Nicolas de Véroce. The helicopter with the doctor were on the spot ten minutes later, just half an hour after the accident. That too is what mountain rescue is about.

Several calls come in at the same time in the afternoon. A small girl bitten by an adder, a Spanish climber hurt and stuck at the famous grade IV step on the Cosmiques Arête, a Dutch pair who arrive at the helipad, with the wife in tears, because they have lost their children on the way down from Montenvers.

Everything is organised, at Major Darrhort's expense, for every time he is on first call-out, there is a rescue on foot, because weather, cloud cover or turbulence prevent flying. As today; thick cloud and a foot rescue for the Spaniard. Astonished at the regularity of his bad luck, Darrhort gets ready with the resignation of a Greek hero pursued by the Fates, whilst I perfidiously recommend he doesn't forget to take what is needed for a possible bivouac.

As for the Dutch, I try and help, touched by the mother's tears, and explain in English there is nothing to worry about. The children, who were in front of them, must have taken another way down. Dr Duperrex notes what they were wearing. The helicopter is busy. I suggest they return to Les Bois, which is where they had come out and then try the main Montenvers track to Chamonix. The mother calms down. A bit later they come back all smiles, the boys had been found sitting at the back of the car.

August 19
Unfortunately, a death today: a nineteen-year-old German in the Whymper Couloir. A rope of three, he the oldest. They'd left very early yesterday for the Moine Ridge of the Verte. Fairly slow and somewhat lost, they had decided not to go for the summit after thirteen hours climbing. Not at all sure of the way down, they ended up wandering around between the Moine and Grande Rocheuse ridges, crossing the Whymper from time to time. In order to try and minimise the risk, they had eventually unroped. The last man, who had the rope in his sack, was carried off by a fall of stone and ice. Lost in the cloud, seeing nothing and without a rope or a clue where they were, the other two had nevertheless managed to get down, crossing the bergschrund at night.

They were pretty frightened, I was told ... 'They'd had a brush with death'.

At daybreak, the alert having arrived during the night, the helicopter had located the body. A sad story.

Less stressful, more anodyne, although rare: a guide reporting someone apparently playing the pirate guide with clients on Mont Blanc du Tacul. Another guide made the same complaint shortly after.

As gendarmes, the matter fell into the PGHM's domain, even though policing in the mountains is not a particularly pleasant role. In a case where someone is passing himself off as a guide, and the clients are witness to the fact, it can have serious consequences. So the second pair on duty, Pierre Bernier and Thibaud Ribiollet, were given the task of investigating the matter, but in the event it turned out to be a proper guide, from the Vosges. Perhaps his ice technique was not up to date, or he was out of practice. But he wasn't illegal.

A rescue on the Frontier Ridge (Kuffner). Two clients with a guide who was not a local. One client hurt. A wound in the thigh. He arrived here pretty upset, indeed furious.

'Give me a sedative! Give me a sedative!' he was yelling to Dr Duperrex in the helicopter, who explained he could not give him an injection whilst in flight.

But on arrival he gave him a shot of Nubain.

'Put me on a drip, a drip!' the man demanded.

Duperrex placed a venflon in the crook of his elbow, so it might be used if needs be at the hospital.

While awaiting the helicopter the guide had bound up his thigh over his climbing breeches, and Guy Duperrex thought it best to leave the bandage in place for transporting him.

The ambulance still has not arrived. Jean-Jacques Malineau started taking details for the formal report. The man was forty-seven and not best pleased.

'You were with a guide?'

'Yes,' grunted the victim. 'So as to be sure not to have an accident!'

'What happened? Did you get hit by a stone?'

'A stone! A ruddy great block! All the fault of the old fart who was with us. He was in the middle, me at the back because I was the best! And Grandad knocked off a block.'

'You mean he pulled on a flake which gave way?'

'Flake? I've told you, a block! Larger than that stretcher over there! Big as the helicopter! If I had not bent my head to one side, I would have got it on my head! The guide went past it OK, but the old fart, of course, had to knock it off on me.'

On the helipad, one often sees stoics. But not this one, who moaned when he was given the injection, and let out a deep roar of pain when he was carefully placed on the ambulance stretcher. He leaves for the hospital. We don't see the other two who didn't ask to be brought down and finished the route.

That evening we learned that the injured man had indeed had a pretty deep gash, and had been even more excitable at the hospital where François Lecoq took charge.

'Yet you gave him a shot of Nubain,' I said to Guy Duperrex.

'Yes, he seemed to be suffering, but not really from pain. Its rather a Tranxene I should have given him.'

Outside the range, Gilles Mathé had to pick up someone pretty badly damaged after a parapent accident, and a rider who had been kicked by his horse and had his leg broken. These outside rescues are often atypical.

August 20 – 21

Not much on the 20th. A lady golfer who had hurt her back a few days ago had an attack of lumbago at the Argentière Hut. Mountain or golfing accident?

On 21st a feeling that the season is coming to an end. Only one serious rescue, in a crevasse at the Envers where an Italian man and woman had done the Ryan/Lochmatter on the Plan and were descending the glacier. She slipped and he was unable to hold her, both ending up in a crevasse. He was unhurt and able to get out under his own steam, and then extracted her by hauling on the rope, which must have been very painful for her, but without doubt better than letting her chill. By the time the helicopter arrived, about thirty minutes after the accident itself, her temperature had already fallen to 35°. Hypothermia sets in faster when someone is seriously injured – a symptom warning the doctor. She had a broken femur and hip.

August 22
So relieved to be able to tell myself it is finished, the season is over, that I do no more than telephone the helipad. Dr Marsigny replied;
    'Helipad at Les Bois. How can I help?'
    'It's Anne Sauvy... Nothing, I suppose?'
    'Nothing ... depends what you mean. I collected a serious death on the Frontier Ridge this morning. It's what can be termed a therapeutic failure.'
    The alert had come in at 5.05. Two Italians, twenty-two and twenty-four. Shortly after leaving the Fourche Hut where they had spent the night, the leader climbed on to a block which gave way and was carried off on the Combe Maudite side. The block had cut the rope. A guide had taken charge of the uninjured man back to the Fourche and given the alert.
    The same day a parapenter broke a leg, and a Pole fell into a crevasse in the Durier area and broke an arm and a leg.
    Will the season never end?

Saturday, August 23
Stand easy! For me, at least who was going with John to Geneva to pick up the English translator of my short stories, Anthea Bell, who was bringing a lovely present, a Burman kitten: Ninotchka.
    It is after all the end of the season. And yet, six rescues. Nothing very dramatic, but one typifies the sort of welfare state mentality that perfectly healthy climbers can develop.
    Call-out for a twisted ankle in the Grands Mulets area, on the way down from Mont Blanc. The helicopter lands.

'Ah, those parasites who collect the moment the 'copter arrives anywhere near Mont Blanc,' Jackie Paillé expostulates when he gets back.

Not far from the pair with the injured man were another couple, a father and a fourteen-year-old daughter.

'Take us down too,' the father said. 'We don't know where we are.'

Jackie Paillé doesn't like that kind of casual attitude.

'Can't you see the track?'

'Yes, but we were following the others. And in any case my daughter has gone quite pale.'

'I don't find her at all pale… But hey! Where's your rope? On a glacier you haven't put the rope on! Its unforgivable… You'll kindly put it on straight away.'

'But we'll fall in a crevasse.'

'No, you've already got through most of it and you'll get through the rest… And properly roped up, please!'

'We'd be happier if you could take us down.'

'This is not a taxi! In one hour from here you'll be at the cable-car. When you want to do a route you start and finish it!'

'Yes, but we didn't realise it was going to be so long.'

'Sir! There are two organisations that are there to advise, open every day, the Office de Haute Montagne, and the PGHM. At the PGHM I was on duty before you left and I did not see you come in. So now please be kind enough to assume your responsibilities and finish the route properly… Off you go. You've only another hour to walk.'

August 24

More people out climbing, this Sunday. Seven rescues, plus another investigation concerning a pirate guide. This time, an Englishman. For an English guide to practise in France his diploma must be recognised by the Ministry of Sport. It was the Chief Inspector of the profession, an instructor at ENSA, who was advised and reported it to the PGHM. Questioned by telephone, the hut warden at the Albert Premier, replied that indeed an Englishman had arrived alone, left the hut alone in the morning, but had spoken with four others who were not signed in with him, and had left for the Aiguille du Tour.

Alain Place and Jean-Louis Oustry were designated and the

helicopter dropped them off near the bergschrund. They spotted the rope of five. An open and shut case, caught in the act!

The guiding profession is protected by law against illegal guides, unqualified but being paid. They can, if caught, be prosecuted and fined and are also liable to have problems with the fiscal authorities, etc. And in this particular case prosecuted as a foreigner illegally working in France.

Place and Oustry stopped another party with a guide to give the impression of a routine check. Then the suspects. But in the end it was in order. A group of soldiers on training in France. Those in charge brought the official papers to the PGHM that evening. No pirate guide, again!

Much sadder is the matter of the Italian killed in the Goûter Couloir. A forty-year-old man, from Milan, carried off by stone-fall. The Goûter Couloir on the normal way to Mont Blanc is a dangerous place. This year it seems to have been benign. But no. It has claimed a death.

The body is taken to the mortuary. At the helipad the rucksack is examined, covered with dark blood. I ask Guy Duperrex what he died from. He makes a helpless gesture:

'He had lost half his head, so...'

The sack is emptied, the papers in it examined. I find it upsetting. There is everything that is needed for a route in the sack, for efficiency, survival, comfort: a green anorak, a violet polar jacket, gaiters, gloves, a blue helmet.

I remark: 'He wasn't wearing his helmet...'

One of the rescuers replied: 'With the way he was hit, helmet or not, it would have made no difference.'

The inventory continues; two ice axes, two receipts from the hut. So, he was on the way down, with someone else, we don't know who yet. Papers, his photo... I wonder if he has a wife, children... We learn that night he was unmarried... Perhaps a good thing in that case. But he'd still have family. He worked in a bank. I notice that yesterday was his birthday, August 23. Perhaps, surely, he had done Mont Blanc to mark that psychological turning point, forty. The death of this unknown person, now revealing himself, is becoming poignant.

Fortunately, there is no longer the throng of journalists, like in the high season. No one for this particular accident.

August 25

The main rescue comes in the middle of the afternoon. A guide who, I hasten to add, is not from the Chamonix Company calls for help for one of his clients who has fallen into a crevasse on the Argentière Glacier. The helicopter leaves and comes back with her in her knickers. It is to be hoped that a more suitable covering had been removed, soaked by the melt water.

Nevertheless, nothing had been done safely. The route was over. So they amused themselves by jumping crevasses, without crampons, rope, harness or helmet. The young woman had fallen five or six metres into a twisting crevasse, hitting the sides twice and was jammed, thanks to her sack. The guide descended to her, tied her on and, since there were several of them, he and his clients were able to haul her to the surface. She was suffering from bruising and a wound on her chin.

'And if she laid a complaint against the guide she would win,' commented a rescuer, moved by the adventure.

It should be added that fortunately there are very few charges laid, which indicates that in general people assume their own responsibility. At least when there isn't anything serious.

'Better to appear an idiot by roping up on a glacier where everyone walks without a rope,' Dubrulle summed up sententiously, 'than to take some of the risks we see!'

August 26

Sky covered. Clouds swirling. Few breaks. Turbulent at altitude.

An accident on the aspirant guides course. One of them had slipped at a point where the quality of the ice changed, in the Chéré Couloir on the Tacul. He had an instructor and Philippe Pouts on his rope. The ice screw belay held, but he fell awkwardly and broke his femur. So it's serious and caused a bit of a stir here because he was a colleague from the Modane PGHM.

August 27 – 29

The 27th, two cases of acute mountain sickness at Vallot: in reality two Belgians, drunk as lords, I was told. Torn ligaments, small rescues then more seriously, a pulmonary œdema case at the Couvercle. Yet the altitude, less than 3000 metres is not very great. But the victim is young: a boy of nineteen.

The 28th, so much rain that the helicopter hangar is not even opened.

The 29th. Some pretty mundane incidents, but getting on for 7pm a foot rescue had to be organised for the IV step on the Cosmiques. An expedition that soon took on epic proportions. The helicopter was able to drop Fulbert, Yvon, Place and Poirot at the Plan d'Aiguille. It couldn't go farther because of the wind and cloud. But the lift that was to take them and their material, hand winch, Piguillem etc, to the top of the Midi wouldn't start and it took a full half hour for the operator to get it going again. So the team was at the summit about half past eight and it would soon be nightfall.

There, Louis, forty and the most experienced of the climbers who had given the alert, was awaiting them. The other two were beginners, unable to do the IV step. The adventure had all the characteristics of the major epic which befalls beginners. First they had not left early enough, but taken the 10 am lift. It must be admitted that when one looks at the route description it has nothing to get alarmed about, two, two and a half hours...

But there was a thick covering of fresh snow, sufficient to make a guide and his client turn back. Not them. They attempted to follow another rope, but when they got to the IV step, they did not see how the others had done it. They considered it too hard and tried elsewhere, to find themselves at the base of a slab, forty metres high. On its left a corner full of ice...

The adventures which beginners experience are often much more exciting than those of the climbing stars. Hearing about them may make you want to laugh, and yet in reality they are characterised by relative prowess, strong and genuine emotions, dangers overcome, sometimes quite incredibly. The Cosmiques Arête is like a small section of a major route, all the more so since it lies at 3800 metres: but it is considered easy because it can be reached by the cable-car. How many tragic comedies, perhaps even tragedies, have taken place there in the forty years the cable-car has been open? No one knows, but the chronicle of them would certainly be long. And an adventure, after all, is proportional to the scale of the objective and the human capacities challenging it. It is not any the less just because the objective is as modest as are the abilities.

So Louis, the oldest, had managed to climb the icy corner, bring up Olivier, twenty-seven, the stronger of the two others, but Brice, the youngest, at twenty-six, couldn't do it. The pitch was buffeted by the wind. Things must have been pretty tense!

So the leader decided to go and get help. When he left his companions, Olivier was above the IV pitch and Brice on the platform below. They had a rope between them and they could hear each other, but neither was warm nor happy. One doesn't know how things would have turned out had they spent the night. Badly, doubtless. At that time of the year, the nights get longer and colder and, of course, they hadn't foreseen a bivouac and had not taken the necessary gear.

Place and Poirot, once at the summit, hurried off down to them whilst Yvon and Fulbert started fixing the upper section with ropes. Neither was roped up, on such easy ground for them, but they had brought along four ropes. To get to them quickly, Place and Poirot rappelled the big slab, Patrick Poirot looked after Olivier while Alain Place joined Brice, frightened and freezing. No need to say that both were much relieved and happy to see rescue arrive. The rescuers learnt that Olivier was a priest.

'Bet you said your prayers.'

'Yes indeed ... for us and for you.'

At that point a clearing seemed to be developing and it was hoped that the helicopter could come, highly desirable for Brice. Alain Place had lowered him to a spot where he could be winched up and joined him there. For ten minutes the helicopter made the attempt, but the clouds were moving on and off the ridge, the following wind was gusting, and the area is littered with cables which made flying hazardous. They failed. Night was falling. The rescue would definitely have to be done on foot.

The most difficult problem to overcome was getting Brice up. They thought they might do so with the use of a jumar and Patrick Poirot pulling from above, but without success. The only answer was to use the portable winch to haul him, and as that had not been foreseen initially, it had been left on the landing platfom. With great haste Poirot, Fulbert and Yvon went to get it. It was installed on the big slab.

This 'small' rescue, near a cable-car, was being undertaken in difficult conditions. The thermometer at the Aiguille du Midi showed –10°C, and with the chill of an icy 40 kph wind, more like –15°.

On the big slab, the rappel rope had remained in place and so could be used as a running belay. Alain Place and Brice were winched up together, to the level of Olivier who was then joined by Alain Place. By attaching the ropes to those that had already been fixed, one of them took Brice to the summit. Alain Place was then winched with Olivier up the remaining bit of slab, and accompanied him to the summit. And whilst those saved tried to warm up in the room used by the cable-car operators, the four rescuers set about packing the portable winch, and recovering the equipment and coiling ropes.

In the cable-car on the way down, looking at the spectacle of Louis and Brice slumped on their sacks, cags hanging off them, glasses askew, totally out for the count, Patrick Poirot remarked

'Looks like an old photo of the famous rescue epic of the Dru.'

And turning to Olivier, Jean-Luc Yvon said:

'Rescue is free, OK, but for you all the same it will be two *Our Fathers* and three *Hail Marys*.'

August 31

When I arrive at the helipad and I hear about the fatal accident in Paris that has involved Princess Diana and Dodi Fayed and two others, a driver and a bodyguard (who survived). At first I cannot believe it but then learn it was real.[1] They were being pursued by journalists, intent on adding a bit more spice to their story.

We have to cope with what's happening here on the last day of August – six rescues, two of which are important.

Two hurt after a fall in snow on the North Face of Mont Maudit. A man and a woman. François Lecoq sums up the cases from a doctor's point of view.

'Two uninjured, no problem. Two dead, no problem. One dead, one uninjured, no problem. One hurt and one unhurt, no problem. But two seriously injured, that's quite a different matter. Normally one looks first at the one who is making the most noise.'

This morning the man was screaming, but she was in a coma. So it was with her he started. Then he turned to the other, placed a venflon and gave him an analegesic. Both had facial injuries. But they will survive, they will live, that's the essential.

Another accident this afternoon, exceptional, unforeseeable. Six people with three guides, doing the traverse of Mont Blanc – a

---

[1] The author's views and the views of the rescuers on this matter are more fully developed in the French edition of this book: *Secours en montagne*, Arthaud, 1998

venture organised by the board of a computing company. The chairman, the most brilliant of their scientists, had arranged this outing with François Marsigny, brother of Bernard.

Everything went well. But at the end, on the path that leads to the Plan d'Aiguille, whilst François Marsigny was bringing up the tail with a client who was tired and falling behind, he saw this engineer, a huge man, sitting on a rock, doubled up. When he got to him he said:

'Come on, it's almost finished. We're just getting to the cable-car station.'

But the other got up, attempted to knock him to the ground, yanked him by the shoulder, tearing his clothes, and threatened him with his ice axe.

According to Dr Lecoq, one can kill someone in such a crisis. Happily, he killed no one, but he continued to behave abnormally, made off towards the gully of a mountain torrent, descended into it and started rolling around, knocking his head against the rocks.

There was an immediate call out for 'someone unbalanced' near the Plan d'Aiguille. That could have meant anything or everything. But it was the latter. To master this normal person who had thrown such a fit needed two rescuers, Jackie Paillé and Olivier Renard, plus the doctor.

François Lecoq tried to discover how serious a case he was. The man understood.

'Open your mouth.'

And he opened it but could not speak, not a single word. His mind had lost language, and doubtless many other things. The back of his neck was rigid. He had suffered a brain haemorrhage, probably due to the bursting of an aneurism, that is a deformation of the artery to the brain. That may be caused through physical effort, but can happen at any time, usually around the age of thirty, with no precursor symptoms. This man had just turned twenty-nine and was in perfectly good shape.

Naturally, an urgent flight to the helipad of the hospital.

Later the rescuers and Dr Lecoq return.

Jackie Paillé and Olivier Renard had the unfortunate man's rucksack whose contents they had to list as required; identity papers, driving license, professional visiting cards, cheque book, still largely unused, electronic address book, mobile phone. (Had he called from the summit of Mont Blanc: 'Guess where I am'?) The personal sack always says something of its owner. True, this man was not dead, but the prognosis was not good and there probably would be sequels.

François Marsigny and a young man and woman from the group arrived at the helipad. All very upset in their own way. It certainly was as unusual a case as it is rare.

François Marsigny was still mightily shaken at the reactions of his client, for whom the route had gone so well, and was so nearly finished.

The young man, a colleague, could not take on board the suddenness of so unexpected an event.

'Don't you realise, he was a specialist engineer in computing. He was the most brilliant of us. The firm will never recover from his loss. How's he going to be?'

'I would be lying if I said he was going to be OK,' replied François.

'But it's terrible! How are we going to manage. And his mother must be told!'

'Was he married?'

'No. But he has a father, half-brothers and sisters. The father will know how to get in touch with the mother. We must telephone!'

'If I were you, I'd wait for a more definitive prognosis.'

'Yes. You're right'

This incident shook us all and the discussion around the sack that had been emptied on the helipad tarmac was somewhat febrile.

With this rescue, ended the month of August.

33

END OF THE SEASON

Monday, September 1
There does happen sometimes the kind of accident which accords with the public image. Not often, but occasionally. Particularly on Mont Blanc. There's one today, on Mont Maudit, probably on the traverse of Mont Blanc.

A lone climber. By no means young; sixty. But at least not in trainers. Real boots, of leather. In jeans. A leather belt serves as harness with a krab on it. For the rest, a T-shirt and a fleece jacket, no anorak. Crampons with anti-balling soles. If he had an ice axe or a ski stick it was lost in the 300-metre fall. Half-scalped, cheek bone broken, broken ribs, and a pneumothorax. That evening I was shown his rucksack: a little green bag like teenagers wear on the Boul' Mich in Paris, with a water bottle, a screw-gate karabiner and a small sling.

Pretty light gear for soloing. What was he doing there? Another of those mountain mysteries.

The weather is becoming less good. One feels autumn approaching. The willow herb feathers blow across the helipad. There is a slight haze. Some clouds blow over. It's warm. The crickets are chirping.

Seated outside I catch up on my notes. Daniel Poujol who has taken over with *Bravo Lima* today comes and sits on the steps. We chat. That is what's still best about the helipad this summer and what I like, a community, a continuous change round of those there and with whom conversation is always worthwhile.

A new rescue. Same place; the Maudit. Four Germans who have slid a 150 metres. A slow party for it is already late in the afternoon. *Bravo Lima* has to make some quite considerable manoeuvres, with intermediate drop-offs, to recover them.

We learn later the reason for the accident. Those Germans seemed unaware that, in descent, the best goes at the back, so he is above and can check a slip. They had put their best man at the front and the rest in reverse order. All very correct – the proper hierarchy – but with the worst outcome. The last climber fell and dragged his mates off.

Nevertheless, one must acknowledge the high level of organisation, equally Germanic, which determined their rescue. They had with them a large sheet of cloth with HELP on it which they spread out on the snow and which was seen from the Tacul. They built an igloo to spend the night if necessary. And when the helicopter arrived they fired off a red rocket at it. It made us laugh, the idea of a helicopter brought down by the friendly fire of those to be rescued.

And they must have found a bit anarchic these French who rode the gusts of wind to come and save them and who joyously greeted them, including a female of the species, me, at the helipad. There were two unhurt, with short white beards, no youngsters. Two were injured, with cuts on the head which one of them had bound up, and the fourth was grazed all over. Nothing really broken. One was limping. The worst hurt was installed on the ambulance stretcher while the other posed by him and a third took the photo for the record. Everyone else grouped around them, laughing. A good rescue, nice human touches.

Tuesday, September 2 – 5
September 3, a rather surprising rescue, particularly as it involved a guide with his client who had left two days earlier for Mont Blanc and spent the night at the Goûter. The Meteo had announced a depression for the next day, which duly arrived. The pair were caught in the storm and lost the way near the Col du Dôme during the descent. Casting around to return to the Goûter, they had passed on to the east side instead of the west and found themselves in a difficult zone. The two men fell several times into crevasses but managed to get out. They wandered around. Then, seeing that night was falling and that they would spend it in the open, they installed themselves in a sort of hole. The guide, by no means young, had no radio. Neither had anything left to eat nor to bivvy: one doesn't expect to bivouac on the Ordinary Route on Mont Blanc.

Next morning, the worried wife of the client advised the PGHM. A recce located them. They were on steep slopes, liable to avalanche, and extremely tired. In fact there was a major chance of a serious accident and they were lucky that all ended well.

September 5
No rescue but a curious scene at the PGHM which I witnessed, for Jackie Paillé and I were seated on the little armchairs in the hall, chatting.

Daniel Duret was at the reception. Enter a pretty curious personage, rather dirty, long kinky hair, dark glasses, clutching a plastic bag. Had he come about a rescue? No. Speaking at a speed that made him almost incomprehensible, without any greeting, he went to Duret and posed the following question:

'Can you tell me where I can find a Judeo-Christian church in the area?'

Duret wide-eyed, kept a straight face and courteously replied:

'I'm sorry! I am afraid I haven't quite understood your question.'

The man grew angry

'You understand French? I asked you where I could find the nearest Judeo-Christian church. A church, you know what it is?'

Had the man been more normal I would have said that the expression 'Judeo-Christian' was one of those terms now used, which means nothing at all: but even with two or three gendarmes around the place, I did not feel like entering into discussion with this guy.

Despite his desire to laugh, all the more so as Jackie Paille was splitting his sides, Duret politely replied that a church, as it happened, was to be found opposite, the other side of the roundabout.

'Good,' replied the other. 'That's all I wanted to know.'

He shot out, slamming the door. Was he about to place a bomb in the Saint Michel church, deemed to be 'Judeo-Christian'? Anything seemed possible. Anyway, no explosion occured in the period following.

It appears that many similar scenes occur at the PGHM office.

The reason I was at the PGHM was because I had arranged to meet Nicole Michoux. Our talk was confiding and touching. I explain why I decided to stop this book after the death of her husband, and why finally I carried on with it. I am happy that she approves.

'Me too,' she says, 'I say – carry on! It's what Régis himself would have told you, had it happened to one of his comrades. You must continue.'

She told me too how much Régis adored his profession of mountain rescue, a real passion for him, and that she, now alone with their two children, felt the PGHM as a family, so much support, understanding and love had she received, so much attentiveness, friendship and help since the accident had happened.

That's as it should be. In old social systems, in large households, where parents, grandparents, numerous children, formed a close group, leading the same communal life, mourning was a more collective act and mutual support forthcoming. The PGHM is a similar social structure and so fulfills that supporting role, so often missing elsewhere.

Michel Médici and Pascal Saudemont leave the PGHM for the CNISAG[1] next door. We are going to their farewell party, which also takes on the atmosphere of a family get together, with presents, bunches of flowers, and children generally joining in.

September 9

Early, this week's GA calls me. It's Jean-Noël Crettier, and he wants to join the PGHM one day. Most GAs have the same feeling after seeing what happens here. There have just been two accidents on the Aiguille du Chardonnet.

The more serious involves three young climbers doing a route between the Forbes Arête and the North Buttress (the Migot). A local girl and two young men, one a ski instructor, the other a CRS[2] man. The girl was in the middle. The leader suddenly skidded off, he doesn't know why. The snow seemed good, but still fairly frozen. He managed to stop himself on a ledge, but the girl fell forty metres and was held by the last man who was on the other side of a rib which helped slow her down. Only the girl is injured: broken ribs, vertebrae and perhaps the pelvis, a broken tooth. The alert came in very quickly, from the summit by someone with a radio who saw the accident but knew no more.

---

[1] Centre National d'instruction de ski et d'alpinisme de la Gendarmerie.
[2] Compagnie Républicaine de Sécurité that deals with civil disorder and in some places with mountain rescue.

The helicopter brings down the two friends of the girl while the rescuers stay with her, refuels and takes Dr Duperrex up.

So at the helipad there only remains the GA, the two lads and me. They tell of how the accident happened. The wait is long for the injured girl has to be fixed into a lined shell. Dr Lecoq, on duty at the hospital, rings to ask what we know of her state. She is taken direct to the emergency helipad, after which there are several flights concerned with this accident, and the less serious one on the Forbes Arête.

I have taken the names; it will save time and not keep the young men hanging around, and I'll take them to collect their car at Le Tour. Feeling that it would be good for the girl not to be left alone, they want first to contact the girl's mother. The one who phones does so with considerable circumspection:

'Good morning, madame. We've come back down. There was a slight problem, nothing to get concerned about! But we came back in the helicopter. Nothing to get worried about! I am simply telephoning because your daughter is a bit shaken and at the hospital. No! No! Nothing serious! But I think it might be a good thing if you could join her there, because we are at the helipad and are still waiting for our sacks... No! Don't get upset. Everything is fine!'

Scarcely had I time to congratulate him on his diplomacy than Guy Duperrex returns from the hospital with a message for the boys:

'She says, "Whatever you do, don't tell my mother!"'

However the news is better than we feared; the girl can leave the hospital in two or three days.

It was an accident that could have been much more serious. I go up to Le Tour with one of the lads, the one in the CRS. I ask him about his work. He has been stationed in the Parisian region for a year, not had to deal with a demonstration but has been involved with security in the suburbs and finds it fascinating, patrolling and those he meets.

Having to leave a note at Rue du Lyret, I see Pouts and Iglesis who have just done one of the Blaitière pillars, still in their climbing clothes and sacks, with that same spaced out look one has on just getting back. We exchange affabilities and I say to Pouts: 'Good morning, Mister Putz', because that is how the program *Zone interdite* presented him a couple of days before. But I remain struck by the impression on the faces of those who have just come back from the mountains, of having been in another world.

The helicopter makes a recce of Les Courtes with Poirot and Lafouge.

'We've spotted our corpse,' Michel Pierre announces on return.

Poirot telephones the PG. The body remaining in the crevasse is now partly visible, but it is jammed under ice and rocks, twenty metres down. Poirot reckons it could be disengaged in a half hour with picks. It will be done tomorrow morning when there is less risk of snow and rockfall, for the crevasse is just below a narrowing which acts as a funnel.

September 10

The body was recovered this morning. Iglesis, Malineau and some others went. It wasn't in a very good state as a part had remained exposed to the air. When I arrived at the helipad around 10 am, the recovery had long been completed. Iglesis was cleaning a yellow and black anorak belonging to the victim and said that even with a strong detergent it was difficult to get it looking right. His red rubber gloves were drying in the sun. In the course of the season I heard a doctor bring up the risk of AIDS that could arise from handling injured people who were bleeding when one might, without realising it, have a graze. No regulations have yet been issued by the Gendarmerie but all now wear rubber gloves, thin or thick.

End of September

At a decreasing rhythm the rescues continue: dislocations, breaks, sprains, tendonitis, exhaustion, wounds, snow blindness, altitude sickness, œdemas. Climbers, walkers, parapenters, work accidents. French, Swiss, Belgians, Italians, British, Poles. A windslab avalanche on the Petit Plateau resulted in three injured and one dead. Four English doing Mont Blanc by the Grands Mulets. One, the least hurt, was able to call the rescue. Two others were more seriously injured. The fourth, who fell in a crevasse, was dead and difficult to get out.

The night of September 17 there was a huge rockfall on the Dru, which left a vast grey scar capped by an overhang. The evening before, a Swiss guide and his client had asked for help, terrified by the sound of the rock groaning under them as they climbed. The next day two young people who were at the jammed block during the night had escaped the collapse, but dared not budge.

Sunday the 28th, the end of season lunch offered to all the rescuers, crew, doctors, wives and children at the helipad. I came back from Paris for it. It was fine, superb weather. While it was on three rescues took place. A Pole was caught by a sérac fall under the Charpoua Glacier; his body had not been found. Another, but I did not know it at the time, involved Annick Guérin, a superb mountaineer who had, during the summer, done major routes on the Italian side of Mont Blanc with Godefroy Perroux. She had had suddenly found herself incapable of climbing back from the Cosmiques Hut to the Aiguille du Midi. She had been suffering from an extremely rare disease which no one had diagnosed and, even if they had, would have been able to do nothing about it. She died on the Wednesday in the cardiology section of Grenoble Hospital. I hardly knew her but I was moved by the end of so courageous a young woman.

There were four more rockfalls on the Dru, during the afternoon.

So we have reached the end of the season. Was it a 'normal' one? In reality no season is like another. This one was marked by the black week where so many accidents followed on that every-one was shaken to the core. Statistics, nevertheless, allow one to see things in better perspective and to say that in June, July and August there were 415 rescues, 36 deaths (3 more than the previous year), 1 missing, 84 ill, 281 wounded, 183 unhurt, for the most part people in difficulty or the partners of the victims. But for the same period how many have been up in the mountains or walked the paths? Hundreds of thousands certainly. Hundreds of thousands to whom nothing happened, hundreds of thousands who found happiness. That is what the mountains are all about, and when one talks of rescue it must always be borne in mind that it is the dark edge, which has its own nobility, but which is but the fringe of a huge radiant garment.

34

RESPONSIBILITY IN THE MOUNTAINS

Some Difficult Cases

Responsibility in climbing is a serious matter, for by definition the high mountain terrain offers a wide range of dangers and risks. While it has been possible to lay down certain basic rules in piste skiing, because the situation is relatively simple, summer mountaineering risks are quite another matter. Accidents will inevitably occur – whether due to gravity (falls, avalanches, wind slab, stonefall, séracs, crevasses, slipping off paths), variations in the weather (cold, blizzards, mist, wind, storms) or failures of the body (fatigue, illness, altitude problems).

There are also incidents of human error where a third party may be involved through an error of judgement, inattention, or a technical mistake. This may involve incorrect gear placement, unjustified failure to put on the rope, bad decisions over choice of route to match the abilities of the person or persons participating, poor judgement of the nature of the terrain. Finally, those involved can vary – friends, professionals, club amateurs (though often very competent), people who do not know each other, those still learning their skills, oldsters returning and overestimating their fitness and stamina – each permutation of participants offering a range of judgements and potential strengths and weaknesses.

Should a mishap occur, modern society tends to look for someone to blame. Among mountaineers there is generally a reluctance to pursue such cases as the mountain arena is normally considered a place of freedom, one of the last, a place for comradeship, of shared joys and risks. Law suits attending mountain accidents that could have been avoided seem to suggest that human error is the cause of mishap.

Cases of mutual recrimination
It is rare for the issue of responsibility to be raised amongst friends climbing together. There is a notable example (albeit in a team that

included a guide) and by no means recent. The first winter ascent of the Diables Ridge on Mont Blanc du Tacul in 1938 ended with serious frostbite injuries to the three involved, and resulted in a bitter dispute between one and the other two, with court cases lasting for years.[1]

Claims by relatives

Formal complaints most frequently comes from the relatives of the dead person, either to obtain financial compensation where the deceased has left a family without means, or where the parents want those responsible sanctioned, no so much for vindication (which happens sometimes anyway), but more to serve as a warning for other similar organisations or professionals.

At the beginning of this book, two such cases were discussed, one concerning Smiler Cuthbertson, a guide who was not considered negligent by the French authorities but was later found responsible in a civil case in the UK. This case caused a stir in Great Britain since it seemed to lay down inviolable rules concerning belaying without taking into consideration other aspects of the dangers involved.

Also discussed was the the Aiguille Verte accident in June 1997 when the three climbers who were moving at different speeds on the Couturier Couloir, all non-professionals, separated. The alarm was raised too late for the one who had lagged behind who died while descending for want of an abseil rope which his companions had taken. I learnt subsequently, when the insurance companies of the victim's two partners requested to see the PGHM's file on the case, that the family of the victim had laid a formal complaint.

During the summer season of 1997 in Haute Savoie three really contentious legal cases were raised:

---

[1] The climb, which left out the Corne du Diable and l'Isolée, would still have been very advanced for its day – a tough rock climb in winter and above 4000 metres. This may be the first report in English. It was made by Mlle Erica Stagni and Marcel Gallay with Raymond Lambert on February 9-10, 1938. They were overtaken by a storm on the night of their first bivouac on Pte. Mediane and thereafter the climb turned into a multi-day epic that is more fully developed in the notes of Appendix III on page 361. See Lambert's A l'assaut des 'quatre mille', Editions de la Fregate, Geneva 1946, and his report in Les Alpes, 1939. Also Une Tragique aventure au Mont-Blanc by Marcel Gallay, Private publication, Geneva 1940.

A rock climbing accident

The first accident occurred on May 15 on the Grande Jeanne. It involved a woman in her forties who had signed on for a CAF introductory rock climbing course conducted by two voluntary certificated instuctors. One of these had installed a moulinette (lower off) at the top of the cliff through which she was being lowered by her second. She had not managed to climb as far as the ledge where this belay was installed and so could not have changed it in any way. As soon as she started to be lowered, she fell, fifteen metres, bringing the rope down with her – suggesting that the moulinette had not been correctly set up. She was not wearing a helmet. Helmets were only recommended where there was a risk of stonefall and are rarely worn on cliffs, for if one is properly belayed, falls are neither long nor serious.[2] But this particular fall had important consequences. The victim suffered from skull damage resulting in coma, various breaks, ribs, ankles, shoulder blades, teeth, and impaired vision.

A formal complaint was made, initially by the father and then by the victim herself after she recovered consciousness.

Two explanations are possible, but the various accounts make it difficult to work out. Either the rope was not actually clipped through the moulinette, so that when the victim took off the last clip she had no rope above her. Or the karabiner had not been screwed up, which is what one witness who checked immediately afterwards claimed, but had been screwed close subsequently. The problem remained unresolved, the victim having no memory of the accident when she came out of coma.

Such an accident, on a course with voluntary instructors and probably free, raises further issues. Voluntary helpers, certificated or not, are usually less competent than professional guides, and often find themselves looking after several people, which a guide would not be allowed to do. Their advantage is that they allow modest climbing or walking training for beginners at little cost.

A high mountain accident

The second contentious case is the sad one of July 27 already described, which resulted in the deaths of a sixteen year old boy

---

[2] The author is referring to French bolt or piton equipped cliffs for leading or top-roping. Pupils receiving introductions in other countries might well be equipped with helmets as protection against a variety of eventualities.

and a girl of seventeen, who made up a rope under the direction of a guide. They were part of a course to learn to become independent climbers organised by Social Section of the EDF.[3] The parents were asked to sign a waiver, a formality that may be obligatory when it concerns minors. In the light of the victims' ages, their experience could only be limited, even though they may have been well suited for the training. Their final project was to climb Mont Blanc du Tacul from the Col du Midi, a route which, though not considered difficult, goes above 4000 metres and was, on that day, in icy condition, though there was a beaten track. The guide was only responsible for two ropes, and was soloing between one and the other, giving advice. The accident happened because on the descent a traffic jam had developed at one of the bends on the track. To avoid the jam and the time that would be lost, the guide, after checking the slope, advised the youngsters to cut down between two séracs and rejoin the track below. It was in so doing that the accident happened. The two young people fell a long way, ending up against a sérac wall with no hope of survival.

The guide had just been taken on by the centre and did not know the youngsters. That of itself is of no great importance. Numerous guides, selected by the *tour de rôle*, frequently find themselves accompanying clients whom they do not know. It was the decision to quit the beaten track and the fact that five inexperienced youngsters had been allocated to a single guide that seem to have been the sole causes of the tragedy.

In the eyes of the law, the fact that an accident happens with a professional is potentially no more blameworthy than any other person, but the penalty is much harsher. So if a voluntary monitor leads a group, is he not equally responsible? That is the question the third case raises.

A case of abandonment

This was another accident that occurred on the same day, July 27, and at the same place. The fall in fact took place earlier, but the victim died in hospital a week later. It concerned a twenty-four-year old engineer who had recently come to live in the Alps, of which he knew little. He signed on for a route with the CAF of Chambéry. The text of the prospectus for the outing is incredible,

---

[3] Electricité de France – a powerful union organization that runs holiday centres for its members.

since it was for Mont Blanc via the Tacul and Maudit, a route at altitude, tiring and committing, yet was described as a 'walking trip', and categorised as 'M4', the same level as the Buet and the Aiguille du Tour, which is far shorter and easier.

The leader was an amateur, having no special qualifications either from the CAF or the FFME, but who had been mountaineering for some thirty years. A second leader had been planned for, but he had a problem that had arisen a couple of days before departure and had to call off. The group was thus ten people under the control of a single person. A professional could not take so many for such a route – perhaps no more than three. The man in charge, quite rightly, took on his own rope the two least experienced members of the party, one of whom was the engineer.

The outing did not proceed without incident. One person quit at an early stage and returned alone to the Aiguille du Midi. Another member suffered from mountain sickness at the Dôme du Goûter on the way back and had to be helicoptered off (see Chapter 16). But the serious accident took place between these two events, when, on reaching the shoulder of the Tacul, the young engineer complained he was too tired to carry on. After making an effort to continue as far as Col Maudit, he firmly restated his request to return. It was four o'clock in the morning, cold and still dark for a further hour.

So what could be done? Either the person in charge went back with the whole party and the others thus failed to get their route, or they could continue on their own, something they were unlikely to be able to do since they had specifically joined an outing under guidance. Alternatively, the young man could be pushed to continue, which he was clearly in no condition to do, or be left to return to the Midi cable-car on his own, which is what was done.

He was consequently left alone and no one knows what he did during the next two hours. Probably he waited for daylight, or for other ropes that might be descending after having climbed the Tacul. In any case it was after 6 am that he started down and fell. A guide saw it and immediately raised the alert. At that stage it was believed he was soloing. He was found deep in the snow, hypothermic and with multiple contusions. He survived a week but the efforts to save him were unsuccessful. His parents lodged a formal complaint.

This case, even more than the others, raises important issues. Professionals are judged more severely than amateurs or voluntary leaders. But most associations that organise walks, outings or routes in the mountains, do so with leaders who are not paid but who nonetheless assume the same responsibility as guides. They are usually in charge of novices who are looking for a modest and cheap initiation and have no way of assessing the skill of their instructors. If it is a matter of a walk in the countryside, there is no problem. But on more dangerous terrain, would it not be better to make use of guides, who in turn would only accept, for safety reasons, a more limited number of participants?

Who is really responsible in these cases? The person in charge, or the institution which allows such risks to be taken? A death which occurred in a similar case in the Calanques led to a judgement against both the leader and the institution, in that case the Paris CAF.

There is no doubt that if, in this third case, it had been a professional in charge he would have been charged and perhaps held in prison. Is the fact of not being professionally qualified an argument for diminished responsibility? Is it justifiable for a climbing organisation to use voluntary amateurs, with varying experience, in such serious high mountain situations? This matter needs careful consideration as it is often the young, with few financial resources, who place themselves under their charge.

We should note the broader dimension of these issues, notably the victims and their families who pay a high price, but also the professional leader, the voluntary helper, the comrade or the group responsible also suffer the heavy consequences, not just legal but moral and psychological too.

Responsibility in the greater ranges

We have been speaking of France where it is most desirable that mountaineering remains an unregulated activity, and that lawsuits and trials remain few and far between. This means that each and everyone (parents, clients, guides, instructors, sponsoring institutions) assumes seriously their own responsibilities.

But if we look elsewhere in the greater ranges, the Andes and above all the Himalaya at the present time, where no rescue is really possible, since helicopters cannot fly at such altitudes, there we can find horrifying cases that reveal a total lack of sense of solidarity among groups of climbers from different countries, each bent on their own success. The climbing press talks of it and Joe Simpson, in his book *Dark Shadows Falling*, provided some frightening examples.[4]

Conditions, obviously, are different, far more savage – very high altitudes, dangers incomparable with our own mountains, an expensive expedition, high peak fees. Add to that rarefied air and extreme meteorological conditions, both cold and wind, and the vicious storms. Thus a mindset of extreme determination to succeed develops – 'shit or bust' – as the rather crude dictum puts it.[5] The problem is that if it's the others who bust, so much the worse for them: it's an 'everyone for himself' attitude that starts to prevail, getting to the top at all costs, that leads to passing by corpses and even those dying without rendering assistance.

When things turn bad in the Himalaya the accidents are terrifying. One only has to think of the twelve dead on K2 in summer 1986, amongst whom were Alan Rouse, Maurice and Liliane Barrard and Renato Casarotto.[6] At least on that occasion there was mutual assistance between the different parties, between the various nationalities, all European. Amongst those who got away with it were Benoît Chamoux, Wanda Rutkiewicz and Jerzy Kukuczka, all of whom met their deaths in the Himalaya on subsequent trips.

In 1995, a storm led to a further six deaths on K2.

In May 1996, there were eight deaths on Everest, but the circumstances there were very different.[7] Selling Everest had become a matter for tourism for Nepal and China. In 1991, the price paid to Nepal for an Everest expedition was $2,300. In 1996 it had risen to $70,000 for a group of seven, plus $10,000 for each added climber with a maximum of twelve. Thus it is no longer mountaineering ability that decides the membership of a trip but financial resources, and some, as Joe Simpson explains, mortgage themselves to the hilt to achieve their dream. In one of the groups clients were each paying $65,000 to join.

---

[4] Jonathan Cape, London, 1997
[5] The original French is slightly more elegant 'il faut que ça passe ou que ça casse'.
[6] See the accounts of this tragedy given by : Christine Grosjean in *Alpirando* No 92 : Jim Curran in *K2 Triumph and Tragedy* (Hodder, 1987) and *K2, The Story of a Savage Mountain* (Hodder, 1995); and Kurt Diemberger in *The Endless Knot* (Grafton, London, 1989 and collected in *The Kurt Diemberger Omnibus* (Bâton Wicks, London / The Mountaineers, Seattle 1999)
[7] See Jon Krakauer in *Into Thin Air* (Villard, New York 1997)

Those who died in 1996, including two experienced guides who were making a profession out of such trips, the New Zealander Rob Hall, for Adventure Consultants, and the American Scott Fischer for Mountain Madness (a curiously prescient name, as it turned out), were not all members of commercial groups, for a Taiwanese and three South Africans were members of conventional national expeditions. The Taiwanese survived, but lost his lower right arm and all the fingers of his left hand. The leader of the South African expedition, who in any case did not make the summit, refused to lend his radio to help the others. Some, in contrast, like the Kazakh Anatoli Boukreev, who later fell to his death on Annapurna, gave of their all.

On Everest's Tibetan side similar tragedies took place in the same storm. Japanese climbers passed by dying Indians without offering help, for there was one, unique objective for them. On their way down they passed the last survivor, again without giving assistance. One of them declared on his return 'above 8000 metres one cannot afford the luxury of morality.'

Simpson cites another case, perhaps even worse, on the South Col of Everest in May 1992. Five Dutch climbers, knowing that an Indian, frozen, but still alive, was feebly waving an arm only thirty metres from their tent, did nothing to carry and shelter him for his last moments. They left him to die, alone.

It seems, from these two unfortunate examples, that the limits of horror and barbarism have been reached. These mountains, so vast and marvellous are polluted, fouled by rubbish, empty oxygen bottles, corpses left in place, not even covered, and now, worse, profaned by human indifference.[8]

The hope that the attitude of each for himself does not proliferate has to be expressed. There are presages of it sometimes even in our own mountains

And it must again be stated, to end this work, how much the rescue system as carried out in our Alps, spontaneous at first, often starting with the guides, then organised professionally, with respect, conscientiousness, commitment and love, deserves the tribute of a book devoted to it.

---

[8] Since this book was written things have improved somewhat; oxygen bottles and other detritus is being removed and human remains are being covered or interred as is feasible at the height and in the terrain.

EPILOGUE

Since the summer season of 1997 certain things have changed in the Chamonix mountain rescue world. There is now a major new building complex at the helipad. All the helicopters are based at Chamonix – the Gendarmerie air unit moving there in the last days of 1999. Since then the helipad at Les Bois is open all the year. The Alouette III has been replaced by the EC 145 and the Gendarmerie's famous blue helicopter, *Bravo Lima*, that first entered service in 1972 was finally retired in 2004 with more than 14,000 hours flying time and over 15,600 rescued.

Some things have also changed amongst those rescued. The mobile phone, only carried by a few at the time this book was written, is now a commonplace and alarms are often passed on more rapidly, but not frivolously – there seems to have been no great increase in unnecessary call-outs though the number of incidents is increasing.

It is possible too that the nature of mountaineering is changing. Anecdotal evidence points to far fewer people in the high mountains in 2004 (except on the most popular classics) and far more activity on the safely bolted rock routes in the Aiguilles Rouges and similar haunts. This may reflect the apparent climatic change of recent years. Certainly the hot dry summer of 2003 was exceptional and the number of rescues shot up (forty or so on the Walker Spur alone). But there are other factors involved in the view of experts, including that mountaineering is too much like hard work.

By contrast, activity in the high mountains has increased in winter, whether for skiing or ice climbing, and experienced mountaineers are often doing the big routes well after the traditional season ends, when things are colder. Helicopter rescues in winter from Chamonix average about 700, of which about a fifth are alpine and a third skiers in the Vallée Blanche. But as this book shows, high mountain rescues, and indeed climbing rescues of any kind, form a far less important proportion of the service than is generally believed, albeit they may provide the most dramatic,[1] and the general figures for rescue have not changed for a statistically significant period of time (with the exception of 2003). In the year 2,000 for example, for all the mountainous departments of France, 63% of rescues were for walkers, 17% for alpinists and 20% for other incidents. The latter includes mountain biking, canyoning, via ferratas, ski touring, parapenting, hang-gliding etc.[2]

So whilst details may have changed and indeed mentalities (along with the media) following September 11 (9/11), the main features of this book are still perfectly valid. These are French circumstances however, albeit in an internationally popular range, and it is up to readers from English-speaking countries to decide how far some of the features, particularly the approach of the media to mountain rescue, are peculiar to France.

Certain French aspects of our story are summarised for the benefit of the English-speaking world in the following appendices.

In any case, there are certain aspects of that country affecting our story with which most inhabitants of what the French would call the Anglo-Saxon world will not be familiar, and for this reason a short summary of some relevant background follows.

---

[1] In summer 2000 there were 417 rescues involving 661 alpinists, 60% of whom were injured or dead (defined as before reaching hospital). Of these 60%, 9.3% (ie 6% of the total) were dead. In contrast to virtually all alpinist accidents, 60% of walkers deaths were non traumatic. This is also reflected as would be expected as a mirror image of age groups. It is also worth noting that whereas a vast proportion of non-alpinist rescues are for French, a third of those in the mountains are foreigners.

[2] In the summer season 2000 for the mountainous departments of France there were 102 deaths comprising 43 walkers, 38 alpinists, 4 rock climbers, 11 parapenters/hang-gliders, 2 canyoners, 1 ski-tourer, 1 via ferrata person, 2 mountain bikers. The percentage of alpinists, of course, will be much higher in Haute Savoie.

APPENDICES

APPENDIX I

THE EMERGENCE OF THE PGHM

by John Wilkinson and Anne Sauvy

THE PGHM (Peloton de la Gendarmerie de Haute Montagne) is a special and small part of the Gendarmerie that has gradually developed expertise for dealing with incidents in mountain terrain. Like all organisations that have a history, the rescue services in France have evolved, not always logically, and they by no means present a straightforward picture.

Post-war rescue organisation
Mountain rescue is as old as mountaineering itself. Originally provided locally by guides and amateurs, a more formal structure began to develop at the beginning of the 20th century, but it still remained fundamentally the affair of local guides, sometimes helped by non-professionals. The modern history really starts after World War II. At the national level mountaineering was still considered essentially a sporting activity and so came under the general aegis of the Directeur Général des Sports in the Ministre de l'Education Nationale which by now trained and qualified all French guides at ENSA (École Nationale de Ski et d'Alpinisme) at Chamonix.

The main interface between Government and the sport was the FFM (Féderation Française de la Montagne), presided over then by the highly influential Lucien Devies, which amongst other things arranged insurance for properly organised rescues. But otherwise rescue remained basically in local hands. In Chamonix there were three organisations capable of rescue with qualified and experienced guides, the Compagnie des Guides de Chamonix, the Army's E(M)HM (École Militaire de Haute Montagne) and ENSA.

Each however was quasi-independent with its own hierarchy. The Chamonix Guides' Company, was essentially a closed shop and conservative in its direction – increasingly resentful of talented and innovative outsiders, professional and amateur alike, many of whom were young Parisians. They had also suffered considerably in operations when in 1950 the *Malabar Princess* crashed in winter near the summit of Mont Blanc. The EHM, particularly after the war had a wealth of talent, and also had access to helicopters, but it was subject to military order. ENSA, as we have seen, was a public service, subject to its own ministry. To complicate matters further a vehement local quarrel placed one half of the French side of Mont Blanc itself in the *commune* of St-Gervais which had its own local organisation. Theoretically, the coordination of rescue was in the hands of the SCSM (Société Chamoniarde de Secours en Montagne, founded 1948).

Vincendon and Henry
The potential weaknesses of the system came to a shameful head when two students, the Parisian Jean Vincendon, a qualified aspirant guide, and the Belgian François Henry, made a laborious winter ascent of the Brenva Spur on Christmas Day 1956. (Winter climbing was at that time in its infancy and considered by many to be unjustified.) In deteriorating weather they joined up with Walter Bonatti and Silvano Gheser (who were also on the climb) and after a bivouac the four fought their way out to the Col de la Brenva where the weather briefly improved. Dividing again into two ropes they set off to cross the wind-hardened slopes over the summit of Mont Blanc to gain the Vallot Hut, but Vincendon and Henry fell behind and after a bivouac in the vicinity of the Rochers Rouges made the fatal error of trying to descend by the steep northern slopes towards the Grand Plateau. The details of what happened in the saga that followed need not concern us, except to note that the Chamonix Guides Company refused to let its members take part in the rescue (which led Lionel Terray to resign temporarily). The EHM took over control and attempted a helicopter rescue during which their Sikorsky crashed. No assistance was given to the rescue teams on foot that Terray and various friends and non-Chamonix guides had mounted. The outcome was tragic and a matter of national scandal. The bitterness was slow to heal.[1]

However, in the aftermath overall responsibility for mountain rescue moved to the Direction de la Sécurité Civile under the Interior Ministry (see below) and the potential of helicopters for mountain rescue was acknowledged, most notably when the Alouette II was brought into action. It was also clear that the military pilots were insufficiently trained and experienced in mountainous terrain. The outcome was the forerunner of the PGHM.

---

[1] The accident is described (with the lie of the land fully illustrated) in 'The Tragedy on Mont Blanc' by René Dittert, *Mountain World* 1958/59 (Allen and Unwin, London 1958) and also by Lionel Terray in *Conquistadors of the Useless* (Gollancz, London 1963, Bâton Wicks/ Mountaineers 2001), and Walter Bonatti in *On the Heights* (Rupert Hart-Davis, London 1964).

The Dru rescue 1966[2]

The next major turning point occurred in the famous rescue on the West Face of the Dru in August 1966 when two Germans became stuck on the ledge after the pendulum above the Ninety Metre Dièdre at the point where an old fixed rope of dubious quality gave access to the North Face. Regardless of the Prefect's instructions of 1959, rescue remained rigidly divided into periods of duty between the same three organisations that were involved in the Vincendon and Henry debâcle. This time it was the EHM that was on call and it proved incapable in an attempt to try to reach the climbers by descending from the summit.

For ENSA and the Chamonix Guides, by 1966 a more youthful and experienced body, the obvious approach was via the North Face and making use of the original rope traverse route of the first ascent.[3] The military seemed almost bent on a competition and proved uncooperative. In the process a German climber strangled himself in a rope manoeuvre trying to descend to his friends. So the guides approached via the North Face.

In the meantime, disregarding these official rivalries, a group of amateur climbers, skilled in big wall techniques (including Gary Hemming and Mick Burke), plus the Chamonix guide René Desmaison attempted a direct ascent by the West Face route that Hemming himself (with Royal Robbins) had pioneered. This party managed to reach the Germans and brought them successfully to safety by their route of ascent. In the acrimony that followed, exacerbated by the sensational media coverage in *Paris Match* and *Das Bild*, Desmaison was expelled from the Guides' Company.

The continuing shortcomings of the mountain rescue bodies were exposed by these events, leading to further organisational changes. The PGHM emerged as the main rescue service in Chamonix.

The gendarmes were initially accompanied by civilian guides for important rescues. They gradually acquired experience so that today many Peloton members are fully qualified guides or aspirants, as well as being high class climbers. Such specialisation was coupled to the increased use of helicopters in rescue, with the advent of the Alouette III and greatly improved training techniques under the auspices of CNISAG.

The Gendarmerie

The Gendarmerie is a military service, parallel to the army. Its precise responsibilities are complex, but briefly it fulfills the same role as the police outside urban centres (25,000+, approximately). The essential difference is that the Gendarmerie comes under the Defence Ministry, while the Police come under the Interior Ministry. There is a long history behind

[2] Described in various magazines and in *Total Alpinism* by René Desmaison (Granada, London 1982) and *Gary Hemming* by Mirella Tenderini (Ernest Press, Glasgow 1995).
[3] *The West Face* by Guido Magnone (Museum Press, London 1955).

this (the word 'gendarme' goes back to the *gens d'armes* of the Middle Ages), but the essential reason is that in an already centralised state system, power should not be over-concentrated in one ministry. All gendarmes are non commissioned officers (NCOs) with the equivalent army rank of sergeant whose training includes adequate knowledge of judicial procedures to be *assermenté* (give sworn testimony). Indeed, one of the original reasons for the emergence of the PGHM was the need to accompany rescue parties in mountain terrain where judicial interest might be involved. The next rank up, Chef, needs the qualification of being an Officier de Police Judiciaire (the PJ) and in the case of the PGHM a qualified guide. Above that comes adjutant, adjutant chef and major (the highest NCO rank). The officer ranks are more or less the same as in the British army (lieutenant, captain, commandant = major, colonel etc).

So the Gendarmerie is responsible to the judiciary for many aspects of its work and from the point of view of the PGHM all intervention reports (PVs – *Procès verbal*) go automatically to the Parquet (Public Prosecutor's Office). The judicial system in France is again quite different from that in Britain and America, but need not concern us except to note that for the Chamonix PGHM the immediate judicial authority is the Procureur de la République at the first level tribunal (Tribunal de Grande Instance) at Bonneville. If the Procureur decides that the matter may involve potential penal proceedings (*délit* – misdemeanour, offence; *crime* – crime etc), or is liable to give rise to complications such as a formal complaint by an 'injured' party or claims to compensation (as for example when the accident involves a professional), he may refer it to a *juge d'instruction* (investigating judge) who may well call for supplementary reports and investigation. These will be made available for pleadings should the case come to court. In France, it should be noted, an 'injured party' may constitute itself *partie civile* in penal proceedings.

Security and rescue:
The State Security, as we have seen, since the Vincendon and Henry affair is the responsibility of the Ministry of the Interior, whose arm is the CRS (Compagnies Républicaines de Sécurité), largely associated in the public mind with beating off peaceful protestors exerting their democratic rights to hurl paving stones at the bourgeois forces of order. But in fact they have a much wider role than keeping control at *manifestations* (demonstrations): they fill a parallel position to the Gendarmerie Mobile and consequently their roles can overlap, and indeed cause rivalry. Involved often with certain major accidents, avalanches, aeroplane crashes etc, the CRS consequently also developed a section specialising in mountainous terrain with its training centre at Les Bossons (near Chamonix). While the CRS is little involved in Haute Savoie, it often alternates with the PGHM in other mountainous departments and it has played an important role in

developing equipment, notably the Piguillem, a pliable (folding) stretcher named after one of its former commandants.

The main organisation of the Interior Ministry responsible for safety and rescue, is the Sécurité Civile with a service in each Département (Department). The Département is the fundamental unit of administration in France, with at its head a Préfet (Prefect) reporting to the Interior Ministry. One of the two helicopters (the red one) used in rescue at Chamonix belongs to this local division. Also under the Ministry is the fire service who are also obviously trained in rescue. The *sapeurs-pompiers* play a vital role in climbing rescue in many non-mountainous areas, such as the Gorges du Verdon or the Calanques, and they also help the PGHM for rescue in mountain areas outside the Mont Blanc range. In 1994 they provided the ambulance service from the helipad but by the time of this book (1997), that had been privatised and managed from Annecy, with not altogether happy results. (This ambulance service should not be confused with the emergency medicalised service provided by the SAMU.) However, much of the cost and administration for the fire service, as too certain other aspects of rescue, largely devolves on local organisms, run by publically elected representatives, from the level of the *mairie* (that is the administration of the *commune* under an elected mayor assisted by a municipal council) to the region. There are more than 38,000 communes in France, ranging from the tiny hamlet to large cities (Bordeaux, Marseille, Lyon, etc). That, of course, raises the thorny issue of who bears the cost of rescue. In certain *communes*, notably those frequented by cavers, that can be a heavy burden and the right to charge is recognised and evolving. However, this need not concern us here, since basically the rescue service operated by the PGHM or any other state organisation is free and that principle has been confirmed recently (2004), despite many arguments raised against it. That nevertheless, it should be noted, does not extend to skiing, except in the high mountains (though the question of the Vallée Blanche in winter is a thorny issue).

Rescue in mountain areas

So in each department there is an organisation responsible for fire and rescue overseen by the Prefect, but its structure and emphasis obviously varies according to the main risks involved, urban, marine, mountainous, etc. In mountain regions there is a specific 'Plan Départemental de Secours en Montagne', that regulates and coordinates all those potentially involved with the problems and consequences of natural hazards in such terrain, with various levels of alert that may, in the case of a major emergency extend to higher echelons than the department. The PGHM is represented by the Commandant of all the department's Gendarmeries, a colonel. Also deeply involved are the *mairies*. In the Chamonix valley the main *commune* is Chamonix itself (which includes Argentière) but there is also Vallorcine towards the Swiss frontier and Les Houches. Of some importance too, because Mont Blanc itself partly comes within its domain is St-Gervais (the old local quarrel). By 1997 the PGHM at Chamonix was reduced to a detachment at St-Gervais, but since then this has closed and been replaced by one at Annecy, also under Chamonix PGHM command, to provide a more effective coverage of Haute Savoie. In 1997 the Chamonix PGHM was commanded by a captain (Jean-Claude Gin) and assisted by two majors, one at Chamonix (Major Mathieu), the other at St-Gervais (Major Darrhort). The unit strength was approximately fifty (today forty in Chamonix, ten in Annecy).

As at 1997, the PGHM had sixteen units operating in the high mountain regions of France, plus a new one in Réunion, and a further five units of PGHM in the Jura, Vosges and Massif Central. Of those sixteen there are five large units, in the Pyrenees, and in the Alps at Grenoble (with detachments at Bourg d'Oisans), Bourg-St-Maurice (detachments at Modane), Briançon, and Chamonix, by far the most important. The Chamonix PGHM which is responsible for Haute Savoie carries out over 50 per cent of all the rescues in mountain areas effected by the Gendarmerie throughout France (today approximately 3000 a year, roughly 1000 by Chamonix and 500 by Annecy).[4] The area covered extends from the French side of the range to the lower hills and mountains on the other side of the valley, the Aiguilles Rouges, the limestone Platé désert, the Aravis chain etc. All this area is much frequented by walkers, ramblers and tourists out for a simple stroll in terrain that can prove treacherous, as well as mountaineers, climbers, parapenters, hang-gliders etc.

Local organisations and medical arrangements
However, that does not mean that all is in the hands of the PGHM. As mentioned, the Sécurité Civile crew and helicopter alternates with that of the Gendarmerie, while for a long time the fire service provided ambulances. But all these are, in essence, state structures. Local support, both physical and moral, remains vital. The essential is provided by the above mentioned SCSM presided over at the time of this book by the mayor of Chamonix (Michel Charlet), with its vice-presidents the President of the Chamonix Guides Company (Xavier Chappaz) and the head of the emergency medical service at the Chamonix Hospital, the SMUR, Dr Bernard Marsigny, himself a powerful mountaineer like many of the other doctors from the hospital. All the doctors attached to rescue operations in 1997 were volunteers from the Chamonix Hospital, though since then this recruitment has widened. This attachment to the rescue service of doctors with the specialised training to deal with injuries on the spot, coupled to the ability of the helicopter to land directly at the emergency helipad at the Chamonix Hospital and elsewhere has more or less eliminated the need for the SAMU and the privatised ambulance service provides little more

[4] Another indicator is that 40 of the 58 deaths in the mountain departments in 2000 were in Haute Savoie.

than transport. This medicalisation, it is estimated, resulted in saving some 15 per cent of those who previously died before reaching hospital

The role of the Société is basically one of liaison, and its Secretary, Robert Petit-Prestoud, frequently features as a visitor to the helipad. But since it also receives indirectly the monies collected from piste ski accidents, with a further subvention provided by the *mairie*, it furnishes much of the equipment used by the PGHM which receives little from the state.

Operational organisation
Briefly, there are two centres of operation. The PGHM headquarters in Chamonix itself and the helipad out at Les Bois. It is at the latter that the author spent her summer of 1997. As explained, the former receives the alerts and coordinates the programme of action, with a gendarme on duty at night. Every day there are four rescuers on immediate duty (*les premiers à marcher*), relaying each other in pairs, with two fully prepared at the helipad and the other two in the Chamonix centre; they go straight out to the helipad when the first pair become involved in a rescue. There are another two pairs (*seconds à marcher*) in short readiness, should operations require. It should be remembered that not all rescues are airborne.

The helicopter alternates weekly between that of the Gendarmerie (blue) and that of the Sécurité Civile (red). At the time of this book the former was based with the Détachement Aérien at Megève, the latter at Annecy (the *chef lieu* – administrative capital) of the department.

A word about the helicopter, the Alouette III. As shown, operations can become complex with intermediate drop offs, etc, essentially because of weight limitation and the maximum number it can carry (six, at a push). The all up maximum take-off weight is 2250 kg and the machine consumes roughly 150 litres of fuel per hour's flight, obviously using more power at altitude. Conventionally the available operational weight is divided into seven units, each person being one unit, as too each 100 litres of fuel. Two people are essential on board, the pilot and the mechanician. The latter is also responsible for basic maintenance of both the machine and the winch, theoretically every five hours or fifty hoists, but operations are not interrupted since they rarely exceed the ten hours flying time that is tolerated. It is however worth noting that every hour's flight requires in total three hours maintenance and revision. In flight the mechanician sits beside the pilot facing the opposite way to observe, and he also operates the winch. Since at least one rescuer is usually required that already means three units are being used for a minimal operation, plus a fourth for fuel. So it is a question of juggling between the numbers to be carried (rescuers, the doctor, and the injured), fuel and time (including returns to the helipad to refuel and pick up further personnel).

In 1997 the total operations at Chamonix exceeded the one thousand mark for the first time. Flying time, including training is also roughly a thousand hours.

THE MEDIA[1]

TO INFORM. What a fine task. So all the more important that it is done properly.

It is certainly well done by some. By others, no, and unfortunately the majority of the representatives of press and television we have seen at Chamonix this summer have fallen into the latter category, hence my sometimes sharp reactions. It has been a continuous problem throughout the season. Impossible not to take the subject up again, as a whole.

It should be remembered, first of all, that the diffusion of news is a recent phenomenon, in historical perspective, and it is a direct product of technological innovations. There existed, in early times, news written in manuscript, even in the earliest civilisations, but it was of minor importance and it is the printing press in the 15th century that allowed news to be disseminated. That gave rise to occasional bulletins, the *canards*, which from the 16th century sometimes reported news items (*faits divers*, crimes, etc). From that derived the popular press. The first regular paper, was the weekly *La Gazette* which appeared in 1631, but it was not until the 19th century with the invention of paper made from wood, at the same time as the development of rapid printing techniques, that we see the extraordinary flourishing of the press that was associated with the rise in general literacy and a new mass market. Then came the wireless, the cinema, and television which conveyed information in a more basic way, by oral and visual transmission.

But before all that people existed, and perhaps not so badly after all.

In the old days, the burden of village and local dramas were quite sufficient for people to reflect on the miseries of accidents, sickness, poverty, suffering and death. On a scale when everyone felt involved, in a solidarity that could be supportive. That has gone! If, through a television campaign, we are moved into giving money for cancer it can still manifest itself, but it can also be to fill the pockets of crooks, as happened recently. We don't know, we have no means of telling. It is the same with all propaganda, political or otherwise.

The news has taken a disproportionate place in our lives. But there is nothing we can do about it. So at least we can hope that it will be served up with a modicum of honesty, exactness and human respect.

Its importance is such, in any case, that it needs a constant source of

[1] It should be remembered that this chapter is written from a French perspective. It is for the reader to judge how far it is applicable to the English speaking world.

supply – one event immediately replaced by the next – in a sort of never ending race. Television, this modern bottomless barrel of the Danaïdes, has to be incessantly filled with new items and images. In the end, the input does not really matter so long as input there is, always more, always faster. Any thought processes necessary to accompany the images are of secondary importance.

At the receiving end, we swallow it, we ingurgitate it, we suck it in, we zap, we take in the news along with the crisps and the nuts, we watch the bloody wounded in a terrorist attack as we carve the lamb, we consider the misery of others as a sort of daily bread, we fill our eyes with a suite of atrocities, sportive performances, dishonest political declarations. And we no more even perceive the scandal that is before us.

Two worlds are confronting each other: you, who are alive and reflective, at least more or less, and a virtual world, filled to the brim with exploits, provocative wealth, titillating sex, robberies, sordid murders, scandals of all kinds, planes crashing in the sea with the loss of all aboard, oil-polluted tides washing over flora and fauna, fires blazing over hundreds and thousands of hectares, babies dying of hunger, mothers broken and weeping, human masses fleeing from genocide, and so on.

All these images have been captured. Sometimes at considerable risk. Always in haste. Broadcast likewise. And it starts again tomorrow, and for ever.

Often, the commentary aggravates the picture. It only shows the worst. 'If one talked more about the 90% who have work and less about the 10% unemployed it would be so much more encouraging,' a girl of fifteen said to me.

All that involves the spectators ever less, since it is too much to take in. At the same time, it reassures them that they live in less disadvantaged circumstances, watching their telly. So next time, and the time after, a bit more has to be added to break the barrier of indifference. The power to stir sentiment is therefore frothed up further.

Even more serious is that it has reached the point of changing behaviour patterns in everyday life. Something deep down in the human emotional system has been affected.

One day on Boulevard Raspail in Paris, I saw a twenty or so old female snatch the bag of someone who was probably a Portuguese concierge. In the middle of the day, when the streets were full, everyone stood and gawked. I ran fast, I pursued the thief and caught her, and grabbed the bag shouting imprecations. She made off without more ado. I returned the bag to its owner who fell into my arms, crying with emotion. No one had moved. The passers by had watched the scene with interest. It was as though they were at the cinema. They were no longer affected by the reality of things.

That, if you watch carefully, has become a commonplace. When someone falls down in the street, when someone is caught in the exit doors of the underground shouting for help, people simply look on, stupidly. They don't realise that something is actually happening around them. Their reaction is slow to get going. They are no longer aware. They have seen so many scenes of urgency enacted on the screen, slumped in their armchairs, that the very idea of crossing to the other side and becoming actors themselves is foreign to them, or is slow to awaken. They pass through a period of incomprehension, of emerging thought, of inertia before realising that there is something they can do. And then they probably decide to do nothing.

It is frightening also to see the way information is manipulated. During the major series of transport strikes in Paris at the end of 1996 I used my car if I had to travel and obviously picked up those who had to walk for three or four hours a day in the snow, and without exception they were grumbling, dispirited and generally fed up. But when I turned the television on in the evening what did I see but people happily on foot saying they were solid with the strikers and it was good to get out and walk in the fresh air? That is how 'public opinion' is formed!

Have we no alternative but to accept our world as it is, controlled by the media? Or can one hope to change it in any way?

Mountain accidents are often the prey of the written or spoken press. How do the majority of the media behave in the world of mountaineering? By seeking out the sensational and gross oversimplification.

Let us state from the outset, there are good examples, most obviously, the monthly climbing press written by those who know their subject.

In the daily press, one sometimes meets people who take the matter seriously. For example: since 1982, when I first started writing about the mountains, there have been a series of scrupulous journalists on the *Dauphiné Libéré*. The current one, whom I have never once seen this summer at the helipad seeking sensation, still gave a true reflection of events in his daily reports.

The weekly press swings between the two extremes. It includes the worst offenders, while at the same time in this summer of 1997, *Le Point* carried a double-page article which was well-informed and had no mistakes. And I, who was at the helipad almost every day, learnt something from it I did not know:

> The all powerful ABC chain, with all its influential backing... was virtually thrown off the helipad by the exasperated rescuers. They could no longer stomach being treated as part players in some 'superproduction'.

But television can also report correctly. We have already spoken of *Pioneer Productions*, British, working for the Americans, using a French producer who knows the mountains, spending the necessary time on site, doing everything possible not to get in the way, as exemplified by the miniaturised camera fixed on to the helmet of one of the rescuers – they succeeded in doing a proper job which should result in an excellent documentary series.[2] Those two took the time, cultivated their contacts, and presented what they saw and experienced of the problem caused by other journalists who exasperated the rescuers, crew, doctors, plus me, thrown in for good measure.

But in contrast with these examples, what an invasion of the helipad by the superficial, ignorant, pretentious, shameless, revolting even. And always with the same preliminary: 'What I am seeking, is what the *public* wants.' A discourse, by which any accusation or reproach is automatically disarmed. It's not them, it's the fault of the public! What a pretext.

And a pretext is what it is! If the public were really bloodthirsty and wanted atrocities, ought it to be supplied with them, in any case? If there is a demand for drugs and prostitution does that mean that dealers and pimps should be encouraged? The public is also what one makes of it, once the right to speak for it is arrogated and moulded to pre-established and inappropriate models, which is what is happening more and more. In all honesty, I think I can say I started off this season without any particular prejudices against journalists – other than the sort of thing that most feel about them – and it is the continuously repeated experiences of this summer which have led me to regard many of them in a quite different and critical light.

And yet I should have been forewarned, for I had already received, and have rediscovered, a letter Philippe Claveau, one of those rescued on the August 9, 1994, had written to me the following winter when he and his wife were invited by a television programme to relate their experience:

… we were plunged into the world of the media. Interesting certainly, but what a let down the mentality of these journalists, living in their own little world; no exchange, no common understanding with those existing outside it like ourselves, who are almost despised.

Those lines didn't particularly strike me at the time. I know now what they mean and in what a universe devoid of all reality and human sentiment these journalists concerned with creating news navigate.

Why is the media so concerned with mountaineering? An average of thirty or forty dead each summer on the French side of the Mont Blanc range, true. But it is a small figure compared with the 150 annual drownings. It is few compared with the current massacres in Algeria, as they were before in Black Africa or in Yugoslavia which are spoken of, certainly, but in a different way. At the moment I am writing this, the massacre of 400 people has just occurred yet again in Algeria, that is the equivalent of ten summer rescue seasons. Never mind the sixty-five thousand deaths per year in France alone from smoking.

[2] The series of programmes was indeed very fine, though aimed at a mass audience. They reflected in visual terms many of the aspects described in the book, particularly the elation (for all concerned) of a rescue successfully accomplished.

So why the mountains? In part, doubtless because the scene is accessible. Accessible, but not immediately at hand. Just a few hours driving, and there is a good chance of getting an accident, of filming a helicopter, a captain, a rescuer, someone wounded, even a corpse if one is lucky. Furthermore, it is not something the vast majority of the public is familiar with. So the mountain accident can be shown but without making the spectator feel he is being got at. It is also a matter of habit. Mountain accident reports have become standard fare for the month of August.

But the real reason is perhaps more subtle than that. The mountains are beautiful. They demand a sustained effort – are not facile. They arouse passion, even sometimes the search for an ideal. To approach them is not like approaching the failings and deviant practices widespread in society, but it is to approach something that is rare, beautiful and pure. When one does not understand, the need is to *besmirch* what one cannot have, to denigrate what is seen as risk-running, with standard phrases, platitudes and false ideas

Jean-Claude Gin had a point of view on the press which differed from mine, but which had its own logic. According to him, the journalists who come to Chamonix, particularly those from television, will leave with text, images and commentary from wherever they can get it. If they cannot obtain it from a sound source, they will besiege the helipad, invade the hospital, interview, if needs be, someone in the street who will probably talk a pile of rubbish, and it is with that they will make their news. If one explains properly what it is all about to them, if one gives the right information, the result couldn't be worse and perhaps it might even be better. It makes sense. He has gone to great lengths to see they get the right material. And he succeeded with *Le Point*.

But that aside, how many failures. For certain journalists, it must be recognised, are like leeches. They are looking only for one thing, the sensational, and cannot conceive anything outside their own fixed ideas.

For them, the sensational is obviously an accident. And the worse it is, the better.

One day, a journalist naively, but at least frankly, asked Xavier Chappaz, President of the Chamonix Guides Company:

'Where can I find the most cases of mountain accidents?'

'In the cemetery.'

For that is what they want, deaths! In this simplistic, unenquiring approach they implant in the public mind their own ignorant ideas.

Xavier Chappaz, again, rightly told me that in the eyes of journalists, who have to reduce everything to a facile explanation, alpinists fall into two categories, foolhardy and heroes.

And, he added, one easily moved from one to the other. On July 23, Régis Michoux who, with Olivier Renard and Guy Bochatay saved forty 'foolhardy climbers' on Mont Blanc, was categorised a hero. Five days later when he was carried away by a snow slide on the Aiguille Verte, he shifted into the 'foolhardy' class. To say that in both cases he was an excellent professional, and that he was the victim of one of those choices inherent in the very nature of mountaineering would be too straight-forward, too obviously true, too subtle. It does not enter into the media mould.

In the same way, one can see subsumed among the 'foolhardy' those overtaken by bad weather when trying to open a new route. But the same people, when they exit alive are sought after for interviews, photos, become 'heroes'. Where's the logic of that? None! And yet it is the kind of thing we are subjected to every day.

Two sensational magazines made their appearance this summer. We, the rescuers and I, counted nearly forty errors in each of their texts, neither very long.

One, who appended Chamonix under his article, arrived from Paris one day and left the next. So that he and the photographer who accompanied him should see for their own eyes what the high mountain actually looked like, the PGHM delegated Pierre Raveneau to guide them from the Aiguille to the Col du Midi: a very short, but quite spectacular outing, taking perhaps 2 to 3 hours, which is no more than a preliminary initiation. But the journalist hadn't come to learn but to regurgitate what he wanted to bring up. When he arrived at the top of the cable-car, he refused to set foot on the ridge and shot off back home to Paris, telling his photographer to say that he had stayed for the three or four days he had been sent. That's how his text was written: from afar, in haste, using all the clichés he could drum up. As for the photographer, he stayed, took photos, but because of a disagreement with his editor only one was used and the text was illustrated with whatever came to hand; pictures not taken at Chamonix, rescuers in red who were therefore not of the PGHM... Any old thing!

I can understand the bitterness of Jean-Claude Gin when, having done everything he could to inform the press properly, found himself faced with the same results as though he had done nothing. After the appearance of those two magazines, I saw him totally dismayed:

'We have given them the real information! We helped them! And that is what they produce!'

The unfortunate fact is that those who have an active position to maintain, first and foremost politicians, but also the Gendarmerie and the PGHM have need of the media. They need its attention to strengthen and legitimise their positions. For that's how things work now. It is not sufficient to do things well, it must be publicised too. Even if the news is deformed, defective and skewed.

If the PGHM was not spoken of, the politicians wouldn't know about it. And it is they who command the funds. Public finance is not unlimited, there is a danger of money being taken away to give to others. One has to be to the fore when the cake is being shared out.

So, sometimes it is necessary to take journalists on rescues, carrying them in the helicopter and thus, perhaps, impeding the rescue itself. Public benefit is not of itself sufficient, it requires being broadcast by the media. 'If the PG has survived, it is thanks to the press coverage,' Captain Gin commented. 'The press not only allows the outside to know what's going on but also the inside.'

There are 96,000 people in the Gendarmerie, of which only 250 belong to the PGHM, paid no more than the others and without any danger money. It's not a great burden for the organisation but it is liable to be closed down were it not for the prestige it brings.

One day I was at Poitiers prison. Invited! Because the inmates read my books. At that time I was planning to write *Nadir*. After a long session with them and feeling the current pass, I threw out:

'Guess who I am thinking of writing about next.'

No reply, as expected.

'Gendarmes.'

Expressions immediately hardened.

'The gendarmes who do mountain rescue.'

Relaxation, smiles.

'Ah, that lot's OK. They're not the same.'

But the press, for its part, also needs the PGHM or some similar rescue organisation, particularly during July and August. How else would it fill the pages with news and pictures during these slack periods? It provides text and images. But what kind? How I would love to see shown or described a successful rescue, as it really happens. Certainly it is more difficult to do than showing a sack with a body in it arriving at the helipad and to make that the focus of attention. How much better, just once, to show a fine rescue than to fall back for the umpteenth time on the hack and heartless images – always playing on tragedy and pain as the sole worthwhile news.

So there we are. No going back. We must put up with the period we live in. As best we can. Each in his own way. The most we can hope for is to make our modest portion of this world a little less bad. And it won't be through political parties, intrinsically linked with the whole media game and increasingly removed from reality, that we shall do so.

To do one's best. Make the world a little better. It can be simply the outcome of personal endeavour. When it succeeds one has a Mother Teresa, whose only arm was love. For others it may be mountain rescue, without any desire to make a name for oneself.

And the least we can do is to reject the stupidities which the media bombard us with. It requires considerable effort, for we are bogged down in a mire of set behaviour, of errors, of myths, of lies. But every good fight is worth the fighting.

NOTES ON THE FIRST WINTER ASCENT OF THE DIABLES RIDGE

The climb would have been very advanced for its day – a tough rock route in winter and above 4000 metres. This seems to the first report in English. It was noted in the *Guide Vallot* (though incorrectly dated 1928). It was first reported in *Alpinisme*, June 1938, but there was no later report in *La Montagne*. It was made by Mlle Erica Stagni and Marcel Gallay with the guide Raymond Lambert on February 9-10, 1938. But during the climb they were overtaken by bad weather and the subsequent events proved very dramatic. John Wilkinson has compiled these notes to record the main facts of the story briefly noted on page 337. In view of the much-frequented area of the main events, it is important to remember that the Midi cable-car and the Cosmiques Hut had not been built and this meant that the slopes of Mt. Blanc du Tacul and the Col du Midi were very remote:

Preliminaries:
Raymond Lambert had done the sixth summer ascent of the Diables Ridge with Loulou Boulaz in 1934. Winter ascents on the Aiguilles were in vogue at the time (see *Climbs of My Youth* by André Roch) and Lambert was one of the main participants. In January 1937 Lambert and Marcel Gallay (amateur, but a climbing partner and not a client) made the first winter ascent of Dent du Caïman. After this they make plans to tackle the Diables.

At the end of 1937 Lambert says he is going to bring along Mlle Erica Stagni. She is a remarkable athlete, but new to mountaineering. Nevertheless she has done a solid series of ascents with her guide Lambert during the summer. It should also be noted that nothing in the accounts suggests that in the ascent she did less than her part. Lambert may have wanted to bring her along to secure a fee/expenses. She was rich as too was her mother Mme Amstutz (remarried).

The Climb:
Various delays, illnesses etc – Lambert still suffering from flu when they leave. There has been a long period of fine weather and the conditions are excellent.

Days 1 and 2. (February 7) They climb to the Requin Hut and next day on skis and then snow shoes reach Combe Maudit and the old Col de la Fourche Hut.

Day 3. They begin the climb by-passing Corne du Diable and crossing Pte Chaubert and Pte Médiane where they make a planned bivouac on a good ledge ten metres below the summit. The only mishap during the day was that their snow shoes had been torn from the sack. At midnight the weather suddenly changes, the rock is soon plastered with snow and they are now in real trouble.

Day 4. Problem lies in getting over Pte. Carmen; descent (abseil) to brèche and up the other side. Gallay belays from the abseil point while Stagni gives support (a shoulder to stand on) from the brèche. Following complicated manoeuvres the sacks are hauled across in tyrolean but one smashes into wall and they lose all their provisions. They descend Pte. Carmen, miss out l'Isolée and hasten to the summit of the Tacul. But on the Chamonix side they are hit by the by full blast of the storm. Terrible second bivouac on the lee side, just below Tacul east summit (4247m). They lose one of the sleeping bags.

Day 5. In blizzard and white-out it is impossible descend to Col du Midi and instead they descend towards the more sheltered Col Maudit. Stumble across hole which opens into a sort of horizontal crevasse. Improve site and settle there (*Hôtel de la Mort-Lente* – Hotel of the Slow Death). They have not eaten for two days. All they have is some chocolate, three dried fruits and a Maggi powder soup. Third bivouac: Lick ice, burn slivers of ice axe with last match, cut up leather of a shoe to chew etc.

Day 6. Remain in snow slot (fourth bivouac) – more suffering, drink urine etc.

Day 7. Exit. Discover they are in a precipitous position near Col Maudit. Bitter cold, strong winds and only partial visibility. They realise that by now their friends from Geneva would be searching. Lambert decides only course of action is for him to go and find them since Gallay and Stagni in no fit state to descend. Lambert starts down the NW side of Col Maudit towards the Grands Mulets, but finds himself in an ice-fall and has to climb back up 300m, re-passing the snow hole (but not telling them) and eventually gains Col du Midi (problems of rimaye etc). Near Gros Rognon is spotted by one of the Genevan groups. Insists on going down with them under his own steam to Requin, where they find the Stagni family doctor Ody.

In the meantime: When climbers are overdue Stagni's mother (who thinks they are on the Aiguille du Rochefort because of *radiésthesiste* – a form of clairvoyance) asks Chamonix Guides Office to save her daughter at all costs. Paul Demarchi, Michel Payot (who died in 1950 trying to reach the *Malabar Princess*) and Arthur Franchino set off and luckily meet one of the Genevans who reports Lambert's rescue. At Requin Hut Lambert tells them where the other two are. They set off that night at 10pm, –31° at the level of the hut.

Meanwhile on the Tacul: Stagni and Gallay spend third terrible day and night in ice slot (fifth bivouac). Part of the crevasse has collapsed. Gallay unable to get his boots back on, bare feet. Everything sodden or soaked through.

Day 8. The three Chamonix guides find them and straight away whisk off Stagni, leaving Gallay alone, but telling him there are others coming. Tell other rescue parties gathered at Col du Midi 'he's had it in any case'. Conditions incredibly bitter and some of the other friends and guides decide to wait. But Armand Charlet, Luc Couttet, Jerôme Bozon (Chamonix) and Genevans Francis Marullaz and Walter Macquart press on and reach Gallay. Drag him down rejoin the others at Col du Midi, (adventures, rimaye, Géant Ice Fall etc) and together they descend meeting Dr Ody who gives some basic treatment and says he will see Gallay at Requin Hut. Arrive at hut – Ody and most others have gone and so no treatment for Gallay.

Day 9. Gallay still tied to skis brought down to valley where first treatment is from local doctor. Continues to the clinic at Geneva where the other two plus rescuers of Stagni are being treated, Demarchi being badly affected.

Aftermath:
Here the real problems develop (only briefly summarised here). Clearly Mme Amstutz straight away takes control of matters to cut costs, along with Dr Ody the family doctor. Stagni had promised everything will be done for Gallay and Lambert, but when Gallay arrives at the clinic the first words of the mother were 'Ah there you are, you. Are you insured?' Arguments and discussions: Gallay goes to the public hospital (where in fact he receives equally good treatment as at the private clinic).

The problem is that his frostbite is exceptionally severe, treatment prolonged and he has frequently to return. Stagni recovers completely. Lambert has much amputated but recovers enough to come close to climbing Everest in 1952. Paul Demarchi also has losses but recovers sufficiently to carry on as guide, Marullaz too is also able to carry on mountaineering.

Mme Amstutz finally settles with Lambert and Chamonix guides who seem to be preparing to sue, but Gallay gets covered with debts (his wife leaves him) and has continuous surgery. Becomes paranoid accuses Lambert of disloyalty. Mlle Stagni prevented by her mother from seeing him. On the other hand (reading between the lines) Gallay is not very clever about the way he sets about things and he begins to lose people's sympathies. In his pamphlet *Cas de Conscience* (published by him in 1944, when back again in hospital) we see he has taken out legal proceedings and has been stirring up controversy. (In his first publication of 1940 *Une tragique aventure au Mont-Blanc* he had merely recounted what happened when he arrived at the clinic.)

Some settlement appears to have been reached. Raymond Lambert in the story he recounted to the compiler his *A l'Assaut des Quatre Milles* (Geneva, 1946) says nothing of the aftermath, and adds nothing more in its re-publication that includes his Everest adventures. Gallay too published *La Tragédie des Aiguilles du Diable* in 1952 and says nothing of the aftermath, stopping effectively with the rescue. All he says is 'Thereafter, hospital, treatment, hospital again; but there ends, what is for me, the adventure of my life, for I shall always carry the visible marks, the mutilations of that great wild beast which is the mountain.'

APPENDIX IV

ACKNOWLEDGEMENTS

All my thanks to:

At the PGHM *Officers* – Capitaine Jean-Claude Gin. Majors: Gérard Mathieu, Alain Darrhort and Pierre Raveneau

Rescuers Pierre Bernier, Olivier Bianchi, Xavier Bogo, Frédéric Boidin, Max Buttoud, Henri Cazemajor, Thierry Coquillat, Florian Cuinet, Philippe Debernardi, Marc Dubrulle, Daniel Duret, Roger Émin, Pierre Faussurier and Mrs Faussurier, Olivier Fernandez, Éric Fulbert, Maurice Gardoni, Philippe Garnier, Philippe Godard, Michel Gonzalez, Cyrille Gravier, Bernard Guérin, Alain Iglesis, Lionel Isaia, Franck Junod, Philippe Klein, Christian Lafouge, Jean-Jacques Malineau, Michel Marquier, Gilles Mathé, Michel Médici, Régis Michoux † and Nicole Michoux, Jacques Ottonello, Jean-Louis Oustry, Jacky Paillé, Gérard Peyraud-Magnin, Alain Place, Patrick Poirot, Philippe Pouts, Olivier Renard, Thibaud Ribiollet, René Rosseil, Pascal Saudemont, Jean-Claude Tissot, Jean-Luc Yvon. *And the secretaries:* Jean-Pierre Gallay, Jean-Louis Thomas.

Helicopter pilots (p) / mechanicians Christian Bare-Guillet, Alain Charnay, Philippe Buffenoir, Sylvain Haquin, Didier Méraux (p), Daniel Poujol (p)†.

Gendarme auxiliaries (GAs): Matthieu Berlioz, Olivier Carnet, Arnaud Comte, Jean-Noël Cretier, David Depoisier, Sébastien Ertzbischoff, Sébastien Gosset, Jérôme Grandjean, Yohan Lemoine, Xavier Sonnensheim, Pierre Sy.

Sécurité Civile Helicopters: Gilles Bidon (p), Roland Boutard, Ivan Commène, Jean-Luc Labeyrie †, Yves Maréchal, Michel Pierre (p), Noël Rivière, Vincent Saffiotti (p), Bernard Stoop and Jean-Michel Vialle (p).

Doctors: Emmanuel Cauchy, Benoît Cousineau, Guy Duperrex, François Lecoq and Bernard Marsigny.

Also: Xavier Chappaz, Président de la Compagnie des Guides de Chamonix; Arnaud Pinguet, Secrétaire Général du Conseil Supérieur des Sports de Montagne; Robert Petit-Prestoud, Secrétaire de la Société Chamoniarde de Secours en Montagne.

And in addition: Guy Bochatay, Alexei Boldyrev, Madeleine Bonnard, Gilbert Chappaz, Philippe and Marie Claveau, Philippe Dreux, Michel Durand, Mr and Mrs Guiverec, Guy Labour, Éric Lazzeri, Marc Ledwidge, Marie, Dr. Loïc Mingant, Xavier de Rohan-Chabot and Christian Van Cauwenberghe. *And also members of the families:* Green, Vanderzwan, Heinrich, Payrol, Verger and Voruz

Regarding the UK edition the author and the publisher wish to thank:
George Band, Beth Burke, Margaret Body, Robin Campbell, Dave 'Smiler' Cuthbertson, Lionel de Souza, Daniel Duret, Sue Harper Todd, Patrick Raspo, Don Sargeant, Yvonne Sibbald, Tony Smythe, Patricia Stansfield, Mirella Tenderini, John Wilkinson and Elin Williams.

INDEX